10-22-91

Lullabies OF *Hollywood*

Lullabies of Hollywood

MOVIE MUSIC AND THE MOVIE MUSICAL, 1915–1992

by Richard Fehr *and* Frederick G. Vogel

McFarland & Company, Inc., Publishers
Jefferson, North Carolina, and London

Frontispiece: Leslie Caron and Gene Kelly in the concluding production number of *An American in Paris,* winner of the Best Picture Academy Award for 1951.

"Academy Award" — or "Oscar" — is the registered trademark and service mark of the Academy of Motion Picture Arts and Sciences.

British Library Cataloguing-in-Publication data are available

Library of Congress Cataloguing-in-Publication Data

Fehr, Richard.
    Lullabies of Hollywood : movie music and the movie musical,
1915-1992 / by Richard Fehr and Frederick G. Vogel.
      p.   cm.
    Includes bibliographical references and index.
    ISBN 0-89950-849-9 (lib. bdg. : 50# alk. paper) ∞
    1. Motion picture music—United States—History and criticism.
2. Musical films—United States—History and criticism.   3. Popular
music—United States—History and criticism. I. Vogel, Frederick
G., 1933-   . II. Title.
ML2075.F34   1993
781.5'42'0973—dc20   92-56640
                                                             CIP
                                                              MN

Manufactured in the United States of America

McFarland & Company, Inc., Publishers
  Box 611, Jefferson, North Carolina 28640

"To Mary with Love"
(Mack Gordon–Harry Revel, 1936)

Preface

The twofold purpose for writing *Lullabies of Hollywood: Movie Music and the Movie Musical, 1915–1992* was to examine in detail the vital importance of American popular songs to the astounding three-decade success of the Hollywood musical, and to trace the development and eventual decline of musical pictures from 1929 to 1992.

Most original film songs were written by teams of lyricists and composers under contract to Hollywood studios (Al Dubin and Harry Warren, Mack Gordon and Harry Revel, Leo Robin and Ralph Rainger, Harold Adamson and James McHugh, Johnny Burke and James Van Heusen, Sammy Cahn and Jule Styne, Alan and Marilyn Bergman and Michel Legrand, and Howard Ashman and Alan Menken). The far fewer contributions of such Broadway-based professionals as Irving Berlin, Ira and George Gershwin, Cole Porter, Jerome Kern, and Richard Rodgers, however, are also highlighted, since some of the most familiar songs in their catalogues originated in film musicals.

Also included are comments on numerous "minor" film songs that, despite words and music of outstanding quality, failed to achieve much recognition. The major reason for their anonymity, of course, is that the Hollywood of the 1930s and 1940s released so many musicals that while the public was being serenaded with one or two fresh new songs from a recent picture, another musical with a five- or six-song score was opening at the local first-run movie houses. Overwhelmed by the sheer number of popular songs directed at them not only by Hollywood but also by the Broadway stage and the publishers of nonproduction tunes, people were unable to give many new songs the concentrated attention required to lift them to prominence.

The information is presented in chronological format, beginning with the background music commissioned by such celebrated silent-picture directors as D.W. Griffith and with the occasional theme songs "inspired" by the titles of feature films and published as promotional pieces to advertise the movies or their stars. Within two years after the introduction of "talking" pictures in October 1927, musical production had become a major Hollywood endeavor that was to continue, with only one significant interruption, up to 1958. The film musical rose to spectacular heights of popularity during what the authors consider to be its three "golden ages" (1929–30, 1935–40, and 1942–45). So creative were these periods that the authors have concentrated most of their text on them, as well as on the performers who sang and danced their way through the Great Depression and World War II.

Because of deficiencies in screenplay and music writing originality, the decade of the 1950s is not regarded here as a "golden age." It is, however, thoroughly examined because of the superb craftsmanship exhibited by the various talents involved in film musical production, ranging from the producers (Arthur Freed in particular) to the directors, choreographers, orchestrators, performers (most of them at the pinnacle of their careers), and expert, behind-the-scenes technicians.

The book concludes with a review of post–1958 movie music and musicals, along with an analysis of the social and artistic forces that led directly to their decline beginning in the late 1960s. Nontraditional musical pictures have appeared intermittently over succeeding years. But save for Elvis Presley, the "new" movie musical has so far failed to develop its own roster of stars, those "regulars" who in previous years had been cast in so many musical comedies that they served as competing "stock company" performers hired by the major studios expressly to perform the musical selections inserted into the hundreds of lightweight screenplays so popular at the time. Such was the major role assigned to Dick Powell, Ruby Keeler, Doris Day, and Gordon MacRae (by Warner Bros.); Fred Astaire and Ginger Rogers (RKO Radio Pictures); Eleanor Powell, Judy Garland, George Murphy, Jeanette MacDonald, Nelson Eddy, Frank Sinatra, Kathryn Grayson, Ann Miller, Gene Kelly, and Cyd Charisse (Metro-Goldwyn-Mayer); Janet Gaynor, Shirley Temple, Alice Faye, Tony Martin, Betty Grable, Cesar Romero, and Shirley Jones (Fox Film/

20th Century–Fox); Bing Crosby, Bob Hope, Dorothy Lamour, and Shirley Ross (Paramount Pictures); and Deanna Durbin and the Andrews Sisters (Universal Pictures).

It is astounding that such contemporary performers as Barbra Streisand, Liza Minnelli, and Bette Midler have appeared in so few original musical pictures. Instead of being given adequate opportunities to spark a revival of the Hollywood musical, once assumed to be indestructible, they have been relegated by disuse of their acknowledged talents to witnessing its virtual extinction. Suffering a similar fate have been Stephen Sondheim, Charles Strouse, Henry Mancini, Marvin Hamlisch, Jerry Herman, and a host of other composing notables whose participation in original musical pictures has been severely limited or is indeed nonexistent.

In analyzing the quality — or lack of it — of Hollywood songs, the authors tried to exclude personal preferences, difficult as that admittedly can be. We assumed that selecting songs like "Lullaby of Broadway," "Pennies From Heaven," "Moolight Becomes You," and "The Way We Were" as examples of superb movie music is unarguable. Where we may deviate from popular opinion is in praising relatively minor efforts — "Then I'll Be Reminded of You," "I Used to Be Color Blind," and "I'm Old Fashioned," for example — none of which was acclaimed at its debut or widely remembered today.

The primary criteria used in evaluating film musical tunes are originality of music and lyrics; pertinency to the screenplay sequence in which they were introduced; degree of initial popularity; excellence of on-screen rendition; and recognition, by title or melody, by the average 1990s popular music professional.

All song titles and the names of writers and films were verified as correct by checking the annual *Catalogue of Copyright Entries* volumes maintained by the Library of Congress. A few copyrighted songs scheduled to appear in specific films were deleted at the last minute, although this was not a frequent occurrence. Sometimes these songs were inserted into later films, sometimes not. To make certain that all pairings of songs and films are accurate, the *CCE* information was compared with the credits printed on copies of the first editions of the published sheet music. Throughout the text and the reference lists that make up the appendix, songwriting credits are given with the names of lyricists preceding those of composers.

The writing of the book was stimulated in the mid–1980s by what can correctly be defined as the authors' all-consuming interest in popular music and movie musicals. Actually, basic research was undertaken in the late 1950s, when co-author Vogel was on the book and film reviewing staffs of *The Washington Post* (then *The Washington Post & Times-Herald*). Thanks to frequent showings of film musicals at movie-revival houses in Washington, D.C., and New York City, including the Museum of Modern Art, and television's *Late* and *Late Late* shows, he decided to narrow the enormous field of popular music to Hollywood's huge contribution to it, especially between 1929 and 1958, when the major studios' consistent musical practice gradually elevated the genre from experiment to art. Also of inestimable value to the research effort was the development of the VCR and the subsequent release on cassette of about 300 films musicals dating from the 1927 version of *The Jazz Singer* to the present.

In March of 1986, novelist and publicist Richard Fehr, also a long-standing film buff, joined Mr. Vogel in defining the scope of the proposed book, collecting additional data, and writing the text. Through viewing the films and listening to the radio, collector's-item phonograph records, and solo piano versions based on the sheet music, the authors have heard every song mentioned in the book at least once. Where necessary, the plots of the few unavailable films have been summarized from reviews appearing in *The New York Times, Variety,* and *Billboard.*

"Invaluable" is the apt word to describe the cooperation given to the authors over the years by the 25 songwriters whose names appear in the bibliography. Chief among these professional helpmates was lyricist Sammy Cahn, the winner of 26 Academy Award nominations for Best Song and president of the Songwriters' Hall of Fame. It was he who arranged many of the interviews between authors and songwriters and, like all of them, he was unstinting in sharing memories of his years in the film capital. Sammy died January 15, 1993, and the authors lament the fact that he will never see the book to which he contributed so heavily.

To close friends Virginia Vida and Stewart Siegel we extend our highest regards for disciplining our efforts to improve the manuscript. Busy people themselves, they never delayed responding to requests for assistance or withheld suggestions on how best to carry the project to its conclusion. Deserving special mention are the highly cooperative, ever-gracious staffs of the Copyright Division of the Library of

Congress and American Film Institute in Washington, D.C.; the Lincoln Center Library of the Performing Arts, Museum of Modern Art, and Songwriters' Hall of Fame in New York City; and the Academy of Motion Picture Arts and Sciences in Los Angeles.

Particularly helpful in furnishing the names of current licenseholders of movie songs and significant information on many of the songwriters' non-film achievements was Karen Sherry, of the American Society of Composers, Authors and Publishers, New York City, and we are grateful for her giving us so much of her time and effort. Lucy Salkoff and George Rapée merit our special thanks for permitting us to quote directly from songs written by Erno Rapée and Lew Pollack, as do Jack Rosner, vice president for special projects, Warner/Chappell Music, Inc., Los Angeles, and Len Perry, CPP/ Belwin, Inc., Miami, for granting permission to quote directly from nine other songs. Sheet music collectors/dealers Sandy Marrone, Cinnaminson, New Jersey, and Beverly A. Hamer and Catherine Fredette, East Derry, New Hampshire, were extremely helpful in providing the authors with copies of difficult-to-find sheet music of a number of the earliest film songs.

Co-author Vogel also wishes to acknowledge the singing and dancing talents of a trinity of attractive young sweethearts from his elementary school days — Elizabeth Blair, Barbara Barry, and Betsy Brown — whose delightful renditions of popular songs of the time kindled in him the permanent fondess for popular songs and musical films that, later in life, prompted him to initiate the book project. To this threesome, as well as to the songwriters and musical actors and actresses who brightened his past and continue to endow the present with pleasant reminders of vanished years: "All my love, and thanks for the memories."

Richard Fehr
Frederick G. Vogel
Belmar, New Jersey
July, 1993

Contents

CHAPTER ONE

Overture

*T*HE DEBT that songwriters and publishers, performers and lovers of popular music owe the film industry is staggering. In only the 77 years since D.W. Griffith's *Birth of a Nation* opened in 1915, American films have introduced or reprised an estimated 25,000 songs, a hefty percentage of which rank among the finest ever written in the United States. Propelled by a Charleston beat, early movie songs personified the razzle-dazzle of the high-kicking twenties. Along with the Great Depression of the 1930s came countless sprightly tunes that uplifted sagging spirits by reminding that the money people lacked would not buy true happiness anyway. In fact, riches were scorned as impediments to finding it.

In the first half of the 1940s, popular songs bolstered morale during the most devastating war in history. We will carry on to victory, one film lyric assured us, even if the only things going for us are a wing and a prayer. Praise the Lord, urged another one — but be sure to pass the ammunition, too.

Americans bought millions of these songs on phonograph records and sheet music. They sang, whistled, and hummed them, danced to them at proms and in nightclubs, played them on the living room piano, listened to them on home and automobile radios. In the 1950s, celebrities performed film songs on television; audiences took personal satisfaction when a favorite nudged its way into the number one slot on the weekly *Your Hit Parade* program.

Many of these songs were written by the greatest composers and lyricists in theatrical history, ranging from Irving Berlin and Jerome Kern to Cole Porter, Richard Rodgers, and the Gershwin brothers. They were performed by such celluloid luminaries as Fred Astaire

1

and Ginger Rogers, Dick Powell and Ruby Keeler, Bing Crosby, Bob Hope, Judy Garland, Alice Faye, Betty Grable, Gene Kelly, Frank Sinatra, and Doris Day—even by a Walt Disney cartoon character with the name of Jiminy Cricket. Including the five 1991 nominees, a grand total of 323 film songs have received Academy Award nomination. Actually, that number is only about 25 percent of the high-caliber hits that have arisen from movie sound tracks over the past six decades.

Hollywood actors and actresses took advantage of film songs to entice and spellbind the vast empire of fans that became enamored of "talking" musicals. Singing and dancing their script-written blues away, these personalities doggedly pursued the objects of their affection and ambition. Using merry lyrics grafted to bouncy tunes, they propped up their own spirits while cheerleading viewers into a similar state of optimism, transforming those dispossessed orphans of the Depression and war years into vicarious participants in the joy bubbling from the Big Screen.

So dismal was the real world of the 1930s and 1940s that Hollywood's musical producers declared it off limits. Using their movies as building blocks, they renovated film houses into cocoons perfectly designed to insulate audiences from the ravages of normal life. All that was asked of viewers was to take a cue from the obsessive happiness writ large across the angelic faces of the young cast members seeking to bring out the best in the worst of times. Their reward was the substitution of the fanciful for the actual and, more often than not, at least a transient renewal of hope.

The film musicals of the time served admirably as beacons of the average American's aspirations. In darkened theaters all over the country, people willingly lulled themselves, if only fleetingly, into a relaxed state of mind. They watched Ginger Rogers's lips curve into a confident smile as she encouraged everybody to forget personal problems and "Let Yourself Go." They followed Bing Crosby's advice by figuratively scooping up Depression pennies from heaven. And they applauded youngsters who fought for a part in a Mickey Rooney charity show almost as vigorously as they cheered their soldiers battling a ferocious enemy in Europe and Africa and on previously unheard of islands in the Pacific.

The sermons these musicals conveyed through plot and song echoed the virtue of living life according to the trinity of faith, hope, and charity. Self-reliance and forbearance were cardinal virtues, strengthening character and the belief that better days would soon displace the distressing present. Viewers were taught to grip their fingers around straws of hope, since life without it is meaningless. Love was the God-given glory of mankind that induced even the most selfish and cynical to help the unfortunate without expectation of repayment.

Although the weathervane indicating the public's film preferences shifted direction now and then, it unfailingly returned to one constant from 1929 to 1958. People went to the movies for entertainment. They cared little for social protest, symbolism, brutality, cynicism, or gore. So the studio chieftains gave them exactly what they wanted, knowing full well that musicals provided the ideal forum for dispersing happiness on a grand scale. And they did it willingly, since above all else their films were made to entertain for profit — nothing more, nothing less. The stunning box office revenues earned by these films bore witness to the moguls' astute bottom line reasoning.

Songs became an absolutely necessary lubricant of filmmaking, frequently rescuing even the most amateurish movies from disaster. Music, acting, and screenplay gradually became a formidable coalition, a harmonious *ménage à trois* that, in time, would rival the best that Broadway had to offer.

A Two-Way Street

Just as incalculable as the indebtedness music professionals and fans owe the film industry is the reciprocal debt piled up over the decades by Hollywood producers. Without their stables of tunesmiths, the film musical would never have been able to rise to the very top of the box office.

For it was the songs that compensated, often superlatively, for the fluffy, repetitive, B-picture screenplays, dismal acting, and beefy, lumbering chorus lines that characterized so many of the earliest movie musicals. The handful of ever-reliable craftsmen, including a few women, who wrote the songs were both prolific and highly professional. It was they who, beginning in the mid–1930s, would dominate the Academy Award for Best Song to the end of the 1950s.

Just how vital songs were to the success of musical pictures was underscored by the mindset of audiences. By the end of 1929, they were regarding film musical plots and dialogue as tiresome intrusions with but a single redeeming feature: to lead the singers and dancers from one number to the next. An astoundingly large number of film songs were so superior that they have long outlived both the assembly line pictures they enlivened and most of the stars who performed them.

Without the Hollywood musical as an outlet for their wares, America's composers and lyricists undoubtedly would not have written hundreds of songs, a potentially lamentable loss to performers and public. Broadway could produce only so many operettas, musical comedies, and revues even in the best of times. During the Depression, many of its theaters spent months in the dark or, ironically, showed films instead of stage plays. Or, like the $4.5 million, 3,000-seat Earl Carroll's Theater, then the world's largest playhouse, they succumbed to the wrecker's ball.

Hollywood, on the other hand, released as many musicals as the market could bear. Support for them was powerful and, except for a slowdown in the early 1930s, remained virtually undiminished for three decades. To keep up with the demand, the major studios placed songwriting teams, beginning with Jack Yellen and Milton Ager, Arthur Freed and Nacio Herb Brown, Leo Robin and Richard A. Whiting, Al Dubin and Harry Warren, and Mack Gordon and Harry Revel, under contract, paying them excellent salaries to do nothing but turn out songs and more songs, even if some wound up on the cutting room floor.

Far more song hits came from sound tracks than from the stage in 1929–30 and 1934–48. Although none surpassed the greatness of such Broadway classics as "Tea for Two," "Ol' Man River," "Begin the Beguine," "All the Things You Are," and "September Song," Hollywood need not blush with embarrassment by comparison. Plentiful were the lumps of coal to be found among the nosegays. But about 30 percent of Hollywood songs, ranging from "Louise" in 1928 to "Under the Sea" in 1989, represent notable contributions to our popular musical heritage.

Curiously, though the industry kept calling on the indispensable songwriters for an endless supply of material, it continued for years to shunt aside even the most inspired of them when it came to bestowing laurels attesting to their artistry. When the Academy of Motion Picture Arts and Sciences passed out its first series of Oscars in 1928, it awarded them to the best actor, actress, director, picture, cinematographer, and script and subtitle writers. Composers and lyricists were ignored, an understandable omission since film musicals were confined at the time to taking mere baby steps on the road to glory.

But by 1929 they were off and running, compounding the puzzlement over the Academy's exclusion of songwriters from Oscar contention until the decade of the 1930s was almost half over. It apparently did not matter to the Academy's governors that many of filmdom's all-time greatest songwriters were filling movie palaces with distinguished music. Their only prize, and a consolation one at that, was the writers' knowledge that many of their songs were attracting worldwide attention while adding immeasurably to the popularity of the productions they decorated.

At least 20 of the finest songs ever written specifically for films originated in the first six years of the talking-picture era, 1928–33. Thirty more are first-rate, and another 50 or so undoubtedly would have qualified as Academy Award contenders, had they been written during or after 1934, when the first Best Song Award was presented.

Several of these early, neglected music writers even contributed songs to pictures that won Oscars in categories approved by the Academy. "My Tonia," a lovely tune fashioned by the fantastically successful Broadway triumvirate of Buddy (George Garde) DeSylva, Lew Brown, and Ray Henderson, ran through the all-talking *In Old Arizona* (1928), which earned Warner Baxter the Best Actor award for his portrayal of O. Henry's Cisco Kid. Irving Berlin's delightful ditty "Coquette" appeared in the film of the same name, which starred Mary Pickford, voted Best Actress for 1929.

Selected as Best Picture of 1929 was Metro-Goldwyn-Mayer's *Broadway Melody,* which inspired dozens of successors for decades afterward and was the first of eight Hollywood musicals to win that award. Unnoticed during the 1930 Academy Award festivities were the studio's two workhorses, lyricist Arthur Freed and composer Nacio Herb Brown, whose sparkling score was as responsible as anything else for *Melody*'s heady profit and prestige. After the gala had run its course and all the Oscars were distributed, the two ineligible tunesmiths had nothing to put on their mantelpieces but their elbows.

Other film composers, described as "serious" by music critics, like the multiple Academy Award winner Alfred Newman, simultaneously perfected the lyricless program or "mood" music designed to heighten the emotional intensity of talking epics, romances, Westerns, adventures, and fantasies. Complementing the theme song mania that descended on Hollywood in the late 1920s, background music grew in stature over the years, eventually pervading more and more films practically from beginning to end.

Although they traveled different musical roads, the pioneering serious and pop music writers together bequeathed an imposing legacy to the artists who followed them. Unsung as most of them were during their lifetimes, they generously helped to alchemize what began as a peep-show novelty into one of the biggest commercial enterprises of the century.

With the onset of the turbulent 1960s, both the film musical and the types of songs associated with it suffered a precipitous decline that remains in effect in the 1990s. Practically all the bellwether "classical age" songwriters had died or retired by 1965, along with the industry's early moguls who had fought the Depression and World War II with melodies laced with cheerful lyrics and driven by a lively beat.

A challenging new era dawned while young Americans grappled with the Vietnam War and the civil rights and women's movements. Rather than exult, as had their elders, in their stamina to survive in society, the youngsters of the 1960s and 1970s agitated to change it. The standard film musical plot depended on a consensus mentality to rally audiences to the side of optimism while problems were attacking the fortress of hope. Screenwriters (and lyricists) rarely delved very deeply into the causes of social unrest. They were medicine men, not reformers. Their primary job was to alleviate the nation's ills by wrapping the unpalatable and unwholesome in euphemisms and allowing performers to serenade viewers with happiness songs.

The prescription worked in the 1930s, 1940s, and 1950s. But by the mid–1960s, the nation's difficulties seemed so numerous, pervasive, and complex that Americans segregated themselves into a welter of philosophical camps, each holding strong, contrasting opinions on how to solve them. Operating in an increasingly fragmented society, producers rejected sing-song nostrums, played by the same persistent fiddler, as antidotes. Nor did they dare reincarnate Hollywood's traditional escapist musical comedy formula for a public grown harsh and cynical, and in no mood to be buffeted by contrived happiness.

Musical tastes changed so dramatically in the 1960s that the films' long-standing infatuation with gentle romantic ballads quickly fell out of tempo with the times. The new generation cared little for reminders of a past with which they had little in common, and indeed found difficult to believe ever existed. Youngsters also displayed antagonism for what they justifiably considered the shallow stories and sentimentality endemic to old-time musicals. So for all intents and purposes, by 1965 the conventional film musical was pronounced dead at the age of 37.

Accompanying it in its demise were the graceful melodies, happy-talk lyrics, frivolous dialogue, and stock situations and characters that had entertained more than three decades' worth of moviegoers throughout the world. All had been so immersed in regenerating the human spirit according to neo–Victorian principles that these once-beloved pictures can truly be termed unique in our history. Their comforting presence having been superseded by realism and the wizardry of special effects departments, Hollywood musicals have become such stuff as nostalgia is made of.

CHAPTER TWO

In the Beginning: 1915–1927

*M*USIC has long been an integral part of films, silent or talking, dramatic or musical. In silent-picture studios, live or recorded music was played on the sets to wring emotion out of performers in the throes of acting. As early as 1908, classical composer Charles Camille Saint-Saëns, whose *Samson et Dalila* was among the most popular of grand operas, furnished the background music for the French silent *L'Assassinat du Duc de Guise*. A rash of other semi-symphonic screen scores by less highly regarded composers followed, leading in 1915 to the first movie song hit.

Pre–World War I silent-film producers called on professional live musicians to maintain moods consistent with the action unfolding on the screen. In major metropolitan film houses, the music was played by organists or pit orchestras, some with as many as 100 instrumentalists. Filmmakers formed a partnership with composers that has yet to be dissolved.

In neighborhood theaters and in small-town America, music was furnished by pianists. Seated only a few feet from first-row audiences, they escorted such preeminent personalities as Pearl White from one peril of Pauline to the next, Charles Chaplin from despair to deliverance, and Rudolph Valentino from Bedouin encampment to boudoir. Sometimes the pianist was augmented by a violinist, drummer, or other instrumentalist. But handicapped by the inability to even suggest the lush resonances of a full orchestra, these musicians typically substituted vintage popular songs, improvisations of their own, or snippets filched from the classics for the orchestrated scores.

They were free to play whatever they wished because nobody required them to stick to the orchestrations. Following the lead of the enterprising Thomas Alva Edison, who about 1903 began supplying theaters with printed programs of instrumental music for the movies made by his production company, other studios merely shipped "suggested movie scores." It was up to the individual conductors or pianists to decide whether to follow the scores as written or insert other melodies at will.

Live small-scale musical accompaniment was also part of the bills of fare at movie houses that displayed illustrated song slides—i.e., projections of song lyrics—on the darkened screen. Audiences were encouraged to join the onstage vocalists in singing them. This participatory exercise continued, minus the vocalists, into the late 1940s by means of musical sound tracks and little balls that danced above the lyrics, pausing every so often to indicate accented syllables.

Proof of the inestimable value of musical backdrops to films is readily accessible to even the youngest of generations. All one need do is watch twice a videocassette of two extraordinary silents, *The Big Parade* (1925) and *Wings* (1927), the first time turning off the recorded piano accompaniment, the second time listening to it. The difference is startling. The pianoless version seems strangely incomplete; something is definitely missing. The second viewing, with piano, clearly shows how a film without spoken dialogue can nonetheless pulsate the blood and tug at the heartstrings by virtue of the sound of fingers rippling along a keyboard.

Sensitized early to the artistic worth of music, motion picture producers released scarcely a single major feature film after 1903 that lacked a melody line. Like the background music for sound films, such as Max Steiner's impressive *Gone with the Wind* score, silent-picture orchestrations frequently contained themes that captured the public's fancy.

The first of them—"The Perfect Song," by Clarence Lucas and Joseph Carl Breil—highlighted *Birth of a Nation* in 1915. Aficionados of old-time radio know it as the theme song of the *Amos 'n' Andy* show, which made its debut in 1926 under the name of *Sam 'n' Henry*. In May of 1921, when *Birth of a Nation* was revived at New York City's Capitol Theatre, all the original 1915 Breil music had been scrapped. In its place was a completely new orchestrated score by Erno Rapée, Dr. William Axt, and Hermann Hand. It was arranged by impresario

Samuel L. ("Roxy") Rothafel, then the Capitol's general manager. A born showman, Rothafel was especially adept at commingling live music, including onstage ballets and symphonic concerts, with the films presented at his theaters.

He also tried his hand at incorporating unusual creature comforts into his showplaces, which were among the most magnificent ever built in the United States. For his Roxy Theatre, which opened in 1927, he installed an air conditioning system laced with ozone to make audiences feel better. But his original intention to diffuse laughing gas through the system was dropped.

Rothafel's explanation of the sole purpose of background music for films is as definitive today as it was in 1921: "A score is nothing more or less than a musical adaptation or interpretation of the dramatic values of the picture."

In 1916, Breil composed the music for another masterwork, *Intolerance,* which cost an incredible $2.5 million to produce. Although the 189-page score failed to win popularity, it is one of the very few of its day that have been preserved. Its great length, together with its having been written for as prestigious a director as D.W. Griffith, lent credence to the growing opinion that silent-picture scoring was a noble calling to be undertaken by top-flight composers only. But Breil's *Intolerance* music was blasted by film critic Julian Johnson, whose acid commentary on it appeared in the December 1916 issue of *Photoplay Magazine:* "The music is sadly inefficient—the most inefficient music a big picture ever had."

Disappointing as Johnson's appraisal was to Breil, it did indicate that movie music was being recognized by critics as worthy of evaluation. In later years, how well songs compensated for humdrum musical-picture plots would exert a powerful influence on attendance. Despite the jarring review, *Intolerance* became an acknowledged classic, and in 1989 was among the first 25 features placed by the Library of Congress on the new National Film Registry of significant films.

Also in 1916, composer Jerome Kern, whose ever-lovely "They Didn't Believe Me" was a major stage hit of 1915, wrote the music for the nondescript silent serial *Gloria's Romance.* It was presented, like the better-known *Perils of Pauline,* in weekly "chapters." The same year, Victor Herbert (*Babes in Toyland, Naughty Marietta, The Red Mill, Sweethearts*) became the first prominent American composer to write a complete film score. The picture was the 12-reel *Fall of a Nation,* produced and written by Thomas Dixon, whose book *The Clansman* was the inspiration for *Birth of a Nation.* According to *Fall of a Nation,* America is so ill-prepared militarily to enter World War I that it falls victim to conquest by a foreign power, most likely Germany. A new Joan of Arc arises, however, and she organizes multitudes of suffragettes who help male Americans expel the conquerors and return the United States to democracy.

Herbert, the finest classical cellist of his time and conductor of the Pittsburgh and other symphony orchestras, took his assignment seriously and composed what was regarded as the first original background music that scrupulously followed the action of the film. The score earned the highest critical acclaim and reputation as one of the all-time best of the silent years. Unfortunately, both film and orchestration are lost; only a two-hour piano version of the music exists.

A few years later, into the movie-music spotlight strode another high priest of operetta, the Hungarian-born Sigmund Romberg, who could list several Al Jolson stage shows and *Maytime* among his credits. Steeped in the lyrical melodic tradition of the Austro-Hungarian Empire, Romberg was not a particularly original composer, but he was a wildly popular one nonetheless. According to lyricist Irving Caesar, who collaborated with him on several stage musicals, all of Romberg's music had an undisguised familiarity about it. For *Blossom Time* (1921), Romberg based his entire score on music written in the previous century by Franz Schubert. "First-nighters at the opening of a Romberg show could hum the tunes on the way *into* the theater," Caesar noted.

To Romberg was given the task of composing the musical background for director-actor Erich Von Stroheim's massive 32-reel *Foolish Wives,* premiered in February 1922. Sitting through a film lasting almost seven hours proved too taxing for even the most fervid moviegoer, and so Universal Studios streamlined it to 14 reels, then to 10, excising most of Romberg's score in the process. Putting the ax to Von Stroheim's films became a ritual that other studios would perform on many later works by this long-winded, profligate genius. In 1923 MGM slimmed his *Greed* from 45 reels to 10, desecrating what has since been hailed as a masterpiece in its full-length format, which covered 30 miles of film.

In 1923, George Gershwin became the first major Broadway composer hired to write a song specifically to promote a silent movie,

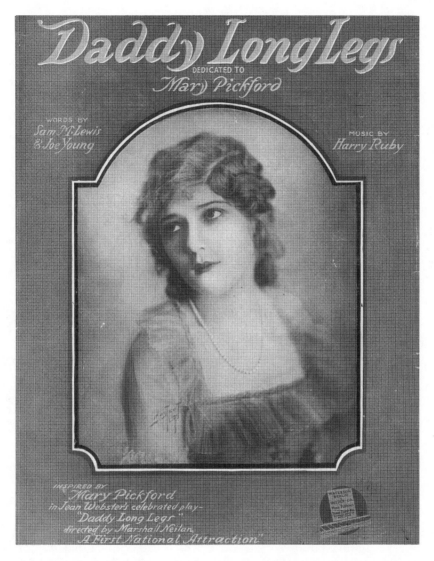

"America's Sweetheart" of the silent screen and the song "inspired" by her 1919 film, *Daddy Long Legs.*

director Thomas Ince's *Sunshine Trail,* which carried the same name as the song. The unsung words were by George's equally gifted brother Ira, then writing under the pseudonym of Arthur Francis, culled from the first names of another brother and sister Frances. That same year, Billy Rose, Mort Dixon, and Ray Henderson, then mere pledges in the songwriting fraternity, wrote a major theme song hit, "That Old Gang of Mine," for the minor Warner Bros. silent *Country Kid.* All five men would return to film writing after the introduction of talking pictures.

Between 1914 and 1927, other composer-lyricist teams earned money from songs "suggested" by popular silent features. Usually not part of the orchestrated scores, these melodies were heard only occasionally inside the theaters showing the films. Instead, the writers sought to capitalize on the films' success by appropriating their titles and splashing them boldly across sheet music covers.

Dozens of such independent songs rattled off the presses of music publishing factories. Their ballyhoo potential was not lost on the moguls, ever alert to new ways to affix the names of their films on the public's consciousness. So they failed to complain about the songwriters' exploitation of their properties.

Singing Commercials

Songs promoting heroes and entertainers, consumer products and reform movements, and victory at the ballot box and in war have long been staples of American music. Typically undistinguished and short-lived, such songs have depended for popularity more on fans of a personality or adherents of a cause than on the public at large. Scores of people wrote them, from respected professionals to the rankest amateurs.

Many U.S. presidential candidates have chased after votes to the tune of a lively campaign song, as Theodore Roosevelt did in 1904 with William R. Haskins–Maurice Staube's "He's Good Enough for Me," or basked in the glory of a stirring tribute to their latest triumph in office. In late 1914, Woodrow Wilson was publicly thanked for keeping the country out of World War I, which had erupted that July, in Blanche Merrill's "We Take Our Hats Off to You, Mr. Wilson." On the sheet music cover was an inset of Fanny Brice, who popularized it. In 1933, even a cabinet officer, William H. Woodin, President Franklin Roosevelt's first Secretary of the Treasury, felt compelled to express confidence in the new chief executive by writing the music for the "Franklin D. Roosevelt March," with a lyric by Irving Caesar. Irving Berlin also paid tribute with "The President's Birthday Ball" on the occasion of the wartime leader's 60th birthday in 1942.

Bert Kalmar-Alexander Steinert's "We Want Willkie," a familiar refrain in the 1940 election, was pitted for popularity against Henry Myers and Jay Gorney's "Mr. Roosevelt, Won't You Please Run Again?" Undeniably, Berlin's 1952 campaign song for Dwight D. Eisenhower, the best known of all presidential songs, was a model of simplicity, relying on only three words that the overwhelming majority of the electorate endorsed: "I Like Ike." Written originally as "They Like Ike" in 1950 for Broadway's *Call Me Madam*, it mustered far more popularity than Berlin's followup 1956 Republican campaign ditty, "Ike for Four More Years." The strictly non-partisan Berlin had campaigned musically for Alfred E. Smith, a Democrat, in 1928 with "Good Times with Hoover, Better Times with Al."

Heroes John J. Pershing and Charles A. Lindbergh were the objects of innumerable affectionate tributes following the general's success in World War I and the aviator's solo transatlantic flight in 1927. Inventor Edison, the film industry's patron saint, was the recipient of a 1929 tribute written by George M. Cohan, the original "Yankee Doodle Dandy," appropriately entitled "Thomas A. Edison — Miracle Man."

That same year, New York city's colorful mayor, James J. Walker, was also celebrated in song. Dr. D.B. DeWaltoff dedicated his "New York Town" to Walker, then as notable for undertaking construction of the monumental Independent Subway System as he was notorious for his fondness for graft. (Walker was forced to resign in 1932.) Not averse to self-promotion, the good doctor inserted an advertisement for his new eternal-youth cream, Agavin, on the inside front cover of the sheet music.

All kinds of free enterprises have been passengers on the singing band wagon. Vincent Bryan-Gus Edwards's "In My Merry Oldsmobile," dating to 1905, has yet to be dethroned as the most recognizable of automobile songs. Three years later, baseball was given the all-time champion of sports songs when Jack Norworth and Albert Von Tilzer came up with the singable "Take Me Out to the Ball Game." In the 1920s, the "March of the Flit Soldiers" promised to make every house bug-proof; "Time to Re-Tire" glorified Fisk tires; "We Are the Blades" defiantly reminded shavers that the Gillette Company's safety razor was their best buy; and David Mendoza's "At the Sign of the Green and White" was installed as the theme song of Quaker State Motor Oil's weekly radio program.

Songwriters have also drawn public relations inspiration from associations and clubs. March king John Philip Sousa promoted the 1908 Boston Food Fair with "The Fairest of the Fair," also a march, and dedicated it to the Boston Retail Grocers Association, which sponsored the affair. "The Sweetheart of Sigma Chi," by Byron D. Stokes and F. Dudleigh Vernon, remains the finest of all college fraternity songs 80 years after publication. In 1920, Charles and Henry Tobias penned the less than immortal "I Spend My Nights at the Knights of Columbus," which catalogued the delights to be found at the local K. of C. chapter. Not to be outdone, J.W. Keefe tossed off "Hooray, Elks, Hooray!" six years later.

Even catastrophes attracted their share of popular songs, tending to raise the knowledge level of their impacts. "Prohibition, You Have Lost Your Sting," gleefully announced J. Russel Robinson and Billy Curtis only months after ratification of the 18th Amendment, which banned the manufacture, importation, and consumption of booze. No classic, the cheery tune won the affection of Sophie Tucker, who introduced it with her singing group, the "Five Kings of Syncopation." As the history of the lawless twenties would show, the lyric was pretty much on the mark.

The comics were looted for publicity purposes, and songs based on cartoon characters proliferated. Billy Rose and Con Conrad adopted "Barney Google," the fellow with the "goo-goo-googly eyes," for their mammoth hit of 1923. In 1930, Conrad joined Benny Davis for "Skippy," borrowed from the comic strip by Percy L. Crosby. As recently as 1967, "Peanuts" was appearing on sheet music covers for Clark Gesner's stage show *You're a Good Man, Charlie Brown.*

Many states and cities have official anthems, ranging from Rodgers and Hammerstein's "Oklahoma!," sired in 1943 on Broadway, to Fred Ebb and John Kander's "New York, New York," written for Liza Minnelli in the 1977 film of the same name. In 1941, visiting songwriter Jack Owens was so gratified by the friendly reception accorded him by residents of Santa Catalina, California, that he repaid them with "Hi, Neighbor," a catchy tune debuted that year by singers Jane Frazee and the Merry Macs in the film *San Antonio Rose.*

Among the best known of movie songs celebrating American cities is the rousing "San Francisco," introduced by Jeanette Mac-Donald, who sang one chorus in uncharacteristic swing tempo, in the 1936 MGM film. Written by Gus Kahn, Bronislaw Kaper, and Walter

Jurmann, the song is unparalleled in expressing the resurgence of hope among the residents of a community just emerging from a disaster, in this instance an earthquake.

For the 1946 film *New Orleans,* lyricist Eddie deLange and composer Louis Alter wrote the classic "Do You Know What It Means to Miss New Orleans." Sung in appropriately sultry fashion by Billie Holiday, it later served as the theme song for *Frank's Place,* an excellent but short-lived television comedy series aired in 1988 by CBS.

Then there is "Hooray for Hollywood," written by Johnny Mercer and Richard A. Whiting for the 1937 Warner Brothers musical *Hollywood Hotel* (Dick Powell introduced it). A first-class publicity piece for both the movies and the movie capital, the tune nevertheless failed to win even nomination for that year's Academy Award for Best Song. But it did complement the earlier popular movie-inspired novelty "You Oughta Be in Pictures," completed in a mere ten minutes in 1934 by Edward Heyman and Dana Suesse.

SERENADES TO THE STARS

During World War I, film stars became America's new royalty, and songwriters, like Roy Barton with "Charlie Chaplin Walk" (1915), were quick to give voice to the public's adulation of them and the characters they played. An imposing cluster of promotional songs went to market in 1919, prompted by the end of the war and Americans' longing to return to what President Harding would call the "normalcy" of prewar years, which certainly included songs not written in a martial tempo.

One of the most lyrical of the movie-based songs, Ballard MacDonald and A. Robert King's "Broken Blossoms," helped to publicize D.W. Griffith's hit film with the same title. From Irving Berlin, who would be nominated for seven Academy Awards between 1936 and 1955, came "New Moon," written to promote the Norma Talmadge opus which "inspired" the song.

Composer Harry Ruby, soon to team with Bert Kalmar for stage and film scores, joined the prolific Joe Young and Sam M. Lewis for the delightful "Daddy Long Legs," taken from the title of the Mary Pickford film of 1919. Albert Von Tilzer promptly chimed in with a second promotional song, "Dear Old Daddy Long Legs," which also carried Miss Pickford's photograph on the sheet music cover.

Fred Fisher, whose hit "Chicago" paid swinging tribute to that "todd'lin' town" on Lake Michigan, wrote the pretty "Evangeline" to alert moviegoers to Fox's screen success based on the Longfellow poem. Then came top-drawer composer Richard A. Whiting's "Fallen Idols," which took its title from *A Fallen Idol,* another of the year's many popular films.

The busiest and most successful of the promotional songwriters was Ernest R. Ball, known best for "When Irish Eyes Are Smiling," "Mother Machree," and other tunes praising Emerald Islanders. The film version of Booth Tarkington's *Boy o'Mine,* also from 1919, planted the seed for Ball's misty-eyed "Dear Little Boy of Mine"; another Norma Talmadge film, *Eternal Flame,* suggested his song with the identical title. Ball continued into the 1920s, with "For the Sake of Auld Lang Syne," the finest of his later melodies, luring paying customers to see *Lights of the Desert.*

When "Ramona" swept the country in early 1927, silent pictures were given their biggest-ever promtional song. Dedicated to Mexican-born Dolores Del Rio, who played the title role, the song was written by L. Wolfe Gilbert and Mabel Wayne, who, along with Dana Suesse, was among the rare women to succeed in the overwhelmingly masculine composing business. The tune added significantly to the popularity of *Ramona,* and was the last smash hit used primarily to inflate attendance for a non-talking feature film.

Paying homage to the talent or beauty of silent stars, from Chaplin to Vilma Banky, was another source of the tunesmiths' income. The cream of this crop, "There's a New Star in Heaven To-Night (Rudolph Valentino)," was published in 1926 "in memory of our late beloved star," who died that year at age 31 after undergoing an operation for acute appendicitis and gastric ulcers.

The best-selling song struck a sentimental chord with the battalions of heartsick fans of Rodolpho Alfonzo Raffaelo Pierre Filibert Guglielmi di Valentina d'Antonguolla the world over. For good measure, publisher Jack Mills saw to it that a large photograph of the Great Lover, at his pensive best, adorned the cover, overpowering the names of the writers, J. Keirn Brennan, Irving Mills, and James McHugh. The latter would go on to far, far better things, including five Oscar nominations and election as mayor of Beverly Hills.

In 1937, 26-year-old Jean Harlow joined Valentino in the afterworld and in song. Her death that year, during the filming of MGM's

Saratoga, inspired Nat Simon and Dick Sanford to collaborate on the dirge "There's a Platinum Star in Heaven Tonight," almost identical in title to the Valentino elegy.

Although the overwhelming majority of these promotional songs and tributes never triumphed in the marketplace, they did represent concerted efforts to further identify music with the movies. The next step, actually a megaleap forward, would occur when, after three decades of frustration, the movies sang.

AN ALL-AMERICAN PURSUIT

A uniquely American art form that has yet to be rivaled by any other country, the film musical was a blessing to show business from the moment of its inception. Besides composers and lyricists, it lifted hundreds of Broadway-trained librettists, dance directors, arrangers, instrumentalists, actors, singers, dancers, and set and costume designers to new heights of popularity, while grooming legions of unknowns with little or no theatrical experience into world-class celebrities. Riding the crest of musical pictures, musical stars zoomed up the rungs of the *Motion Picture Herald*'s annual poll of the "Top Ten" box office leaders. Selected by exhibitors, the lists have been studded with the names of attractive ladies and gentlemen, from Janet Gaynor to Elvis Presley, whose sole task was to cater to the public's ravenous appetite for songs and dances.

Everyone shared in the wealth generated by "all-talking, all-singing, all-color" musicals. The film studios, their executives, stockholders, and stars made a bundle; songwriters watched their salaries and royalties soar. Con Conrad, who contributed songs to no fewer than five motion pictures in 1929, ordered a swimming pool for his Hollywood estate solely for the purpose of stocking it with trout.

Film musicals assisted songwriters in still another way that directly affected their pocketbooks. In the earlier part of the century, the only routes open to songwriters like Conrad for selling their compositions were song plugging (a demeaning task often undertaken by the songwriters themselves), the legitimate stage, vaudeville, and dance orchestras.

Although by the mid–1920s radio was also a primary promoter of songs, it served the writers poorly. Attracting ever-growing numbers of fans, the new entertainment colossus wrought a significant switch in the public's musical habits as it developed into the biggest rival the movies faced until television confined families to their living rooms beginning in the late 1940s.

Pop music filled the airwaves in 1927. With the help of two networks — the National Broadcasting Company, founded in 1926, and the Columbia Broadcasting System, which began life in 1927 — Americans could tune in to 732 stations operating in various parts of the country. Radio sets that year could be plugged for the first time directly into electric current. Models powered by three different batteries that lasted only a few weeks became obsolete; sales of the new electric radio sets took off into the stratosphere.

How musical minded Americans were was underscored by a 1927 survey of 387 successive hours of broadcasting by the largest of the New York City radio stations. It showed that 289 hours (74 percent) were devoted to popular music, mostly jazz. The other 98 hours were given over to talk shows and classical or semi-classical music. Since many of the semi-classical selections had their origin in Broadway operettas, they also could be termed popular music.

Radio accustomed listeners to hearing their favorite songs for free, inadvertently prompting them to abandon music stores. Sales of sheet music and phonograph records, from which songwriters had traditionally derived a goodly portion of their incomes, fell sharply. To make matters worse, the tunesmiths received nothing in royalties from broadcasters. Radio station owners consistently refused to pay for using copyrighted musical material.

A similar royalty predicament, this one caued by owners of nightclubs, dance halls, and small-town theaters in particular, had led in 1914 to the founding of the American Society of Composers, Authors and Publishers. Organized by a talented group of artists headed by Victor Herbert, the society was charged primarily with acting as watchdog for the financial interests of the hapless composers and lyricists (authors), who earned nothing from the countless unauthorized and unlicensed public performances of their songs for profit. Reform was slow — so slow, in fact, that Irving Berlin, a charter member of ASCAP, established his own music publishing company in 1919 to retain control over all his copyrights, which he guarded zealously.

After prolonged litigation initiated by ASCAP, the U.S. Supreme Court finally issued a unanimous decision upholding copyright owners in their claims against infringers. The ruling gave songwriters a decisive victory in the battle for royalty payments, and the motion picture industry became a major source of income. By mid–1928, with the indefatigable Hollywood sound stages working full time for them, songwriters were happy upholders of the studios' conviction that inserting a song into a film was usually sufficient to guarantee the popularity of both.

Talking pictures rapidly became the most influential song pluggers of all time. They unleashed torrents of new and old songs, and mesmerized gargantuan audiences. They resuscitated dormant sheet music and record sales among viewers who wanted to entertain friends by playing the latest movie hits on the piano or to rehear, courtesy of the Victrola, the voices of the stars who had introduced them. Music publishers were spared many of the perils of speculation. They could now focus on Hollywood songs that were constantly being test-marketed in theaters from one end of the country to the other.

So great was the money-making potential of Hollywood that the perennial Movieland detractor Harry Warren (born Salvatore Guaragna in his beloved Brooklyn, N.Y.) moved there in 1932 and reluctantly stayed put till his death almost 50 years later. At the depth of the Great Depression—the summer of 1932—he was earning about $1,500 a week, roughly equivalent to $17,500 in 1992 dollars. The acknowledged "Father of the Hollywood Musical," Warren contributed 309 songs to 79 films between 1929 and 1967. Forty-two of them landed on radio's *Your Hit Parade* (1935–50), the all-time record for composers. In second place is Irving Berlin, with 33.

Early in his career, the Puccini- and baseball-loving Warren played piano, and a few bit parts as a gangster, in Brooklyn's Vitagraph Studios to create mood music for silent performers. In 1915 he began playing accompaniments in Flatbush movie houses. His first movie song, written in 1928 with Bud Green, was reprised by in-theater musicians during the Charleston danced in silence by Joan Crawford in *Our Dancing Daughters*. Entitled "Wob-a-ly Walk," the tune had been written earlier that year for the stage show *Paris* and introduced by Irene Bordoni. To the end of his life, Warren cherished his upbringing in Brooklyn, where, for all he knew, the ringing church bells on Sundays inspired him to write music for a living.

The movie industry had ranked as big business long before its song-and-dance films rescued box offices from the silent-picture doldrums of the mid–1920s. The average weekly attendance in the United States in the silent year of 1927 was 57 million; in 1929, when film musicals burgeoned in popularity, it jumped dramatically to 80 million, then in 1930, to 90 million. Weekly attendance never would pass the 90 million mark, although that figure was tied in 1946, 1947, and 1948.

Box office receipts climbed accordingly. The total for the whole of 1927 was $526 million; in 1930 it shot up to $732 million. That figure would not be surpassed, even with gradually inflated ticket prices, until 1940, and then by only a whisker. That year Americans spent $735 million to see the latest Hollywood offerings.

At no other time in film history were the songwriters' contributions more numerous or more experimental than between January 1929 and June 1930. The studios released 128 musical features during that 17-month period, which averages out to almost two musicals a week, a record that has yet to be equalled. As for the number of hit songs from the screen, the only other years that top 1929 are 1936, 1937, and 1938.

The major credit for leading film music into the first of its three golden ages — the years 1929 and 1930 — and for turning Hollywood into a boom town again and box offices into torrid zones goes to a singer with a powerful voice and towering talent exceeded only by elephantiasis of the ego. His name was Al Jolson. Thanks to him, a technological revolution took root in the film capital, and the manufacturing of motion pictures was changed forever.

Search for Synchronization

The technology that made the movie musical possible took a slow boat for the voyage to Hollywood. For decades, no one had been able to overcome the challenges posed by precisely matching (or synchronizing) spoken dialogue with lip movement as seen on the silent screen. Most of the difficulties were caused not by the lack of scientific talent, but by the polyglot of primitive devices available to sound engineers, who began experimenting in Europe and America in the 1890s.

Even Edison, an authentic genius, failed consistently at incorporating synchronized speech into the motion pictures produced at his breakthrough film studio, known as the "Black Maria," in West Orange,

New Jersey. First came the Kinetograph, widely identified as the world's first motion picture camera, which Edison had developed with the help of co-worker William Kennedy Laurie Dickson in 1888. Regarded by Edison as an extension of the phonograph, which the "Wizard of Menlo Park" had invented 11 years earlier, the Kinetograph was intended to photograph films that would be synchronized with the phonograph.

Like his fellow pioneers, Edison pinned his talking-picture aspirations on an awkward assortment of earphones and other sound-reproducing attachments to link what was being mouthed on the silent screen with dialogue previously recorded on phonograph cylinders. His Kinetophone, or Cameraphone, developed in the early 1900s, required such paraphernalia. But beset with faulty synchronization, sound quality, and amplification, the system soon wore out its welcome with viewers. Its promise unfulfilled, the Kinetophone died an unpublicized death, its novelty ephemeral, its impact negligible.

Although Chaplin, who introduced his "Little Tramp" character in *Kid Auto Races at Venice* in 1914, might have pursued talking pictures, he refused to do so. A partner (with Mary Pickford, Douglas Fairbanks, Sr., and D.W. Griffith) in United Artists since 1919, Chaplin undertook no research projects. When the talkies finally arrived in late 1927, he greeted them with the curt comment that "movies need dialogue as much as Beethoven symphonies need lyrics."

Apparently, Chaplin forgot that Beethoven's greatest symphony, the Ninth, does contain a lyric, in the form of Schiller's "Ode to Joy," in the final movement. Not until 1940 would Chaplin speak his first words on film, although he had sung several verses of a humorous ditty in *Modern Times* four years earlier.

Like Griffith, Chaplin imbued his films with musical accompaniments, most of which he himself composed. His background score for the silent *Circus* (1928) is excellent, as is the one for *City Lights* (1931), with its clever caricature of pompous political speechmaking using distorted musical sounds. His poignant theme song for *Modern Times* was revived in 1954 after John Turner and Geoffrey Parsons added the lyric to a slightly revised melody that became known as "Smile." But Chaplin's, as well as Griffith's, sterling reputation will rest forever on the visual creativity he etched on a screen imprisoned in silence.

Hollywood executives were aware of the advantages to accrue to

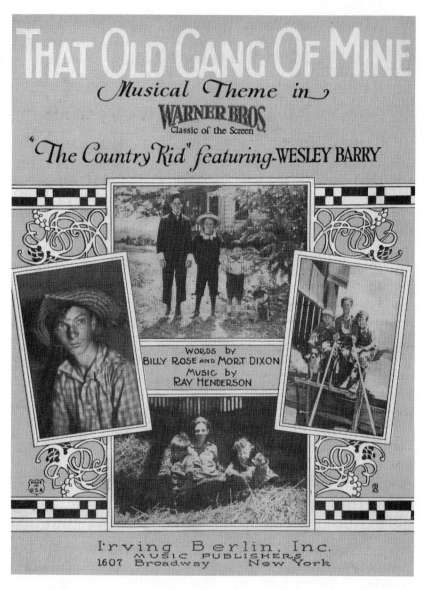

One of the first big hits actually commissioned by the producers of a movie, 1923.

their industry from talking pictures. One of them was prestige, denied for so long by intellectuals, who regarded most silents as simple-minded mime shows. The British writer and theater lover St. John Ervine best compressed the cinéastes' opinion of "shadow plays" versus the stage into a single sentence: "The moving picture is mechanically superb and intellectually contemptible." As for moviegoers, Ervine described them as "celluloid nitwits." To H.L. Mencken the movies were "fodder for half-wits."

Talking pictures would allow the industry to compete more forcefully with Broadway, where spoken words were the heartbeat of drama and comedy. Films could flow smoothly from episode to episode without interruptions to give audiences time to read the printed titles (or dialogue). Above all, Hollywood could produce its own songfests and divert spectators from the stage into film houses. The only persons unimpressed by the potential of talking pictures were the theater owners. And they had a pretty strong argument to support their opposition.

In 1923, New York City's Rivoli Theatre previewed a true technological marvel by showing the first sound-on-film motion pictures. They consisted of a series of short vaudeville and musical acts presented by Lee DeForest, widely regarded as the "Father of Radio" for his 1906 patent of a three-electrode vacuum tube called the triode, or spherical audion detector. His work made wireless telephony practicable and paved the way for the radio industry.

For the Rivoli program, DeForest notched the dialogue directly onto the filmstrips. Relieved of wooing the coquettish phonograph, his pictures actually talked and sang from the screen using the Phonofilm.

In 1924, DeForest released a six-minute campaign speech by New York Governor Alfred E. Smith, who was seeking (unsuccessfully) the Democratic Party's presidential nomination. Later, DeForest invited President Coolidge, the winner of the 1924 election, to orate on the state of the national economy, then about to take off on a spree of unparalleled vigor. Luckily for Coolidge, he did not live up to his nickname "Silent Cal," and became the first chief executive to speak from a sound track.

Neither the 1923 skits nor the 1924 speeches aroused enthusiasm, although the reason had nothing to do with the personalities or dialogue. Most of the public was never exposed to the films. Only a handful of theater owners nationwide were willing to trifle with costly sound equipment while the silents continued to rake in the customers. In 1925, DeForest abandoned his Phonofilm process.

VITAPHONE ENTERS THE PICTURE(S)

It was then left to the Warner brothers (Al, Harry, Jack and the hard-driving Sam) to aerate Hollywood with the fresh breeze of innovation — and music played a prominent role. By early 1926, two major competing systems for sound transmission were available — sound on disc, represented by Vitaphone, and sound on film, which Fox Film called Movietone.

Upset over depressed box office revenues from their latest silent pictures, the Warners took a costly gamble with Vitaphone, and the studio became its first licensee. The hugely complicated, albeit miraculous, system was far from perfect, but it was a significant improvement over every other sound-on-disc process ever developed.

Vitaphone was an offspring of Edison's rather than DeForest's pioneering, in that it relied on the phonograph to give voice to films. What it did was couple an electric record player and the film projector. The turntables were driven by the projector motor to maintain synchronization, while a lathe cut the transcriptions. Sound tracks were played on a series of discs with 16-inch diameters. Thanks to the fast-developing science of electroacoustics, the recorded sound could easily be amplified to fill even the largest theaters.

The fragile disc continued as the chief sound enhancer until 1932, when the far superior sound-on-film system deposed it. With Movietone and its successors, sound was recorded on the same strip of film containing the images. Audio tracks were photographically recorded as variations in brightness. Sensing these changes, a photosensitive element reproduced the audio signal, which was fed to loudspeakers behind the screen. Fox had begun practicing with the process for its talking Movietone newsreels in late 1927.

Warner Bros. debuted Vitaphone at the Manhattan Opera House on August 5, 1926, for its film *Don Juan,* with John Barrymore and Mary Astor. To accent the importance of the sound track, the studio gave special acknowledgement to its new system. "Vitaphone and John Barrymore" were the stars, according to newspaper ads.

No performer spoke a word, but the audience could hear some sound effects, like the clicking of dueling swords, and the musical

Erno Rapée and Lew Pollack's "Diane," 1927.

accompaniment — the first Vitaphone-synchronized background score — by Dr. William Axt. Playing the music on the sound track was the prestigious 107-member New York Philharmonic Orchestra. Melodies also resounded from the Vitaphoned short subjects that filled out the bill. Mischa Elman treated spectators to a violin solo, and opera stars Giovanni Martinelli and Marion Talley sang from the screen.

So complex was Vitaphone that Will H. Hays, a former U.S. postmaster general under President Harding and then the czar of film censorship, tried to explain it to the *Don Juan* audience from his own sound track. His words penetrated few minds, but Vitaphone impressed many of them. The sell-out *Don Juan* was transferred to the nearby Warners' Theater on the reserved-seat basis customary for first-run pictures in New York City. Tickets sold for 50 cents to one dollar for weekday matinees, 50 cents to two dollars for evening performances. Low by today's standards, the prices were high for 1926, considering that a single room with bath in pleasant Times Square hotels ranged between three and five dollars a day.

In October 1926, the executive vice president of Bell Telephone Laboratories (Western Electric), Inc., Edward B. Craft, took his turn at explaining Vitaphone in the short talking feature *Voice from the Screen.* The system, after all, was his company's baby; Craft apparently felt compelled to demystify it.

The film ran 34 minutes and included technological details, a visit to the Warner Bros. Vitaphone sound stage, and a static long-distance shot of a "Witt & Berg," who duetted a novelty Hawaiian tune on a guitar and ukulele. Again, it is doubtful that audiences comprehended the process by the time the speech, tour, and song were over. But little doubt was left that the reality of talking pictures was racing down the pike.

Also in the fall of 1926, film houses were beguiling hoards of customers with Fox's *What Price Glory,* based on the Maxwell Anderson–Laurence Stallings stage play of two brawling World War I U.S. Marines, Captain Flagg (Victor McLaglen) and Sergeant Quirt (Edmund Lowe). Its slapstick notwithstanding, it is as antiwar a film as the later *All Quiet on the Western Front,* also scripted by Anderson. Again, no character spoke. From the standpoint of the bluenoses in the audience, the omission of dialogue was salutary, since the no-no phrase "son-of-a-bitch" can be read clearly three times from McLaglen's silent lips.

The picture remains most noteworthy for Erno Rapée and Lew Pollack's "Charmaine," the first Movietone-synchronized song hit, which followed namesake Dolores Del Rio, the daughter of "Cognac Peter," a small-town French hosteler, practically everywhere she went. Like the film, the song was a tremendous success. The handwriting was on the theater walls: the era of the live orchestra and solo pianist was approaching its end. By the beginning of 1929, some 20,000 theater instrumentalists had lost their jobs.

Rapée and Pollack duplicated their good fortune in early 1927, adding the lovely waltz "Diane" ("I'm in heaven when I see you smile, / My Diane, my Diane") to Fox's otherwise all-silent *Seventh Heaven*, one of the better, and teariest, of the year's films, and the first to couple the vastly appealing love team of Janet Gaynor and Charles Farrell. They would co-star in 11 more pictures up to 1934.

"You Ain't Heard Nothin' Yet!"

But it was *The Jazz Singer* that made the real history. Opening its two-a-day performance schedule on October 6, 1927, at New York City's Warners' Theater, it was the first major film to combine synchronized music, sound effects, and some dialogue. It taught the movies how to sing, and its influence on the future of the Hollywood musical was profound.

Warners cast Al Jolson (born Asa Yoelson in Russian Lithuania) to play Jakie Rabinowitz, the cantankerous son of a fifth-generation cantor who prefers singing jazz tunes in nightclubs to chanting *Kol Nidre* in synagogues. Jolson at the end of 1926 had participated in an experimental Vitaphone short, *Al Jolson in a Plantation Act,* singing "April Showers" and a few other songs in his customary black-masked face. Few theaters could handle sound, and so the picture was not widely distributed. Previously, in 1923, D.W. Griffith had signed Jolson to appear in the appropriately titled *Mammy's Boy*, but the film was never made.

In many ways, Samson Raphaelson's *Jazz Singer* storyline paralleled Jolson's life. His own father had wanted him to be a cantor, but young Asa joined a circus instead, later performing in cafes as a vaudeville singer-entertainer in tandem with brother Harry (Hirsch), and, following his Broadway debut in *La Belle Paree* in 1911, becoming America's premier stage star. He also developed into one of the most disliked performers of his time.

Irving Caesar, a friend and associate who collaborated with George Gershwin in 1919 to write Jolson's biggest hit, "Swanee," never forgot the entertainer's impact on him:

> Al had the most electrifying personality I ever came across. He could
> grab and hold an audience quicker and longer than anybody else.

The jazz singer and his mammy — Al Jolson and Eugénie Besserer in *The Jazz Singer,* **1927.**

> Unfortunately, he could also be cruel, self-serving, and brusque even
> with people who thought the world of him and his magnificent talent.
> In fact, that's the way he usually was. He broke the heart of everyone
> who knew him.

Agreeing with Caesar on the talent angle, critic-humorist Robert
Benchley, writing in *Life* magazine in 1926, called attention to Jolson's
"supernatural hold over an audience." He was the "greatest personality to appear since John the Baptist," Benchley continued, quite
possibly with tongue firmly in cheek.

Jolson's high-octane *Jazz Singer* performance is more theatrical
than cinematic, especially in the closeups, at the time unique to filmmaking and foreign to most stage stars. He jogs through the film with
pop eyes vibrating with unalloyed enthusiasm or glazed over with sorrow. Yet his reprise of "My Mammy," written for him by Joe Young,
Sam M. Lewis, and Walter Donaldson for *Sinbad* (1921), is a thing of

power, regardless of his maudlin black-face delivery and his ever-supportive mother's tearful appreciation. Actually, Jolson should have sung the song to Ma Bell, which had invented Vitaphone three years earlier.

Although *The Jazz Singer* is about 65 percent silent, complete with titles for dialogue, Jolson does insert spoken sentences, including his familiar chant, "Wait a minute! Wait a minute! You ain't heard nothin' yet!," which he hollers to highly receptive admirers in a speakeasy. Midway through the film, about two minutes of dialogue are exchanged among Jolson, his mother (Eugénie Besserer), and his cantor father, played by Warner Oland, an actor of Swedish descent who in 1931 would emerge as the Confucius-quoting, Honolulu-based Chinese detective Charlie Chan. (Also appearing briefly as a chorus girl was Myrna Loy. In 1934, she would star for the first time as the wife of another screen detective, Nick Charles, in the *Thin Man* series.)

As for the songs, *The Jazz Singer* uses seven, all but one of them Jolson-established standards, setting a musical pattern that would continue throughout film musical history. Original songs were always welcome, but no producer was rash enough to turn away reprises of well-known tunes, especially when the singer was the same performer who had popularized them.

The first song—"My Gal Sal," by Paul Dresser, the older brother of novelist Theodore Dreiser, who kept the family name—is sung not by Jolson, but by Bobby Gordon, playing the teenage jazz singer with a "tear in his voice." Gordon also launches into the familiar "Waiting for the Robert E. Lee," but is chased out of a saloon before he can finish it.

Other golden oldies sung by Jolson himself are "Toot, Toot, Tootsie!" and "Dirty Hands, Dirty Face," the first an up-tempo number long associated with the entertainer, the second a heartfelt tribute to boyhood that Jolson had introduced in *Bombo* in 1921. Both singing styles had served Jolson admirably over the years and would continue to do so into the 1930s.

Jolson also gives a rousing rendition and encore of "Blue Skies," an Irving Berlin tune introduced a few months earlier by Belle Baker in a Florenz Ziegfeld stage disaster entitled *Betsy*. Jolson's version helped immeasurably to propel the song, one of Berlin's own favorites, to the top of the year's popularity charts.

The song had been inserted furtively into *Betsy* so that Richard

Rodgers and Lorenz Hart, whose contract with Ziegfeld forbade song insertions by other writers, would not know of it until it was too late to act. Accordingly, Miss Baker sang it at the end of the show. She brought down the house and then further enthralled the audience by reprising it 23 times. On the final go-round, she forgot the lyric. Berlin, sitting in the first row, stood up, yelled out the words, and they finished the song together.

Rodgers and Hart refused to speak to Miss Baker for the next 12 years.

Jolson's only original number in the film is "Mother of Mine, I Still Have You," which he also sings to his mammy. Written by Jolson, Grant Clarke, and Louis Silvers, the song radiates sentimentality, particularly in the concluding praise to his mother's determination to stand by him after all his plans have gone awry and his fair-weather pals have deserted him. Clarke, incidentally, was one of the very few lyricists to collaborate with Berlin, providing the words for his "Everything Is Rosy Now for Rosie" in 1909.

With all its flaws, *The Jazz Singer* permitted viewers who had never stepped inside a legitimate theater to see the face behind one of the most celebrated singing voices of the era. Moviegoers in 1919 had not been so lucky. An even more respected voice, that of Enrico Caruso, was absent from the only silent film the great operatic star made, *My Cousin*. Understandably, it was one of that year's biggest flops.

The tinniness of the sound sequences notwithstanding, the opening-day *Jazz Singer* audience loved the whole package, as did Jolson, who almost succumbed to tears after a Broadway-like standing ovation. The October 7 *New York Times* declared that the "Vitaphoned songs and some dialogue had been introduced most adroitly." To playwright Robert E. Sherwood, then also a film critic, the picture was "fraught with tremendous significance." Writing in the periodical *Silent Drama* for October 27, 1927, he added that *The Jazz Singer* "proves that talking movies are considerably more than a lively possibility; they are close to an accomplished fact."

Rather than embrace the new technology, many moguls remained wary of it. They were preoccupied not so much with the great potential that *The Jazz Singer* had opened up to them as with the huge sums needed to wire their own studio stages and the thousands of theaters that played their pictures. On October 6, 1927, only about 500 forward-looking movie houses were equipped to handle sound. Nonetheless, Warners marched on, and on July 6, 1928, exactly nine months after *The Jazz Singer*, released the first 100 percent talking picture, the 57-minute gangster melodrama *Lights of New York*. Underscoring the growing popularity of sound films, it made an astounding $2 million profit.

Another notable exception to the fear of the new was Paramount Pictures, whose teams of songwriters would eventually win more Oscar nominations for Best Song (51) than those working for any other studio, including mighty MGM (37). In spite of a disastrous fire that leveled several of its sound stages under construction, Paramount promptly rebuilt them and joined the talking-picture parade in mid–1928 with *Interference*. The process used to record it was the Photophone, developed jointly by General Electric Company and Radio Corporation of America.

Rarely outwitted for very long, the nervous movie executives devised the perfect strategy while waiting to see whether their individual nascent sound systems would pass muster with the public. Up to early 1930, they released their print negatives in two versions. One contained audible background music and sound effects, and often bits of dialogue as well. For example, the late–1928 remake of the romance *Evangeline,* this one starring Dolores Del Rio, used sound only for the theme song, by Jolson and Billy Rose, and certain effects. Not a single word was spoken. The second negative was totally silent.

Theater owners could pick whichever version they wanted, and most chose the soundless ones. As late as the fall of 1929, fully two years after *The Jazz Singer* opened, only about 2,500 of the nation's 16,000 theaters had installed sound equipment.

THE MOVIES' COLORING BOOK

Hardly had filmgoers responded enthusiastically to the talkies when the moguls drew up their limousines in a circle and accelerated their competition with musical Broadway. Monochrome, or black-and-white, film made their pictures look stark, even bleak, when compared with the splashes of color common to stage sets and costumes. So the word went out: movies must be shot in color, period.

Like sound, color was not unknown to the 1920s film industry. In the final decade of the 19th century, women workers in France were painstakingly tinting filmstrips with color, frame by frame, by hand or using primitive filters. With the arrival in 1915 of Technicolor, thanks to Dr. Herbert T. Kalmus and a team of physicists at the Massachusetts Institute of Technology, the movies inherited the finest of all color systems. By 1922, Kalmus had expanded the invention's color range and improved the quality by exposing two negatives in the same camera at the same time. Each negative was shot through a colored filter to record distinct parts of the spectrum. They were then dyed to accent red-orange and blue-green as the basic colors.

Much like the human voice, two-strip (or two-process) Technicolor was used sparingly in the infancy of the Vitaphone era. Most producers confined it to a single sequence, typically a musical number. The "Wedding of the Painted Doll" ballet in 1929's *Broadway Melody* was originally photographed in color, but reshot in black and white when MGM's production chief, Irving Thalberg, was disenchanted with what he regarded as a mosaic with shoddy tiles.

In May 1929, the pioneering Warner Brothers released *On with the Show,* the first all-talking musical in 100 percent two-strip Technicolor. Almost simultaneously, MGM brought out its own all-talking, all-color *Rogue Song,* directed by actor Lionel Barrymore.

Far the better of the two, *On with the Show* displayed the consummate artistry of 28-year-old Ethel Waters, who stole the show by singing Grant Clarke and Harry Akst's "Am I Blue?" Thus did the young lady, known as "Sweet Mama Stringbean" in her vaudeville days, and generally regarded as the finest of all jazz singers after Bessie Smith, enter film history as the first black performer to introduce a hit song from a sound track. Also making his talking-picture debut in the picture was Joe E. Brown, the wide-mouth comedian who would play Cap'n Andy in MGM's 1951 edition of *Show Boat.* Newcomers Betty Compson and Sally O'Neill sang the two songwriters' second *On with the Show* success, "Let Me Have My Dreams."

Unfortunately, the "colorization" of movies turned out to be more sensational than appealing over the average 90-minute time span. It was often impossible to separate pure blue from green, or solid red from pale pink. The result was such exotic sights as pink grass, rose-colored hills, and rusty red, or magenta-tinted, skies. Where the colors were distinguishable, they frequently paled into white or light brown, sometimes before the Technicolor sequences had run their course.

As many critics contended, color films often did little more than raise the technical standards of poor movies. In a perverse way, though, the worst of them helped to accent further the importance of the songs. As the old saw regarding failed Broadway musicals warned, it's the score that is crucial to success; after all, you can't hum the scenery.

So rapid was the refinement of Technicolor in the early 1930s that while the two-process version was being improved, out came the three-process followup. As the term implies, three negatives were passed through the camera and dyed cyan, magenta, and yellow. Individual primary colors were now much sharper and more natural than ever before, and they were contrasted or complemented by various shades equally clear and lifelike. Walt Disney was the first to use the new Technicolor for his animated cartoon *Flowers and Trees* in 1932.

The high cost of three-process Technicolor prevented its use throughout a feature film until Rouben Mamoulian's *Becky Sharp* in 1935, although it also appeared in the "Ice Cream Fantasy" in *Kid Millions* (1934) and the final scene of *The Little Colonel* (1935). By 1945, Technicolor was functioning as faithful handmaiden to practically all big-budget musicals and was sometimes derided as "MGM pretty" because of that studio's generous application of it. Indeed, Hollywood lavished Technicolor on audiences to such a degree that when the black-and-white Sammy Cahn–Jule Styne musical *It Happened in Brooklyn* made the rounds in 1947, it was a rare exception to the rule.

It is unfortunate that except for the body of movies shot in durable three-strip Technicolor, only a scattering can be viewed today in their original color. Unless films using two-strip Technicolor or such subsequent processes as Metrocolor and Deluxe were guarded against humidity and abrupt temperature changes, an expensive process, the color might fade entirely in as few as five years. Even worse, many of the movies themselves have self-destructed. All films made before 1951, when "safety stock" was introduced, were shot on cellulose nitrate film, a highly combustible substance that eventually dissolves into powder.

Activated by innovations, but too competitive to appreciate their long-range significance, the studio magnates paid little heed to the history being made on their own sound stages. Preservation of their landmark achievements was given almost no priority.

CHAPTER THREE

Music, Music Everywhere: 1928–1929

*L*IKE SO MANY sand castles swept away in a tidal wave, silent films were overwhelmed by the talkies, which by mid–1928 had become the salvation for filmdom's plunging profits. Apart from the performers, the biggest beneficiaries of Hollywood's initial forays into sound were the writers of theme songs.

The moguls, impelled by their long-standing delight in excess, decided early in the year that every picture they made, including dramas, must have at least one melody of love in the background, and they commissioned an outstanding medley of stage-trained tune-smiths to grind them out. Almost all their songs, except the numerous waltzes, were cast in the standard AABA (32 bars plus release) format.

The obliging partnership of Rapée and Pollack led the theme song pack in 1928 with "Angela Mia," a charming song that lilted its way through Gaynor and Farrell's *Street Angel*; "Someday, Somewhere (We'll Meet Again)," inserted into Dolores Del Rio's *Red Dance*; and "Destiny," from *Four Devils,* also starring Janet Gaynor. An excellent but unheralded songwriter, Pollack in 1905 had composed one of the first successful jazz tunes written by a white man, "That's a Plenty." Its unusual construction contains three themes of 16 bars each, with a 12-bar interlude between the two choruses of the third theme.

Also in 1928, *Lilac Time* introduced L. Wolfe Gilbert and Nathaniel Shilkret's lovely "Jeannine, I Dream of Lilac Time," while Lou Davis and J. Fred Coots's "A Precious Little Thing Called Love" sweetened the sound track of the Gary Cooper–Nancy Carroll version of *Shopworn Angel*. Victor Schertzinger, accompanied by Edmund Goulding

37

and Will Jason as the only American composers to direct films, added "Another Kiss" to the otherwise forgettable *Manhattan Cocktail.*

Greta Garbo, who would not utter a syllable on film until she played Anna Christie in 1930, was among the dramatic stars given themes to glide along with. One of them, "That Melody of Love," insinuated a path through *Love,* Hollywood's first attempt at *Anna Karenina.* (Garbo would also star in the 1935 talking version.) The song was a collaboration by publicist-lyricist Howard Dietz, who designed the MGM logo and gave the studio its motto, "Arts Gratis Artis" ("Art for Art's Sake"), and Walter Donaldson, a superior hit-maker who would receive an Oscar nomination in 1937.

Most 1928 theme songs were recorded as instrumentals. But then Lupe Velez sang the hit "Yo Te Amo Means I Love You," by Al Bryan and Richard A. Whiting, in *Wolf Song.* Her pleasant rendition of the equally pleasing lyric turned the page to still another chapter in Hollywood's musical history. From out of the studios' executive suites came the command: everybody sing. So many songs were available that it was a simple matter for even the least twinkling of stars, musically inclined or not, to obey the new edict. Soon, theme songs were being sung in every category of film imaginable, however inappropriate their inclusion and undistinguished the vocalizing.

Cops-and-robbers screenplays halted their chase scenes long enough to permit a song to swell up from the sound track. One of 1929's finest, Clarke and Silvers's "Weary River," was sung by Richard Barthelmess, playing a musical-minded gangster, in the film of the same name. Frank Fay crooned Ray Perkins's "Under a Texas Moon" in the Warner Bros. film, the first Western in Technicolor. For another melodrama set in Cactusland, *The Big Trail,* Joseph McCarthy and James F. Hanley wrote the charming "Song of the Big Trail." One of the featured performers was a babyfaced cowpoke by the name of John Wayne, then 23.

Other singing theme songs were interpolated into boilerplate adventure films (Arthur Freed and Nacio Herb Brown's "Chant of the Jungle," for *Untamed*); college romps (Bobby Dolan and Walter O'Keefe's "Little by Little," for *The Sophomore*); and tearjerkers like *Woman Disputed,* for which Bernie Grossman and Edward Ward raised the ridiculous to its apogee in a frenzy to match song and film titles. They finally compromised on "Disreputable Woman, I Love You," now a minor cult classic.

Detective yarns also serenaded audiences. Jack Yellen and Harry Akst contributed "(I Says to Myself, Says I, Says I) There's the One for Me" to *Bulldog Drummond,* starring Ronald Colman. Overpowered by the windy, tongue-twisting title, the song suffered an undeserved death shortly after the picture was released.

So many carryover icons from the silents were vying for roles in the talkies that it became incumbent on studio heads to provide basic training in the requirements of the new medium. Elocution lessons were made available to — and sometimes forced on — performers who for years had depended on gestures and titles to convey their emotions and words. Also rampant were singing coaches, hired to instruct holdovers and newcomers alike in the art of putting a song over.

Silent-screen siren Gloria Swanson joined the chorus by singing a Vincent Youmans song ("You're the One") in *What a Widow!,* and another by DeSylva, Brown, and Henderson ("Come to Me") in *Indiscreet.* Mary Pickford, that empress of the silents, sang and danced a Busby Berkeley–directed number in top hat, white tie, and tails in *Kiki.* Norma Shearer reprised the familiar 1919 title song in *Smilin' Through.* Walter Pidgeon, the future Mr. Miniver, baritoned in *Viennese Nights* and other musical films. Claudette Colbert offered her deep-throated version of Leo Robin and Ralph Rainger's "Give Me Liberty or Give Me Love" in *Torch Singer.* Robert Montgomery sang "Go Home and Tell Your Mother," one of four delectable Dorothy Fields–James McHugh tunes in *Love in the Rough,* and Jean Harlow warbled Freed and Brown's melodic title song in *Hold Your Man.*

Accomplished as these heavyweights were in the acting department, they very likely would have starved to death, save for Pidgeon and Miss Swanson, if forced to sing for their suppers, and the practice was eventually dropped in favor of dubbing. In later years, such professional off-screen singers as Marni Nixon would excel at recording the lyrics only mouthed in silence by big-name performers. Hers was the singing voice of Audrey Hepburn (*My Fair Lady*), Deborah Kerr (*The King and I*), Natalie Wood (*West Side Story*), as well as of Jeanne Crain, Janet Leigh, Ida Lupino, Diana Lynn, Hope Lange, and many others.

Unable to hone their skills in the pre-sound era, very few performers able to sing or dance crossed the threshold from silents to talkies. Eddie Cantor managed it easily, though, as did John Boles, Dolores Del Rio, Lupe Velez, and Joan Crawford.

By mid–1928, while Hollywood was wrapping its dramas in theme songs at a frantic pace, the moguls focused their attention on Broadway. Had not a major purpose of talking pictures been to permit films to compete with the stage musical? The talkies were here. What was missing was the competition.

With songs now the locus of their activities, the studio chieftains girded their loins, revved up their sound stages, and rushed helterskelter into the production of bona fide musicals. Every kind of show for which Broadway was noted became the targets of their madcap rivalry. Concentrating first on the operetta, the moguls soon eyed the galaxy of musical comedies awaiting their favor and gobbled them up. Then came their own versions of the stage revue.

The Hollywood musical was off and running.

THE SOUNDS OF MUSIC

Talking musical shows quickly claimed their first casualty in the battle between the film and the stage, or, more accurately, between film and film. By late 1928, the oxymoronic "silent musical" had been consigned to the Hollywood boneyard. Able by then to reproduce Broadway scores and bring the glitz and glamour of that venerable thoroughfare to even the tiniest hamlet, the studios closed the books on non-talking musical pictures that necessarily had concentrated on the usually limp librettos and left the music to theater orchestras and pianists.

Never again to be duplicated were such "unmusical musicals" as Franz Lehar's *Merry Widow* of 1925 (in which Clark Gable played a bit part), the Gershwins' *Lady Be Good*, Rudolf Friml's *Rose-Marie,* Walter Donaldson's *Kid Boots,* all from 1926, and Sigmund Romberg's *Student Prince* of 1927, that rarest of all operettas with an unhappy ending.

Henceforth, Hollywood was able to translate even grand opera, which also had been given the silent treatment in the past. A musicless *La Bohème* had been filmed in 1926 with Lillian Gish and John Gilbert in the leading roles. Fortunately, Henri Murger's novel *Scènes de la Vie de Bohème,* which neatly balances tragedy and romance, proved to be quite filmable, and the picture posted a profit. Not so lucky was the German-made *Der Rosenkavalier,* which opened the same year. Classical composer Richard Strauss did his best to add stature and dignity to the silent film by writing a tad of extra background music and conducting the live orchestra, but it was denied commercial success.

To activate their new musical-production policy, producers first had to embark on talent searches. Naturally, it was to New York City that they scurried to buy properties and rent the services of almost everybody who had ever spoken or sung in public. Next, they set their sights on Europe.

Broadway had long ago set the pattern that Hollywood would stitch into the fabric of its film musicals. The first American stage musical, *The Black Crook,* opened in 1866, and from that year on, hundreds of stage shows testified to the appeal of combining music, dance, dialogue, and plot into bonanza entertainment. Huge phalanxes of beautiful girls strutted down staircases, comedians told jokes, music bubbled up from even the desert, and ingenues wept when their lovers were ensnared temporarily by a rival's come-hither eyes. The librettos, typically lightweight if at times terribly complicated, were yoked as if by law to happy endings. Stage musicals regularly paired off distraught youngsters who reclaimed each other with the mandatory hug, kiss, and tuneful curtain-lowering ballad.

Americans' fondness for Broadway musicals, which Hollywood fortified, has been clearly documented. Of the ten longest-running shows in Times Square history, eight have been musicals, each of which has boasted at least 2,700 consecutive performances on its first run. Heading the list is *A Chorus Line,* which, when it closed in early 1990, had racked up 6,104 performances, almost twice as many as *Life with Father,* the champion of non-musicals with 3,334 performances. Seven of the eight musicals have been made into films; the exception, *Cats* (nearing the 5,000 mark), has yet to close on Broadway.[1]

Like nomads taking identity from their surroundings, the peripatetic Hollywood talent scouts absorbed enough reality along 1928 Broadway to acknowledge that they were neophytes in the intricacies of musical-making. The result was their assurance that the Easterners would be given a free hand in adapting scripts and staging production numbers if they agreed to travel west. So on the studios' behalf, it must be said that the artistic errors the industry committed in 1928-29

---

[1] *The other all-time top Broadway hits:* Oh! Calcutta!, *5,852;* 42nd Street, *3,486;* Grease, *3,388;* Fiddler on the Roof, *3,242;* Tobacco Road, *3,182;* Hello, Dolly, *2,844; and* My Fair Lady, *2,717.*

were imposed rather than indigenous. Hollywood's sound stages lay astride a fault line of repetitiveness that stretched as far east as New York City.

But the Broadway expatriates and Hollywoodites lived in symbiosis, like Siamese twins joined together at the money clip. Only a few took note of how poor most of their toe-in-the-water musical pictures were. Practically all the barbs were thrown by critics, to which producer Joe Pasternak provided the perfect response: "Critics don't buy tickets." And anyway, weren't these films the source of scads of songs that were winning the affection of audiences everywhere?

Unlike the Hollywood producers, the New Yorkers blithely ignored their own unique handicaps, which included an acquaintance with movie-making that was at best skeletal. Consequently, they hurriedly cobbled together dozens of photographed stage musicals festooned with reminders of their own theatrical background: *Broadway; Broadway Babies; Howdy, Broadway; Broadway Scandals; Broadway Hoofers; Lord Byron of Broadway; The Broadway Melody; Gold Diggers of Broadway;* et cetera.

In the meantime, early in 1928, the moguls adopted film pioneer Adolph Zukor's credo that big-name foreign entertainers mean big box office in America. Zukor had been instrumental in coaxing the "Divine" Sarah Bernhardt to make a film in 1912, and accordingly Hollywood bigwigs packed their steamer trunks and headed for the big talent roundup in the Old World.

The music halls of Europe, from which Chaplin had emerged, were renowned as fertile breeding grounds for star material, and it was in them that the studio heads expected to discover another generation of illustrious performers. But by scrupulously avoiding Mistinguette, the legendary but aging Folies-Bergère star, and Josephine Baker, the daughter of a St. Louis laundress and by this time the Continent's leading black entertainer (she had even appeared in several French silents in 1927), the scouts returned home with few potential sensations under contract.

Undeterred, the studios recruited a number of foreign-born Americans as substitutes. Fifi D'Orsay, a Canadian veteran of American vaudeville who had never visited France, was gallicized into the very model of a Parisian chanteuse. She sang her best-known song, James F. Hanley's "Cute Little Things You Do" in *Young As You Feel* (1929), following it up with the equally popular "You're Simply

Delish," by Arthur Freed and Joseph Meyer, delivered as a duet with Cliff Edwards, better known as "Ukulele Ike," in *Those Three French Girls.*

Similiarly, the Scotch singer-dancer Jack Buchanan, on Broadway since 1924, was shipped to Hollywood, where he appeared in the film version of Cole Porter's *Paris,* and then teamed with Jeanette MacDonald in her third feature film, *Monte Carlo,* one of the most memorable musicals of the time. Directed by the versatile Ernst Lubitsch, who almost alone laced charm and wit with irony and made it appealing, the film debuted one of the first and best anti–Depression songs, "Beyond the Blue Horizon" (where, according to lyricist Leo Robin, a beautiful day is waiting to dawn).

The great Irish tenor John McCormack starred in *Song o' My Heart,* which flopped despite Joseph McCarthy and James F. Hanley's lovely title song and "I Feel You Near Me." It was agreed that McCormack certainly could sing. What he could not do very well was act, a deficiency that abruptly collapsed his fledgling movie career.

But it was Zukor himself who landed an authentic celebrity from foreign shores when he imported Maurice Chevalier from the Folies-Bergère in 1928 to play the lead in *Innocents of Paris,* Paramount's first musical. Billed in the opening credits as the "world's greatest entertainer," the same phrase once used by the Shuberts to identify Jolson, Chevalier nonchalantly sings "Louise" in his highly accented but serviceable English, giving scant indication of the tremendous popularity the song would command. Still one of the biggest successes in the pantheon of film songs, it overwhelmed every other number in the picture, including the memorable "On Top of the World, Alone," also by Leo Robin and Richard A. Whiting.

The next year, Chevalier co-starred with Jeanette MacDonald in the first of their four screen sojourns together, *The Love Parade,* a sly and sardonic piece of fluff also piloted by Lubitsch. Writing the four excellent songs were lyricist Clifford Grey and composer Victor Schertzinger. In "My Love Parade," Chevalier merrily chronicles the names and charms of his female conquests, while Miss MacDonald sings the beautiful waltz "Dream Lover" and the militaristic "Song of the Grenadiers." The score is also the source of a true classic comedy song, "Let's Be Common."

Chevalier's astounding popularity made him the beneficiary of the crown jewel in Whiting's catalogue, "My Ideal." Among the simplest and loveliest of all screen songs, it easily would have qualified for an Oscar nomination, and most likely won the prize, but Whiting and his fellow songwriters were not yet allowed to participate in Academy Award competition.

Of all the busy behind-the-scenes craftsmen, none was weighted down with more or tighter deadlines than the songwriters, especially in 1928-29. Shouldering the herculean task of often working on three musical pictures at the same time, Hollywood's contract songwriters were further pressured by commands from above to turn out nothing but hits. They never succeeded at that impossible goal, but they came close — very close.

MUSICAL-PRODUCTION PITFALLS

Unaccustomed to camera and closeups and microphones, most professional actors, whether from New York or Europe, were reduced by film to amateurs, delivering stilted performances replete with the posturing reminiscent of the most mediocre of silents and, in fact, of some stage plays as well. They remained motionless after delivering a punchline or song as if awaiting a live audience's laughter or applause to subside before reactivating themselves.

Stretched-out platoons of dancers were squeezed into much too small a space to accommodate them, and the legwork was celebrated for its clumsy exuberance and almost total lack of innovation. It was not unusual for moviegoers to glimpse perspiration stains on gowns when the dancers raised their arms, so powerful was the heat generated by the studio klieg lights.

Skits were generally unfunny, relying on overexposed jokes and routines that already had made the rounds of vaudeville and legitimate stage houses the country over. Taking a tip from Freud's observation that topicality is a "fertile source of pleasure in a great many jokes," writers gave comedians lines redolent with 1920s slang, personalities, and events. Contemporary viewers, unless students of pop culture, find little reason for guffawing. The ancient truism that nothing in show business has a shorter life span than a joke lived on. Indeed, much of the humor in these early films was unintentional, stemming from occasional faulty lip and sound synchronization, like mismatched song lyrics and door slams.

But the performers can be excused for their lapses in professionalism.

All were hampered from displaying the full range of their talents by the shortcomings of the very machinery that had made talking musicals possible. Instead of permitting singers and dancers to add burnish to their careers, the talkies abruptly ended most of them.

The chief culprit was the new bulky, uncompromising sound camera, which practically eliminated tracking, or following characters on the move from one screen to another. Viewers usually stared at one stationary frame, like a picture hanging on a wall, throughout entire sequences. The typical scene opened on a bare set onto which everybody walked, as if from stage right. Locked in place, they then went about their acting business while straining to avoid peering into the camera lens, and exited en masse.

During much of the 1928-29 gestation period, the camera was isolated in a soundproof booth so that it would not pick up unwanted noises from the set or the whir and grind of the camera itself. The lens recorded the action by focusing on it through a plate glass window. This utter lack of camera flexibility was, in fact, regressive. In the early stage of the silents, tripods were actually nailed to the floor to steady the camera and keep it from shifting out of focus.

Fortunately, Hollywood executives have never been averse to innovation, despite the age-old chorus of complaints that they systematically retreated from it. The sound track was itself a major technological departure that killed the silent film, which even at the time of its death was enjoying a golden age of its own. Driven into continuous trial and error by the complexities of making musical pictures, producers grew accustomed to biting into unripe fruit hoping to taste victory. Milestone followed milestone at such breathtaking speed that Hollywood between 1928 and 1930 was forced into the most intensely creative period in its history.

One of the first significant alterations in musical production occurred during the filming of *Applause* in late 1928. Starring Helen Morgan, who had played Julie in the original 1927 *Show Boat,* the film was directed by the brilliant Rouben Mamoulian, who shot it using two cameras. Furthermore, he gave them welcome mobility by mounting the isolation booth on wheels. A little later, when the cameras were wrapped in their own soundproof casings, they deserted the booth altogether.

Another progressive step was the installation of overhead booms to support the microphones, enabling dialogue to be recorded by swinging the microphones to wherever the performers were positioned. Previously, actors' movements had been severely curtailed. They had to remain close to the microphones, which were stationed inside flower pots, desk drawers, the actors' garments, and sundry other improbable places. But even the actor with a sound attachment pinned to the inside of his lapel could not stray very far. The booth-insulated camera would have been unable to follow him.

Not surprisingly, the switch from immobilized single camera to two or more that traveled presented another set of challenges to the musical makers, whose problems surpassed those of the producers of any other classification of film. Throughout much of 1928, when musical scenes were photographed and recorded simultaneously, the editor's job was problem-free. The practice, which evoked a nostalgic Broadway ambience, was suitable as long as the use of one camera preserved continuity. Fixed at eye level, it was held perfectly still, except when moved occasionally to the left or right to pan, say, a full chorus line. Multiple cameras on the same shooting set quickly dispensed with such simplicity of technique.

Photographing songs and dances from a variety of angles by two or more cameras did clear the way for imaginative cuts that, in essence, interrupted the normal uniform flow of events as represented on the screen. Viewers were treated to alternating long shots of a chorus and closeups of legs and faces, frequently interspersed with medium shots of gleeful patrons of the arts applauding in nightclubs or stage houses constructed on the set.

This new versatility was a film director's dream come true. But it complicated the work of choreographers, performers, and film editors. Dance directors were forced to make their routines conform to the wanderings of the multiple cameras. Editors were charged with the delicate task of splicing into a single filmstrip the best views contained in the jigsaw matrix of bits and pieces generated by the cameras. The vocalizing and dancing seen on the screen had to match perfectly with the lyrics and taps emanating from the sound tracks.

While the filming of *Broadway Melody* was under way in mid-1928, sound engineer Douglas Shearer, brother of actress Norma, devised the solution to Hollywood's latest sound challenge. The recording and photographing of musical sequences would be done separately. The method was a novel approach to the synchronization problem, but it also pushed performers into latter-day Chaplinesque pantomime that was awkward till mastered by the Broadway veterans forced to adapt to it.

First, the song to be used in a movie was prerecorded by the orchestra and singers. When the scene was ready for filming, the re-cording — called a playback — was played through loudspeakers on the shooting set. With the cameras now focused on them, the singers went through their motions while merely mouthing the words as they heard them on the playback. The silent lip movements and recorded lyrics were rarely mismatched. But a number of singers cringed at par-ticipating in what was essentially a dumb show that required them to dub their own voices.

Up to the mid-1930s, playbacks were usually recorded on the shooting set itself, with both orchestra and singers in attendance. Gradually, vocalists and instrumentalists transferred their activities to small recording studios, much like those used to make phonograph records. Singers recorded their songs in virtual privacy, away from the distractions so common to shooting sets. The superior playbacks made by Bing Crosby reflected the relaxed atmosphere of the new re-cording studio setting. His movie singing was every bit as smooth and graceful as what his fans heard on their home phonographs, and his films benefited enormously.

The reverse of the singers' playback routine, a method not nearly so demeaning, was used to record the dancing. Dancers performed their numbers on camera, guided into maintaining the correct tempo by a small rhythm section on the shooting set. The orchestration was then fleshed out and the sequence projected onto a screen on a record-ing stage.

The dancers repeated their steps in unison with the movements they saw on the screen. Sometimes — as happened in the singing se-quences also — the beats of the feet were amplified beyond the decibel level of the dialogue, but neither producers nor audiences seemed to mind such discrepancies in volume, or the static that usually accom-panied the recorded playback.

Further enhancing lip-sound synchrony was the contemporan-eous development of the Moviola. By incorporating a small screen for viewing filmstrips as slowly as desired, the machine allowed the film editor to stop and start the strips at will for the closest examination of specific frames, and then mark them for synchronization.

The immense value of the Moviola was underscored by the great director King Vidor, who humorously relates the travails of one film editor — who remains mercifully unnamed — in his autobiography. According to *A Tree Is a Tree,* it all happened while Vidor was shooting the hit musical film *Hallelujah!* in the pre–Moviola summer of 1929. The sound truck never arrived in the Tennessee hills where Vidor was shooting a sermon, other dialogue, and singing at a baptism ceremony. As was customary in such crises, the sound track was recorded far away, in this instance at MGM in Culver City, California, using the script and lyrics as guides to what was being said and sung. Vidor writes:

> During the editing of *Hallelujah!,* I saw a cutter literally go berserk at his inability to get the job done properly. The walls of his cutting room were lined with multitudes of shiny film cans containing the mass of sound and picture tracks. Returning from a projection room after many hours of labor, he discovered that the scene was still out of synchronization and let fly with a reel against the solid wall of cans. This precipitated an avalanche of loose film that engulfed the two of us. The hysterical cutter fell on the floor sobbing helplessly. I unwound him from the tangled maze and drove him home to the care of his wife. He remained in bed a week before he could again undertake the task of editing the film.

Next came a new mixing process which meticulously combined the separate sound tracks (for music, effects, and dialogue) into a single track. This track was then merged with the picture track to produce the composite print, permitting both tracks to be projected onto theater screens in absolute synchronization.

Cameras began moving more surefootedly than ever and blending wide- and mid-angle shots with pans or dollying into closeups at will. Film editors sped up the pace of musical films while adding variety to the visual menu. Performers seemed to race through their scenes, which had the advantage of lengthening viewers' attention span by inspiring the unlikely fear that one might miss something important in the plot. But the action speedup had its own drawbacks: it resulted in sketchy treatment of the stories and precluded attempts at character delineation.

The moguls solved these problems, too, in their own fashion. Plots were allowed to become trite and repetitive so as not to overtax the harried scriptwriters or jangle viewers' nerves by veering too far from the familiar. Musical screenplays were inevitably anchored to backstage life and love played out by stereotypical characters. Audiences were rarely greeted with suspense or new plot twists meant to suprise. Most of the dialogue reverberated with what had been said in previous boy-meets-girl films, and anyone who had seen only a few could anticipate how the one-dimensional caricatures would react in any given situation.

HITTING HIGH C

The talkies' cadging from Broadway operettas was as logical as it was profitable. The stage versions already had been hailed by audiences far more critical than movie fans, in effect guaranteeing that the film adaptations would be equally successful.

So popular were movie operettas that by the end of 1929 their vast constituency had paid back much of the lavish expenses the studios had incurred by switching from silents to sound. The pictures lent themselves ideally to what moguls and moviegoers loved best: spectacular sets, flashy costumes, and eye-popping production numbers.

Despite its deserved reputation as an era of bootleggers, mayhem, hardboiled flappers, and immediate gratification, the "Roaring Twenties" also delighted in old-fashioned musical shows with never-never land settings. Populating these excursions into escapism were sweet-faced princesses and dashing, clean-living heroes who spent most of their time singing sweeping waltz melodies that sometimes jumped an entire octave between notes. The librettos gave no indication that the writers had heard of jazz, the Charleston, or, for that matter, America.

In April 1929, Warner Bros. released Sigmund Romberg's *Desert Song,* the first all-sound operetta based on a Broadway original, which the studio followed religiously. Starring the handsome tenor John Boles, it also contained a few scenes in two-strip Technicolor. Its success was duplicated shortly afterward by Joseph McCarthy and Harry Tierney's *Rio Rita,* the operetta that had opened Florenz Ziegfeld's upper Times Squre theater in 1926. Boasting a 100 percent Technicolor print, Boles, Bebe Daniels, and about 1,000 extras, the film version introduced one of Tierney's loveliest waltzes, "You're Always in My Arms (But Only in My Dreams)."

Out of Universal came the first of the three film adaptations of

Jerome Kern's masterful *Show Boat*, which had followed *Rio Rita* into the Ziegfeld Theatre on December 27, 1927. Unfortunately, the sound print of *Show Boat* was only 50 percent talking, and so the picture was shorn of most of the original score. The songs that survived were played in the background in a musical prologue. Preceding the film during its New York City presentation, Jules Bledsoe, who had introduced "Ol' Man River" in the stage production, and Helen Morgan sang a few of the Kern songs.

The film featured Laura LaPlante as Magnolia and the distinguished dramatic actor Joseph Schildkraut as the inveterate gambler Ravenal. It dwelled almost exlusively on lyricist Oscar Hammerstein II's libretto, which he had based on the best-selling novel by Edna Ferber. Schildkraut had been a matinee idol on Broadway since 1921, and his portrayal of Judas in the Cecil B. DeMille film *King of Kings* (1927) furnished ample evidence of his acting prowess. He was equally impressive as Ravenal, singlehandedly boosting *Show Boat* to enviable dramatic heights.

Apparently feeling that Kern's score, the finest ever assembled for a stage musical, was too well known to merit another hearing, Universal exercised its collective wisdom by issuing a call for three brand new insertions from other writers. Responding were Sigmund Spaeth and William H. Myddleton, who contributed the nondescript "Down South" to the picture. From Gene Austin and Nathaniel Shilkret came "Lonesome Road," the hit of the film that was later powered into even greater prominence by the extraordinary 1931 Louis Armstrong recording. Joseph Cherniavsky's addition was the immensely pretty "Love Sings a Song in My Heart."

Other operettas lifted from the stage were Rudolf Friml's *Vagabond King*, with soprano Jeanette MacDonald in the feminine lead opposite Dennis King; *Song of the Flame*, with songs by Herbert Stothart and the Gershwin brothers; and *Song of the West*, based on Vincent Youmans's *Rainbow*. Buoyed by the hearty attendance at these musical films, the studios gradually gained the confidence to tackle new operettas all by themselves. Plans were devised to launch a series with original plots and songs that had never graced the Broadway stage.

Another call for help went out, this time to Oscar Straus, whose *Chocolate Soldier* (1909) and its hit song "My Hero" were familiar to music lovers everywhere. He answered and promptly set about filling *Married in Hollywood* with melodies, such as "A Man — A Maid," that could easily have been composed in turn-of-the-century Vienna. But the most successful song from this costume musical was "Dance Away the Night," a charmer by two other Broadway veterans, Harlan Thompson and Dave Stamper. A few years later, Straus contributed the waltzes "While Hearts Are Singing" and "We Will Always By Sweethearts" to Maurice Chevalier films.

Meanwhile, Al Dubin and Joe Burke wrote the beautiful "Like a Breath of Springtime" for the popular film operetta *Hearts in Exile*. Friml, who in 1911 had composed the music for *The Firefly* after Victor Herbert's illness forced him to bow out, lingered long enough in Hollywood to compose the excellent original score for *The Lottery Bride*, also starring Miss MacDonald. The best of the songs were "You're an Angel" and the novelty "Yubla." The reliable songwriting duo of Roy Turk and Fred Ahlert supplied Ramon Novarro, the original Ben Hur, with a winsome item, "Into My Heart," for the operetta *In Gay Madrid*. A good song, it nonetheless failed to match the popularity of Clifford Grey and Herbert Stothart's "If He Cared" and "Charming," written for Novarro's earlier *Devil May Care*.

Sometimes, but not often, Hollywood's home-grown operettas generated enough critical acclaim to qualify as true gems of the screen. One that did was *Dixiana*, starring Bebe Daniels, which brought Harry Tierney and Broadway lyricist Anne Caldwell together and introduced their peppy title tune and the lilting "A Tear, a Kiss, a Smile," two excellent 1930 songs. The film also featured Bill ("Bo-jangles") Robinson in his film debut. The next year the dancer appeared in *Heaven Is Harlem*, a minor but mirthful musical with an all-black cast.

Despite their flaws, the talking, singing, color musicals were creating a groundswell of enthusiasm inspired by the songwriters. Their melodies were pouring from movie cathedrals onto millions of radios and turntables throughout the land, and singing stars became household names. Perfection eluded producers and performers, but few could deny that the film musical, like any wobbly yet precocious one-year-old struggling to lift itself by grasping the bars of its playpen, was poised to walk into a new era of professionalism.

CHAPTER FOUR

The First Golden
Age of Film Music:
1929-1930

B Y MID–1928, enough gold could be seen shimmering in the
Hollywood sunlight to beckon five of Broadway's most notable
songwriters only a few months after the debut of *The Jazz
Singer.* Among them was Irving Berlin, whose genius was best sum-
merized by Jerome Kern. Asked to rank Berlin among the nation's
popular songwriters, Kern replied succinctly: "Irving Berlin has no
place in American music. He *is* American music."

Berlin's very first film song was an instant and lasting triumph,
as might be expected from such an inestimable hitmaker. Entitled
"Marie," it was sung by Vilma Banky in 1928's *Awakening.* In the late
1930s, bandleader Tommy Dorsey revived it in spectacular fashion by
recording it in swing tempo for RCA Victor. Also in 1928, Berlin gave
"Where Is the Song of Songs for Me?" to Lupe Velez, who sang it in
D.W. Griffith's *Lady of the Pavements.*

Berlin's three smash 1929 songs included "Puttin' on the Ritz," introduced in the picture of the same name by Harry ("Yeth, thir")
Richman, who lisped his way through it with Joan Bennett. In 1946
this syncopated classic, satirizing the dreams of a jaunty man of
modest means to emulate the wealthy, was reprised by Fred Astaire
in *Blue Skies,* and forever after belonged to Astaire rather than
Richman. For *Mammy,* Jolson's best starring film, Berlin supplied the
story idea and the winning "Let Me Sing and I'm Happy." No other
song Jolson ever sang better expressed his personal philosophy.

53

Berlin's third 1929 hit, "Waiting at the End of the Road," was the hit theme of the all–Technicolor *Hallelujah!*, the first major American sound film with a completely black cast. Because of the performers' color, the picture experienced booking difficulties in many cities, notably Chicago. The Balaban and Katz chain of movie houses delayed showing it for weeks, fearing it might alienate whites by attracting a preponderance of blacks.

The worry was unfounded. It was the whites who crowded the Chicago theaters, where they were treated to a wholesome and dignified glimpse at snatches of black religious culture. Reminders of this musical's success — and lack of racial epithets hurled at the theater managers — encouraged the filming of more black rituals, as, for example, in *The Little Colonel* (1935) and *Green Pastures* (1936).

Also from the East sped DeSylva, Brown, and Henderson, unquestionably the most popular tunesmiths of the 1920s. Collaborating mostly with DeSylva and Brown, composer Henderson was highly regarded for such stellar stage songs as "Alabamy Bound," "Black Bottom," "Five Foot Two, Eyes of Blue (Has Anybody Seen My Gal?)," "I'm Sittin' on Top of the World," "Birth of the Blues," "Bye, Bye, Blackbird," "Together," "Lucky Day" (later the theme song of radio's *Your Hit Parade,* sponsored by Lucky Strike cigarettes), "It All Depends on You," "Button Up Your Overcoat," "You're the Cream in My Coffee," "Varsity Drag," "The Best Things in Life Are Free," and dozens more.

Because so many of their songs had been popularized by Jolson, it was inevitable that these "Three Musketeers of Broadway" would be assigned to write the mammy singer's most lachrymose film song, "Sonny Boy," which he crooned to three-year-old Davey Lee, the most popular child star since Jackie Coogan, in *Singing Fool*. As was his custom with songs he introduced, Jolson appended his own name to the list of songwriters. So huge was Jolie's following that few writers protested his taking such a liberty with their material. But in Jolson's defense, it must be said that sometimes he, like Billy Rose, who also sought songwriting credit, did come up with ideas for the lyrics and song titles, and deserved some recognition.

"Sonny Boy" was commissioned by Robert Crawford, the songwriting team's business manager, who telephoned DeSylva in Atlantic City, where the trio was holed up trying to finish the score for their newest stage musical, *Hold Everything*. Warner Bros. wanted a song for

Jolson right away, Crawford announced, and he briefed DeSylva on the plot of the picture and on Jolson's suggestions for a lyric. Two hours later, DeSylva called Crawford and informed him that the song was completed, which was not all that unusual for these particular gentlemen, practiced as they were in writing on demand.

"I don't know whether it's any good or not," a weary DeSylva told Crawford, "but it's the best we can do." The song was obviously good enough for Jolson fans, who bought a sizzling 1,500,000 copies of "Sonny Boy" on sheet music in 1928 alone.

DeSylva, Brown, and Henderson rejoined Jolson and Master Lee in 1929 for *Say It with Songs,* actually the second part of *Singing Fool.* They presented Big Al with four slight hits: "Little Pal," "Used to You," "Why Can't You?," and "I'm in Seventh Heaven." But it was Jolson who supplied the movie's best-seller, "Back in Your Own Backyard," which he had written a few months earlier with Billy Rose and Dave Dreyer. Collaborating in virtual anonymity on the story idea was Darryl Francis Zanuck, the boy wonder from Wahoo, Nebraska, who later became potentate of 20th Century–Fox.

Fox Film next released the songwriters' *pièce de résistance,* the utterly charming *Sunny Side Up,* with Janet Gaynor, Charles Farrell, and an industrial-strength score. The peppy title song is a minor classic, as are the ballad "(I'm a Dreamer) Aren't We All?" and the playfully topical "If I Had a Talking Picture of You." Less familiar but equally melodious is the production number "Turn on the Heat," choreographed by Sammy Lee, who had directed the dances for the 1927 *Show Boat.* Not even a bevy of bathing-suited damsels, gamboling awkwardly to the song on a beach, could deflect attention from its rhythmic delights.

The final major DeSylva, Brown, and Henderson movie musical, released in early 1930, was *Just Imagine,* advertised as the "successor to *Sunny Side Up,*" although the title was plucked from one of their tunes in *Good News.* More fanciful in plot than any other musical of the time, the film was set in New York City in faraway 1980, and qualified as science fiction by tracing a rocket ship on its voyage to Mars. The best of the three-song score, for which Seymour Felix served as dance director, was "(I Am Only the Words) You Are the Melody," sung by Maureen O'Sullivan and John Garrick.

The picture marked the beginning of the end of one of the most productive partnerships in popular music history. DeSylva joined Fox as a producer (he later became president of Paramount and a co-founder of Capitol Records) and wrote occasional lyrics for other composers, as did Brown. Together, the two men were instrumental in furthering the career of Shirley Temple, Fox's biggest star ever, who auditioned before them and composer Jay Gorney in 1933.

Another first-wave immigrant to the "other coast" was Richard A. Whiting, father of songstress Margaret Whiting and composer of a string of sensations reaching back to World War I. His "Ain't We Got Fun," in which the rich get richer while the poor get children, was a gigantic Roaring Twenties hit, as were "Japanese Sandman," "Breezing Along with the Breeze," "Horses," "Sleepy Time Gal," and "She's Funny That Way." Whiting also composed "Till We Meet Again," the most sentimental and loveliest song inspired by the war to end all wars. The song ranks among the all-time sheet music best-sellers, having sold more than 17 million copies since 1918.

After "Louise," Whiting stayed in Hollywood to work with a small circle of lyricists on such melodious pre–1934 film songs as "It Seems to Be Spring," "My Sweeter Than Sweet," "My Future Just Passed," "Adorable," "Give Me a Moment, Please" (the theme song of the Russian violinist [David] Rubinoff), and "One Hour with You." The latter song, duetted by Chevalier and Miss MacDonald in the 1932 Paramount film of the same name, was outfitted with a revised lyric and handed to Eddie Cantor as the theme song of his weekly radio program.

WALL STREET TUMBLES

The fear that gripped America after the stock market crash of October 1929 initiated an abrupt change in the studios' production schedules. The first aftershocks of the Great Depression were still six months away, but there was scant doubt that the instability of the financial markets was rattling nervous systems across the land. Something had gone wrong, but only *Variety,* with a nod toward the show businesses it covered each week, was able to explain what had happened. "Wall Street Lays an Egg," read its terse front-page headline.

Instantly motivated by any danger, real or imagined, that might adversely affect their purses, film producers carefully scrutinized box office receipts. What they discovered was that their operettas' rustic Ruritanian settings and tuneful royalty, ever oblivious of such a mundane matter as economic turbulence, had just about lost their appeal. The fact failed to immobilize the moguls for very long. Debates on the wisdom of pursuing other musical paths dissolved from their decision-making, like medieval disputes about the sex of angels. Musical pictures, if not operettas, were still incredibly rich in profit opportunities, and they continued to enjoy most-favored status in the film colony. The studios looked homeward and began dunning Broadway for other trophy properties in the form of down-to-earth, contemporary musical comedies set in the United States.

Barren of members of the nobility, musical comedy scripts were inevitably *au courant,* more realistic than fanciful. Heidelberg was transformed into New York and Atlantic City. Characters were confronted with problems affecting common folks, not with affairs of state or regal love matches. As for the throneroom, musical comedy converted it into a football field or a battleship.

Among the first in the new series of filmed musical plays was *Spring Is Here,* a mild 1929 Broadway hit with songs by Rodgers and Hart. Then Hollywood picked up *No, No, Nanette,* for which Vincent Youmans had written the music in 1925, and *Good News,* the 1927 collegiate triumph by DeSylva, Brown, and Henderson. Youmans was tapped a second time for *Hit the Deck,* another 1929 stage success.

Dancer Marilyn Miller, destined to die at the age of 37 in 1936, made her screen debut in *Sally* in 1930 and sang "Look for the Silver Lining," one of only three Jerome Kern songs retained from the 1920 stage original. A few months later, Miss Miller followed with the filmed version of another of her Broadway smashes, *Sunny* (1925), also with an abbreviated Kern score. Her final film, *Her Majesty Love,* was a fiasco despite Al Dubin and Walter Jurmann's ultra-lovely "Though You're Not the First One."

Also filmed was *Follow Thru,* the highlights of which were DeSylva, Brown, and Henderson's carryover "Button Up Your Overcoat" and the talking-picture debut of Jack Haley, the future "Tin Man" in *The Wizard of Oz.* A modest 1928 Broadway hit, *Follow Thru* suffered similar disregard in the juiceless film version despite appearances by the popular Charles ("Buddy") Rogers, soon to become Mr. Mary Pickford, and Nancy Carroll, the bearer of one of the prettiest faces ever to brighten the decor of a light-hearted film. Luckily

Joan Blondell as a chorus girl in the opening "We're in the Money" production number of *Gold Diggers of 1933*.

for George Marion, Jr., and Richard A. Whiting, several of their interpolated melodies ("A Peach of a Pair" was one) lingered on long after the picture was forgotten.

Four of the five Marx Brothers signed with Paramount for their first film, *Cocoanuts,* based on their 1925 Broadway musical about the

Florida land boom. As dismayed real estate investors were to learn, their highly speculative get-rich schemes burst when the waters of Biscayne Bay, propelled by two successive hurricanes, turned home-building plots into swamps.

The original show is best remembered today for dropping Irving Berlin's "Always" from the score. He composed it as a love song to Ellin Mackay, who had been spirited off to Europe that year by her aristocratic father, the founder of Postal Cable Telegraph Company, to block her marriage to the Russian-born, Lower East Side–bred songwriter, whose birth name was Isador Baline.

Berlin had publicly chronicled his courtship with Miss Mackay by revealing its lack of progress in two earlier songs, "All Alone" and "Remember." It is safe to say that no other lady in history has been the inspiration behind three enormous song hits by the same composer. Soon after she returned to America, the couple married in January 1926 and remained together for 62 years, until her death in 1988. Berlin died the next year at the age of 101.

Long before their deaths, Papa Clarence Hungerford Mackay, whose own father was one of the discoverers of the generous Nevada silver mine popularly known as the Comstock Lode in 1859, had become reconciled to their marriage. It did not hurt Berlin's cause that he was able to bail his father-in-law out of financial woes during the Great Depression.

George S. Kaufman, who wrote the *Cocoanuts* libretto (with Morrie Ryskind, who received no credit), insisted that the tender "Always" would be out of sync alongside the Marx Brothers' enlightened buffoonery, and he won. But the song has succeeded very well under its own steam, showing up in many later films, most notably as the theme song of *Pride of the Yankees* (1942) and as a love song for Deanna Durbin in *Christmas Holiday* (1944).

Cocoanuts was shot at Paramount's Long Island studio in Astoria, Queens, which the company maintained for its proximity to the stars appearing on Broadway. For the film, Berlin added several new songs, the best being "When My Dreams Come True," sung by soubrette Mary Eaton and Oscar Shaw. Carried over from the stage play to win renewed popularity was the sublimely catchy "Monkey-Doodle-Doo," rich in the sophisticated syncopation that distinguished many Berlin songs.

As they would continue to do for decades, the moguls cut out many of the original songs from these musical comedies and assigned their contract writers to fill the gaps. Harry Warren, for example, wrote six new melodies for *Spring Is Here*. Only two of the Rodgers and Hart stage songs were kept, thankfully including "With a Song in My Heart."

The purpose of these song substitutions was to generate more profits for the studios, many of which had set up their own music publishing subsidiaries to complement their talking-musical revenues. Royalties paid on songs that had appeared in the stage productions went to independent houses; those from the interpolated tunes were paid directly to the studios' publishing firms.

Rarely did the insertions add very much to the songwriters' glory or the studios' coffers. The songs were almost uniformly poor, although a few, like Freed and Brown's "If You're Not Kissing Me" (*Good News*), Herman Ruby and M.K. Jerome's "Were You Just Pretending?" (*No, No, Nanette*), and Sidney Clare and Vincent Youmans's "Keepin' Myself for You" (*Hit the Deck*), merited more than fleeting attention.

The finest of the song interpolations undoubtedly was Gus Kahn and Walter Donaldson's "My Baby Just Cares for Me," introduced in black-face by Eddie Cantor in United Artists' all–Technicolor *Whoopee!* (1930), Cantor's first talking film. It was co-produced by Samuel Goldwyn, a one-time glove salesman, and the legendary Florenz Ziegfeld, whose Follies ranked among the most professional divertissements ever packaged for Broadway. The first of them hit the boards July 9, 1907; 19 more followed up to July 1, 1931. Only four years were without a Ziegfeld Follies — 1926, 1928, 1929, and 1930. Ziegfeld also produced numerous other stage spectaculars that ranged from *Show Boat* to the 1928 version of *Whoopee!*, which also starred Cantor as probably the best-known girl-shy hypochondriac in American theatrical history.

Testifying to the bouncy charisma of "My Baby Just Cares for Me" was its inclusion in the 1979 New York stage revival of *Whoopee!* Sadly, to make room for the song in the 1930 film, "Love Me or Leave Me," the hit of the 1928 stage show and one of the biggest songs of the entire 1920s, was chopped. The 1979 revival committed no such error: "Love Me or Leave Me" was reprised.

"Makin' Whoopee" was retained in the film, giving Cantor the opportunity to treat moviegoers to his rolling-eyes routine, as familiar to stage audiences as his hopping in unison with the rhythm while clapping his hands to maintain the beat. Also of musical interest was "I'll Still Belong to You," a pretty love song contributed by Edward Eliscu and Nacio Herb Brown, whose names are omitted from *Whoopee!*'s opening credits.

UPSTAGING BROADWAY

Midway through the 1929 season, the studios decided to roll into one film a cornucopia of everything the musical stage had to offer: spectacular sets, skits, mammoth chorus lines, lovable characters, stronger-than-usual storylines, and totally new scores that became show-stoppers of the first magnitude. The films were immense money-makers, attracting long lines wherever they were booked.

Warner's *Gold Diggers of Broadway* may have tapped Avery Hopwood's 1922 *Gold Diggers* play as its source, but the plot and characters were so thoroughly revamped that any similarity between the two is minimal. Of the six Al Dubin–Joe Burke songs, two became towering successes — "Tip Toe Through the Tulips (with You)," with its major league melody unfortunately wedded to a rather childish, alliterative lyric that touched the raw nerve of ridicule from the start, and "Painting the Clouds with Sunshine." Both were sung by Nick Lucas and danced by Broadway star Ann Pennington.

The year 1929, however, belonged to MGM's *Broadway Melody,* which opened in February and promptly shattered film attendance records. The first original all-talking musical comedy on film, it ended Broadway's stranglehold on musicals. Clearly, Hollywood had learned how to make them, too.

Tracing the struggles of Hank and Queenie Mahoney, a sister act from the sticks, to succeed in the rough-and-tumble world of Broadway, the picture is unquestionably one of the best of its kind in Hollywood history, a remarkable achievement considering its birth year. The story, by director Edmund Goulding, is strong and believable; the dialogue, much of it written by character actor James Gleason, is crisp. The acting, especially by Bessie Love, a one-time child actress who had played the Bride of Cana in *Intolerance,* is appealing, if not always competent.

In a startling departure from the enforced happy endings, Miss Love winds up a loser at the conclusion. Having lost her boyfriend

(Charles King) to Queenie (Anita Page, the real-life wife of composer
Nacio Herb Brown), she leaves the Big Town to return to the hinter-
lands. Now saddled with a new partner whom she dislikes, and bereft
of a lover, Hank is determined to work hard, learn all she can, and
one day fulfill her consuming desire to be a star on the Great White
Way. The audience is left with the impression that the effervescent
bumpkin's big break will come true. But after seeing how cruel Broadway can be to neophytes, one cannot be absolutely sure.

Freed and Brown's title tune remains one of the best and best
known of the many anthems to Broadway. The ballad "You Were
Meant for Me" developed into one of the most popular songs of 1929.
The charming ballet celebrating the "Wedding of the Painted Doll" is
a visual and aural delight. All three songs, as well as 11 more by Freed
and Brown from other 1930s musicals, would be reprised in the
historic *Singin' in the Rain* (1952), which lovingly poked fun at MGM's
own befuddled efforts to cash in on the talking-picture craze that blew
into Hollywood in 1928.

Cheerful was the word for *It's a Great Life,* MGM's next *Broadway
Melody* lookalike, but it and the score failed to measure up to the standards set by its predecessor. Charles King and Bessie Love were
reunited in another Metro carbon copy, *Chasing Rainbows,* in the
midst of which King delivers the rousing "Happy Days Are Here
Again." Three years later, the Yellen-Ager song was enlisted as the
theme song of Franklin D. Roosevelt's first campaign for the presi-
dency. The film was also the repository of the two songwriters' excellent production number "Everybody Tap," executed by a chorus of
true professionals in superb fashion.

Musicals on film provided so many spectator assets that the
stage, from mid–1929 on, would be hard pressed to compete. Films
ran continuously all day and well into the evening, and every day of
the week. The players could be seen and heard no matter where one
was seated, and no understudies usurped their roles. Movie stars were
truly bigger than life, and in such cavernous perimeter galleries as
New York City's 6,400-seat Roxy, which could accommodate 2,200
persons in its lobby, were magnified to 100 times their actual size.
Movie ticket prices were less than half those charged by the legitimate
theaters, and even cheaper at the second- and third-run houses.

The first-run houses, and many in the neighborhoods, were opulent rococo mansions that would beguile a sheik of Araby, making a

visit to them a treat in itself. "We sell tickets to theaters, not to movies," declared Marcus Loew on behalf of his fellow theater magnates. Adolph Zukor's strikingly beautiful flagship Paramount Theatre in Times Square, which opened November 19, 1926 (with *God Gave Me Twenty Cents* as the feature film), cost a whopping $3 million. The lobby contained a semi-circular colonnade of veined marbles supported on a black and gold base, itself about one story high. The dome of the space was 50 feet above the floor. A bank of elevators carried patrons to all four levels.

From the lobby, visitors went into the "Hall of Nations," which devoted one wall to a collection of stones from 37 countries. The French-renaissance Grand Hall, also 50 feet tall, measured 150 feet long and 40 feet wide. Massive marble columns surrounded the dome; at one end of the hall was a marble stairway that widened as it approached the mezzanine. To obtain the special marble he wanted, Zukor had to reopen a quarry in Italy that had been closed for 40 years.

The Paramount organ was one of the largest anywhere in the world. The stage was flanked on the left and right by two fountains that glowed in a splash of colored lights. A velvet and silk valance embroidered with gold hung from the proscenium arch, with curtains to match. A ventilating and refrigeration system, known as the down-feed system, brought air in through openings in the ceiling. The air was then drawn off at the floor by blowers and fans.

The theater staff numbered 400, including 150 uniformed ushers. Persons wishing to meet their party inside the 4,000-seat theater could designate the exact room, replete with its own stippled plaster walls, niches, urns, murals, and chandeliers, where they could be found. The choice of site was dazzling: the Venetian Room, Club Room, Hunting Room, Jade Room, Marie Antoinette Room, Music Room, Colonial Room, Empire Room. Or maybe the Peacock Promenade, Powder Box, or Chinoiserie (the ladies' smoking room). Some 56 original paintings gleaned from all over the world adorned the walls of these waiting rooms.

Impresario Zukor had landed in the United States from Hungary in 1889, when he was 15, with either 25 or 40 cents in his pocket (he never could remember which). His novel 1908 approach to talking pictures, the innovation of stationing actors behind theater screens to read dialogue aloud while watching the film in reverse, earned him the title of pioneer, a totally warranted designation.

At the time his theater opened, Zukor, at one time a Manhattan furrier, was president of Famous Players–Lasky Corporation, the forerunner of Paramount Pictures. His estate in New City, N.Y., boasted an 18-hole golf course. The most enduring of the moguls, Zukor died at the age of 103 in 1976, 12 years after his Paramount Theatre was razed.

BRANCHING OUT

No matter how tuneful their musical productions, Hollywood producers soon discovered that even the deluge of musical comedies was insufficient to quench the paying public's thirst for screen songs. So they raided other New York City entertainment centers, from vaudeville to nightclubs, for fresh stories and song-and-dance headliners to star in a veritable bazaar of one-man and one-woman movies that owed little to the legitimate stage.

Songwriter-comedian Eddie Leonard's *Melody Lane* chose vaudeville as its stamping grounds. Two other popular vaudevillians, (Gus) Van and (Joe) Schenck, appeared in familiar surroundings in MGM's *They Learned About Women,* a mild musical with six brief hits by the overworked Yellen and Ager. The world of burlesque, still oriented toward family viewing, furnished the backdrop for *Dance of Life* and *Applause.* For Will Rogers's first talking picture, *They Had to See Paris,* Sidney D. Mitchell, Archie Gottler, and Con Conrad wrote the charming theme song, "I Could Do It for You."

To star in *Pointed Heels,* Paramount hired Helen Kane, the pixieish "boop-boop-a-doop" girl, who sang Mack Gordon and Max Rich's catchy "Ain'tcha?" as well as Robin and Rainger's "I Have to Have You," which she shared with comedian Skeets Gallagher. For *Dangerous Nan McGrew,* she popularized Richard A. Whiting's cutesy "Aw, C'mon! (Watta Ya Got to Lose?)."

As vivacious as any singing star of the time, Miss Kane made six musicals in 16 months. Overexposure, especially of her coy blinking of eyelashes when things went nicely, and her pronounced little girl pout when they did not, cost her a career that seemed promising at the beginning.

Other stars in these tuneful quickies were many first-rank personalities who today are acknowledged as show business legends. Sophie Tucker was recruited to sing "Some of These Days" and other of her all-time standards in *Honky Tonk* (1929). Among the new songs written for her by Yellen and Ager were "I'm Doing What I'm Doing for Love" and "He's a Good Man to Have Around." Fanny (sometimes spelled Fannie) Brice also revived many of the songs in her rich repertoire in *My Man,* including the Channing Pollock-Maurice Yvain title tune, which she had immortalized in *Ziegfeld Follies of 1921.* Fortunately, she was able to sing the entire song in the picture; seven years later, when she reprised "My Man" for *The Great Ziegfeld,* only the first half survived the editing.

It was in the same film that Miss Brice introduced "I'd Rather Be Blue Over You (Than Be Happy with Somebody Else)," with a lyric by one of her husbands, a five-foot-two dynamo by the name of Billy Rose, and music by Fred Fisher. Another brief hit was the prophetic "If You Want the Rainbow, You Must Have the Rain," written by Rose and Mort Dixon to the music of Oscar Levant, whose song-writing reputation rests almost exclusively on "Lovable and Sweet," sung by Betty Compson in *Street Girl,* which was also released in 1929.

The acid-tongued, chain-smoking, hypochondriac Levant later switched careers from workhorse film composer to foremost piano interpreter of George Gershwin's concert pieces. Along the way, he was a witty regular panelist for six years on radio's *Information, Please,* and beginning in the late 1940s an actor in MGM musicals, in each playing his favorite character—himself.

Miss Brice's renowned gift for Yiddish-dialect humor wound through her second film, United Artists' *Be Yourself,* particularly in her riotous rendition of "Sasha (the Passion of the Pasha)," by William Rose (not to be confused with hubby Billy), Ballard MacDonald, and Jesse Greer. Schlemiel though he is, he's still got sex appeal, she informs the audience, referring to the pasha.

As clever a specialty number as any other written in 1930, the song perfectly counterpointed her other songs, the sentimental "When a Woman Loves a Man," the first screen hit by Ralph Rainger, to a lyric by William Rose, and "Cooking Breakfast for the One I Love" (William Rose–Henry Tobias), which permitted comedienne Brice to indulge in heart-throbbing wistfulness, at which she was equally adept.

Waco-born Texas Guinan (*née* Mary Louise Guinan) served as hostess of several Prohibition-era bistros in midtown Manhattan, but was more noteworthy for coining two phrases that quickly developed into popular code words for brashness. The first, "Hello, sucker," was her usual gratuitous greeting to guests as they streamed into her night spots. The second, "butter-and-egg man," targeted wealthy farmers who might well be suckered into paying exorbitant prices for the bootleg booze dispensed by her staff of waitresses.

In 1929 she went into the movies to star in the semi-biographical *Queen of the Nightclubs,* which also featured George Raft, who danced for the first time on film. Practically every later nightcub hostess would be fashioned on the sassy Miss Guinan with the exception of Gladys George in *Roaring Twenties* (1939). Sedated by an overdose of the sentimentality of the late 1930s, Miss George could be tough as nails, but she displays a heart every bit as big as all outdoors in her unrequited love scenes with gangster James Cagney.

Bandleader-entertainer Ted Lewis, the "high-hatted King of Jazz," reprised many of his personal evergreens in *Is Everybody Happy?*, in addition to such sparkling albeit short-lived new Grant Clarke–Harry Akst tunes as "Wouldn't It Be Wonderful?" and "I'm the Medicine Man for the Blues."

Crooner-saxophonist-bandleader Rudy Vallee also made his film debut in mid–1929 in *Vagabond Lover,* a nickname that identified him to his adoring public. He sings the hit "I'm Just a Vagabond Lover," which Vallee had co-authored with Leon Zimmerman about one year earlier, during the opening credits only. A chorus of obviously apprentice ballerinas cavorts to it toward the end of the picture. Happily, Vallee's co-star was rubber-faced Marie Dressler, the woman of a thousand grimaces and gestures, who was blessed with a chameleon voice that changed tone to match any predicament in which she found herself. As usual, she was superb.

Not so the picture. Like most of the "superstar" movies, the plot is ridiculous, and Vallee's performance is agonizing to watch. Giving the impression he had been embalmed just minutes before the camera rolled, he underwhelmed the audience to such a degree that, except for a brief stint in a second 1929 feature, already under way, Hollywood would not call on him to perform again for four years.

Also typically, the songs in *Vagabond Lover* are very good, and Vallee managed to lift "If You Were the Only Girl (in the World)," written in 1916 by Clifford Grey and Nat D. Ayer, "Little Kiss Each Morning," by Harry Woods, and Edward Heyman and Ken Smith's beautiful "Then I'll Be Reminded of You" to hit status despite his deadpan deliveries and annoying habit of closing his eyes while singing the concluding lines.

But bandleaders as a whole have been irredeemably poor actors, including even Benny Goodman, Tommy Dorsey, and Glenn Miller. Actually, their major film function, apart from lending the publicity value of their names, was to accompany performers in full view of the audience. It would take producers years to feel comfortable when permitting music to arise as if from nowhere. Audiences, they felt, would neither understand nor accept musical backgrounds for lovers' ballads or dance routines without an orchestra or instrumentalist visible somewhere on the screen.

Vallee made only a cameo appearance, as did Eddie Cantor and Helen Morgan, in *Glorifying the American Girl.* Paramount's highest-grossing picture of 1929, it echoed in its title a phrase associated with Florenz Ziegfeld, who made a rare trip to the Astoria studios to supervise the production. That the master showman succumbed to the lure of films is a curiosity, even if his mighty spending on his stage shows was bankrupting him. Long suspicious of talking films as harmful competitors, Ziegfeld had advertised his 1927 Follies as "Glorifying the American Girl in the flesh — *not canned.*"

In *Glorifying the American Girl,* Vallee and Miss Morgan turn a neat trick by encoring songs they had sung in two earlier 1929 films. Vallee again sings "I'm Just a Vagabond Lover," while Miss Morgan repeats "What Wouldn't I Do for That Man," the same excellent E.Y. Harburg–Jay Gorney song heard in *Applause,* also produced by Paramount. But it was Walter Donaldson who wrote the picture's hit, "There Must Be Somebody Waiting for Me (in Loveland)," sung by Mary Eaton amid expressionless, leggy girls wearing skyscraper headdresses in traditional Ziegfeldian tableau.

Luckily, Vallee had other things going for him to account for his popularity as a pioneer schmaltz king. Almost immediately after graduation from Yale in 1927, he formed his band, known as the "Connecticut Yankees." He and it took the country by storm, specializing in saccharine, Guy Lombardo–sounding arrangements that were immensely danceable.

With equal alacrity, Vallee conquered the airwaves. As both producer and host of the *Fleischmann Hour* from 1929 to 1939, he was responsible for the radio debuts of a constellation of top-level talent:

Eddie Cantor, Milton Berle, Beatrice Lillie, Edgar Bergen, Carmen Miranda, Phil Baker, Alice Faye, Olsen and Johnson, Bob Burns, Lou Holtz, and others.

Also raising a baton in Hollywood was Edward Kennedy Ellington, better known by his royal designation of "Duke." He and his fabled orchestra in early 1930 joined Amos 'n' Andy (Freeman Gosden and Charles Correll) in *Check and Double Check* to serve up Kalmar and Ruby's "Three Little Words." Twenty-one years later, the song would serve as the title of the MGM "biography" of the two tunesmiths, with Fred Astaire as Bert Kalmar and Red Skelton as Harry Ruby.

One of the most gifted of American composers, arrangers, pianists, and bandleaders, Ellington compiled an impressive catalogue of independent song hits, including "Mood Indigo," "Solitude," and "Sophisticated Lady" in 1934 and the swing classic "Don't Get Around Much Anymore" in 1942. Never commissioned to write film songs, Ellington did compose the background music for several pictures, including *Symphony in Black*, a 1935 Paramount short feature, and *An Anatomy of a Murder*, in 1959.

Another popular orchestra leader, Fred Waring, led his "Pennsylvanians" in *Syncopation*, which laid claim to two of 1929's biggest hits, "Jericho" and "I'll Always Be in Love with You." Appearing with Waring in his screen debut was crooner Morton Downey, who sang Bud Green and Sam H. Stept's up-tempo "Do Something." In Downey's second feature, this time opposite George Jessel in *Mother's Boy*, he warbled another Green-Stept tune, "There'll Be You and I."

It was incumbent on Jessel, who spoke and sang much like Jolson, to render a touching albeit lugubrious mammy song, which is exactly what he did in *Mother's Boy*. The task was not a demanding one: Jessel had played the Jazz Singer in the original 1925 Broadway play, and so was quite mother-oriented. In the film, with his lips trembling and his voice quavering with emotion, he uncorks "My Mother's Eyes," ever oblivious of the excessive sentimentality of its lines.

But the song did serve as the basis of a supreme satire in an early 1950s *Show of Shows* telecast. Sid Caesar, playing a hardened criminal in the middle of a prison break, is about to jump to freedom from atop a wall. Caught in the beam of a searchlight, the frightened Caesar drops to one knee and sings the lyric of "My Mother's Eyes." The audience was convulsed into one of the longest periods of sustained laughter on record.

According to the script for the skit, Caesar was supposed to get angry, shake his fist at the light, and scream at it. The idea of spreading his arms and bursting into song while balancing himself on his right knee "came to me on the spot," the comedian confessed to an interviewer. "That's the way things happened on live television in those days."

In the mistaken belief that *Mother's Boy* needed a second mother-of-mine song, the producers gave "I'll Always Be a Mother's Boy" to Downey. Infinitely better than Jessel's serenade, the pleasant Stept melody was marred by the usual sugary sad lyric by partner Green, which again defined a mother's love as the last source of comfort for adult males confronted with misfortune.

Jessel's acting career plummeted like the stock market, as did Downey's after *Lucky in Love* (not to be confused with DeSylva, Brown, and Henderson's hit song from *Good News*). Green and Stept's "For the Likes o' You and Me" was a pretty newcomer, but saddled with a poor script and string of listless Irish jingles by the same two songwriters, Downey failed to dig deeply into pay dirt and soon disappeared from the screen.

The Metropolitan Opera was not overlooked in Hollywood's search for new talent, and from it, in 1929, came Lawrence Tibbett and Grace Moore to play the lovers in *New Moon,* Hammerstein and Romberg's perennial Broadway favorite. Tibbett, who had failed his first audition at the Met only a few years earlier, also appeared in *Rogue Song,* booming out his baritone version of Clifford Grey and Herbert Stothart's lovely "When I'm Looking at You." Next, and last of all, came *Cuban Love Song,* best remembered for Tibbett's manly interpretation of James McHugh's stunning title song.

BIG AND BOUNTIFUL

In a sterling example of biting the hand that was feeding it, Hollywood in mid–1929 charged into a new round of competition with the stage by producing its own variations of the revue, which for decades had served Broadway faithfully. On the West Coast it was blown up into star-crammed, plotless extravaganzas that alternated skits with stylish production numbers using all-new songs, and plenty of them. The films also reflected their debt to Broadway by incorporating stagelike revolving sets, plywood scenery reeking of artificiality, and blackouts denoting the end of a skit.

For *Fox Movietone Follies of 1929,* the studio tapped almost everybody caught strolling on the back lot and, to insure its blockbuster appeal, photographed several sequences in color. The six-song score by Sidney D. Mitchell, Archie Gottler, and future Academy Award–winning composer Con Conrad included the festive "Walking with Susie," "That's You, Baby," and "Breakaway," the only titles even faintly familiar today.

In rapid monkey-see, monkey-do fashion, four more revues slid off the assembly lines. Warner Bros.' entry, *Show of Shows,* presented cameos of both dramatic and musical stars under contract. Irene Bordoni showed up, as did John Barrymore (who recited a soliloquy from Shakespeare's *Richard III*), Beatrice Lillie, and Frank Fay, all Broadway veterans, and even Rin-Tin-Tin, one of the studio's most popular "actors."

Ten songwriters contributed the five songs, the best of which was "Singin' in the Bathtub," by Oscar winners-to-be Herb Magidson and Ned Washington to Michael H. Cleary's melody. Another catchy tune, Al Bryan and Edward Ward's "Li-Po-Li," was danced by Myrna Loy while Nick Lucas sang it.

Marching along in *Paramount on Parade* were Gary Cooper, Helen Kane, Virginia Bruce, Jean Arthur, Jack Oakie, and William Powell, among others. The picture spun off the mellifluous duet "Any Time's the Time to Fall in Love," written by Elsie Janis and Jack King, but the major attraction was Chevalier, who sang the biggest hit in the eight-song score, Sam Coslow's "Sweepin' the Clouds Away."

Also in the cast was singer Lillian Roth (Rutstein), who subsequently appeared in four more pictures up to 1933. Devastated by a long bout with alcoholism, she was married eight times and divorced the same number. She dropped out of sight until her autobiography, *I'll Cry Tomorrow,* was published in 1954. The film version, released the next year, was equally explicit in detailing her downfall and Alcoholics Anonymous–supported recovery. Portraying Miss Roth was Susan Hayward, an excellent dramatic actress who went beyond the call of duty by singing all the songs herself (and very well), including Miss Roth's 1930 movie hit, "Sing You Sinners," from *Honey.*

Next came Universal's 100 percent Technicolor *King of Jazz,* by far the most innovative of the fantasy factories' newest series of spectaculars. The star was "King of Jazz" Paul Whiteman and his orchestra. The most imaginative bandleader of the time, Whiteman had

An example of the artificial sets and large choruses common to 1929 and mid–1930 film musicals appears in this scene from Universal's *King of Jazz* (1930). The singer is John Boles, the song, Billy Rose and Mabel Wayne's "It Happened in Monterey."

been trained as a classical violinist, but it was in the popular music realm that he earned his reputation and fortune. In 1925 he banked $680,000, much of it garnered from his recording of "Three o'Clock in the Morning," which sold 3,400,000 copies.

Unfortunately missing from the film was the legendary Bix (Leon) Beiderbecke, the greatest of all white cornetists and most gifted of Whiteman's instrumentalists. Beiderbecke was in a sanitorium battling acute alcoholism when the picture was being made. One year later he was dead at the age of 28.

King of Jazz was the only spectacular to hit a bull's-eye on Hollywood's musical dart board in 1930. It remains most notable for a condensed version of Gershwin's *Rhapsody in Blue,* which Whiteman had commissioned and introduced at New York City's Aeolian Hall in 1924. It also featured a Walter Lantz animated cartoon set to music and marked the film debut of the orchestra leader's singing "Rhythm

Boys." Two of the young gentlemen were Al Rinker and Harry Barris; the third happened to be Bing Crosby, and therein hung a career.

Crosby had made his first solo recording for Columbia Records in November 1929, crooning "Can't We Be Friends" and "Gay Love."[2] He appeared in four of the film's sequences and established the easy, almost conversational singing style that would be his trademark for the next four decades. But it was John Boles, the romantic lead in *King of Jazz*, who sang its two biggest successes, Billy Rose and Mabel Wayne's "It Happened in Monterey" and Yellen-Ager's "Song of the Dawn."

The most exciting of these film revues, though technically primitive compared with *King of Jazz,* was MGM's black-and-white *Hollywood Revue of 1929*. It showcased 17 songs by 13 composers and lyricists, including Fred ("Chicago") Fisher, Gus ("School Days") Edwards, and Louis ("Manhattan Serenade") Alter. The hit, the memorable "Singin' in the Rain," was supplied by the studio's trustworthy contract-writing team of Freed and Brown. The song was sung by Cliff Edwards, whose major task was protecting himself from being jabbed by the umbrellas used as props by the disporting amateurs who were compressed accordion-like into a chorus.

The cast, truly an all-star roster, included Joan Crawford, Marion Davies, Buster Keaton, Laurel and Hardy (film partners from 1926 to 1950), Marie Dressler, Norma Shearer and John Gilbert (who recreated the balcony scene from *Romeo and Juliet*), and Jack Benny and Conrad Nagle as masters-of-ceremonies.

The Hollywood-made revues so overpowered all other screen fare that a number of high-quality, cheapie musicals practically dropped from attention within weeks of their release. One such casualty, Gaynor and Farrell's *High Society Blues,* an early 1930 lyrical romance, surely deserved a better fate. The five songs, composed by James F. Hanley, were plainly the work of a true professional, which Hanley unquestionably was.

His "Rose of Washington Square"—to be picked up for the title of an Alice Faye musical film in 1939—had been popular since its debut by Fanny Brice in Ziegfeld's *Midnight Frolic* in 1920. The next

---

[2] *"Can't We Be Friends," by Paul James and Kay Swift, originated in* The Little Show, *a Broadway revue of 1929. Sidney Clave and Oscar Levant's "Gay Love" first appeared in the 1929 film* Delightful Rogue.

year, Hanley provided Miss Brice with "Second Hand Rose," which the lady sang in *Ziegfeld Follies of 1921* to rousing nightly ovations. "Just a Cottage Small (By a Waterfall)," was a solid 1925 hit; thanks to Judy Garland's vocalizing in the 1938 film *Listen Darling,* "Zing! Went the Strings of My Heart"—originally sung by Hal Leroy, moviedom's "Harold Teen," in the 1935 stage show *Thumbs Up*—is the most familiar of the composer's later melodies.

With assists from Joseph McCarthy and Fred Fisher, Hanley gave Gaynor and Farrell plenty to sing about in *High Society Blues*: "Eleanor (the Song I Sing in My Dreams)"; "I Don't Know You Well Enough for That"; "I'm in the Market for You"; "Just Like a Story Book"; and the lilting title tune. But not even Miss Gaynor's singing voice, as pleasurable as any other dramatic star's, could save the songs from eventually tapering off into oblivion.

To charge Hollywood with overloading theater circuits with songs from the beginning of 1929 through the first half of 1930 is belaboring the obvious. Obvious, that is, to everyone but the studios' sachems and their midwifery of yes-men and hangers-on. Their firm grip on the irrelevant frozen in place, they released so many musicals so fast that they should have been issued speeding tickets, or at least warnings. None came their way, and so by the late spring of 1930, film musicals were turning up D.O.A. at the box office.

If the sheer ubiquitousness of movie songs was not enough to dissuade audiences from galloping back into theaters to hear still more, producers added to the overkill by overplaying many of the ones they were convinced were desinted for stardom. Freed and Brown's "Pagan Love Song," the theme of MGM's lush *Pagan,* for instance, is reprised 27 times in the film after Ramon Novarro first sings it. In essence, when producers got hold of a good song—and this one is very good—they rarely knew when enough was enough.

The incoming Great Depression also took a heavy toll on box office revenues. In the spring of 1930, about 4 million Americans were without jobs compared with 1.5 million at the end of 1929, fewer than six months earlier. Breadlines were reappearing in large cities for the first time since the severe but brief recession of 1921, adding validity to one of then President Harding's less profound observations that "when a lot of people are out of work, unemployment results."

Deficient in reflecting reality, Hollywood's musicals were running along on such threadbare plots that even the classiest scores were unable to save them from financial disaster. Market saturation had not paid off; the product had grown stale. First exhaustion and then ennui were the typical responses to the appearance of another musical in partially filled movie houses.

A pause was prescribed by those consulting physicians known collectively as the public, and the movie musical was sent to a rest home. There it would stay, with occasional time-outs to flex its muscles, for almost three years.

But moguls and moviegoers alike sensed that the musical would flower again, and they were proved right. When it did, beginning in 1934, it ushered the industry into a spectacular second golden age of film music that would surpass anything Hollywood has ever achieved, before or since.

CHAPTER FIVE

The Lean and Mean Years: 1930–1933

*I*T WAS in mid-spring of 1930 that the studios watched their dreams of perpetual profits backslide into nightmares. Box office apathy and recurring financial pinches caused by the stumbling national economy combined to foreshorten expectations that musical films would continue relentlessly into eternity.

The studio chiefs, their visions of the future devalued by the specter of bankruptcy, moved swiftly to cut costs to the marrow. For the next three years, survival was the be-all, end-all of their existence. If they had to downgrade the flashiness of their films to attain that goal, so be it.

Even in the fantasy world of Southern California, optimism was a precious commodity, so short was the supply. Like the man who came to dinner, the Depression overstayed its unwelcome presence contrary to frequent government and business predictions that it would soon move on. The 4 million jobless at the beginning of 1930 doubled to 8 million in 1931, and then almost doubled again to more than 15 million by March 1933. That month's unemployment rate stood at 24.9 percent of the labor force, perhaps as high as 27 percent if the formerly self-employed, like shopowners and professionals, were included.

Bank failures became commonplace, with 5,500 occurring between November 1929 and March 1933. Without deposit or unemployment insurance, Social Security, or any other federal benefit, the lower economic classes grappled with unrelenting debt and despair. The middle class suffered loss not only of income, but also of their businesses, savings, houses, and farms. Even the well-to-do took a beating. They sustained huge losses when forced to sell their securities in a bear market, and many of their companies were crushed under the weight of unpaid bills. Sales of Cadillacs, which totaled 40,965 in 1929, tumbled to 6,655 in 1932 despite lower retail prices.

Mired in a disaster that hung on tenaciously, people drifted farther and farther from movie houses. Weekly attendance in 1931 was 15 million fewer than in the benchmark year of 1930. In 1932 and 1933 it was 30 million lower.

Nervous MGM executives vetoed the projected film version of Vincent Youmans's *Great Day,* which was to star Joan Crawford, as well as the followup extravaganza *Hollywood Revue of 1930.* Kalmar and Ruby's Broadway hit *Five o'Clock Girl* died on Hollywood's drawing boards, as did *Rosalie,* which boasted a score by George Gershwin and Sigmund Romberg.

The ever-accommodating Romberg, then on the downside of his career, wrote 12 European-sounding originals for *Viennese Nights* (1930) and another nine for *Children of Dreams* (1931). Only one hit emerged from his 21 at-bats, "You Will Remember Vienna," sung by Walter Pidgeon and Vivienne Segal.

Reviewing *Viennese Nights, New York Times* critic Mordaunt Hall rendered his—and most other viewers'—opinion of this and all the other contemporary movie musicals in an insightful comment: "Appealing musical compositions, agreeably sung and well played, compensate for imperfections in the dialogue and story." After the review, Warners paid Romberg and his sometime collaborator Oscar Hammerstein II $100,000 each to cancel their contracts. For DeSylva, Brown, and Henderson, the ax was wielded almost as severely: of the 15 songs they wrote for *Indiscreet,* 13 were chopped.

Also crossed off purchase lists were *Funny Face,* with an extraordinary score by the Gershwins and a cast headed by Fred and Adele Astaire, and Howard Dietz and Arthur Schwartz's *Band Wagon,* the brother and sister's final stage show together. These two Broadway smashes would not make the Hollywood scene until the 1950s—with Fred, again, as the star of both.

Nor did the studios vie with one another to buy the film rights to Noel Coward's *Bitter Sweet,* as they most likely would have only a few months earlier. Ironically, the successful operetta opened in midtown Manhattan the same week that the New York Stock Exchange collapsed downtown under the tidal wave of selling on Monday, October 28, 1929, and the next day, "Black Tuesday," when the Dow-Jones Industrial Average plunged a harrowing 24.5 percent. Not until 1940, when the economy was more sweet than bitter, would the Coward musical finally be filmed as a three-strip Technicolor vehicle for Nelson Eddy and Jeanette MacDonald.

Film executives rarely learned from their errors because they were convinced they were committing none, a byproduct of their superiority complex. So it was the theater owners who were the first to concede that musical films had lost the voodoo that had hypnotized moviegoers for the past 18 months. "This picture is NOT a musical," read many chains' mid-1930 newspaper ads for new arrivals, in an obvious attempt to cater to a public grown sated with songs and dances.

Temporarily out of work, Harry Warren followed Hammerstein and Romberg and Rudolf Friml back to New York, where he would remain for almost three years. But he kept busy writing songs for the stage. Four were instant hits: "Cheerful Little Earful" and "Would You Like to Take a Walk?," both from *Sweet and Low*; "You're My Everything," from *Laugh Parade*; and topping them all, "I Found a Million Dollar Baby (in a Five and Ten Cent Store)," which appeared in *Billy Rose's Crazy Quilt*.

Dorothy Fields and James McHugh also returned East to supply songs for *International Revue*, which bombed despite an excellent cast headed by Gertrude Lawrence. From the show came two of the songwriters' perennials, the anti–Depression "On the Sunny Side of the Street" and the sprightly love song "Exactly Like You." In 1932 the partners collaborated on four songs for producer Leon Leonidoff's first live show presented on the mammoth revolving stage of the Radio City Music Hall, which opened December 27.

Richard A. Whiting and Nacio Herb Brown exited to the East Coast to write the songs for *Take a Chance*, with Ethel Merman and Jack Haley, who sang "You're an Old Smoothie" and "Eadie Was a Lady." Ray Henderson's *Hot Cha!, Strike Me Pink,* and *Say When* (with a very young Bob Hope in the cast) were only mild stage hits in spite of several delightful songs. Far more successful was his score for *George White's Scandals* (of 1931), starring Miss Merman, Rudy Vallee, and Ray Bolger. Included were such standards as "Life Is Just a Bowl of Cherries," "My Song," "The Thrill Is Gone," and the patronizing

"That's Why Darkies Were Born," which, according to the lyric, was mainly to pick cotton.

Irving Berlin returned to New York to write *Face the Music,* which produced "Let's Have Another Cup of Coffee," "Soft Lights and Sweet Music," and two of the best popular songs celebrating big-city life: "A Roof in Manhattan" and "Manhattan Madness." In 1933 came his *As Thousands Cheer,* with Marilyn Miller and Clifton Webb, who shared "Heat Wave" and "Easter Parade," the latter a reworked version of the songwriter's "Smile and Show Your Dimple," written in 1917.

Unfortunately, Hollywood was not the direct beneficiary of any of these tunes, which, if nothing else, proved that the master writers had suffered no loss of talent. The loser was the bedridden film musical, purged of these writers' services throughout the period.

BELT-TIGHTENING

Like other businesses in the early thirties, the film industry had been turned into a pyramid precariously balanced on its narrowing point and in danger of toppling over. Rattled by the Depression, the moguls virtually outlawed Technicolor, once the glory of the Big Screen. Also prohibited were the expensive sets required for backstage musicals, along with the huge star casts that typically populated them. Chorus lines were reduced to a handful of dancers or eliminated altogether. Budget-busting, bedazzling spectacles, so tantalizing in days of yore, also went out the window.

The closest Warners came to reviving the splashy musicals for which the studio was renowned was to hire 1930's 11-member All-American college football team for the pedestrian campus-based musical *Maybe It's Love.* Besides Joan Bennett and Joe E. Brown, the other star of the picture was the pleasant title song by Sidney D. Mitchell, Archie Gottler, and George W. Meyer.

Paramount settled for eight recent beauty contest winners representing only six states (two of the lovelies came from California) and the District of Columbia. They were handed swimsuits, a few lines to speak, and pairs of oars for brief appearances in the chummy, low-key musical appropriately entitled *Eight Girls in a Boat.* The movie's single hit, Sam Coslow and Harold (Lefty) Lewis's "This Little Piggie Went to Market," became a favorite with singer Ethel Shutta, who popularized it on the radio. In the studio's halcyon days of 1929, it most likely would have constructed a mock battleship and jammed it with every young lady who had so much as entered such a contest — and from all the 48 states.

The moguls also cut ticket prices. Throughout most of the 1930s, small-city children normally paid a mere ten cents for a double bill of dreams. Those over 12 were classified as adults and forced to shell out an extra nickel. Prices in New York City, Chicago, and other big towns were about three times higher, but the first-run houses offered an hour or so of vaudeville featuring many of the nation's top bands, singers, and comics.

Producers also filled the screen with humorous shorts, animated cartoons, and such kiddie treats as the *Baby Burlesk* and *Frolics of Youth* series. Topping the list of these one- and two-reelers were the *Our Gang* pictures (now known as *The Little Rascals*), initiated by producer Hal Roach in 1922. Following closely behind were the *Mickey McGuire* shorts, also carried over from the silent days, based on a comic-strip character and starring the versatile Brooklyn-born son of vaudevillians Mickey Rooney. Largely unnoticed was the film debut of a tiny atomic bomb of a dancer, seven-year-old Sammy Davis, Jr., in the all-black featurette *Rufus Jones as President* (1933).

The June 1930–March 1933 musical eclipse was not total. Idling rather than shutting off their song-and-dance motors, the studios released 36 musical pictures during those 33 months — a number that pales alongside the 100 for just the 12 months of 1929. But performers still sang a song or two and tripped a few lights fantastic. Even Broadway musicals, stripped of most of their Coolidge-era trappings, made infrequent visits to movie houses.

Talking pictures and the Depression killed vaudeville, but they had little adverse effect on radio. The year 1932 was the networks' most successful to date, and they regaled huddled families with endless entertainment that cost even less than a film ticket.

On January 30, 1933, the day that President-elect Roosevelt celebrated his 51st birthday and Adolf Hitler his appointment as chancellor of Germany, listeners heard the initial installment of one of radio's longest-running shows.[3] First came the strains of Rossini's rousing overture to *William Tell*. Then hoofbeats, then a cowboy's piercing

---

[3] *The longest-running radio serial drama,* One Man's Family, *racked up 3,256 broadcasts from April 1932 to May 1959.*

cry, then gunshots and more hoofbeats. Enter the announcer: "A fiery horse with the speed of light, a cloud of dust, and a hearty 'Hi-yo, Silver!' The Lone Ranger!"

Into living rooms across the country galloped the masked marvel of the Old West and his escort Tonto, referred to as "Kemo-sabe," or "faithful friend." They would travel the sagebrush circuit for the next 21 years, until September 3, 1954, when the Lone Ranger (then played by Brace Beemer) lost the showdown with his sponsors and rode into the sunset. An occasional early bit player on the program was Amos Jacobs, later known as Danny Thomas, who would reprise Al Jolson's role in the 1953 remake of *The Jazz Singer.*

The program's influence on the movies was curiously insignificant. The Lone Ranger (the pseudonym of cowboy character "John Reid") would not appear on the screen until 1938, when Republic Pictures released a 15-chapter serial on his exploits with Lee Powell in the title role. Well before then, in 1933, another heyday of pulp magazine-inspired Westerns had dawned—this time with spoken dialogue and thundering hooves—and they repeated the success, and most of the stories, of the silent cowboy yarns.

What was significant was the talking Western's impact on film music. Besides horse, saddle, and six-guns, the 1930s cowboy heroes were also outfitted with a guitar, the better to sing with. And sing they did. Thanks largely to Bing Crosby, whose 1933 recording of the late 19th-century ballad "Home on the Range" was a smash hit, cowpokes began singin' and strummin' along the trail straight into movie houses.

One of the first, Gene Autry, triumphed in 1934 with Bob Nolan's "Tumblin' Tumbleweeds," introduced in the picture of the same name. In 1941, Autry also became the first screen performer to be nominated for an Academy Award for Best Song, "Be Honest with Me," which he sang in *Ridin' on a Rainbow.* Comic sidekick Al "Fuzzy" Knight scored in 1936 with Sidney D. Mitchell and Louis Alter's exquisite "Twilight on the Trail," from *Trail of the Lonesome Pine,* which also contained the first outdoor scenes photographed in three-process Technicolor. According to Alter, the song was President Roosevelt's favorite, contrary to popular belief that it was "Home on the Range," which F.D.R. actually disliked.

Many of Hollywood's best "oater" songs were satirical in tone and written by Easterners who rode not on horses, but in taxicabs around

Tin Pan Alley. For *Rhythm on the Range* (1936), Johnny Mercer supplied the witty Crosby hit "I'm an Old Cowhand (From the Rio Grande)." In it, Crosby confides that he is a poor cowboy, having never seen a cow. Nonetheless, he concludes each stanza with a bogus cry of contentment: "Yippy-I-O-Ki-ay!"

Cole Porter, as sophisticated a composer-lyricist as America has produced, presented Roy Rogers and the Andrews Sister with a classic satire for the 1944 film *Hollywood Canteen*. Purportedly reflecting the despair of a "rovin' kind". of desperado sentenced to jail, "Don't Fence Me In," is basically a melancholy reminder of the cowboy's traditional love of open spaces, which were already fast disappearing. A graduate of the "Sons of the Pioneers" singing quartet and a former stand-in for Gene Autry, Rogers issues his lament while perched atop his horse, Trigger. He simply "can't look at hobbles and can't stand fences." What he wants to do is "ride to the ridge where the West commences, / Gaze at the moon till I lose my senses." But he cannot. The rangeland of Rogers's movie forebears is being crisscrossed by highways, allowing new communities to encroach on what was once grazing land.

In 1948, Ray Evans and Jerry Livingston combined their exceptional talents to give Bob Hope one of the finest of all satirical Western songs for *Paleface*. The winner of the Oscar for Best Song, "Buttons and Bows" has the disoriented Hope, playing an apprentice cowboy, lamenting his decision to desert the East to journey to the West. Agreeing with Hope is cowgirl Jane Russell, fully aware that Hope is singularly unequipped to deal with anything that happens west of Pittsburgh (see List #2, "'Western' Songs from American Films").

With radio developing its own superstars, it was natural that 1930–33 Hollywood would eschew backstage plots for the much simpler world of broadcasting. Stories centering on radio were relatively inexpensive to produce, and chances were good that casting films with popular airwave personalities would prime the box office.

For Paramount's *Big Broadcast,* which, like *Broadway Melody, Gold Diggers,* and *Hit Parade,* evolved into a serial musical bearing the same title but different years, the studio engaged some of radio's biggest names: Crosby, Kate Smith, Arthur ("Street Singer") Tracy, the Mills Brothers and Boswell Sisters, and the Vincent Lopez and Cab Calloway orchestras. Also on hand were George Burns and Gracie Allen, whose weekly *Robert Burns Panatela Program* was one of 1932's most popular shows. (Guy Lombardo and His Royal Canadians served up the music.) Assigned to write the *Big Broadcast* songs were trustworthy Robin and Rainger, who handed Crosby two of his biggest all-time hits, "Please" and the mournful "Here Lies Love."

Another musical using radio partially as a backdrop was Walter Winchell's gossipy *Broadway Through a Keyhole,* which merged such luminaries as Russ Columbo, Texas Guinan, Blossom Seely, Abe Lyman and his orchestra, and Frances Williams, who had introduced Herman Hupfeld's "As Time Goes By" in the 1931 stage revue *Everybody Welcome.* The picture also debuted an early Mack Gordon–Harry Revel charmer, "You're My Past, Present, and Future."

Columbo, second only to Crosby as the leading radio crooner, was a respectable actor and, like Ramon Novarro, a Valentino lookalike. He died in 1934, at the age of 26 and at the height of his career, when he was hit in the eye by a bullet from an antique pistol shot off accidentally by gun collector Lansing Brown, Columbo's best friend.

Also from radio via the stage came Ed Wynn, the "Perfect Fool," who appeared in *Follow the Leader* and *The Chief.* Both films were eminently forgettable, although the first at least had the Al Segal–Pierre Norman–Sammy Fain song "Satan's Holiday" going for it. Twenty-five years would elapse before Wynn, the father of actor Keenan, set his baggy-pants comedy routines aside and made his mark in Hollywood as a dramatic actor. His performance in *Diary of Anne Frank* (1959) earned him an Oscar nomination for Best Supporting Actor.

Kate Smith, radio's chubby "Songbird of the South," introduced the lyrical "Moon Song (That Wasn't Meant for Me)" in *Hello, Everybody.* Her weekly guest-filled *Kate Smith Show,* also known as the *A & P Bandwagon,* scored a coup by coaxing publicity-shy Greta Garbo into appearing on it — once. The show also introduced the Aldrich Family, Bud Abbott and Lou Costello, and Henny Youngman.

Myrt and Marge, whose soap opera attracted legions of listeners, made *Laughter in the Air* in 1933. Experienced as the twosome was at speaking dialogue, neither Myrt (Myrtle Vail) nor Marge (Donna Damerel Fick) could act, and the picture failed. To compound the problem, they were cast as sisters. Myrt was actually Marge's mother, and the disparity in their ages was painfully evident in the closeups. But the film did include a very good tune, J. Jasmyn and M.K. Jerome's "Isle of Blues."

In the meantime, the radio industry was throwing a spitball at Hollywood over Gordon Clifford and Nacio Herb Brown's "Paradise," written for silent star Pola Negri in *A Woman Commands*. Worried that some people might salivate from salacious thoughts during the humming sequences, censors banned it temporarily from broadcasting studios. A similar rebuke would be meted out to the Gershwins' equally harmless "Nice Work If You Can Get It" in 1937. This time the censors were distraught over how the public might interpret "it."

A PAPER MOON, A DREAM, AND A WOLF

Any list of the best June 1930–March 1933 Hollywood songs would cover many more that are at least vaguely familiar to contemporary popular music fans. Buddy Rogers performed "It's Only a Paper Moon," inserted into the film version of *Take a Chance*. Russ Columbo crooned Dubin and Warren's "Coffee in the Morning, Kisses in the Night" into a standard, although the songwriters' biggest hit from the same picure (*Moulin Rouge*) was "Boulevard of Broken Dreams."

Three more winners were penned by Jay Gorney — the excellent "You're My Thrill," with a lyric by Sidney Clare, for *Jimmy and Sally;* and "Ah, But Is It Love?" and "Moonlight and Pretzels," again with Clare, for *Moonlight and Pretzels*. Ginger Rogers and Jack Haley collaborated vocally on "Did You Ever See a Dream Walking?" in *Sitting Pretty*. The first towering success by the formidable writing partnership of Gordon and Revel, the song won ASCAP's first prize as the outstanding hit of 1933.

"Inka Dinka Doo," one of the more ingenious nonsense songs, highlighted *Palooka*, based on the comic-strip prizefighting character. It was sung by its co-author, the bulbous-nosed Jimmy Durante, in the role of Knobby Walsh, Joe Palooka's manager. "Schnozzola" Durante had boarded the show biz bandwagon 25 years earlier on Coney Island, playing piano in Carey Walsh's saloon for another newcomer with ball-bearing eyes, Eddie Cantor.

One of America's most popular radio stars ever, Cantor himself sang two movie song hits in 1933, Dubin and Warren's "Build a Little Home" and "Keep Young and Beautiful," in Samuel Goldwyn's elaborate *Roman Scandals*. The film was spirited along by three Busby Berkeley–directed dance interludes and a climactic chariot race, a

spoof of the better-known contest in *Ben-Hur.* Also in the cast were singer Ruth Etting, whom Doris Day would portray 22 years later in *Love Me or Leave Me,* and Lucille Ball, in her first bit part, and Paulette Goddard as chorus girls.

The supporting role that music has played in animated cartoons got off to a healthy start in the early 1930s. Ann Ronell and Frank Churchill's "Who's Afraid of the Big Bad Wolf?" placed high on popularity charts after its debut in *The Three Little Pigs* (1933), one of Disney's best "Silly Symphony" shorts. Some people read social commentary into the lyric, with the wolf symbolizing the Depression.

Folks are in for bad times when he comes to town, the lyric declares, and the wolf promptly threatens to blow apart the houses built by the trio of piglets. The wolf manages to crumble one house made of straw and another of twigs. But the third house is a different story. Its little pig owner has built it with bricks, and not even the wolf's heaviest huffing and puffing are able to demolish it.

The moral, according to several interpreters: one can weather any storm when one's life, including the financial part of it, is based on the firm foundation of sensible planning. It is questionable that this was the message Disney intended the film to convey, despite his flair for propagandizing (see List #3, "Academy Award-Nominated Songs From Walt Disney Productions").

Another cartoon song stressed nutrition over architecture. Devouring cans of spinach worked wonders with one fellow, transforming his spine from jelly to steel and his biceps into boulders of muscle. "I'm Popeye the Sailor Man," which Sammy Lerner whipped up in fewer than two hours for cartoonist Dave Fleischer, remains one of the best-known songs written for an animated character. Lerner also wrote the theme song for animator Myron Natwick's *Betty Boop* cartoon series, introduced in 1930. Singer Helen Kane supplied the voice for Betty, a curvaceous, short-skirted flapper with a Kewpie-doll face that appropriately mirrored her virginal coyness.

Meanwhile, in the world of flesh and blood, Shirley Temple became the youngest person in the annals of film — and very likely in all

Opposite: **Indicative of the reduction in the size of Depression-era choruses is this nine-member lineup for Al Dubin and Harry Warren's "Keep Young and Beautiful" production number in *Roman Scandals* (1933). The third girl from the right is Paulette Goddard in a blonde wig.**

the other entertainment media as well — to help popularize a song. In her case it was Harry Woods's independently written mock lament "We Just Couldn't Say Goodbye," wherein even the lovers' furniture bursts into tears at the prospect of their breakup. (Not to worry: they stay together.)

A robust four years old at the time, Shirley delivered the song while parodying Marlene Dietrich as Morelegs Sweetrick in *Kid'n' Hollywood,* the sixth of the talented tot's *Baby Burlesk* featurettes. Her first screen song, a reprise of Arthur J. Lamb and Harry Von Tilzer's well-known "A Bird in a Gilded Cage," was sung in *Glad Rags to Riches* earlier in 1932.

In the midst of filmdom's musical Sahara arrived Broadway's distinguished Richard Rodgers and Lorenz Hart, whose initial assignments were to furnish three songs for *The Hot Heiress* (1931), starring Walter Pidgeon, and another trio for *The Phantom President* (1932), with George M. Cohan and Claudette Colbert. Perhaps reflective of the dismal times in which the partners were working, the songs were largely ignored, even though "Give Her a Kiss," from the second film, is as graceful as anything else Rodgers ever wrote.

George and Ira Gershwin also made their talking-picture debut in 1931, furnishing the score for Fox's *Delicious.* The songs, definitely not among the twosome's top-ranking compositions, included the title tune (spelled phonetically, "Delishious"); "Blah, Blah, Blah," a pleasant satire on moon-and-June love songs; and the pretty ballad "Someone From Somewhere."

The film is historic, however, in that it features in the background about one minute of the six-minute orchestral work George wrote for it. The music is heard only briefly to accent the noise and jarring tempo of swift-moving Manhattan while Janet Gaynor searches its streets for her shipboard lover, Charles Farrell. Gershwin later expanded the work and published it under the title *Second Rhapsody.*

Also bivouacking briefly in the film capital was musical giant Jerome Kern, the first American composer to successfully blend the Viennese genius for melody with popular rhythms of the day, including jazz. Beginning his Broadway career with *The Red Petticoat* in 1912, Kern in 1917 set an all-time Broadway record: seven of his musical comedies were running there at the same time. But on his 1931 visit to the "other" coast, he was treated so shabbily that one would assume he was a mere dabbler rather than the dean of the musical theater.

His job was to help Universal Studios capitalize on the spectacular bottom-line success of films about aviators—*Wings, Hell's
Angels,* and *Hell's Divers* among them. Accordingly, Kern and lyricist
Otto Harbach produced a score for *Stolen Dreams,* which carried the
same title as one of Kern's ballads. The picture was supposed to be
lifted to fame and fortune by three lightweights: Jack Whiting, Irene
Delroy, and Bramwell Fletcher.

Disaster quickly befell Kern, the picture, and the studio. News
that the anti–film-musical public was equally indisposed to World
War I aerial dogfights caused Universal to waver temporarily. Stubborn to the end, although with scant hope of success, it released the
film anyway, but under a new title, *Men of the Sky,* which repelled audiences further by advertising that the cast would be airborne most of
the time. Worse still, all of the 11 Harbach-Kern songs were deleted.

But Kern would have the last laugh on Hollywood. His stage-
based operettas *Cat and the Fiddle,* with Jeanette MacDonald and
Ramon Novarro, and *Music in the Air*, with Gloria Swanson and John
Boles, made money in 1934. Between 1936 and 1946, six of the composer's songs would receive Academy Award nominations.

Several Broadway musicals, none so opulent or tuneful as their
1929 predecessors, found their way into movie houses, only to suffer
banishment to the nether world of marginal success. *Flying High,* with
music by DeSylva, Brown, and Henderson, hit wind shear and fell
back to the tarmac, although it did introduce Bert Lahr—Dorothy's
"Cowardly Lion" pal in *The Wizard of Oz*—to films and the sparkling
"We'll Dance Until the Dawn," a Dorothy Fields-James McHugh interpolation.

Still another casualty was the remake of *Fifty Million Frenchmen,*
with the Cole Porter stage score heard only dimly in the background.
Not even the zaniness of ("Ole") Olsen and ("Chic") Johnson enticed
many sightseers to that one. More successful was the slapstick comedy
duo of (Bert) Wheeler and (Bob) Woolsey, whose filmed version of
Kalmar and Ruby's *Cuckoos* gave birth to the hummable "I Love You
So Much," added to the original Broadway score in Hollywood.

Numbered among the once-popular performers whose careers
were dimming was Marion Davies, whose *Peg o' My Heart* (1933), also
adapted from the stage, was a turkey, with Freed and Brown's "I'll
Remember Only You" its sole asset. Genuinely and widely loved in
real as well as reel life, Miss Davies (born Marion Douras) acquired

and retained shaky star status by virtue of her off-screen role as mistress of newspaper tycoon William Randolph Hearst.

He had become attracted to her while she was appearing in *Ziegfeld Follies of 1917.* He was 54, she was 20. Hearst was entirely willing to marry his young heartthrob, but Millicent Hearst, a one-time chorus girl herself, refused to divorce him under any terms, no matter how generous.

Hearst kept Miss Davies in the public eye by establishing Cosmopolitan Pictures, later an independent unit of MGM, strictly to produce films with her as the star. Although she displayed only limited talent as a singer and dancer, she was a respectable light comedienne in spite of a slight stammer. A spoof of the studio's own *Grand Hotel,* MGM's *Blondie of the Follies* (1932) paired Miss Davies with Jimmy Durante, and their brief recreation of the Garbo and John Barrymore roles qualifies as one of the year's film highlights.

The Hearst-Davies relationship, in barely disguised format, entered Orson Welles's *Citizen Kane* in 1941. In it, Kane (Welles's pseudonym for Hearst) builds an opera house for his wife and forces her to sing on stage. Instead of applause, the poor woman is deluged with ridicule, as was Miss Davies herself by many film critics. A vengeful Hearst took umbrage and ordered his Hollywood columnist, Louella Parsons, to blast *Citizen Kane,* which she did, even though it was already on its way to enshrinement as one of the best sound films ever produced in America.

Harry Warren, whose several songs for Miss Davies included "I'll Sing You a Thousand Love Songs," looked upon her with special and rare fondness. "She never took herself seriously," he said, echoing the yardstick by which he measured a Hollywood celebrity's claim to his affection.

MEANWHILE, IN THE BACKGROUND . . .

Lost in the miasma of the period's uninterest in film music was the trial balloon floated by director King Vidor in the romance *Bird of Paradise* in 1932. For the first time in a Hollywood film, the musical background, consisting mostly of Edward Eliscu and Max Steiner's theme song "Out of the Blue," continued under the dialogue between the stars, Dolores Del Rio and Joel McCrea. Previously, when performers spoke, the orchestrated accompaniment disappeared from the sound track, presumably so that it would not compete with, or drown out, their words. As early as *The Jazz Singer,* in the sequence that set this musical-background pattern, cantor Warner Oland's singing voice is heard off-screen while Bobby Gordon creeps into his flat, adjacent to the temple, and pilfers a picture of his mother before running away from home. But Gordon neither speaks nor makes any other sound.

As regards popular songs, the camera would sometimes shift from singer to audience, while the pop song continued in voice-over format, with occasional spoken interruptions by the spectators. The melody of "I Surrender, Dear" is heard clearly during the verbal exchange between James Cagney and Jean Harlow in *Public Enemy* (1931), but such use of standard songs was rare.

For the most part, dramatic pictures were barren of background music, including theme songs, during the cost-cutting interregnum, a most unfortunate development. It was unfortunate because the very earliest talkies had given rise to a number of distinguished sound track scores by the likes of Louis Silvers, who also conducted the Vitaphone Orchestra for *The Jazz Singer;* Herbert Stothart; Leo Forbstein; and Hugo Riesenfeld, among other composers.

Essentially talking pictures' answer to the orchestrations written for the silents, these typically overpowering, lush, sometimes derivative musical accompaniments often attained concert hall quality. One such score was by Alfred Newman for *Street Scene,* director King Vidor's 1931 film adaptation of Elmer Rice's acclaimed 1929 stage drama. Straitjacketed to a single set — a tenement stoop and the sidewalk it abutted — the film starred Sylvia Sidney and Beulah Bondi, two of the screen's most skillful actresses. Newman's music deserved equal billing. In several forward-looking scenes, the composer interspersed the dialogue with musical phraseology that effectively intensified the lines. In several instances, the musical backdrop also echoed the actor's voice.

"The finest example of the latter technique," Vidor notes in *A Tree Is a Tree,* "occurs in the scene in which the fiercely jealous husband unexpectedly arrives at the tenement where, upstairs, his wife is entertaining her lover. As the husband enters the building, a neighborhood boy calls out the wife's name as a warning. The orchestra repeats his cries in the exact tone of his voice. As each warning becomes more frantic, the orchestra paraphrases his words and increases in intensity until the fatal shot is heard. Then the crescendo that has been achieved is cut short by a cacaphonic climax."

Indebted as the familiar major theme is to Gershwin's *Rhapsody in Blue* and *Concerto in F,* Newman's *Street Scene* music, as well as that for *Dead End* (1937), *Gunga Din,* and *Wuthering Heights* (both 1939), wielded tremendous influence on later generations by opening new vistas of film-music composition that are abundantly apparent to this very day. The most celebrated of the background-music writers, as well as the composer of the well-known drum roll and blast of martial music that swell up from behind the 20th Century–Fox logo, Newman worked on the scores of more than 200 films before his death in 1970. He won nine Academy Awards as composer, conductor, or musical director.

Another composer frequently tapped by Hollywood was Max Steiner, whose march for *The Charge of the Light Brigade* (1936) ably escorted Errol Flynn and 599 other warriors into the battle at Balaklava Heights. He was also responsible for the beautiful musical interludes that distinguished such other dramatic films as *Jezebel* (1938), *Dust Be My Destiny* (1939), and *Since You Went Away* (1944). For *They Made Me a Criminal* (1939), Steiner inserted snatches of the same "Tara Theme" heard later that year in *Gone with the Wind.*

Effective background scores have also been provided by Erich Wolfgang Korngold (*Adventures of Robin Hood,* 1938); Aaron Copland (*Our Town,* 1940); Bernard Herrmann (*Citizen Kane,* 1941); Victor Young (*For Whom the Bell Tolls,* 1943); Miklos Rozsa (*Spellbound,* 1945); David Raksin (*Forever Amber,* 1947); Dimitri Tiomkin (*It's a Wonderful Life,* 1947); Franz Waxman (*Sunset Boulevard,* 1950); Alex North (*A Streetcar Named Desire,* 1952); Leonard Bernstein (*On the Waterfront,* 1954); non-relative Elmer Bernstein (*Man with the Golden Arm,* 1956); and Henry Mancini (*Touch of Evil,* 1958). Virgil Thompson's score for *Louisiana Story* (1948) won him the only Pulitzer Prize ever awarded for background music.

It is no disservice to contemporary composers to credit much of their success to the efforts of Newman, Steiner & Company on Hollywood's scoring stages. Without their trailblazing, such later artists as Quincy Jones, a one-time trumpeter and arranger with Lionel Hampton's band and composer of more than 30 recent sound tracks, and John Williams (*Star Wars*) would have faced tough sledding selling their talent to film producers. Nor might 1989's highest-grossing movie, *Batman,* have been embellished with a praiseworthy background score by Danny Elfman that deftly alternates between the dramatic and the sensuous.

Certainly, no laborers in Hollywood's vineyards have faced more difficult artistic challenges than the background-music writers. Their job has always been to match music to a film already completed, and into which they had no input whatever. Their scores are never to impede the director's intentions or include musical comments or overtones of meaning of their own. Their music must flow through the picture as an almost unnoticed undercurrent. The most effective background music, now as always, is unobtrusive. It is to be vaguely sensed rather than heard.

One notable exception to the dearth of theme songs in the 1930–33 period was the haunting title song by Edward Heyman and John W. Green for Claudette Colbert's *I Cover the Waterfront.* Unsung in the film, it nonetheless developed into one of the finest of all theme songs, as well as one of the most popular.

A man of diverse talents, Green has served the music field as bandleader, concert hall conductor, arranger, and composer. "Body and Soul," sung by Libby Holman in Broadway's *Three's a Crowd* (1930), is his masterpiece, with "(You Came Along From) Out of Nowhere" not very far behind. In later years he would be MGM's general musical director and the winner of Oscars for scoring such musicals as *Easter Parade* (1948), *American in Paris* (1951), *West Side Story* (1961), and *Oliver!* (1968).

Composer Allie Wrubel, meantime, carried on the time-honored tradition of writing promotional songs for movies bearing the same titles. Two of his 1932–33 entries were particularly good: "As You Desire Me," for the Garbo film, and, with lyricist Abner Silver, "Farewell to Arms," which publicized the Helen Hayes–Gary Cooper picture based on the Hemingway novel of a tragic love affair between a soldier and a nurse in World War I.

A GIRL NAMED MIMI

In the summer of 1932, when the Dow-Jones Average dropped to 41.22 (on July 8), its lowest level of the 20th century, the Hollywood studios adopted another round of spartan cost reductions. They dispensed with many of the high-salaried directors who had established their reputations in the silent days, opening the portals for the easy passage of directors from Broadway. The assumption was that the latter would not charge as much as the former for their services. But within a year, the expatriate stage directors began upping their salary demands, basing them, logically, on their newly acquired experience making films. The studios promptly reversed course and rehired the out-of-work silent veterans en masse.

Luckily for the film musical, the new open door policy coaxed director Rouben Mamoulian back into action. Paramount teamed him with Rodgers and Hart, in brilliant form again, and Maurice Chevalier and Jeanette MacDonald, and out came an authentic beauty, *Love Me Tonight.*

Containing innovative "rhythmic dialogue" (much of the dialogue is sung in rhyming couplets, as in the prologue to "The Son of a Gun Is Nothing but a Tailor"), the film awarded Chevalier with another personal theme song, "Mimi," as well as one of his best ballads, "Isn't It Romantic." Rodgers, a master architect of the waltz, bestowed one of his stateliest, "Lover," on Miss MacDonald, who wasted the song by singing it to a horse. Not till *The Major and the Minor* in 1942 would Paramount do justice to a truly beautiful song by reprising "Lover" as the opening number at a military school dance.

The two songmen expanded their use of rhythmic dialogue in their next picture, the five-song *Hallelujah, I'm a Bum!*, among the best of the Depression musicals. Scripted by playwright S.N. Behrman, the film revolves completely around Al Jolson, back in Hollywood after a three-year hiatus brought about by the disappointing reception to his *Big Boy* (1930), which had only a vivid racetrack atmosphere and Bud Green and Sam H. Stept's "Tomorrow Is Another Day" in its favor. In the 1933 film, Jolson plays "Bumper," a carefree panhandler whose abounding good humor wins him the honorary title of "Mayor of Central Park," even if he does lose the girl (Madge Evans) to Frank Morgan, in the role of the mayor of New York City. Jolson sings the superlative ballad "You Are Too Beautiful" and throws a bone of consolation to his fellow unemployed with the lighthearted "What Do You Want with Money?"

In early 1933, Sam Coslow joined Arthur Johnston, who had revealed inordinate talent for orchestration by scoring Chaplin's *City Lights,* to write the songs for two Bing Crosby bonanzas, *College Humor* and *Too Much Harmony.* From them came such perennials as

Mae West practicing her wiles on veteran character actor Victor Moore in
***The Heat's On,* 1943.**

"Moonstruck," "Thanks," "Black Moonlight," "Learn to Croon," and "The Day You Came Along." The singer's biggest hit of the year, however, was by Freed and Brown, whose seductive "Temptation" was the champion of their six-song score for *Going Hollywood.*

That same year witnessed the rejuvenated presence of the swaggering Brooklyn-born avatar of Cleopatra, equally adept at arousing a generation of males with her irresistibility. A true one-of-a-kind, Mae West was nearing 40 when she appeared in her two 1933 pictures, *She Done Him Wrong* and *Belle of the Nineties,* dishing out a delectable ragout of sexual innuendo and provocation, titillating but never prurient, while bending the barriers of film censorship.

Her reputation had preceded her to Hollywood, where she landed in 1932, and she had every intention of living up to it. Actually one of her era's great satirists, Miss West had the audacity in 1926 to perform the forbidden shimmy on stage in *Mimic World.* Predictably, her undulating hips and obvious delight in shocking audiences into attention brought down the house. They also brought her career under the scrutiny of the law.

In 1927 she and the producers of her *Sex* were convicted of staging an indecent play, and Miss West was incarcerated on Welfare Island, New York City's little Alcatraz, for eight days. A short time after liberation, she reopened her bag of tricks, only to witness the city of Detroit shut down her new show, *Diamond Lil,* after censors branded it as "silly, holding no moral, and teaching no lesson."

As if the themes of her plays were not bold enough, the actress also dabbled in wisecracks. Only slightly less subtle than her studiously exaggerated gestures, they operated on a layer cake of levels. Her saucy greeting to a male acquaintance, "Is that a gun in your pocket, or are you just glad to see me?," is but one example. Her films pestered movie censors, but they were at a loss in 1933 over how to contain her brazen sultriness.

Acting out her priceless adage that "too much of a good thing is wonderful," the buxom Miss West sashayed rather than walked through her films, her fluttering eyelashes and falsetto voice indispensable to her portrayals of the eternal temptress. Her stocky hourglass figure, poured like molten lava into tight-fitting dresses, regularly left males smoldering in her wake. Her invitation to Cary Grant to "come up sometime and see me" rang with promise, but she clearly had no intention of fleshing out the visions of ecstasy dancing in his head. She loved to excite, then deflate, then ridicule. And she practiced her art better than anybody else.

The double entendre lyrics of her 1930s screen songs ably complemented her leering renditions. Miss West enjoys "A Guy Who Takes His Time" and an "Easy Rider," she admits in *She Done Him Wrong,* using Robin and Rainger songs as confessionals. Calling on Sam Coslow and Arthur Johnston for the tunes in *Belle of the Nineties,* she reveals that "I'm in Love with a Tattooed Man" and "I Met My Waterloo." She invites the audience to "Meet the King" and expands on what happens "When a Saint Louis Woman Comes Down to New Orleans." In a fifth song, this one by Harvey Brooks, Gladys DuBois, and Ben Ellison (for *I'm No Angel*), Miss West demonstrates why "They Call Me Sister Honky Tonk."

In mid-1933, with the all-star drama *Dinner at Eight* under way, MGM assigned Dorothy Fields and James McHugh to write songs for it. Accordingly, they submitted two sparklers with as much candlepower as the cast, which included Marie Dressler, Jean Harlow, John and Lionel Barrymore, Wallace Beery, Edmund Lowe, and Billie Burke.

But the songs were the victims of injudicious decision-making; neither is heard anywhere in the film. The major tune, "Don't Blame Me," became an acknowledged classic independently, even though it was also dropped from a minor stage musical, *Clowns in Clover,* with Larry Adler, master of the harmonica. The second song, "Dinner at Eight," was used to promote the film. It also ranks as one of the most cherished of all 1930s sheet music pieces for its illustrations of the leading players and facsimiles of their autographs on the front cover.

Composer McHugh and lyricist Fields were numbered among the finest songwriting teams of the early 1930s. They had been collaborating since Broadway's *Blackbirds of 1928,* which introduced Bill Robinson to the stage and their first big hit, "I Can't Give You Anything But Love," to music fans.

Although the song has sold more than three million sheet music copies over the years, it got off to a shaky start. It was not written for *Blackbirds,* but for the 1927 failure *Delmar's Revels.* The original singers, who would later grace the screen in numerous comic roles, were Patsy Kelly and Bert Lahr, the latter a vaudeville headliner since 1910. Playing two poor Brooklyn youngsters dressed in rags, they duetted the song while sitting atop the stairs of a tenement cellar. Producer Harry Delmar dropped it from the short-lived show.

Miss Fields was the daughter of star vaudevillian Lew Fields (of Weber and Fields) and sister of librettist Herbert Fields, whose credits include *Annie Get Your Gun* (1946). She continued writing into the mid-1960s, winding up a brilliant career by poeticizing the songs in *Sweet Charity.* In 1936, McHugh teamed up with another exceptional lyricist, Harold Adamson, for a series of screen songs that are among the best remembered from the years 1936 to 1945.

Both film fans and moguls made an egregious error in judgment when they turned their backs on musical films in mid-1930. If ever the public needed to hear cheerful little ditties and chuckle at the antics of stock comic characters, it was at the outset of the Great Depression. What it got instead was an outpouring of dramatic films centering on gangsters, executives traumatized by the stock market crash, tearful ladies dispossessed of their virtue by philandering lovers, and copycat melodramas with tough private eyes, like Sam Spade (Ricardo Cortez) in the first movie version of Dashiell Hammett's *Maltese Falcon.*

Offering neither comfort nor distraction, some of these pictures were unquestionably fist-rate: *Little Caesar, I Am a Fugitive from a Chain Gang, Public Enemy,* and *Scarface.* But they were relentless in depicting the assorted economic and social ills besetting almost every American, who above all else wanted to escape from them.

It cannot be stated unequivocally that big-budget musicals would have perked up morale and box offices. But when Hollywood finally released a few new ones, customers ganged up at movie houses and profits again painted the studios with sunshine. Perhaps inevitably, the studio responsible for reviving the backstage film musical was the same one that had pioneered both the talkies and singing from sound tracks.

Warner Bros. was back in the business it knew best.

Sons of Blockbuster

In August 1932, the Warners decided to renail their colors to the film-musical spectacular that once had served them, and all the other major studios, so nobly. They made a deep-pockets $400,000 commitment to renovating their own *On with the Show*, successfully filmed in 1929, and finessed it with a bubbly new score, unsentimental tone, attractive cast, and convoluted but sturdy story that neatly balances six intertwining subplots that are merged logically at the end.

By borrowing the main storyline from the past, the studio validated the umbilical dependency the forthcoming series of movie musicals would have on the 1929-30 period. The songwriters' challenge was to clothe the films with enough new popular songs to disguise the similarities in settings and characters, which were by then as instantly recognizable as Christmas crèches.

Released in early 1933 as *42nd Street,* the film reignited the musical comedy flame that MGM had lit with *Broadway Melody* almost exactly four years before. Viewers were again given a tour of Times Square, but it was not glamour that predominated, but rather the sweat, tears, frustrations, and temperamental outbursts afflicting producer and performers anxiously trying to put on a show under a tight deadline and peppered with pitfalls.

Warner Baxter hands in his usual professional job as the harassed producer — a role he would repeat many more times — who desperately needs the then titanic sum of $40,000 in order to stage one more smash hit before he retires or dies, whichever comes first. Ginger Rogers and Una Merkle excel as caustic chorines. Only slightly less effective are Bebe Daniels as the star who breaks her ankle on opening night, George Brent as the gigolo, and Dick Powell and Ruby Keeler, matched for the first of their seven films together, as the ingenues looking for their Big Break.

The four songs by the tireless Dubin and Warren, who appear briefly at the beginning of the film, are superb, ranging from the spirited to the romantic. The Busby Berkeley–staged title tune is performed in a brief melodrama complete with an obviously artificial stage set depicting the towers surrounding honky-tonk 42nd Street, for years the epicenter of the legitimate stage.

The picture's only flaw was continuing the stage and film musical tradition of inserting songs haphazardly, without recourse to the storyline. Most stage songs could be shifted effortlessly from act to act, and film songs from scene to scene, without in any way endangering plot development. Musicals, live or canned, rarely furnished a context for the songs to be taken out of.

Jerome Kern had deviated from the policy as early as 1914 in his series of intimate musical comedies produced at the 299-seat Princess Theatre on West 39th Street. In the first, *Nobody Home,* he stitched together the seamless blend of music and libretto in which the lyrics advanced the storyline, sometimes foreshadowing the action, other times exposing subtleties of character. But Broadway resisted Kern's pioneering for decades. So did Hollywood.

"Shuffle Off to Buffalo," the slightly suggestive second-ranking hit from *42nd Street,* is mere decoration, giving the chorus another opportunity to display their cherubic faces and physical attributes. More than ever before, Warners was picking up chorus members from the road shows of Broadway musicals playing in Los Angeles, and the footwork benefited from their expertise.

The ballad "You're Getting to Be a Habit with Me" has no purpose other than to provide Miss Daniels with an excuse to sing one of Dubin and Warren's all-time best. Similarly, the bouncy "Young and Healthy" serves only to indicate the kind of tunes producer Baxter wants for his forthcoming musical show, as well as to accent Powell's tenorizing and Miss Keeler's demureness.

Although the sensation caused by *42nd Street* reverberated with seismic proportions across the country, only Warners was shaken into further activity. With the film, the studio proved that the recent musical comedy slump was an aberration rather than an omen. Off it went on another song-and-dance binge that would continue for almost six years, when it took another breather. (In 1980, producer David Merrick's stage version of *42nd Street* began its highly touted eight-year run at three of Broadway biggest theaters, the Winter Garden, Majestic, and St. James. Added to the score were nine songs from other Dubin-Warren 1930s musical pictures.)

Their timidity buttressed by hindsight, the other studios were understandably reluctant to join Warner Bros. in the backstage-musical comedy sweepstakes. When F.D.R. succeeded Hoover in the Oval Office in March 1933, the country was technically bankrupt, lacking even the funds to redeem the $700 million in government securities payable March 1. At the March 4 inauguration, no hotel in Washington, D.C., would accept checks, so infirm was the banking system.

Like all the studios, Warners had been losing money. In 1931, when RKO Radio lost $5.5 million, the brothers posted an even bigger $8 million loss; in 1932 they went $14 million into the red. Paramount was in worse condition, losing $16 million in 1932 and tumbling into bankruptcy. Fox lost $17 million.

Paramount finally climbed out of receivership in 1935 after its directors hired Joseph P. Kennedy, the father of the future president, as financial adviser. Fox was saved from extinction the same year by merging with Twentieth Century Pictures, which had entered negotiations mostly to buy Shirley Temple's contract, the hottest property in the picture business. The studio was renamed 20th Century–Fox and, under the leadership of Darryl F. Zanuck, succeeded as one of Hollywood's most profitable enterprises.

Even MGM, which had earned profits of $12.1 million in 1929 and $15 million in 1930, was whiplashed by the Depression. In 1931 its profits fell to $12 million, then in 1932 to $8 million. But the studio never operated in the red through the 1930s. Indeed, general manager Louis B. Mayer's 1937 earnings of $1.3 million made him the highest-salaried person in the country. Another problem facing the studios on the eve of the 1933 musical revival was grooming youngsters with the potential to become song-and-dance celebrities of the first magnitude.

Training would take time, and time was money to the moguls, who were struggling to keep their heads above financial quicksand.

Few popular personalities of the 1929-30 period were available to appear in musical movies in 1933. Many had returned to the stage, their first love to begin with, complaining that filmmaking was simply not their bag. Film acting played havoc with the careers of confidence-brimming entertainers, like Jolson, who could entrance live audiences but found it difficult to stand still and sing before microphones on silent sound stages.

Film-musical stars like Mary Eaton, Winnie Lightner, Sue Carol, Vivienne Segal, Bernice Clare, and Nancy Carroll were petering out by early 1930. So were Bessie Love, Anita Page, Cliff Edwards, Nick Lucas, and Charles and Dennis King. John Boles and Janet Gaynor retained much of their glitter, although to do so they gradually veered into dramatic parts. Dolores Del Rio and Lupe Velez continued, but after 1934 were being cast in character roles in second-rate pictures. Fanny Brice and Sophie Tucker were similarly downgraded to secondary or specialty billing — Miss Brice in *The Great Ziegfeld* (1936) and Miss Tucker in *Broadway Melody of 1938*. Not even radio giants Amos 'n' Andy appeared in another film after 1930.

The archaic musicals that had launched these and other stars' film careers were ignored like so many spent cartridges. They were curios of a lost age when business was king and booming, when people were happy and therefore uncritical. Because of advances in filmmaking, grainy artifacts like *Show of Shows* and *Vagabond Lover* gave the distinct impression they had been produced in Edison's time, rather than a mere three to four years before.

The unique ability of films to freeze performers in time is both an asset and a handicap. Viewing a 60-year-old musical is a priceless experience. We see the same artists earlier generations saw, forever young, still shedding starlight while reflecting faint images of the vanished summer of a distant America. The stage surmounts revival problems by updating old scripts, adding songs, and fielding new casts whose skills are attuned to current acting standards. Unless a decades-old film musical is remade, what we see is the untouched original, warts and all. Today, many persons find these backward looks fascinating. But in 1933, moviegoers had no sense of the nostalgia that would pervade later generations, and so the mass of the 1929-30 musical films became one with Ninevah and Tyre.

THE DANCING GANGSTER

With a corner on the backstage-musical market, Warners confidently dipped further into its treasury to piggyback the success of *42nd Street*. *Footlight Parade* and the second in the studio's *Gold Diggers* series quickly went on stream, winning plaudits from public and critics alike. *Foolight Parade,* pulled taut by a feisty James Cagney, also revisits Broadway, though not in the customary manner. Here, instead of his usual role as a scrappy hood, Cagney plays a producer of musical "prologues," which consisted of brief skits with songs and dances performed by live actors on the stages of the largest silent-movie palaces in big cities. Each prologue centered on a slight story that referred, usually satirically, to the theme of the feature film to follow.

The practice continued into the infancy of talking pictures. So many were released that prologue producers were forced to commission scripts and songs and train casts at breakneck speed, often working day and night to ready them for theatrical presentation.

Always at his acting best when confronted with problems demanding on-the-spot decisions, Cagney performs admirably as the hard-driving entrepreneur who nontheless is protective of his mobs of tired troupers. He is abetted by the thoroughgoing professional Joan Blondell, with whom Cagney had been paired for the first time in the 1929 stage musical *Penny Arcade*, with songs by Lew Pollack. The next year they appeared in the film version, renamed *Sinners' Holiday,* and proceeded to outshine everything and everybody else in that mediocrity. Their talismanic touch endowed *Footlight Parade* with a vitality and incandescence that survive to this very day.

No slouch as a dancer, as he would confirm in his role as George M. Cohan in *Yankee Doodle Dandy* (1942), producer Cagney is forced to replace an amateur too frightened to do his routine. Cagney dons a sailor suit, hops atop a bar, and sings and prances to Dubin and Warren's "Shanghai Lil," played by Ruby Keeler, in Busby Berkeley's most inventive dance number up to that time. The song is also good, even though the chorus bears a striking resemblance to the first few notes of the verse to Gershwin's "Swanee." The finale is a downscaled reenactment of New York City's gigantic NRA parade, including a huge picture of President Roosevelt.

Flush with the success of "Shuffle Off to Buffalo," Dubin and

Warren wrote a sequel, "Honeymoon Hotel," during which happy newlyweds cavort in the corridors and suites of a Jersey City hotel rather than on a Niagara Falls–bound train, as occurred in *42nd Street.* The hit of *Footlight Parade,* Sammy Fain's "By a Waterfall," is sung by Dick and Ruby and reprised no fewer than 12 times by a chorus of bathing beauties both above ground and in a highly artistic underwater ballet. Curiously, all three production numbers are jammed into the final 45 minutes of the 104-minute film.

Arranging chorus girls in geometric patterns suggesting, for example, flower petals lounging atop a water garden was not a fresh idea. *Cocoanuts* included a brief stylized grouping of arms and legs, as did Busby Berkeley's own *Whoopee!* In that film, with the camera pointed downward, the Indian headdresses worn by the chorines double as petals that gradually expand, like flowers awakened by sunlight arising above the surrounding mountains.

Through such inventiveness, William Berkeley Enos elevated the movements of a chorus line to the highest imaginative level. In fact, no other artist of the period was more responsible for establishing the format of 1930s big-budget production numbers than he. A veteran of Broadway, he invoked his limitless creativity to unfetter the chorus from single-set scenes, permitting it to engage in surreal activity. Regarding the camera as a tool in the dance director's kit, he deployed it in every conceivable way to photograph his girls and boys from bizarre angles beyond the ken of his contemporaries — from overhead, from beneath a glass floor, from between outstretched legs.

Excessive may well be the proper word to describe some of Berkeley's flights of fancy, but the demeaning of his work as atypical of the stage misses his purpose entirely. Unlike his predecessors, who had directed the close-order dance drills for the 1929-30 films, Berkeley refused to accept the movie set as a West Coast proscenium. The camera was free to roam at will, and Berkeley had no desire to dampen its flexibility. His routines were as intricate yet harmonious as a Persian carpet.

Practically all his film-musical production numbers were supposed to be a part of stage shows, but it was evident that no stage anywhere could hope to duplicate the rapid shifts of scene, multitudes of participants, or elaborate sets that distinguish the typical Busby Berkeley dance. By crossing all boundaries of space and imagination, he gave his musicals a uniqueness, different from anything that had come before.

Harry Warren, who wrote most of the songs that Berkeley choreographed, tempered his admiration for Berkeley's ingenuity by complaining that "he never knew when to quit." Berkeley reprised Warren's "I Only Have Eyes for You" so many times (12) that the composer tired of hearing his own song.

Berkeley's influence was wide and enduring. The chorus of swimmers in Billy Rose's *Aquacade,* part of the 1939-40 New York World's Fair, paddled along the Olympic-size pool in Berkeley-like ritualism. Well into the 1960s, the June Taylor Dancers were reintroduced bits and pieces of his Warner Bros. routines for their own ensemble dancing on television's *Jackie Gleason Show.*

In the fall of 1933, Warners released *Gold Diggers of 1933,* still one of the best Hollywood musicals and a worthy successor to *Broadway Melody.* Not so well crafted as *42nd Street,* it does suffer from an overabundance of conversation that, sharp as it usually is, slows the action to a near crawl, especially in the nightclub talkathon. Lapses in the chatter are welcome, not least because they allow Dubin and Warren, by then inured to working in a pressure cooker, to fill the gaps with five songs that easily match any other score they wrote.

The opening production number, "We're in the Money" (or "Gold Diggers Song"), sets the tone: optimism in the future. Ginger Rogers sings it, partly in pig Latin, while a cluster of chorus girls dances between huge replicas of silver dollars. Their confidence rising as the song continues, the ladies are actually serenading the demise of the Depression, which, they imply, is gasping on its deathbed. Nowadays, when they see the landlord, "We can look that guy right in the eye." Recovery, however, was not quite so apparent in the world outside film houses.

The hit of the picture, "Shadow Waltz," one of the numerous ballads of the time with a verse as melodious as the chorus, is performed by Dick Powell and Ruby Keeler, along with strolling chorus girls playing, or at least holding, illuminated violins. It ranks among the most acclaimed of Berkeley's production numbers, surpassed only by his superlative "Lullaby of Broadway" spectacle in *Gold Diggers of 1935.* Dubin and Warren's other two songs were the catchy "Pettin' in the Park" and the bluesy "I've Got to Sing a Torch Song," the latter among the prettiest of the composers' secondary efforts.

Part of Busby Berkeley's "Shadow Waltz" production number in *Gold Diggers of 1933*. The Al Dubin–Harry Warren song was the hit of the picture.

The climax of the film is an undisputed minor classic that clings to the memory as do the concluding 65 seconds of *City Lights.* Warners was already noted — or notorious — for its gangland "message" pictures, and *Gold Diggers of 1933* also crusades against a perceived social injustice. Its plea to "Remember My Forgotten Man" is both poignant and powerful, yet delivered as an appeal to conscience rather than as a clarion call for revolution.

Rich in the documentary-like chiaroscuro that only black-and-white film can impart, the final scene is dominated by a stark backdrop guaranteed to transfix the attention. A huge ferris wheel holds tiers of ex-soldiers (America's forgotten men) marching in Busby Berkeley–directed unison. Caught on a treadmill, they thump their feet in monotonous cadence, oblivion their eventual destination. In a series of intercuts, the jobless men are shown eating in soup kitchens and selling surplus apples from the bumper crop of 1932-33. Their lives, which only 15 years earlier they had risked on the battlefield, have become meaningless.

Standing before them is Joan Blondell, who recites the lyric while her saucer-like eyes commingle sorrow and hope. What comes out is one of the great torch songs of the period, almost equal to the champion of all Depression anthems, E.Y. Harburg and Jay Gorney's "Brother, Can You Spare a Dime?," introduced in 1932 by ex-vaudevillian Roy Weber in the Broadway revue *Americana.*

"Remember my forgotten man," Miss Blondell pleads. "You put a rifle in his hand, / You sent him far away, / You shouted 'Hip Hooray!' / But look at him today!"

Audiences knew what she was advocating: immediate payment of the $500 to $1,000 bonuses that President Coolidge had promised veterans in 1925. Issued as federally guaranteed bonds, they were scheduled to be redeemed in 1945, 27 years after World War I ended. Even the massive "Bonus March" on Washington in the summer of 1932 had failed to persuade Coolidge's successor, Herbert Hoover, to loosen the purse strings and hand out the bonus money then and there. In fact, the marchers were routed and their ramshackle encampment in nearby Anacostia Flats destroyed by the Army, led by Chief of Staff Douglas MacArthur.

After Miss Blondell lip-syncs the song for a second time—she rarely sang in films—she stares in near despair into the lens and cries out one last time: "Remember my forgotten man!" A pause. Scattered applause from the spectators ganged around the ferris wheel. The screen goes black. The picture is over.

In spite of this dramatic final scene, Miss Blondell's appeal went by the boards. Although President Roosevelt did meet with veterans' spokesmen (Hoover had refused to), he also withheld the bonus money, explaining that his administration was intent on providing jobs for all the unemployed as well as direct relief for the needy, including veterans, until his various New Deal programs took effect.

WINGS ON HIS SHOES

In 1933, MGM was the only other studio to pump a little oxygen into the comatose Broadway-based film musical. With the immensely popular Clark Gable and Joan Crawford heading the cast, the unoriginal *Dancing Lady* trod the same path as *42nd Street,* but far less successfully. Harold Adamson and Burton Lane's "Everything I Have Is Yours" is an exceptional ballad, and the only song in the film still remembered.

Dancing Lady, however, did make two contributions to films. Among the participants were the Three Stooges, members of comedian Ted Healy's vaudeville act since 1928. By the time of *Dancing Lady,* Jerome ("Curly") Howard had succeeded his brother Samuel (or "Shemp"), and it was this film that united the familiar slapstick trio that would star in about 200 short features for Columbia until Jerome's death in 1952. The second, far more significant milestone was the picture's introducing Fred Astaire in a small part as a hoofer. Within the next two years, his genius would lift the film musical to its absolute zenith.

Astaire had tried to break into the movies with sister Adele in 1928, when they made a screen test for Paramount. The test consisted of a few numbers from their recent stage hit, the Gershwins' *Funny Face,* which would not be converted to film until 1957, with Audrey Hepburn as Astaire's co-star.

The tryout flopped, at least according to one studio factotum who scribbled his impression of Astaire in a terse memo: "Can't act. Can't sing. Balding. Can dance a little." Perhaps cowed into anonymity by committing such an egregious error of judgment, the man has never been satisfactorily identified. Or perhaps, as some commentators maintain, the story is a fabrication. Either way, Astaire would not appear in a film until *Dancing Lady,* minus Adele and five years after the screen test. In the meantime, Adele had married an English duke, Charles Arthur Cavendish, and retired.

Born Frederick Austerlitz in Omaha, Nebraska, Fred took his father's suggestion and adopted Astaire as his stage name. In 1906, at the age of six, he entered vaudeville with Adele, subsequently appearing in 12 stage musicals from 1912 to 1933 in New York and London. His first published song, "You've Such a Lot," appeared in the London show *The Co-Optimists* in 1923. Altogether, he made 33 film musicals, at least half of them among the best ever, and co-starred with Ginger Rogers in ten of them. He danced professionally for the last time in 1976 at the age of 77.

"The greatest and most original dancer of all time" was how ballet virtuoso Mikhail Baryshnikov described Astaire shortly after Astaire's death in 1988. Few dancers before Astaire were given lines to speak in films, and only rarely did their names appear very high up on the list of cast members. With the exception of Marilyn Miller, Ann Pennington, Joan Crawford, Ruby Keeler, and a scattering of others, dancers of both sexes were dropped into films strictly as specialty acts. Their sole purpose was to break the monotony of the dialogue or lend individuality to production numbers.

Astaire revamped the formula. He was the star. He dominated the plots. He acted and sang as well as danced. Songwriters were among the first to recognize his uncommon precision of footwork, ever in balance like identical weights on a scalepan, and extraordinary vocalizing gifts. Only the best of them wrote his film songs: Berlin, Kern, Gershwin, Porter, Youmans, Warren, Harold Arlen, Frank Loesser, Arthur Schwartz, Burton Lane, and Johnny Mercer, who, like Loesser, sometimes wrote music as well as lyrics.

Irving Berlin, who supplied songs for six Astaire films, said of his close friend: "As a talent, Fred Astaire was pure gold." According to Ira Gershwin, who collaborated with George on Astaire's *Damsel in Distress* and *Shall We Dance,* the final words spoken by his dying brother in 1937 were "Fred Astaire."

Usually covetous of the talent in its stable, MGM let Astaire slip away after *Dancing Lady.* He returned to RKO Radio, which had hired him first and promptly farmed him out to MGM. Astaire's ten RKO musicals, made between 1933 and 1939, earned enviable profits for the studio and a soaring reputation for himself. In 1945, MGM hired him again, and off he went on a second string of spectaculars that ended with *Finian's Rainbow* in 1968.

In *Dancing Lady* he appears briefly and performs three songs: Adamson and Lane's "Heigh-Ho, the Gang's All Here" and "Let's Go Bavarian," the latter while adorned in top hat, white tie, and tails, and Fields and McHugh's "My Dancing Lady." Also in a cameo role is Nelson Eddy, who had made his own screen debut only weeks earlier in MGM's *Broadway to Hollywood.* For *Dancing Lady,* he sings Rodgers and Hart's jubilant "Rhythm of the Day."

Two superstars were born.

CHAPTER SIX

An Earful of Music: 1934

*I*T WAS ALMOST 20 months after the release of *Dancing Lady* that the Academy of Motion Picture Arts and Sciences awarded its first Oscar to songwriters, in this instance for the Best Song of 1934. Why this recognition had been delayed for so long is open to conjecture, but it surely was not because of the songwriters' lack of talent or failure to do the studios' bidding.

They obligingly mastered a wide variety of rhythms and rhymes to accommodate moviegoers' shifting tastes for two-steps, foxtrots, waltzes, novelties, Western ballads, blues, swing, specialty dance numbers, and even a few songs with a Latin beat. Their thanks consisted mostly of disdain from the moguls, some of whom were convinced that the melody-makers earned too much money for too little work, and in addition raked in even more from their quarterly ASCAP dividends.

Nor was it rare for Hollywood producers to further affront songwriters by hiring teams to complete film scores begun by other contract writers. Things were different on the stage, where new hirees could interpolate songs only after the original writers agreed. Their permission was likewise required before a producer could drop any of their songs. In Hollywood, arbitrarily lopping off songs from the finished print was rampant.

Then there was the not inconsequential matter of artistic pride. Although the best-known Broadway songwriters usually experienced the satisfaction of seeing their names standing alone in large letters on a title (or credit) card, their contract counterparts had to squint to find acknowledgments aimed at them. For most of the 1928–33 period, and sometimes beyond, their names were squeezed into the smallest visible

Ruby Keeler stands head and shoulders above the chorus of lookalikes in this scene from Al Dubin and Harry Warren's "I Only Have Eyes for You" spectacle in *Dames* (1934). Photo courtesy of *Movie Star News*.

type available, if not omitted altogether. Or they shared the same title card with three or more other equally unheralded craftsmen, like the art director, scriptwriter, and film editor. Even Irving Berlin's name was missing from the opening credits of *The Jazz Singer,* as were those of every other composer and lyricist whose songs appeared in that landmark film.

Adding more insult to injury, too many of Hollywood's rank and file, according to Harry Warren, regarded the songwriters' contributions as mere hooks for other people to hang their talents on. After all, they only wrote the songs. It was up to the directors, cinematographers, dance directors, lighting and sound engineers, and set and costume designers to showcase the songs for visual consumption. Then along came the singers, dancers, and instrumentalists to inject life into the tunes, to "sell" them to moviegoers and record and sheet music buyers.

The indifference and anonymity under which the 1930s contract writers toiled was summarized by one of them, Al Dubin, in the title song of Warner Bros.' *Dames* in 1934. Singing a Warren melody, Dick Powell asks rhetorically:

> Who writes the words and music
> For all the girlie shows?
> No one cares, and no one knows . . .
> Who cares if there's a plot or not
> When they've got a lot of dames!

It was only through stubbornness and fierce determination to excel that Warren was able to contend with what he termed the "demeaning punishment inflicted by producers and others on the contract-writing profession." His prescription for longevity, which for him spanned the 38 years between 1929 and 1967: "Ignore everybody and do the best you can."

Along the way, he kept churning out hit after hit in all the mandated rhythms for almost every significant musical personality as if to spite everybody who had predicted he was bound to run out of inspiration. As writer-entertainer Abe Burrows once observed: "Let's face it, nobody can have a better reward than to have somebody, years after, singing his song." Many of Warren's and his fellow contract writers' best efforts are still sung and enjoyed throughout the world, a fitting coda to their musical artistry.

Sadly, the Academy Award came too late to honor a number of songwriters who had performed yeoman services during the first six years of talking pictures. Such stalwarts as Lorenz Hart, one of the premier lyricists in theatrical history, never was nominated for an Oscar. Nor were Nacio Herb Brown, Sam Coslow, Erno Rapée, Yellen and Ager, Ray Henderson, Victor Schertzinger, Joe Burke, and Clifford Grey. Others, like Lew Brown, DeSylva, Whiting, and Johnston, would receive nominations but lose out to competitors. Each might well have won during the earlier awardless glory days.

Then, too, one can only guess how many more Academy Award–caliber songs these talented men might have written if the industry had not slashed musical production between 1930 and 1933. Fortunately, many of them did live to see themselves installed in the Songwriters' Hall of Fame, an honor society founded in 1971 by Johnny Mercer and headed for 20 years by lyricist Sammy Cahn, who holds the record for Oscar nominations (26) and winners (4).

But in February 1935, songwriters joined the cast of leading players in the annual award festivities. The Academy had accepted them. From audience to stage they would rush, like all the other winners, to pick up the Louise deBertollet–sculpted lead and goldleaf statuettes reserved for them. They would thank the folks who had helped them along the road to recognition, and return briskly to their seats while grasping the cherished Holy Grail of professionalism.

Hollywood had begun to pay off the immense debt it owed to the word- and tunesmiths whose contributions had helped to make American films the envy of the world.

Shaking Hands with Oscar

Spotlights raked the mid–February 1935 sky above Hollywood's Biltmore Hotel, the site of the eighth annual presentation of awards to the industry's highest achievers. Reporters from major metropolitan dailies and the wire services were there, along with newsreel cameramen, those lucky gossip columnists assigned to cruise the coveted Hollywood beat, and commentators whose words brought the activities to life for the millions of stay-at-homes congregated around their radios.

Multitudes jammed the front of the hotel, like the faithful on a pilgrimage. As time passed and they grew even more impatient and excited, the ropes set up to segregate commoners from Hollywood's ruling aristocracy started to heave under the pressure of cascading bodies. Soon, screams of joy rent the air as the luxury vehicles laden with Movieland's heavyweights began pulling up to the curb.

Impeccably garbed in tuxedos, the actors in the processional — "King" Clark Gable, William Powell, Ronald Colman — dutifully acknowledged the applause of the huddled masses with a smile and regal wave of the hand. Their exquisite ladies — Claudette Colbert, Myrna Loy, Jean Harlow, and other queens of the sound stages — were likewise dressed to the hilt. As in their films, nary a hair was out of place, not a single blotch destroyed their immaculate, enticing beauty. The contours of their floor-length gowns swirled symmetrically with each step, as if their wearers were executing impromptu *pas de deux.*

But the festival still resembled the rather formal semi-private affair that it was at the 1928 inaugural. Not until the late 1950s would it evolve into the Mardi Gras–like spectacular so familiar to television viewers, and which, on April 1, 1989, *The New York Times* ridiculed as "too long, unfunny, tacky, and top heavy with schlock." The to-the-point headline above the article read: "Oscar's Endless Night."

Operating under an almost medieval concept, the Academy of Motion Picture Arts and Sciences was, and still is, a loose confederation of 13 guilds, or crafts, ranging from songwriters and producers to writers and film editors. Art directors are lumped together, as are cinematographers, sound technicians, and administrators. Faithful to its founding purpose — to "improve the artistic quality of the film medium" — the Academy bases membership on meritorious accomplishment. No one can join it; he or she must be invited to become a member.

Each guild (or a special committee) votes annually in secret for the nominees for its respective Academy Award. Only songwriters, for example, choose the Best Song candidates. Then the entire Academy membership (now almost 5,000 strong) votes for the winners from the lists of nominees. All the guilds vote for Best Picture nominees; again, the winner is selected by the full Academy.

Specific rules were applied in 1935 to qualify a song for Oscar contention. The picture in which each nominee appeared must have run at least seven consecutive days in a Los Angeles theater between January 1 and December 31. The songs had to be original and written for a new film, which could be a musical — from which all the 1930s winners came — or a Western, drama, or epic.

Non-production tunes that became popular on their own before making their way onto Hollywood sound stages were eliminated from competition. So were songs that had appeared in an earlier film or a stage show. Thus Cole Porter's great "Night and Day," which appeared in 1934's *Gay Divorcee*, was omitted. It had been composed in 1932 for Broadway's *Gay Divorce*.

Preferably, the songs nominated were sung or danced in the film by at least one leading player, unless doing so would upset whatever logic the screenplay contained. Also preferred were songs that had acquired hit status during the year the film was released. A melody played only instrumentally in the background as a leitmotif or theme song was disqualified, even if it had a lyric.

No limit was placed on the number of songs to be nominated in any one year, or on the number written by the same composer or lyricist. Only one song from a picture, however, was eligible, meaning that later films, like *Top Hat,* paid a penalty. This stunning 1935 Irving Berlin musical introduced four songs that unquestionably met all the requirements, but only one entry was permitted. And it lost.

The three nominees for Best Song of 1934 included two from RKO — "The Carioca" (a carioca is a native of Rio de Janeiro), from *Flying Down to Rio,* with music by the celebrated Vincent Youmans and lyric by Gus Kahn and Edward Eliscu, and "The Continental," from *The Gay Divorcee,* music by Con Conrad and the lyric by Herb Magidson. The third hopeful, "Love in Bloom," by Leo Robin and Ralph Rainger, appeared in Paramount's *She Loves Me Not.*

As would occur so often in the future, the first two songs came from Fred Astaire films, and the third was introduced by Bing Crosby. Altogether, Astaire would perform 12 Oscar nominees, 2 of them winners; Crosby would sing 14 nominees, including 4 winners. No other performing artist approaches either star's Academy Award records. Among female performers, Judy Garland and Barbra Streisand top the list with six nominations apiece.

Primitive as it looks today, *Flying Down to Rio* has earned a reputation among generations of film buffs for two reasons. It was the first picture to unite Astaire (as "Fred Ayres") and Ginger Rogers ("Honey Dale"), although they did not share top billing; Dolores Del Rio and Gene Raymond were the stars. Another Broadway expatriate, Miss Rogers had played the lovelorn postmistress Molly Gray in the Gershwins' *Girl Crazy* in 1930, summing up her lack of romantic involvement with the familiar "But Not for Me." Astaire struck up an acquaintance with the actress while doing freelance choreography for Ginger's other hit song, "Embraceable You." (Ethel Merman introduced "I Got Rhythm" in the same show.)

Flying Down to Rio was also the vehicle for staging one of the most innovative, if downright ludicrous, production numbers in the history of Hollywood musicals. Toward the end, after Astaire's performance of the lively title tune, dance director Dave Gould set out to dazzle viewers while scaring the wits out of those with acrophobic inclinations. Cavorting to the melody is a bevy of lightly clad chorus girls, their bodies strapped and their shoes bolted to the wings of a fleet of vintage airplanes in flight from the Rio airport to the grand opening of the downtown Hotel Atlantico.

How the ladies managed to get off in one piece after their high-risk, open-air voyage was left to individual imagination. Lapses in explaining the bizarre were common to Hollywood musicals. What was said and done was inconsequential compared to what was sung and danced. That was the way it was back in 1929. Nothing had changed. It never would.

In any event, RKO's special effects department, which also hoisted King Kong atop a miniature Empire State Building the same year, assured the chorus girls' safe arrival. The airborne scenes were shot in a hangar. A few planes were hung from the low-level ceiling and whipped into motion by a battery of wind machines.

"The Carioca," which is played and danced for 13 consecutive minutes, became an instant smash, serving to continue the long list of songs with complicated rhythms designed to introduce a dance craze. Broadway had come up with many such songs over the years, ranging from "Everybody Ought to Know How to Do the Tickle Toe" in 1917 to the "Conversation Step," "Black Bottom," and "Varsity Drag" of the 1920s. The hope of RKO bigwigs and the songwriters was that an enamored public would request the song from orchestra leaders and disk jockeys to practice the steps, thereby adding to the popularity of the film.

What everybody failed to realize was that in order to dance "The Carioca," one had to be either an Astaire or a Rogers to manipulate the complex footwork and body undulations, including forehead-to-forehead contact. So the dance failed to take the country by storm. But the song did.

Lyricist Irving Caesar, who collaborated with Youmans on several stage scores, always considered the versatile composer as the "greatest master of melody ever to write for Broadway." His praise might seem a trifle fulsome, particularly when one recalls that Berlin, Gershwin, Kern, Rodgers, and Porter, each boasting his own splendid theatrical pedigree, were creating stage music at the same time.

But there is no doubt that the typical Youmans song is hummable and unforgettable. As recently as 1988, his and Caesar's "Tea for Two," from *No, No, Nanette,* ranked as one of the ten most frequently played songs in the world, according to ASCAP. Older music fans remember its 1953 resurgence as a cha-cha, selling many more millions of records dressed up in its new tempo.

The Youmans-Caesar partnership presented a sterling example of the vital importance of the lyric to moving a song up the success ladder. In 1923 they collaborated on "Come On and Pet Me" for the stage show *Mary Jane McKane.* Even Caesar criticized his lyric as "rather too cute and foolish." Youmans agreed and the song was dropped.

Four years later, during rehearsals for *Hit the Deck,* the composer pulled the song from his trunk of discards and decided it was sufficiently bouncy to fit nicely into the new production. He urged Caesar to rewrite the lyric. Retitled "Sometimes I'm Happy," the song became the biggest hit of the show.

Youmans is best known for "Bambalina," "I Know That You Know," "Hallelujah," "Rise 'n Shine," "Drums in My Heart," and "Time on My Hands," an exquisite tune performed by two of the century's greatest stage dancers, Astaire and Marilyn Miller, in *Smiles* (1931). The composer's "I Want to Be Happy" was another *No, No, Nanette* sensation. With lyricist Eliscu he wrote "Great Day," "More Than You Know," and "Without a Song," three perennial beauties from *Great Day* (1929). The lovely "Through the Years," one of his last compositions, was played at his funeral.

Youmans's other two hits from *Flying Down to Rio,* which was released in 1933, were "Music Makes Me," sung by Miss Rogers, and "Orchids in the Moonlight," sung by Paul Roulien and danced by Astaire and Miss Del Rio. "Orchids" is one of extremely few film tangos to burgeon into a standard. The sequence containing it was colortinted.

After *Flying Down to Rio,* Youmans's health deteriorated and he retired from composing. Born one day after George Gershwin, on September 27, 1898, in a Central Park West townhouse (now the site of the Mayflower Hotel), Youmans died on April 14, 1946, of tuberculosis. He did not publish a single song during the last 13 years of his life, an inestimable loss to both stage and film music.

The second nominee for Best Song of 1934, "Love in Bloom," was adopted as the theme song of Jack Benny, who typically played it offkey, but on purpose; he was an excellent violinist. Outfitted with a haunting melody and effective lyric, the song was the finest to emanate from the early Robin and Rainger years. The talented twosome collaborated, mostly for Paramount, until Rainger's untimely death at 41 in 1942.

Rainger's first hit, *sans* Robin, was "Moanin' Low," introduced by Libby Holman and Clifton Webb, then a leading stage dancer, in 1929's *Little Show.* Movie fans will recall that it was Claire Trevor's stumbling rendition of the song, commanded by a vengeful Edward G. Robinson in *Key Largo,* that contributed mightily to her winning the 1948 Academy Award for Best Supporting Actress. Robinson, playing gangster "Johnny Rocco," wanted to win something, too — namely, confirmation that the lady's singing voice had fled along with her youthful beauty. Her solo proved Robinson right.

Robin and Rainger cultivated a talent for writing film songs for Crosby, greatly assisting the crooner along the 1930s fast track to movie and musical superstardom. But their towering success was sung not by Crosby, but Bob Hope and Shirley Ross — the Oscar-winning "Thanks for the Memory" — in 1938. Used to commemorate milestones in the comedian's career, the tune has served Hope well as his personal theme song right up to the present day.

Voted Best Song for 1934 was "The Continental," the year's other enormous best-seller with a dance routine for the title. For the benefit of persons bold enough to attempt it, the back cover of the original sheet music displayed 27 action photographs showing how Fred and Ginger executed some of the trickier steps. A full-scale production number, "The Continental" is reprised over and over for a full 27 minutes. Unlike "The Carioca," which was performed midway through *Flying Down to Rio,* "The Continental" adhered to tradition by appearing near the end of *The Gay Divorcee.*

Two of the picture's other assets were the direction by Mark Sandrich, on his way to becoming a master of movie musicals, and the breezy, feather-light screenplay by lyricist George Marion, Jr., Dorothy Yost, and Edward Kaufman, who integrated the five songs into the amusing plot. Vaguely similar to the later *Top Hat,* also directed by Sandrich and peppered with *Divorcee* cast members, the storyline is one of the best of Astaire's pre–*Holiday Inn* (1942) films. The picture also featured a brief singing and dancing interlude by Betty Grable — it was her eighteenth film — and viewing her tapping toes and appealing vivaciousness makes one lament that she and Astaire were never paired as partners, even though they would appear together one more time, in *Follow the Fleet* (1936).

GRACE PERSONIFIED

The *Gay Divorcee* was the first film to indelibly define the essence of the Astaire persona, something that *Flying Down to Rio* largely neglected to do. He is self-confident, for sure, but with a modesty and gentleness that deflate pomposity. He is the well-groomed, congenial, debonair man-about-town, yet never shallow or vindictive. He is as graceful strolling in a moonlit garden as he is performing on a dance floor, whether solo or with a partner.

Ever the optimist, Astaire is willing to overcome any obstacle to winning the girl of his dreams. And at the end, he gets her. Or at least a perfectly respectable substitute (as in *Holiday Inn*), whom he accepts warmly and without rancor toward his male rival. In short, Fred Astaire was the perfect gentleman and somebody everybody would like to call a friend.

As do the finest stage librettos and screenplays, much of the plot and character delineation in *The Gay Divorcee* unfolds through the lyrics. Two songs by Gordon and Revel set the merry tone at the outset — the curtain-raising "Don't Let It Bother You," possibly referring to the implausible storyline — and provide later comic relief via Miss Grable's "Let's K-nock K-nees." In that number, as the title implies, dancing couples bump knee joints, producing a series of minor leg injuries among the less agile.

Early in the picture, when Fred is trying to find the missing Ginger, he launches into Magidson-Conrad's "Needle in a Haystack," clearly indicating that even a city as large as Paris will not deter him from searching for her. He follows up with one of his all-time best dance routines, and for the first time uses pieces of furniture as props.

Dancing Cole Porter's "Night and Day," Fred and Ginger make it quite obvious from their first few steps that they are about to show the world what perfection is all about. The dancing duo may have duplicated the gracefulness of this number in later films, but they never surpassed it. Each is relaxed throughout, but surefooted in the thrillingly professional way that makes their most intricate movements seem effortless, as if they were a pair of Joe DiMaggios shagging flies in the Yankee outfield. Certainly, they never danced to a better song.

Among the greatest of the Broadway greats, Porter had composed four Hollywood songs — "They All Fall in Love" was the best — for Gertrude Lawrence's *Battle of Paris* in 1929. He would not write another until 1936, when he was at the height of his genius.

The other four songs from his original 1932 *Gay Divorce*, which also

starred Astaire, with Claire Dodd in Ginger's part, were uncere-
moniously dropped from *Divorcee.* Such occurred frequently when
Hollywood vacuumed Broadway theaters for material. Much was left
behind when the moguls packed for the return trip to California.

Just as "Night and Day" soothed Ginger's savage breast, so does
"The Continental" direct her back into Fred's embrace. "Not a bad
tune," he volunteers in one of the classic understatements of the year.
After both sing it, they join other swaying couples on a resort dance
floor, where the song is reprised, even by a waiter (Eric Blore), for
almost one-quarter of the film's running time.

A great leap forward from *Flying Down to Rio,* the dance direction
is thoroughly professional, the editing flawless, the set roomy and
lavish. The camera glides smoothly along the chorus line, switching
from wide-angle views to closeups, sometimes of individual smiling
faces, other times of toes hitting the boards.

Fortunately, all the youngsters visiting or working at the resort
are magnificently adept at singing and dancing. Ziegfeld himself
would have hired them on the spot. But talented performers in Hollywood musicals were always available at the first roll of a drum. A few
years later, when Mickey Rooney and Judy Garland began putting
on their "amateur" shows to bail parents, friends, college, and settlement house out of financial difficulties, they needed to look no further
than their own neighborhood for cast members. Every kid on the
block was a prodigy.

A Triumph of Familiarity

Because of Astaire's presence, *The Gay Divorcee* stands as a distinc-
tive musical, even if one without significant differences from others.
Except for the songs, nothing about it is original, nor did it have to
be. The producers knew they could count on Pavlovian responses
from film-musical partisans, back on the song-and-dance kick again.
A willing suspension of disbelief was all the picture required, and
moviegoers gave it.

The new 1934 barrage of film musicals incorporated most of the
clichés flash-frozen in their 1929-30 precursors. Being the offspring of
the earlier films, the plots that resurfaced were as predictable as the
eye and hair color of an unborn baby. For example, into *Divorcee* step
the stock secondary leads, their absurd eccentricities magnifying their

appeal, scaffolding the rickety plot to keep the picture from crumbling. Edward Everett Horton, that busiest of character actors, master of the double-take and slow burn, given to fits of indignation when he discovers he has been outfoxed again, plays Sancho Panza to Astaire's Don Quixote. Alice Brady, the epitome of the addlebrained matron who would reach her zenith in a similar part in *My Man Godfrey* (1936), is Ginger's much-married aunt.

Ginger herself is married when the picture opens, a rare circumstance for a musical-film heroine. The marriage was most likely consummated, but she wants to dissolve it: her husband is a restless geologist who prefers fossils and feldspar to home and hearth. Apart from those two uncommon ingredients, the recipe for the plot admits only the slightest of variations on ageless themes that would be played out repeatedly for the next 25 years:

- *Love at First Sight.* With schoolboy alacrity, Fred blurts out a marriage proposal to Ginger, whom he has just met, a scant ten minutes into the film.

- *The Long-Suffering Male.* Like all other musical actors, Fred is afflicted with a terminal case of love; the spirit may be exhausted but hope refuses to die. It is evident from the outset that he is not easily rebuffed in affairs of the heart, but ever poised to take up the gauntlet of challenge.

- *Coincidence.* Not only do Fred and Ginger meet accidentally in Paris, but also at an English seaside resort, equally unexpectedly.

- *The Lovers' Spat.* The standard film musical plot required at least one argument between leading actor and actress. Typically caused by the lady's misinterpreting her pursuer's motives, such altercations existed solely to be overcome. Fred and Ginger's running feud continues for about 95 of the film's 107 minutes.

- *The Deus ex Machina.* Denouements were created mainly to snip off the loose threads hanging from the hem of the screenplays. In *Divorcee*, a waiter spills Ginger's hubby's beans: he already had a French wife when he married her. His first marriage exposed and his second foundering on the shoals of annulment, husband "Cyril" quickly departs the plot.

- *The Happy Ending.* Unencumbered by legal technicalities, Fred resumes his courtship. As usual, the happiness umbrella is spread over the other principals in the cast, including Horton and Miss Brady. They also plan to marry, even though Horton earlier embarked on an elephant safari in Africa to escape her advances.

The magic of *The Gay Divorcee* music is eternal, lending stature to another celluloid trip along the well-traveled bumpy road to love. The songs obligingly relieved hardscrabble Depression audiences of the tensions of day-to-day living, returning them home temporarily happy. Along with making money, that has been the major purpose of every film musical ever made, particularly in the 1930s and 1940s. The consummate artistry of "The Continental," together with the joy and effervescence it conveyed, remains a timeless example of how successfully Hollywood's happiness machine worked — and of how expertly many of the musical sequences were crafted.

THE RHYMERS

The musical comedy formula, however, did place special demands on the ingenuity of lyricists. Love was the major theme not only of the films, but of almost 100 percent of the songs as well. Trained to honor the content of the ritualistic screenplays, lyricists were expected to devise new idioms to echo familiar themes — new love, true love, once-upon-a-time love, love lost and love regained, sometimes inserting a dollop of whimsy, while never falling back on such a straightforward title as "I Love You."

Although their overuse of such end-rhymes as "heart/part" and "love/above" is obvious, convincing evidence that lyric writers have been extremely skilled at adapting love messages to a myriad of declarations is available from the most cursory glance at their finest works over the years. In the inspired lyric of "Two Dreams Met," a boy and girl dream conspire to bring the lovers together, then happily depart, their assignment completed, when their hearts are joined.

Actors sang of their sweethearts' lovely-to-look-at attractiveness, dreamed about them in the still of the night, or pictured them clearly in the center of all they held dearly. Fear of rejection forced one swain to cloak his feelings with silence, assuring his lady love that "The Words Are in My Heart." Others conceded their inability to verbalize love to anybody who was simply too marvelous for words.

Other singers saw their lovers in the face of a rose, even smiling down from the doorstep of heaven itself. And though love is often tearful, a problem, a heartache, one singer assured listeners that it's "But Beautiful" nonetheless.

One actress pleaded for male assertiveness by comparing her chilly romance to yesterday's mashed potatoes. Another freely admitted that her lover's absence produced a lull in her life. To a third, flowers sang a love song whenever her partner was present, filling soft breezes with its melodious refrain.

Like nightingales too melancholy to sing, loveless youngsters sought a vagrant kiss to build a dream on. Temporary partings were less painful to the imaginative couples who could kiss again in their dreams while waiting for the stars to keep their promise to meet them tomorrow. Love gone astray was summarized in a catalog of bittersweet memories of one former affair that was fun, harmless, and forever worthy of remembering fondly.

Ethereal love resonated from one singer's gracious admission that before hearing his lover's voice, "I Never Knew Heaven Could Speak." Another envisioned an angel when a knock came at his door, revealing that he'd be in heaven "If It's You." Another eagerly awaited evening, when he could relax in the embrace of *his* angel, who lived on the "East Side of Heaven."

Aging males too old to dream found solace in remembering their long-ago first love. One mature widow and widower, about to embark on their second marriage, happily agreed that love is indeed lovelier the second time around. If asked by angels after death to recall what had been the most thrilling encounter of his life, another devoted lover promised to tell them that "I Remember You."

Two teenage sweethearts forecast eternal love, vowing that even in old age, they would still be sharing "Our Love Affair." The bliss of married life was celebrated by two sentimental sleepyheads, wishbones in hand, far too deeply in love to say goodnight.

Of such dreamy, literate sentiments were love songs made, turning Hollywood lyric writers into respectable popular balladeers and their tender love notes into some of the best-remembered lines in all of American music.

THE SONGS THAT GOT AWAY

The fact that the 1935 song nominees totaled a mere three made the Oscar show even more striking, in an offbeat sense. Undeniably, the trio of tunes was exemplary. But also beyond argument was the paucity of nominees, which revealed the Academy's lack of interest in the Best Song award. (Or perhaps the songwriting members did not want to endanger the future of their part of the program by prolonging it with a surfeit of candidates.)

Since 1934 generated an upsurge of vintage film music, some observers wondered why so many equally great songs were dismissed from consideration. They were certainly plentiful, giving 1934 the reputation as a most generous transitional year bridging the relatively lackluster 1930–33 period and the high renaissance that flourished from 1935 through 1940 (see List #4, "The Leading 60 Songs from 1934 Films").

For example, Dubin and Warren donated the classic "I Only Have Eyes for You" to Dick Powell, who sang it to Ruby Keeler in *Dames*. Few film songs have enjoyed a longer shelf life over the decades. Powell also joined Ginger Rogers for the same songwriters' beautiful "I'll String Along with You," in *Twenty Million Sweethearts*.

Carl Brisson and Kitty Carlisle duetted Sam Coslow and Arthur Johnston's exceptional "Cocktails for Two" in *Murder at the Vanities,* and Mae West sang their second 1934 triumph, "My Old Flame," in *Belle of the Nineties*. Still on her love-is-a-game spree, she casually admits she's long forgotten his name.

Mack Gordon and Harry Revel gave Bing Crosby something to sing about with "Love Thy Neighbor," "May I?," and "She Reminds Me of You," all from *We're Not Dressing*. For Lanny Ross, the only popular singer to earn both a bachelor of arts and a bachelor of laws degree from Yale, the partners wrote the lovely "Stay as Sweet as You Are" and "Let's Give Three Cheers for Love" (*College Rhythm*); while for the comely Dorothy Dell they wrote "With My Eyes Wide Open I'm Dreaming" (*Shoot the Works*).

Crosby's *Here Is My Heart* contained the lilting title tune, plus "June in January," "With Every Breath I Take," and "Love Is Just Around the Corner." Irving Kahal and Sammy Fain's "How Do I Know It's Sunday" and "Simple and Sweet" added zest to *Harold Teen*. For Joan Crawford's *Sadie McKee,* Freed and Brown inserted the still-familiar "All I Do Is Dream of You," sung by Gene Raymond and Gene Austin.

From *Flirtation Walk,* which revolved around cadet Powell's West Point romance with Ruby Keeler, came "Flirtation Walk" and "Mr.

Eddie Cantor peers over the shoulders of George Murphy and Ann Southern while they duet Harold Adamson and Burton Lane's "Your Head on My Shoulder" in *Kid Millions* (1934).

and Mrs. Is the Name." Another Powell hit was "Happiness Ahead," an optimistic charmer from the picture of the same name. Rudy Vallee sang "Fare Thee Well, Annabelle" and "Ev'ry Day" in *Sweet Music* (the croonable title tune was by Dubin and Warren); John Boles sang Robin and Whiting's delectable "Waitin' at the Gate for Katy" in *Bottoms Up*.

Lyricist Ted Koehler rejoined the melodic genius Harold Arlen (Hyman Arluck) for "Let's Fall in Love," sung by Ann Southern in *Let's Fall in Love;* their second hit was "Love Is Love Anywhere." A real-life jazz singer who first sang in his cantor father's Buffalo, N.Y., synagogue at the age of seven, Arlen had combined talents with Koehler for "Stormy Weather" in 1933, and he continued writing for films as well as the stage into the 1960s, gaining recognition as one of the greatest of all American popular composers.

The eminently successful Gus Kahn and Walter Donaldson

brightened *Kid Millions* with "An Earful of Music," belted out by clarion-voiced Ethel Merman, who, one suspects, would have been heard even without a sound track. The same songwriters' anti-Depression "When My Ship Comes In" was sung by Eddie Cantor, along with their concluding "Ice Cream Fantasy," which was filmed in Technicolor.

Kid Millions also featured "Your Head on My Shoulder," vocalized by Miss Southern and another newcomer from the stage, George Murphy, as well as one of the best production numbers of the decade. Sadly enough, because of the plethora of song hits emanating from the screen and elsewhere throughout 1934, it was largely ignored. So was Lucille Ball, who was again confined to the chorus, this time wearing a top hat.

Entitled "I Want to Be a Minstrel Man," the Harold Adamson–Burton Lane song serves as backdrop for a blackface sequence brilliantly performed by Cantor and Miss Merman, who were never better. To fill out their routine, the two stars also sing and dance to a reprise of Irving Berlin's "Mandy," popularized in *Ziegfeld Follies of 1919,* the show that included another Berlin diamond, "A Pretty Girl Is Like a Melody." Among the "Mandy" dancers were the very young and spectacularly talented black Nicholas Brothers, Harold and Fay.

Of greater consequence, though not recognized as such at the time, was the interpolation of Juan Y. D'Lorah's adaptation of the South American favorite "La Cucaracha" ("The Cockroach") in the Technicolor short of the same name, featuring little-known dancers Steffi Duna and Don Alvarado. Another five years would elapse before Latin rhythms would make significant headway in American films, spearheaded by the hip-swaying, fruit salad–hatted Carmen Miranda, 20th Century–Fox's colorful import from Brazil. Like Moises Simon's independently written "Peanut Vendor," *La Cucaracha* was definitely ahead of its time.

Columbia Pictures, throughout its long history an also-ran in film musicals, released *One Night of Love,* complete with the enchanting title song by Gus Kahn and Victor Schertzinger, who directed the film. Opera soprano Grace Moore was given the lead by the abrasive Harry Cohn, the pit bull of moguldom who, according to his many detractors, was tone deaf. Luckily, she was a gifted and attractive singer and actress, and the picture marked her triumphant return to movies after a three-year absence brought about by her tendency to gain weight.

Miss Moore was nominated for Best Actress for her role and, for some unaccountable reason, *One Night of Love* was among the candidates for Best Picture. Both lost out to Frank Capra's *It Happened One Night,* which walked off with the two leading acting awards, Best Picture, and Best Director. Not until 41 years later, in 1975, would another film — *One Flew Over the Cuckoo's Nest* — win the same four top Oscars. In 1991, *The Silence of the Lambs* duplicated the feat.

With the calm nonchalance born of routine, the screenwriters concocted a plot for *One Night of Love* that was unashamedly silly, but on a grand scale. Present in the film are the temperamental Warner Baxter–like singing coach (Tullio Carminati) and the young, slimmed-down heroine dreaming of making it big, not on Broadway this time, but at the Metropolitan Opera. Miss Moore succeeds, of course, but not before singing the title tune, the traditional "Last Rose of Summer," two folk songs, and arias by Bizet and Puccini. Both actress and film scored soaring successes, prompting a number of other opera stars to join her in Hollywood, among them Gladys Swarthout, James Melton, and Lily Pons.

Al Jolson returned to the screen after a year's absence to star in *Wonder Bar,* advertised as a "continental novelty of European night life." In it, he reprises his role as the owner of a plush Parisian nightclub, which he had originated in the 1931 stage version. Dubin and Warren substituted a completely new score for the Irving Caesar–Robert Katscher stage songs, all of which were deleted. One new song was "Tango del Rio," one of only two vaguely popular film songs to carry the surname of the star who performed it, Dolores Del Rio. (The other was Ralph Rainger's instrumental "Raftero," danced by George Raft and stripper Sally Rand in *Bolero,* also in 1934.) The hit of *Wonder Bar* was the very pretty "Why Do I Dream Those Dreams," sung by Dick Powell.

The most famous — or infamous — of the *Wonder Bar* songs was "Goin' to Heaven on a Mule," which developed into an embarrassment to Warren, although he was responsible only for the quite respectable melody, not the words. Even in 1934, when black performers were stereotyped into demeaning film roles, this finale production number borders on the outrageous.

For it, Jolson again burnt-corked his face in the traditional Lew

Dockstader minstrel fashion to imitate an elderly black who has died and gone to heaven accompanied by his faithful mule. Still playing the happy host, he welcomes other deceased blacks into the Promised Land with the song. Al Dubin's lyric succeeded only in heaping insults on the newcomers to Paradise. They are depicted as low-level "pickaninnies" inordinately fond of watermelon and pork chops while wandering around their new surroundings in stupefied bewilderment. Even Jolson's dutiful nod to Abraham Lincoln rings hollow after he has sung the derogatory lines preceding the paean of praise.

Alice Faye, Fox's resident songbird and the finest of Hollywood's 1930s female pop vocalists (Frances Langford was a close second), made her screen debut opposite Rudy Vallee in 1934's *George White's Scandals*. Two brief hits emerged from the score (by Jack Yellen, Irving Caesar, and Ray Henderson), the delightful "Nasty Man" and "Hold My Hand."

The top candidate for the year's musical oddity was Warner's lavish *Fashions of 1934*. Starring non-singers William Powell and Bette Davis as a con man and a dress designer in the Parisian fashion world, the picture drifted aimlessly into a mediocre carbon copy of Broadway's *Roberta* (originally entitled *Gowns by Roberta*), but without a score anywhere near the brilliance of the one Jerome Kern wrote for the 1933 stage masterpiece. Busby Berkeley's dance direction for Irving Kahal and Sammy Fain's melodic "Spin a Little Web of Dreams," the best of the songs, is overcooked, clearly indicating that Berkeley was being victimized by overwork.

Also prominent on 1934 screens was Maurice Chevalier, whose two 1933 films, *Bedtime Story* and *The Way to Love*, detracted from his once-formidable reputation. His frisky rehash of *The Merry Widow* fared much better, aided immeasurably by Jeanette MacDonald, his co-star for the final time, and director Ernst Lubitsch, also on his last outing with Chevalier. Most of the old Franz Lehar songs were retained but, in a novel and effective switch, the lyrics were rewritten by Rodgers and Hart and Gus Kahn to accommodate the updating of the 1905 script. Herbert Stothart added some lyrical incidental background music.

Lyricist Hart was also a central figure in the biggest song casualty of the 1934 film season. First, he and partner Rodgers wrote "Oh, Lord, Make Me a Motion Picture Star" for Jean Harlow's *Reckless*, but MGM dropped it. Then, for *Manhattan Melodrama*, Hart gave the song a new torchy lyric and retitled it "The Bad in Every Man." The song failed to impress MGM a second time, and it again wound up on the cutting room floor.[4] Later that year, urged on by music publisher Jack Robbins, who fancied the melody, Hart revised the lyric a third time into "Blue Moon," still among Rodgers's most beautiful love songs.

It was *Manhattan Melodrama*, incidentally, that the world-class bank robber John Dillinger and his "woman in red" watched at Chicago's Biograph Theatre the night his own life ended shortly after the picture did. The woman, Anna Sage, had agreed to inform the FBI of Dillinger's whereabouts in order to collect the $15,000 reward. The G-men sharpshooters spotted Dillinger leaving the lobby and shot him to death at 10:35 p.m., July 22, 1934, in an adjacent alley.

Arthur Caesar, brother of songwriter Irving, won the Best Original Story award for the picture. But the real-life gangster melodrama starring Dillinger overshadowed the Manhattan-based one depicted on the Biograph screen, quickly becoming a part of Chicago history.

[4] *The song was restored to the film for the 1991 release of* Manhattan Melodrama *on videocassette.*

CHAPTER SEVEN

The Second Golden Age—
The Child Stars:
1935–1940

HE GREAT DEPRESSION musicals were like no other series of films ever produced in Hollywood. Projecting no problem too deeply ingrained that it could not be weathered by anyone with a heart full of joy and gladness, they sought to lift the rain from all parades. They left no aftertaste of despair or doubt; the manufactured end-of-the-picture rainbow was meant to be real and permanent. Coping with economic disaster depended on one's outlook. According to the moguls' dispositive remedy, the answer was simplicity itself: sing and the crusty old world will sing with you; give up and it will shrug you aside.

Like the merchants of merriment they were, the moguls were determined to make lives more golden than leaden by spreading movie-set happiness from ghetto to suburb. They repeatedly accentuated the positive, exhorting the distraught into sublime optimism. Their Valentine musicals were essentially hosannahs to hope designed to put the country on a strict regimen of cheerfulness.

Victims of disappointment were not to be deserted to suffer alone. They merited regeneration by caring people indoctrinated in the belief that society is basically good and never neglectful of neighbors crushed by forces not of their making. Setbacks were to be accepted as a natural part of life, not the destroyers of it. "Life is never perfect," Bing Crosby sings in *East Side of Heaven*, "but it isn't always wrong."

The fellows and girls in these pictures surely faced troubles, but they had enough fire in their bellies to defy fate, cloak fears with a joke, a wink of the eye, or a catchy song, and fight on. So pronounced a national goal was success in anything, especially persevering against overwhelming odds, that audiences found delight in the performers' ultra-confident and unselfish quest for it.

The typical Depression musical tune was quite similar to the ballads and production numbers of the 1929-30 period. The lyrics, however, as well as the plots, were far more purposeful. In the earlier age of capitalism unbound, movie musicals reflected faith in the present and in the ideal that the most far-reaching of ambitions was attainable. When factories and offices began closing, fear displaced optimism. What, the unemployed working classes wondered, had all their years on assembly lines and behind desks brought them. Pinpointing the major cause of the Depression was easy; the fault lay with the owners of failed enterprises, the wealthy people whom President Roosevelt labeled "economic royalists." How to end the problem was a far more difficult matter, and it was pitting supporters and opponents of government intervention in the economy against one another.

Unsurprisingly, the most popular game of the period was Monopoly. Invented in 1935 by Charles B. Darrow, himself an unemployed heating engineer, it turned jobless millions into play-money entrepreneurs, buying up streets of dreams. The movie industry paved them. It did so mainly by advocating grace under pressure while providing much-needed diversion.

Hollywood's equivalent of home cooking, the Depression musical also rearranged the average American's priorities. No longer was the breadwinner to dream of the riches that would accrue to him as he stepped up the corporate ladder; one by one the rungs were disappearing under his feet. With family survival at risk, the prevailing movie wisdom of lowering one's expectations, even in love, to the level of practicality was given urgency. In Dick Powell's *Thanks a Million* happiness song, "I'm Sittin' on the Top of a Hill," he is ecstatic over winning not an election, but the girl of his dreams. In the heyday of Coolidge prosperity, when love found Al Jolson, his jubilation lifted him to an exaggerated height. "I'm Sittin' on Top of the *World*," Jolson sang.

Dreaming, however, was still accepted as a cardinal virtue,

provided that it never exceeded the bounds of possibility or centered solely on the accumulation of wealth. It should come as no surprise that two of the period's best-loved songs rang with the conviction that yes, Virginia, dreams do come true, regardless of one's social standing or amount of money in the purse.

Ned Washington and Leigh Harline's "When You Wish Upon a Star," the only Depression-inspired homily to win the Academy Award, encouraged the most abject to dream themselves into a better world, noting that if it's love that guides them, anything their hearts desire can come true. Sung in *Pinocchio* by "Ukulele Ike" Cliff Edwards, the song confirmed the basic tenet that influenced Depression filmmakers: fate is basically kind, ever on the side of the dreamer.

The second song, this one by Buddy DeSylva, earned a 1939 Oscar nomination. Sung by a trio and then a full chorus of youngsters in *Love Affair,* the graceful lyric firms up faith in dreams by declaring that "Wishing (Will Make It So)," if only people wish long enough and strong enough. To the loving and caring, optimism is not false hope, and patches of blue behind the clouds are no mirage.

The chief lesson of the musicals' dialogue and lyrics was crystal clear and unalterable: happiness was a divine right to be shared equally by king and pauper, even by the "Pessimistic Character with the Crabapple Face," ridiculed by songwriters Johnny Burke and James V. Monaco in *If I Had My Way.* Those without a song or a smile were quickly put in their place. In Walter Bullock and Sam Pokrass's "Dream Sequence" near the end of *The Little Princess,* the mean, money-grabbing headmistress of a girls' boarding school is physically ejected from the aristocratic society she has coveted.

Harboring with almost religious intensity the conviction that to give is far better than to receive, even the most ambitious characters who strove for a stage career did so not for money or publicity, as in *42nd Street, Gold Diggers of 1933,* and *Dames,* but simply to raise spirits. And typically the money earned by their makeshift amateur shows was donated to charity. It mattered little that most film plots were essentially the same. Their familiarity lent a certain stability to a time of sudden and vast change; the dutiful happy endings reminded more than a few dispirited viewers of the comparatively placid, sunny days of the 1920s.

Musical stars made cheerfulness infectious, propping up the national will to chase after it with renewed vigor. And of them all, none were better equipped to rebuild confidence than unusually attractive youngsters, their faces scrubbed clean of all traces of pessimism and with spunk to spare.

Fortunately for the studios, the 1930s' screen children were extravagantly talented and exhibited the well-groomed wholesomeness so vital to winning converts. Circulating eternal hopefulness through scores of youth-oriented pictures honeycombed with songs, they jump-started the biblical teaching that a little child shall lead everybody into the Promised Land. Clearly, few movie fans agreed with W.C. Fields's opinion of children. Asked whether he liked them, the grumpy comedian replied, "I do — if they're properly cooked."

Instead, the very young were accepted as the visual metaphors of the Victorian tradition that placed them above the marketplace and adult world of insincerity. As such, they were ideally qualified to chaperon their elders on Movieland's occasional visits to the lowest economic depths. Although kindness was their chief tool of persuasion, the boy and girl actors were not shy when it came to influencing the actions of elders who lacked the youngsters' convictions and became stalled in their own caution.

Child stars, of course, were not new to Hollywood. Seven-year-old Jackie Coogan ranked as the world's number one box office attraction in 1922. But the Depression youngsters differed from their silent-screen forebears in one vital aspect. Not content merely to protest conditions by banging their spoons on high chairs, they initiated the rehabilitation of adult family members and friends, and by extension the whole of American society. Master Coogan and his contemporaries were largely passive to events swirling around them. For the most part, they were props, charming and cuddly to be sure, but hardly movers and shakers.

The children of the 1930s, on the other hand, were faithful to their political and social environments. The centerpieces of their pictures, they strode the world of make-believe as activists. Totally uninvolved in any counter-culture ferment, they upheld the rock-hard social and moral values they had inherited. They entreated grownups to reform by readmitting hope into the human breast. When that failed, they took it upon themselves to show them how to do it, typically with the tenacity of Ronald Colman struggling against nature to return to Shangri-La. Adjusting to discouragement with customary aplomb, the children reemerged intact from their brief encounters with misfortune.

Tears cascaded from the eyes, but their pluckiness precluded complaints falling from the lips.

Little wonder people idolized the screen children throughout the Depression. They constantly brought out the best in everyone for their sake. So adept were they at piping audiences over to the sunny side of life that their films qualified as passports out of the doldrums. Cockeyed optimists all, the child stars put into motion what Oscar Hammerstein II would later commit to paper: the human race is not about to fall on its collective face. Like the mythological basilisk, their expressive eyes vanquished despair; like the phoenix, their smiles arose from the burned-out embers of dreams.

The Big Crackdown

Also luckily for the studios, the availability of a new stable of talented children arose at the same time that film censorship moved into its most restrictive cycle. Complaints from pulpit, press, and public whenever Hollywood strayed from orthodox morality had been grist for the mill of crusaders almost from the beginning of motion pictures. For decades, screenplays had been examined closely by easily outraged parents and clergy worried about intimations of immorality acted out before the innocent eyes of children, the most impressionable of movie fans.

As early as 1909, the film industry bowed to the champions of goodness by establishing the nation's first voluntary policing agency — the National Board of Censorship, later renamed the National Board of Review. But its avowed goal of cleaning up Hollywood's act by clamping down on implied naughtiness was so unsuccessful that in 1921 New York State passed its own censorship law, followed in rapid succession by many other states. Censors were given incontestible authority to expurgate whatever they deemed too vulgar for viewing. In Ohio they chopped scenes with actresses smoking cigarettes; in Pennsylvania they eliminated scenes showing people imbibing alcohol.

In 1922, Will H. Hays was named to head the Motion Picture Producers and Distributors of America, which had one super weapon in its morality arsenal. Its members controlled the leading theater chains and could refuse to book films that failed to bend to the will of the "Hays Office." Their profits in jeopardy, the studio heads agreed to clear any book or play before producing it for the screen. In 1924 alone, the master censor rejected 67 candidates. But without any in-house mechanism to enforce its rules, the organizaton was unable to expunge all breaches of proper taste, leaving protesters still less than satisfied.

The MPPDA in 1930 created the stricter, self-regulatory Motion Picture Production Code, which went further to launder spicy screenplays by dousing them in detergent. Scenes involving sexuality beyond a suitably bourgeois framework, such as seduction, rape, perversion, and indecent or undue exposure of the body, were banned. Also taboo were trafficking in illegal drugs, excessive and lustful kissing, miscegenation, venereal disease, and profanity. In short, anything that might "demean" the morals of ticketholders, as the code phrased it, was nixed.

The code augured well but pleased nobody. Again, the MPPDA had neglected to set up an agency to enforce compliance. The major offenders continued to be popular gangster films, like *Scarface,* despite the Hays Office's dictum that the "sympathy of the audience should never be thrown to the side of crime, wrongdoing, evil, or sin."

Some film musicals also disturbed the censorious. Many chorus girls were underdressed well into 1934, though judged by current standards they look like clotheshorses. Oglers could revel in the sight of backless and sideless costumes and peekaboo blouses. About 25 chorines seem to undress completely in the "Pettin' in the Park" number in *Gold Diggers of 1933,* although only their silhouettes are seen on an opaque curtain. A leering Peeping Tom of a midget hands Dick Powell a can opener after he has sung the slightly risqué words to Ruby Keeler. She is clad in an armor-plated dress, into which Powell plunges the opener with gusto. But the scene ends before he jimmies very far down her back.

Dialogue, too, was often saucy. The name of Ginger Rogers's character in *42nd Street* is "Any-Time Annie," who, according to her dance director, said no only once, and then she hadn't heard the question. In the same film, Una Merkle deflates one chorus boy by telling him he has the "busiest hands." The accusation fails to bother either very much. The "Shuffle Off to Buffalo" sequence is filled with coyly suggestive gestures and phrases, although they come from newly married couples in sleeping cars on the rails to Niagara Falls.

The James Cagney–Ruby Keeler number "Shanghai Lil" in

Footlight Parade was filmed partly in a Warner Bros.-inspired opium den with plenty of laid-back, skimpily costumed actresses put there for the benefit of girl watchers. Moreover, as Al Dubin's lyric makes abundantly clear, Lil is an Oriental hooker with a special yen for American sailors.

In *Flying Down to Rio,* an envious Anglo-Saxon woman hints at Dolores Del Rio's expertise in flirtation: "Maybe Brazilian women have more going for them below the equator then we do." In *Footlight Parade,* Joan Blondell caustically urges Claire Dodd, her rival for Cagney's affections, to quit the new show since the scheming Miss Dodd can make more money elsewhere. "As long as they've got sidewalks, you've got a job," Joan tells Claire. *Murder at the Vanities,* a tuneful but maladroit admixture of songs, drama, and homicide, had as its backdrop a Parisian girlie show, complete with chorines in flimsies, praises to marijuana, and bloodied bodies.

Biblical dramas, in the hands of Cecil B. DeMille, their chief exponent, so scatologically blended immorality with music that any lesson he might have wished to teach was suppressed by the vulgarity that frequently identified his pictures. The director's *Sign of the Cross* (1932) came close to outright nudity in the pagan Joyzelle's sadistic "Dance of the Naked Moon." Two years later, *Cleopatra* presented Claudette Colbert and assorted ingenues in almost transparent milk baths and the briefest of costumes, while the series of dances by the chorus of slave girls to celebrate Cleo's seduction of Mark Antony (Henry Wilcoxon) was as erotic as the public was ready to accept.

Such borderline flaunting of the Hays Office blacklistings resulted, in October 1933, in the formation of the Episcopalian Committee on Motion Pictures and, almost simultaneously, the far more potent Roman Catholic Church's National Legion of Decency, which promulgated a film-rating checklist. Published usually weekly in parish newspapers, the listings ranged from "unobjectionable" to "condemned," greatly influencing the faithful in their choice of film fare. Moreover, it exerted tremendous influence on the frail MPPDA to force strict observance of the censorship rules already on its books.

Within a few months, on July 1, 1934, the MPPDA appointed a former policeman, Joseph I. Breen, director of the new Motion Picture Production Code Administration. Preferring the ax to the rapier, Breen wielded his dictatorial powers with so much authority that *Film Weekly* described him as the "Hitler of Hollywood." He regarded the code as ironclad without very much in the way of wiggle room. Any scene containing dialogue or even sound effects he found offensive, including Scarlett O'Hara's belching, was rewritten or deleted. Producers kowtowed, realizing that Breen could deny their pictures the precious seal of approval for the slightest of infractions.

The 1934 musical *Dames* satirized censors, but with a light touch. Hugh Herbert, one of Hollywood's classic "fools," plays Ezra Ounce, an extreme example of Mr. Bluenose who disapproves of females, liquor, nicotine, the stage, actors, and New York City. When spoken or spelled out, the surname Ounce can easily be misconstrued as "Dunce." As the head of the Foundation for the Elevation of American Morals, Herbert aims not to expurgate material, but to shut down every "wicked" theater in New York, which to him means all of them. Only when he becomes drunk after consuming a bottle of cough medicine with a high alcohol content does he rescind his crusade. Besides, as the film clearly indicates, Dick Powell's stage show is as clean as the proverbial whistle.

With its creative energies harnessed to the eagle eyes and ears of enforcer Breen, the Hollywood musical in early 1935 segued into a long liaison with romantic love that would last until the pivotal year of 1966, when permissiveness and safe sex made it a theme of the past. Shorn of suggestiveness in incident and speech, films were prettified and permeated with the sweet scents of traditional family values as never before. Their depictions of mutual support in crises, shared goals, and unqualified love of one another and of the less fortunate equated compassion with happiness, which through repetition was expected to trickle down from screen to audience.

Singled out as the crucibles to test the market for unalloyed purity, the musicals passed with flying colors, thanks to the squeaky clean fuel that propelled them. Weekly film attendance burgeoned from the decade's lows of 60 million in 1932 and 1933 and 70 million in 1934 to 80 million in 1935 and 88 million in both 1936 and 1937. The $482 million in total 1933 receipts rose to $556 million in 1935, $626 million in 1936, and $676 million in 1937.

Musical producers happily subscribed to writer Ambrose Bierce's definition of cynicism as a "defect of vision which compels us to see the world as it is, instead of as it should be." Accordingly, they homogenized their song-and-dance diversions for mass appeal by setting them in fairyland. They resembled candy boxes filled with sugary delights that, however often enjoyed, rarely dulled the taste. They were buttressed by the quality of the music, outranked only by 1923–28 and 1949–54 Broadway in the history of the stage or screen for a comparable time span.

Rhythmically repetitive dance routines became back-lot processions of floats in a Rose Bowl parade. Singers and dancers were metamorphosed into cheerleaders. Chivalrous male stars and character actors added an avuncular presence, forever available to counsel wisely with a homespun lecture or lyric. Musical films now were the answer to the most fastidious parent's prayers. The stories could hardly invite dissent, and the performers were fit objects of their children's affection.

THE MILLION-DOLLAR BABY

At the 1935 Academy Award show, songwriters were unexpectedly thrust to the forefront of filmmaking, thanks to the craving for spotless screenplays acted out by pretty, tuneful little people able to shed troubles like an ill-fitting suit while coating the national psyche with a soothing patina of happiness.

It all happened when onto the Biltmore stage walked the major attraction of the evening's festivities. Fast approaching the advanced age of seven, she already had sung, danced, smiled, and cried her way into hearts beating in every corner of the globe. A pint-sized Helen of Troy, she had launched armadas of male suitors into what would become Hollywood's longest-term love affair between actress and fans. Her name was Shirley Temple.

America's newest sweetheart, she had been invited to accept from author Irvin S. Cobb a Special Academy Award for "bringing more happiness to millions of children and millions of grownups than any child of her years in the history of Hollywood." Previously, only Chaplin (for *The Circus*), Warner Bros. (for *The Jazz Singer*), and Walt Disney (for Mickey Mouse) had been similarly honored.

The significance of the child's award should not be underestimated. Along with it came confirmation that film music had definitely rearrived in the movie capital. For despite her performances in dramatic roles, practically every picture she appeared in up to age 14 contained at least one tune written with her in mind. The first film personality to combine childhood and musical performance, Shirley

Temple was primarily a musical star, the biggest of the time and one of the biggest of all time.

Their sextant fixed on Shirley's tumultuous fan approval, rival studio heads were stampeded into developing competing child and adolescent stars similarly encased in song and profitability. Judy Garland, Mickey Rooney, Deanna Durbin, Jane Withers, and to a lesser degree Bobby Breen, Gloria Jean, Donald O'Connor, and Virginia Weidler, similarly sang their way through the hardship thirties.

Songwriters took special note of little Miss Temple's 1935 award and world-class celebrity. In a way, as Harry Warren recalled in later life, he and his fellow melody-makers shared in her miniature Oscar, since they had participated in furthering and sustaining her career. Her Academy Award, according to Warren, relieved contract song-writers of the nagging suspicion that they were mere footsoldiers in Hollywood's huge behind-the-camera brigade, all of them inevitably subservient to the stars who spoke their lines, wore their costumes, emoted on their sets, or sang and danced their songs. Now star and songwriter were on the same professional footing; each was equally indebted to the other for the success of the films on which they collaborated.

From 1935 to 1938, inclusive, Shirley Temple's name stood at the very top of the box office popularity charts, in recognition of her substantially outdrawing everybody else the world over for four successive years. Her stunning feat has been surpassed only once, by Bing Crosby, who reigned as Top Ten champ from 1942 through 1946. But Shirley's record of six consecutive Top Ten listings (1934–39) has yet to be broken.

Between her and Crosby, the throne was occupied by the multi-talented Mickey Rooney, who reigned as the world's number one movie star from 1939 to 1941. Like Shirley, Mickey played numerous dramatic and comic roles, but the films for which he is best remembered, except for *Boys Town* (1938) and a few of the 17 *Andy Hardy* pictures, coupled him with Judy Garland in a series of four "let's put on a show" musicals. He sang, danced, pianoed, and drummed his way through *Babes in Arms* (1939), *Strike Up the Band* (1940), *Babes on Broadway* (1942), and *Girl Crazy* (1943), all but the third based loosely on 1930s stage hits and featuring a smattering of the original Rodgers and Hart and Gershwin songs.

Shirley Temple had the good fortune of easily recruiting the support of a number of Hollywood's most competent musical practitioners who guided her along her meteoric rise. Foremost among them was composer Jay Gorney, a one-time Michigan lawyer, who spotted her on a rainy winter afternoon in 1933 in the lobby of Santa Monica's Fox-Ritz Theatre. (Appropriately, the feature film was a musical, *42nd Street.*) Waiting there with her determined but shy mother, Gertrude, for the shower to lift, the four-year-old paraded past the Gorneys to inspect the illustrated poster advertising the main feature.

Struck, as was his wife, with the child's face—lyricist E.Y. Harburg would later describe it as "molded to perfection by the loving hands of star-struck angels"—Gorney approached Mother Temple and suggested that she take her daughter to see Winfield Sheehan, head of Fox Film. Sheehan had been auditioning dozens of children for a part in a musical that, after a few title changes, would emerge as *Stand Up and Cheer!* Responding happily to the Gorneys' interest in her, the child did a brief tap dance for their benefit, indicating quite clearly that she was talented as well as cute.

The two Temples visited Gorney a few days later at Fox, where he introduced them to songwriter Lew Brown, a charter member of the former DeSylva, Brown, and Henderson team. In a real-life episode that anticipated the radio-audition sequence in Shirley's *Rebecca of Sunnybrook Farm* five years later, the youngster sang Brown a song, Hoagy Carmichael's "Lazy Bones," while perched, Helen Morgan-style, atop his piano.

Like the Gorneys, Brown instinctively recognized the girl's prodigious magnetism and potential and put her on the Fox payroll. She now had two influential tunesmiths on her side, and it was a minor matter for them to persuade Sheehan into accepting her for the role of Shirley Dugan in *Stand Up and Cheer!* Brown co-produced the film, wrote the dialogue and lyrics to Gorney's music, and collaborated on the story, which was suggested by Will Rogers.

Buddy DeSylva carried his support for the child into his Fox executive suite, serving as producer or associate producer of four of her all-time biggest films (*The Little Colonel, The Littlest Rebel, Captain January,* and *The Poor Little Rich Girl*). He also revised, with Sidney Clare, "Polly-Wolly-Doodle," the song hit of *Rebel,* that was based on the popular 1850's minstrel tune. Ray Henderson, the third man in the former songwriting partnership, wrote the music for *Curly Top,* the first musical that saw her name standing alone above the picture title, a distinction devoutly desired by all performers but realized by only a handful.

"POLKA DOTS AND MOONBEAMS"

Stand Up and Cheer! merits its reputation as a tacky musical largely because of its stark unrealism and excessive stereotyping. But thanks to the songs and Miss Temple's showmanship, it is also unique. Playing his customary role as the dapper, quickly energized Broadway producer is Warner Baxter, whom the president appoints to the new Cabinet post of Secretary of Amusement. The president is unquestionably F.D.R., though only the back of the actor's head is visible, a pose that would be duplicated for a second time in *Yankee Doodle Dandy.*

Secretary Baxter, armed with a budget of $100 million, is charged with hiring show folks to bolster everybody's spirits through songs, dances, and guffaws. These are exactly what is needed to perk up a despairing nation, the president explains, and Baxter proceeds to stage four big production numbers, all directed by Sammy Lee. Winding up the film is the highly optimistic albeit premature "We're Out of the Red," sung by columns of happy paupers marching jauntily along the newly paved road to recovery.

Joining her father, played by James Dunn, in the hit of the picture is Miss Temple, wearing a polka-dotted ballet dress and exuding all the confidence and sweetness that became her trademarks. Gorney had coached her on the routine, and the little blonde's performance leaves no doubt that she was an attentive pupil. Crawling out from between Dunn's legs, she pops onto center stage, curtsies, sings her own special lyric to "Baby, Take a Bow," and dances a chorus with Dunn. Her talent and poise were remarkable for a young lady who had only recently passed her sixth birthday. So was her loyalty to Lee and Gorney.

A quick study from infancy, she was already memorizing almost overnight the lines and gestures of everybody in the cast, in addition to her own. Midway through the song, she pulls on Dunn's sleeve to remind him that he has not taken his first bow on cue. He does appear flustered at her tug, but follows instructions. The studio heads decided to leave her coaxing in the finished print, and it does lend a rare touch of spontaneity and a great deal of charm to the sequence. About 18 months later, Shirley would score 155 on the respected Pintner-Cunningham Intelligence Test, placing her beyond prodigy into the genius classification.

In her next feature, *Baby, Take a Bow,* picked up from the song title, she and Dunn sing and dance the catchy "On Account-a I Love You," written by the prolific Bud Green and Sam H. Stept. The occasion for this father-and-daughter duet is the youngster's birthday, celebrated by equally impoverished neighbors on the roof of a tenement. Nothing, least of all the lack of money, was allowed to interfere with observing a child's birthday with a huge party. Essentially, the musical films of the time idealized and sanctified childhood, enfolding it with Wordsworthian reverance.

Never before had songwriters so generously assisted anyone as young as Shirley Temple. Their perspicacity in gauging her talents was amply rewarded, and they topped off their bank accounts with royalties from songs she turned into best-sellers. Her ability to erase worry wrinkles, curve pursed lips into smiles, and reset the sparkle in Depression-dulled eyes also gladdened her Fox bosses.

Her 18 feature films up to 1940 were enormous moneymakers, most of them paying off their entire production expenses well before they played the second-run neighborhood houses. Her 1936-37 pictures alone earned the then astronomical combined profit of $12 million. Her 1937 salary of $307,014, earned when $3,000 was a comfortable annual income for a family of four, was among the highest in filmdom, even though she made only two pictures that year. Clark Gable earned only $272,000, Fred Astaire $266,837, and James Cagney a paltry $243,000. So widespread was her popularity that as early as mid–1935 an estimated 90 percent of the world's population could recognize her by name from her photograph.

A New York Yankee pitching great of the 1930s, Vernon ("Lefty") Gomez, once attributed his mound mightiness to "thinking cheerful thoughts and a fast outfield." The same definition explains much of Shirley's success, which far exceeded even Lefty's. She was a naturally cheerful lass and looked it. Impelled by wedding-like fidelity to accepting life for better or worse, she was unrivaled as the "Little Miss Recovery" and premier Ph.D. in caregiving throughout the waning years of the Depression. Her fast outfield consisted of a Milky Way of skillful stars, from Randolph Scott to Victor McLaglen, who appeared in so many 1930s films that audiences came to look upon them as family. Then there were the supporting, or character, actors and actresses, those roving Hollywood mercenaries who flitted from studio to studio like honey bees to flower gardens. Familiar of face but rarely by name, they provided much of the humor, conflict, and pathos in dozens of musicals. The roles played by Helen Westley, Mary Nash, Sara Haden, Donald Meek, Claude Gillingwater, Sr., Franklin Pangborn, et al., had been established early in their film careers and, after repeating them endlessly, they fairly excelled at them.

Then there was Bill Robinson, the most endearing of Miss Temple's associates. Better known as "Bojangles," an old Southern expression meaning mischief-maker, he appeared in four of her films, adored her (and she him), and taught her some of the most intricate dance steps she was called on to perform. Freely admitting that she astounded him over and over again with the rapidity with which she learned, he further verified his devotion by papering the walls of his Harlem apartment with pictures of her. It was Robinson who best summarized the uniqueness of Shirley Temple: "God made her just all by herself—no series, just one."

The twosome danced seven numbers together, beginning with the widely acclaimed "staircase" duet in *The Little Colonel* (1935), unfortunately cut short by Grandfather Lionel Barrymore's shout to stop all the racket. Their partnership continued into *The Littlest Rebel, Rebecca of Sunnybrook Farm,* and ended with Walter Bullock and Harold Spina's "I Love to Walk in the Rain" in *Just Around the Corner* (1938). Robinson also served as her dance director for *Dimples* (1936), in which he does not appear. Their high-stepping duets were indeed praiseworthy, and the chemistry that linked them was a rare distillation of mutual fondness and respect.

Ranked with John Sublett, the "Bubbles" of the Buck and Bubbles dance team (unfortunately, seen only briefly in Warners' *Varsity Show* in 1937), as the greatest of the century's tap dancers, Robinson had the most brilliant technique of all. His beat was so fast and full of swing that his taps sounded like the rolls of a great drummer. Even Fred Astaire paid homage to him. Appearing in *Swing Time* (1936) in blackface and wearing derby and spats, Astaire performs an outstanding interpretation of the Robinson style in Dorothy Fields and Jerome Kern's admirable "Bojangles of Harlem." It remains one of Astaire's best dance numbers.

Robinson was given one of the biggest funerals in New York City's history on November 25, 1949. He would have appreciated knowing that flags were flown half-mast that day, not only in the Union metropolis, but also in his birthplace, the former Confederate capital of Richmond, Virginia.

It is doubtful that films will ever find another Shirley Temple, or that contemporary moviegoers would be receptive to one. But if a successor is found, the chances of pairing her with another Bojangles is virtually nil. Each was one of a kind, her "Uncle Billy" and his "Darlin'," their tapping toes still carrying them joyfully along memory lane.

"Dance, Little Lady"

The Depression notwithstanding, there is scant doubt that Miss Temple's charm, talent, and picture-book femininity were the major ingredients in her success, not the plots of her pictures or the cheerful economic counseling she dispensed. Add a touch of impishness to her innate self-reliance, and it is not difficult to subscribe to President Roosevelt's reason for her popularity: "When the spirit of the people is lower than at any other time during this Depression, it is a splendid thing that for just 15 cents an American can go to a movie and look at the smiling face of a baby and forget his troubles."

Unusually gifted at singing and hoofing, Shirley was given ample opportunity to display both, even in films based on classic tales of childhood. *Heidi*, for instance, features a small production number, by Sidney D. Mitchell and Lew Pollack, revolving around a pair of little wooden shoes. *The Little Princess* finds her and Arthur Treacher singing and cavorting to "Old Kent Road," a popular ballad of turn-of-the-century England (see List #5, "The 25 Biggest Shirley Temple Film Songs").

For the ultra-successful *Little Miss Marker* (1934), Robin and Rainger wrote "Laugh, You Son of a Gun," only the first of the flaxen-haired moppet's numerous songs to advocate smiling, rather than whining, through life's occasional detours into unpleasantness. For another 1934 hit, *Bright Eyes,* Sidney Clare and Richard A. Whiting gave her "On the Good Ship Lollipop," which, more than any other tune, qualifies as the little star's theme song. More than 400,000 sheet music copies were sold within one month after the film's release, an outstanding total for any year, particularly an economically depressed one. The success of Irving Caesar's Shirley songs, "Animal Crackers in My Soup" and "That's What I Want for Christmas," prodded him into writing his instructive series of *Songs of Safety, Health,* and *Friendship,* all designed to keep toddlers free from accidents, illness, and discrimination.

Her high-pitched singing voice had an untrained, amateurish sweetness. An occasional chuckle at a humorous word or phrase made it sound all the more natural. Her sense of rhythm, as revealed in her swaying rendition of "But Definitely," for example, was astonishing. Even though she had taken some lessons, her dancing seemed spontaneous, as if the teacher had called upon her unexpectedly to entertain her classmates. That she could hold her own opposite pros like Alice Faye and Jack Haley was made abundantly clear in Gordon and Revel's "Military Man" finale in *The Poor Little Rich Girl.*

She walked in rhythm, like Astaire, and when music swelled from off-screen, as in Bullock and Spina's "We Should Be Together" in *Little Miss Broadway,* her transition from walking to tapping was effortless, again like Astaire. Harry Warren, who wrote songs for both, compared them favorably. Pound for pound, Warren once said, Shirley had more natural talent than anybody else he had ever worked with, except the "great Fred, who, after all, had 30 years and 75 pounds on her." To Irving Caesar, she was "one of filmdom's greatest troupers, a female Jolson with matchless charm."

Altogether, her contract songwriters through the years were nominated for 67 Oscars and won 8. Professionals they definitely were, as were dance directors Geneva Sawyer and Nick Castle, apprentice composer Jule (*Gypsy*) Styne, one of her early vocal coaches, and Louis Silvers and Alfred Newman, the chief musical directors for most of her films. No stranger himself to dispensing optimism, Silvers in 1921 had collaborated with Buddy DeSylva on "April Showers," assuring listeners that the clouds they saw upon the hills would soon give way to crowds of daffodils.

"Stay as Sweet as You Are"

"There is no human problem so bad that it can't be solved with kindness," John Boles declares to Jane Darwell in *Curly Top.* Idealistic as the statement may be, it was gospel insofar as the Depression

Dancing to Ted Koehler and Ray Henderon's title tune in *Curly Top* (1935), Shirley Temple uses John Boles's concert grand piano as her dance floor.

musicals were concerned. Kindness, the most visible manifestation of a heart consumed with love and the desire to help anyone in need, promptly became the first law of these pictures.

Operating in tandem with it was the second law: everyone in the cast qualifies for happiness, regardless of how disillusioned they are or how unwilling to change their outlook. And in no way could materialism

**Shirley Temple imitating Al Jolson in Mack Gordon and Harry Revel's
"You Gotta S-M-I-L-E to Be H-A-double-P-Y" in** *Stowaway* **(1936).**

be equated with happiness. That was something — maybe the only
thing — that money could never buy.

Entrusted with enforcing these two laws nationwide were Shirley
Temple and her affable young associates, their eyes as vivid as the tex-
ture of hope, down on their luck but never lacking in spirit, and as
versatile a collection of professional scene stealers as ever appeared on
the screen. Each was kindness personified, and all trod similar paths
to convert world-weary, cynical grownups into true believers.

To Shirley fell the heaviest problem-solving caseload. She diplo-
matically brought shy or reluctant lovers together. She reformed

gangsters, the selfish, the haughty. She showed how pleasant life can be without money, provided there is plenty of love around to take up the slack. Her smile reversed flagging hopes. She faced the future with a contagious confidence, while dismissing present perils with the grace and surefootedness of a charismatic evangelist. And she went briskly about her business of uplifting the downtrodden with the lyrics of most of her songs, which she sang to everybody burdened with cares, from wounded soldiers in the Boer War to out-of-work sailors in 1936 Massachusetts.

Times may be tough, but that's no excuse for succumbing to pessimism. Remember, she sings in *Stowaway* (courtesy of Gordon and Revel), "You Gotta S-M-I-L-E to Be H-A-double-P-Y," chin up and arms swinging merrily like those of a soldier parading past a reviewing stand. When things are bad, don't scout around for expensive trinkets to cheer you up, she advises in *Captain January*. Seek and ye shall learn that the greatest joy is found with one's arms around "The Right Somebody to Love." He or she will share your dreams and restore confidence in the future.

So what if Mom and Dad can't afford presents for the holidays? Take a tip from Shirley. She doesn't want expensive model trains or airplanes, she explains in "That's What I Want for Christmas." She'll be totally happy to have her parents with her all year long and to give gifts of shoes to every poor child who needs them. Then, referring to the war clouds gathering over Europe and the Far East, she expresses delight in receiving a few toy soldiers—provided that they never fight.

In *Little Miss Broadway,* she urges everybody to "Be Optimistic"; nobody can possibly love a mourner with a brow furrowed with frowns. "How Can I Thank You" she sings in another Bullock-Spina tune, not for money and gifts, but for the love from her adopted family, and for the birthday party arranged by a hotel full of broke vaudevillians who remember whose day it is. In *Rebecca of Sunnybrook Farm,* she declares that her sole wish is not for money, but for an old straw hat, suit of overalls, and worn-out pair of shoes to wear on a Saturday night hayride.

In the same movie, she invites one and all to "Come and Get Your Happiness" (by Sam Pokrass and Jack Yellen), which will never be found on Wall Street. Rather, the lyric maintains, if only we open our eyes and hearts, we'll find that it exists in the glories of nature.

The pre-*Wizard of Oz* Judy Garland, then appearing in her first feature film,
Pigskin Parade, 1936.

Moreover, one need not pay any income tax to enjoy them. Wealth
is elusive, she suggests; beauty is permanent, all around us, and, like
all the best things in life, free.

In *Dimples,* given the choice of being adopted by an upper-

Manhattan dowager or remaining with her penniless, light-fingered grandfather in a dingy Lower East Side tenement, she chooses Grandpa. She simply can't "Picture Me Without You," or, for that matter, him without her, she sings while enfolded in the tearful old man's arms. Again, it is love that makes the world go 'round, not riches. The time frame of the picture — the Depression of the 1850s — is the source of a second lecture: the country survived that one, and it can do it again.

Stoic renunciation of all attempts to put a price tag on love is the theme of "I Wouldn't Take a Million," the Mack Gordon–Harry Warren hit of *Young People*. Shared by a down-but-not-out Shirley and Jack Oakie as father and adopted daughter, they sing:

> I don't care for treasures,
> I don't care for fame,
> Or the fortunes others may possess.
> You're my only treasure,
> You're my claim to fame;
> My career is here in your caress...
> If I were just a pauper
> And didn't have a sou,
> I still would have a million,
> If I just had you.

OTHER HELPFUL HOPEFULS

Judy Garland's first film, a two-reel 1936 MGM featurette co-starring Deanna Durbin, was actually a screen test for the 14-year-olds. Metro put Judy under contract and Universal took Deanna, and both studios prospered from their choice. Later that year, Judy sang the first of her string of popular songs, Mitchell and Pollack's "Balboa," in the minor collegiate musical *Pigskin Parade*. One of the most outstanding talents in screen history, she went on to introduce the Academy Award–nominated songs "Over the Rainbow," "Our Love Affair," "How About You?," "The Trolley Song," "On the Atchison, Topeka and Santa Fe," and "The Man That Got Away." Deanna introduced four: "My Own," "Waltzing in the Clouds," "Say a Pray'r for the Boys Over There," and "More and More."

In *Every Sunday,* the girls save the jobs of a bandmaster and his instrumentalists, whose classical concerts in a park are attracting ever-dwindling audiences. Eager to help by setting an example, the teenagers convince him to vary his musical menus by sandwiching in a few swing tunes. Judy sings them; Deanna sticks to the classics. Spectators crowd back to the park, everybody's job is preserved, and the young ladies exude the delight that bubbles up from doing someone a favor.

The next year, in *100 Men and a Girl,* Deanna activates William Powell's declaration in *My Man Godfrey* that the only difference between a man and a bum is a job. She conspires to find work for her unemployed violinist father (Adolphe Menjou) and his friends — and with classical conductor Leopold Stokowski, no less. Along the way, she cheers the despondent musicians with a happiness song from the active pen of the resourceful Sam Coslow. They see only raindrops during a shower. Miss Durbin sees something else: "It's Raining Sunbeams," she informs them.

Also contributing, if less mightily, to the compassionate serenading of the screen children was the boy soprano Bobby Breen. Overtly optimistic under the most challenging of circumstances, he sends a message to "Trust in Me" to troubled adults, converting them to his ever-hopeful outlook on life. The grownups may have to look down to address him, but they look up to him for his courage in adversity, and steel themselves to emulate it. Not even violinist Jascha Heifetz was immune to the pleading of youngsters. In *They Shall Have Music* (1938), he agrees to perform for free at a benefit to raise money to keep alive a nearly bankrupt music school for slum children.

The films of Jane Withers, the tomboy princess of B pictures, added to the storehouse of antidotes to pessimism. Using for the most part Harry Akst placebos to purvey her upbeat philosophy, she urges family and friends to "Keep That Twinkle in Your Eye" no matter what (in *Paddy O'Day,* 1936), and cheerleads them into joining with her to shake the blues away in *Holy Terror,* also 1936, and *Rascals,* 1938.

Family Togetherness

No film expressed the youngsters' determination to lure elders onto the happiness path better than *Babes in Arms.* Charged with invoking this second law of film musicals was Mickey Rooney. His father, played by Charles Winninger, the original Cap'n Andy in the 1927 *Show Boat* and one of the finest of the movies' character actors, is suffering from loss of income and self-esteem. Talking pictures have just about killed his beloved vaudeville, and the Depression is savaging live show business in general, causing him to forgo hope of ever performing again. But Mickey will not abide such foul-weather talk. His plea to Winninger not to abandon either show business or hope is dismissed with a shrug. Mickey then realizes it is one thing for youngsters to cling to optimism, but quite another to transfer it to older persons who have outlived it. If kindness will not do the trick, Mickey will have to show by example that dreams need not die unfulfilled.

So along with ever-faithful Judy Garland, he formulates a plan of action at the local soda fountain, which served as corporate boardroom in musical films with stage-struck high schoolers. Everyone deserves happiness, the teenagers agree, but no one will get it unless and until hope has been revived. Without it, the older generation will surely descend into self-pity and squander away their last chance for a life worth living. Still worse, their despair may well redound on their children, the pawns in an economic disaster they had no hand in creating.

The solution to the father's misery, according to a supporting pillar of many Depression musicals, is for the youngsters to put on a show. Utterly unselfish — an offshoot of the kindness theory — they plan to give all the proceeds to their parents to pay off bills. No one in the audience would question Rooney's munificence. Had the actor not already donated the $100 he received from the sale of his first song, "Good Morning" (actually written by Freed and Brown), to his mother?

Of equal importance, the project is to bring Winninger back into show business, through the back door if necessary. The old trouper is offered the job of stage manager for his son's new show. Embarrassed by what is clearly a handout engineered by Rooney, Winninger first refuses. But he finally accepts the job when he realizes he still has something important to give, namely the training necessary to transform his son and his neophyte friends into professionals.

In effect, the son will carry on from where the old-timer leaves off. The family name will again appear on a playbill, and Winninger's contribution will help to put it there. He has learned that the highest duty of the older generation is to sacrifice everything, even pride, for the sake of the children. That unselfish act alone resuscitates in Winninger the happiness that had eluded him for so long.

Ideally cast as the scrappy take-charge guy, Rooney could be brash without being offensive. His agile brain, the major underpinning of his hopes, never ceased to create an alternate scheme to staging his charity shows. He was an acknowledged expert at surmounting discouragement by reinvigorating the promise of fulfillment. His occasional solo assertiveness was softened by absolute sincerity of motive, always directed at insuring the good of all concerned.

Unique among the youthful stars, Rooney took roles that descended into selfishness now and then. In *Babes on Broadway*, his desire for personal gain supersedes his original goal of subsidizing a two-week trip to the country for inner-city settlement house children. Judy Garland recoils from Rooney's self-centeredness and reprimands him in no uncertain terms. Cut to the quick, he meditates on his ethical lapse and passes through Hollywood's traditional five stages of character reformation: denial, guilt, *mea culpa,* resolution, and sacrifice.

Shunting his personal ambition aside, Rooney helps the children after all. His show earns the vacation money and also boosts his own career by attracting the attention of a receptive Broadway producer. Again, the happiness formula has been invoked: kindnesss and unselfishness combine to solve everybody's problems.

No other films presented small-town American adolescence in a kinder and gentler light than the sweetly innocent *Andy Hardy* series, nowadays the most dated of all teenage movies. They began in 1937, and several of them were sprinkled with cheerful little earfuls. The ravages of the Depression failed to infiltrate Judge Hardy's comfortable home, but that was no excuse to omit a lyric designed to comfort people who lived outside the fictitious town of Carvel.

In *Love Finds Andy Hardy* (1938), the second of the nine films shared by Mickey and Judy, the little lady mounts the pulpit of optimism and takes Gordon and Revel's self-mocking "It Never Rains But What It Pours" as her text. Judy's message is the familiar promise that a rainbow will be along by and by.

The rainbow did appear in the late summer of 1939, when moviegoers were informed by songwriters Harburg and Arlen that their chronic financial worries were coming to an end. "Ding, Dong, the Witch Is Dead," sing Miss Garland and the Munchkins in L. Frank Baum's *The Wizard of Oz,* the clanging of bells sounding the symbolic death knell of the Great Depression. Then, to keep the harsh lessons taught by the period uppermost in audiences' minds, the picture ends where it began, in the modest Kansas home of the well-traveled Dorothy. For it is there, bundled in the love of family and farm hands, that she finds happiness, not in a magical kingdom somewhere over the rainbow of life.

The year after the 1930s ran out of time, Shirley Temple summarized the humanity and spiritual richness of the common people whom she and her youthful adjutants had helped to weather the decade's economic turmoil. In Maurice Maeterlinck's *Blue Bird* (1940), she is invited to live in the opulent castle owned by the Luxury family. The class-conscious Mrs. Luxury announces that the youngster's search for happiness is over; she need never return to her family's humble hut. Certainly, the old lady contends, her peasant parents could never bestow the world of gifts that is now hers for the taking.

But the child wants no part of the life of the Luxurys. What distinguishes it is not happiness, but the mean-spiritedness and self-indulgence that wealth spawns. In no way can that life compare favorably with the generous helpings of love and kindness her mother and father have always lavished on her.

"Oh, they're not poor," Shirley snaps, determined to exit the castle. "They just haven't any money."

CHAPTER EIGHT

The Second Golden Age—
The Adult Stars:
1935–1940

C HANCES ARE that today millions of Americans will hear at least one film song written during the latter half of the 1930s on radio or television or in a supermarket or elevator. So numerous were these songs—about 1,900—and so durable their staying power that the second golden age of film music stands at the pinnacle of Hollywood's achievements during the sound era.

Still instantly recognizable, by melody if not by title, are "You Are My Lucky Star," "I'm in the Mood for Love," "September in the Rain," "Bei Mir Bist Du Schoen," "I've Got My Love to Keep Me Warm," "Blue Hawaii," "Sweet Leilani," "Too Marvelous for Words," "In the Still of the Night," "That Old Feeling," "Two Sleepy People," "You Must Have Been a Beautiful Baby," "Jeepers Creepers," "Over the Rainbow," and a powerful lineup of other songs that used movie house loudspeakers as their conduit from Hollywood to Everywhere, U.S.A.

Always at their best when offering something for everybody, the moguls balanced dramas and comedies against adventures and Westerns while tilting their efforts toward musicals, producing almost 400 between 1935 and 1940.[5] From their stately pleasure domes in Xanadu West, these new Secretaries of Amusement served up a sumptuous banquet of quintessential stars and show tunes to win the

---

[5]*Comedies with as few three songs were classified as musicals.*

cachet of gourmet and gourmand alike. The salutary result was that the studios were able to ride out the Depression in a golden chariot pulled by the twin steeds of popularity and profit.

Of the 25 biggest moneymaking films in 1935-36, 10 were musicals. In 1936-37, musicals accounted for 16 of the top 37, and in the 1937-38 season 8, or more than one-half, of the 15 box office winners were musicals. Audiences clearly preferred the light touch to the heavy hand in their film fare.

Every contract songwriter was in his or her prime, as were Broadway's heaviest hitters, whose frequent visits further enriched the Hollywood musical scene. Cole Porter returned after a seven-year hiatus to write the score for *Born to Dance,* which contained two of his all-time best songs. Dramatic actor James Stewart, who had begun his illustrious film career in 1935 as a corpse in the trunk of a car in *The Murder Man,* sang "Easy to Love"; Virginia Bruce introduced "I've Got You Under My Skin," that matchless lighthearted assertion of sexual obsession. Stewart also vocalized on "Hey, Babe, Hey!," a rare Porter waltz.

For the filmed *Roberta,* Jerome Kern added "Lovely to Look At" and "I Won't Dance" to his original stage score, marking the first time that two songs interpolated into a Broadway remake by the same composer attained hit status. From *Swing Time* came six more Kern perennials: "Waltz in Swing Time"; "Bojangles of Harlem"; "A Fine Romance," a rare sarcastic love song; "Never Gonna Dance"; "Pick Yourself Up"; and "The Way You Look Tonight," one of the loveliest of all Oscar winners. Although legend has it that the melody brought tears to the eyes of lyricist Dorothy Fields when she first heard it, the song was actually inserted for comic relief: Fred Astaire sings it to Ginger Rogers while she is washing her hair and looking less than her usual beautiful self.

Irving Berlin's *Top Hat* was the source of five more Astaire and Rogers standards, "Cheek to Cheek," "Isn't This a Lovely Day (to Be Caught in the Rain)?" "The Piccolino," "Top Hat, White Tie and Tails," and "No Strings." For another of the twosome's hit musicals, *Follow the Fleet,* Berlin contributed the lively "I'm Putting All My Eggs in One Basket," the lyrical "But Where Are You?," and the dramatic "Let's Face the Music and Dance." *Carefree,* also starring Fred and Ginger, was highlighted by three more Berlin beauties: "I Used to Be Color Blind," danced in slow motion; "The Yam"; and "Change Partners."

The Fred Astaire–Ginger Rogers roller skate dance to the Gershwins' "Let's Call the Whole Thing Off" (*Shall We Dance*, 1937).

The Gershwins' two Astaire films were the repositories of nine song successes. They ranged from "Let's Call the Whole Thing Off" and "They Can't Take That Away from Me," the brothers' only Academy Award nominee and a rare musical insight into the emotional pain inflicted by an impending divorce, to "A Foggy Day (in London Town)" and "Nice Work If You Can Get It." *Shall We Dance* also included the delightful unpublished and lyricless "Walking the Dog" background interlude that escorts Fred and Ginger while they are exercising several canines aboard a New York–bound luxury liner.

The death of George Gershwin on July 11, 1937, midway through film music's most glorious era, in which he had been a major participant, was a significant tragedy. Dead two months before his 39th birthday of a massive brain tumor, Gershwin was working on *The Goldwyn Follies*. The quality of the songs—"Love Walked In," "Love Is Here to Stay," and the only partially heard "I Was Doing All Right"—gave proof, if more was needed, that this melodic genius had another 30 or so years of great music inside him.

Gershwin's death, however, brought his close friend Vernon ("April in Paris") Duke to the attention of producer Samuel Goldwyn. (Born Vladimir Appollonavitch Dukelsky in czarist Russia, he shortened his name, at Gershwin's suggestion, when the two were rooming together in London in 1927.) For the film, Duke composed the verses for Gershwin's three songs and reconstructed the unfinished "Love Is Here to Stay" from Gershwin's handwritten notes with Oscar Levant's assistance.[6]

Duke also wrote two additional *Goldwyn Follies* songs, the pretty "Spring Again," sung by Kenny Baker, and "I'm Not Complaining," which was deleted. Also by Duke was the ballet music for "Romeo and Juliet" and "Waternymph," both choreographed brilliantly by George Balanchine and danced to perfection by his future wife, Vera Zorina, and the American Ballet of the Metropolitan Opera.

Other than *Mississippi* in 1935, which featured Richard Rodgers's superior "It's Easy to Remember," with one of Lorenz Hart's most plaintive lyrics, the writers saw scant service on the Hollywood front. Their score for Carole Lombard's *Fools for Scandal* (1938), which included the melodious "How Can You Forget?," was dropped entirely. But the tunesmiths' names were united often on movie screens for a succession of their 1930s Broadway musicals: *On Your Toes* ("There's a Small Hotel"), *Babes in Arms* ("Where or When"), *The Boys from Syracuse* ("This Can't Be Love" and "Falling in Love with Love"), *Too Many Girls* ("I Didn't Know What Time It Was"), and *I Married an Angel* ("Spring Is Here").

"I'LL SING YOU A THOUSAND LOVE SONGS"

Collaborating on musicals that produced more than a single hit song, a feat achieved only occasionally in previous years, became standard operating procedure with the contract writers. Adamson and McHugh's *Mad About Music* boasted three hits: "Chapel Bells," "I Love to Whistle," and "Serenade to the Stars." Gordon and Revel's *Two for Tonight* included the title song, "From the Top of Your Head

---

[6]*Novelist John O'Hara reflected the sentiment of many Gershwin admirers when, after learning that the composer had died, he declared that "I don't have to believe it if I don't want to."*

College kids as viewed by 1930s film musicals: Priscilla Lane and an unbilled partner dancing a swing tune played by Fred Waring and his orchestra in *Varsity Show* (1937).

to the Tip of Your Toes," "I Wish I Were Aladdin," and "Without a Word of Warning." From their *Wake Up and Live* came another popular title tune, "Never in a Million Years," "There's a Lull in My Life," "I'm Bubbling Over," and "It's Swell of You."

Robin and Rainger's *Paris Honeymoon* introduced "I Have Eyes (to See With)," as well as "You're a Sweet Little Headache," "Joobalai," and "Funny Old Hills." For *Big Broadcast of 1938*, they wrote the Academy Award winner "Thanks for the Memory," "Mama, That Moon Is Here Again," "You Took the Words Right Out of My Heart," and "Don't Tell a Secret to a Rose." Johnny Mercer and Whiting's *Varsity Show* launched six hits: "We're Working Our Way Through College," "Have You Got Any Castles, Baby?," "Let That Be a Lesson to You," "Love Is on the Air Tonight," "Old King Cole," and "You've Got Something There."

Walt Disney's *Snow White and the Seven Dwarfs* (1938), the first full-length animated cartoon, featured "Heigh-Ho," "I'm Wishing,"

"Someday My Prince Will Come," and "Whistle While You Work." The next year, Paramount released *Gulliver's Travels,* a tepid animated version of Swift's immortal satire on human folly and prejudice. Also a feature film in Technicolor, it gave rise to Robin and Rainger's third Academy Award nominee, "Faithful Forever," as well as "Bluebirds in the Moonlight (Silly Idea)," "We're All Together Now," and the peppy "It's a Hap-Hap-Happy Day."

Dubin and Warren's *Singing Marine* produced "I Know Now," "'Cause My Baby Says It's So," "The Lady Who Couldn't Be Kissed," "Night Over Shanghai," and "The Song of the Marines." The march won distinction when the U.S. Marine Corps adopted it as its second official anthem, and its popularity exploded during World War II. Many a Marine veteran recalls Dick Powell's visits to boot camps and embarkation ports to sing the familiar words, "Over the sea, / Let's go men! / We're shovin' right off, / We're shovin' right off again. . . ." ("The Marines Hymn," based on a melody of Offenbach, has retained its first-rank status as the Corps' theme song.)

Powell also introduced Warren's stirring tribute to the U.S. Navy, "Don't Give Up the Ship," in *Shipmates Forever* in 1935, and reprised it frequently before cheering crews of World War II sailors. Curiously, Warren's finest military song, "Wings Over the Navy," never achieved the popularity of the earlier two, being used mostly in the background of the 1939 film *Wings of the Navy,* with non-singer George Brent.

James V. Monaco returned to screen composition in 1937 expressly to write tunes for Crosby musicals, and he did nobly with six of them up to mid-1940, including the first of the seven Crosby–Bob Hope–Dorothy Lamour *Road* pictures, the one that took them to Singapore. The writer of such all-time standards as "Row, Row, Row" and "What Do You Make Those Eyes at Me For," Monaco also composed "Dirty Hands, Dirty Face," which Jolson reprised in *The Jazz Singer.* His "You Made Me Love You," from 1913, is best remembered by moviegoers in Arthur Freed and Roger Edens's slightly revised version, "Dear Mr. Gable," Judy Garland's puppy-love fan letter to the actor in *Broadway Melody of 1938.*

Between 1930 and 1931, Monaco contributed songs to a dozen minor films without much success, except for "I Feel That Certain Feeling Coming On," which appeared in Constance Bennett's *Common Clay.* But Monaco had a knack for molding hits for Crosby, four of them for *Rhythm on the River*—the swinging title number, "That's for Me," "Ain't It a Shame About Mame," and the Oscar-nominated "Only Forever," one of the loveliest songs of 1940.

Marlene Dietrich's libido-provoking singing voice was heard in almost every 1930s film she made and, except for Coslow and Rainger's "You Little So and So," from *Blonde Venus* in 1932, none was better than "Awake in a Dream," from *Desire* (1936), and the three in *Destry Rides Again* (1939): "Little Joe," "You've Got That Thing," and the rousing "See What the Boys in the Back Room Will Have."

Their composer, London-born Friedrich Höllander, followed Miss Dietrich across the Atlantic, anglicized his name into Frederick Hollander, and provided the actress with practically all her movie songs. The best known and most closely identified with her is, of course, his "Falling in Love Again," from the German-made *Der Blaue Engel,* released as *The Blue Angel* in the United States in 1930. Like Victor Young and Leigh Harline, Hollander excelled at both background music and popular songs. His haunting Oscar nominee "Whispers in the Dark" was one of the major sound track hits of 1937.

For Sonja Henie, the only figure skater to win the Women's Singles championship at three successive Olympiads (1928, 1932, and 1936), Fox froze pools of water into mirror-like dance floors and inundated the sets with artificial snow to display its new star's magic at transforming a sport into a cinematic art form. To ice what Esther Williams later would be to water, the diminutive Miss Henie spoke with an accent that charmingly revealed her Norwegian heritage, though little in the way of acting, but the songwriters made up for the lack. Revel, Pollack, Berlin, Warren, and Nacio Herb Brown furnished numerous melodies fitted snugly to equally charismatic lyrics that graced seven years' worth of skating ballets for *One in a Million* (her first), *Thin Ice, Happy Landing, My Lucky Star, Second Fiddle, Sun Valley Serenade, Iceland,* and *Wintertime.*

Competing with Miss Henie and Alice Faye as Fox's most popular adult star, Tony Martin quickly developed into one of film musicals' leading men by virtue of a strong baritone voice and pleasing personality. Beginning with "When I'm with You," which he sang in a brief, unbilled solo in *The Poor Little Rich Girl,* Martin crooned more hit songs from 1936 through 1938 than any other male vocalist, except Crosby, in 13 pictures. Three of them starred Miss Faye, and four were musicalized by the indefatigable Gordon and Revel. Their lyrical

Olympic ice skating champion Sonja Henie in a 20th Century–Fox publicity photograph announcing her American film debut in *One in a Million* (1936).

contributions to Martin's career advancement included "The Loveliness of You," "Sweet as a Song," and "Thanks a Million," all as beautiful as any other trio of songs written in the late 1930s for a single performer.

New Kids on the Block

Hoagy Carmichael, who had composed "Stardust" in 1927 (the lyric was added in 1929 by Mitchell Parish), joined the Hollywood songwriting brigade in 1936 with "Moonburn," interpolated into the first film version of Cole Porter's *Anything Goes,* starring Bing Crosby and Ethel Merman. So did Johnny Mercer, lyricist (and sometime composer) who would win 14 Academy Award nominations from 1938 to 1971. An entertainer as well as a writer, Mercer had been in Hollywood since 1932, writing his first hit, "Eeny Meeny Miney Mo," to a tune by Matt Malneck for *To Beat the Band* in 1935.

Also weighing in was Sammy Cahn, who over the next five decades would collaborate with almost every major contract composer to produce a compilation of hits unparalleled by any other lyricist. Also a first-rate entertainer, the decisive, ever-busy Cahn frequently belittled his professionalism by referring to the lightning speed with which he put words to paper. "Other people might write better lyrics," he remarked recently, "but they won't do them any faster."

Not even Mercer, Mack Gordon, Johnny Burke, or Leo Robin, four other extraordinary lyricists, enjoyed a longer film career than Cahn, nor did any lyricist who wrote primarily for the stage. Cahn's suppleness of imagery and facility with words are most notable in his collaborations with such gifted composers as Jule Styne and James Van Heusen. Cahn's first major movie song, the jaunty "Bei Mir Bist Du Schoen," was introduced by Priscilla Lane in *Love, Honor, and Behave,* but it was the recording by the Andrews Sisters (Patti, Maxene, and LaVerne) that put the 1932 Yiddish musical song, originally entitled "Bei Mir Bistu Shein," on the musical map.

Another Hollywood newcomer was Frank Loesser, who was eventually to be recognized with Porter and Berlin as one of the few geniuses in both of the two demanding disciplines of writing words and composing melodies. From his pen flowed innumerable lyrics for late 1930s Paramount songs: "Two Sleepy People," "Heart and Soul," "Small Fry," "Says My Heart," and "The Lady's in Love with You."

Kurt Weill, an immigrant composer from Nazi Germany, became available to producers on his arrival in California in 1935, but they neglected to take advantage of his enormous talent. After collaborating with Sam Coslow on a few songs for the George Raft–Sylvia Sidney 1937 melodrama *You and Me,* Weill embarked on a distinguished Broadway career crowned by "September Song," sung by Walter Huston in 1939's *Knickerbocker Holiday.* (Huston was absent from the cast of the 1944 movie version, which starred Nelson Eddy, as were most of the Maxwell Anderson-Weill songs. Cahn and Styne's interpolations included the delightful "One More Smile.")

Established Broadway playwright and short story writer Dorothy Parker took the reverse trip, traveling from New York to Hollywood, where she wrote screenplays (*Dead End*, e.g.) and the lyrics for several songs, among them the Crosby success "I Wished on the Moon," with Ralph Rainger.[7] Another Broadway writer and one-time lyricist, Preston Sturges, also worked on screenplays for several motion pictures, including *College Swing*. He received no title-card credit for his work, but the witty, fast-paced 1938 musical capitalized on his unique gift for satire. The same year, Sturges wrote several of the verses attributed to the 15th-century French poet François Villon as recited by Ronald Colman in *If I Were King*.

It took the Academy of Motion Picture Arts and Sciences a little time to catch up to the rush of song hits that popped up faster than corn in a hot pan. Once again, as for the year 1934, only three were nominated for the 1935 musical Oscar. As would become a tradition with him, curmudgeon Harry Warren did not want to attend the festival. But when studio boss Jack L. Warner called him the evening before the Big Night and informed him that his entry, the sensational "Lullaby of Broadway," was the winner, Warren decided to please the big man and show up. The telephone call pestered Warren for a second reason. How, he wondered, did Warner know the name of winning song before the sealed envelopes were opened? He charged it up to Hollywood's reputation as a center of chicanery, poured himself into a tuxedo, and joined his lyric-writing buddy, Al Dubin, in the audience.

The next year, however, the Academy reached out to embrace more song candidates, doubling the nominations to six for 1936. Only five were selected for 1937, a bizarre happenstance since that year debuted more hit film songs than any other. For 1938 the total redoubled to 10. Only 4 competed for the 1939 Oscar, but for 1940 the number was 12.

The most startling aspect of the Best Song sweepstakes was the consistent writing quality of the relatively few prolific men who created the overwhelming majority of the contenders. Since most of

---

[7]*Dorothy Parker's first film lyric, to Jack King's "How Am I to Know?," appeared in 1929's* Dynamite.

them had already reached the highest echelon of their profession, the Oscar competition was a fierce but gentlemanly rivalry in which only thoroughbreds could participate. No second-rate writer stood a chance of entering the winner's circle.

Although the movie songs of the time were designed largely to ameliorate the rigors of the angst-ridden thirties, they have endured as survivors in the truest sense of the word. A respectable number have appealed to succeeding generations, in addition to their nostalgia-heavy elders, despite the myriad changes in the substance and style of popular music over the past half-century.

THE HIGH ROAD TO WAR

It did not require detailed study of employment statistics to convince people that times were still bad in 1936. In *Swing Time,* Ginger Rogers calls a cop to recover a mere quarter pilfered from her purse by character actor Victor Moore, who only a few years earlier had played the vice president of the United States in Broadway's *Of Thee I Sing.*

Still without regular full-time work at the beginning of 1935 were some 8 million persons, or about 14 percent of the labor force, which was expanding dramatically as a result of the coming of age of the millions of babies born during World War I. In mid-year, Congress passed legislation creating the Works Progress Administration, like the earlier Civilian Conservation Corps a form of "workfare" aimed at the unemployed on relief. Millions found jobs with the agency, but the employment rolls failed to include them. Persons working for the WPA were not counted as "employed" throughout its eight-year existence. Unlike the post–World War II years, workers holding temporary and part-time jobs were likewise excluded.

Bleak as the domestic scene was, far more threatening was the news from abroad. Benito Mussolini conquered Abyssinia (Ethiopia); the Nazis spirited General Francisco Franco out of Spanish Morocco into Spain, where he promptly launched a three-year civil war against the Republican government. When the first shot was fired, the 18-year quiet on the Western Front was broken. In 1938, Hitler annexed Austria, then the Sudetenland, then the rest of Czechoslovakia, and in the late summer of 1939 he bludgeoned his way into Poland. For the second time in 25 years, Europe went to war on a massive scale.

Faithful to its patented escapist formula, Hollywood struck new dramatic shallows by glossing over such troublesome occurrences in its musicals, and in most of its dramas as well, partly to escape isolationists' charges that the industry favored American participation in the new war. Flying into theaters on Cole Porter's gossamer wings of triviality, widely accepted by the mid–1930s as inherent to the genre, the musicals enticed viewers into letting smiles be their umbrellas throughout the new age of anxiety. Relieved of present shocks and immunized against future ones, the public poured into movie houses for periodic morale-building, blinkered from trauma by the hybrid morality plays they saw there.

They heard knightly beaus and saintly virgins, their ramparts forever threatened but never breached, sing pretty ballads amid papier-mâché flowers illuminated by bulbous Warner Bros. moons. They watched chorus girls dance along the rim of an abyss to banish their dread of falling into it. People who eschewed newspapers, newsreels, and radio for song lyrics were unaware of what was going on in the larger world. And the musical moguls had no intention of expelling them from their manufactured Camelot.

Some Hollywood dramas did challenge audiences with significant screenplays to chew on, if only between chomps of popcorn. *Dead End, They Made Me a Criminal, Dust Be My Destiny, San Quentin, Castle on the Hudson,* and *Each Dawn I Die* sought to awaken public consciousness to the dismal living conditions of the most impoverished Americans, while indicting society for pushing slum-reared youngsters into lives of crime and then dehumanizing them in prison. In 1939, *Confessions of a Nazi Spy* issued an early alert to the growing Nazi menace, and in America at that.

But the titles of many mid–1930s musicals were themselves invitations to cheerfulness: *Keep Smiling, Sing and Be Happy, Everybody Sing, Pack Up Your Troubles, Let's Sing Again, The Singing Kid, The Singing Marine,* and *Sing, Baby, Sing.* The few that touched on social commentary did so briefly and subtly, typically intertwining it around a charity show subplot.

After George Murphy, in *Little Miss Broadway,* ridicules the mummified members of an exclusive club as a "bunch of old men who worked all their lives to make a million dollars, and now sit around wondering why," he calls on them for help. But his appeal that they subsidize a show to salvage unemployed performers living in the nearly bankrupt Hotel Variety was aimed tangentially at Congress. By mid–1938, many members were demanding that F.D.R. cut the budget for the wpa's five arts programs. In addition to feeling that musicians should be given shovels rather than violins, legislators were offended particularly by the works of the Federal Theater. They regarded most of its plays as falling somewhere between radical and subversive, like Marc Blitzstein's pro-union musical, *The Cradle Will Rock.*

Murphy's show, finally presented in a courthouse-turned stage, is so successful that a commercial producer offers to transfer it to the Great White Way. His triumph was also meant to induce other entrepreneurs into filling the void when and if the federal government ceased to fund such endeavors. It did just that in 1939, and the few remaining wpa arts programs were transferred to the states, where they quietly died. But helped by the booming wartime economy, the private sector theater adequately compensated for the absence of federally financed plays.

In *Just Around the Corner,* a band of neighborhood ruffians produces a successful charity show for the benefit of "Uncle Sam," a gruff old industrialist falsely believed to be in financial difficulty. Because of his nickname, bony face, and white beard, he is confused with the federal government, leading to the assumption that putting coins in his palm is the same as donating them to the U.S. Treasury.

Inherent in the episode was the up-from-the-bootstraps theory that Americans should stop inundating the White House with requests for "handouts." Better they use a little initiative on their own, like whipping up charity shows, to help themselves and give the president more time to reinvigorate the economy, then mired in a short recession, on his own terms.

"A Touch of Class"

The musicals' biggest rivals were the "screwball" comedies (*Libeled Lady, My Man Godfrey, Easy Living, Holiday, Fifth Avenue Girl*), which, except for the dearth of songs, contained most of the same plot ingredients that were contributing to the appeal of Hollywood's musical renaissance. The scripts of both categories of film treated the wealthy in a similar manner. More than a few pictures included a Daddy or Mommy Warbucks in the cast; money, after all, was not totally absent from American society. People were shown living in spiffy

Manhattan penthouses, riding in chauffeur-driven limousines, and dining in tuxedos and gowns at elite nightclubs.

But the stock market crash had mellowed them, and Hollywood displayed no interest in shooting the wounded. Like battered refugees from a blighted kingdom, they were portrayed as lovable, scatter-brained bumblers who had learned an invaluable lesson the hard way: greed goeth before a fall. Now they, too, were trying to coexist in a changed world along with the deprived commoners whom, once upon a time, they would have gleefully ignored. The Depression had meshed all economic classes; the wealthy's high horses had run out of the money on Wall Street.

Alice Brady's anguished howl in *Gold Diggers of 1935* after learning that one company has cut its dividend from 60 cents to 40 cents was meant to be amusing, even if her one million shares of the stock repre-sents a substantial loss of income. Few could sympathize with any lady holding assets of $10 million. Worthy of audience empathy is Dick Powell, who accepts the distasteful role of paid escort for Miss Brady's unglamorous daughter (Gloria Stuart) to earn a measly $500 to pay for his final year at medical school.

Where the screwballs and the musicals parted ways was in per-spective. The former preserved the worship of money by serving as Baedakers to viewing the woof and warp of mainstream America. But in depicting characters striving for wealth and position they rarely restrung hope in the laborer's breast. Most of the characters succeeded by accepting executive positions from entrepreneurs who took a shine to them, regardless of the young people's occasional tendency to engage in business-bashing.

Conversely, the musicals both created and reflected the aspira-tions of the middle and lower economic classes, the people who had once worked for the screwballs' management teams. Hoping one day to be recalled to their jobs, they awaited prosperity by participating in tribal dances and singing duets that either dismissed the lack of paychecks as a minor inconvenience or advocated extraordinary pa-tience until their anticipated return.

Like soap opera installments spread over many years, the musicals sought to prove that adversity is somehow ennobling. They continually preached that the have-nots were infinitely better off than the haves. Movie house patrons who identified with the unemployed cast members became convinced, like so many restive natives, that rough as life was for the sharecropper on the fringe of the plantation, it was even worse in the manor house. Indeed, it was the upper class that suffered more than anyone else; they stood in perpetual fear of losing the assets they still had. This was the one crisis the lunchpail set never confronted. The only way they could go was up.

NEW STATUS FOR WOMEN

The philosophy of selflessness and hopefulness expounded by Shirley Temple and her filmmates ingratiated itself into the national consciousness to such a degree that it permeated the roles portrayed by adult musical actresses. In many ways they reverted to their own childhood, ribbons in their hair, shiny Mary Janes on their feet, to promote sangfroid through dialogue and lyrics.

By early 1935, the film musical had so abruptly modified conventions of plot, characterization, and tone that earlier song-and-dance vehicles, even those only one or two years old, were dismissed. They were deemed too sandpapery to please audiences on the roll for depictions of happiness among the ruins, shared compassion, and the intrinsic worth of middle-class motives and ambitions.

Musical-film heroines with gracious manners and tears trickling from forlorn eyes were not unknown before 1935. Janet Gaynor had been a model of feminine decorum and incredible naïveté since *Sunny Side Up,* and Ruby Keeler since *42nd Street.* But most of these ladies existed in a vegetative state, their every activity subordinated to the male leads or their parents, typically aristocrats with elevated social position that had to be preserved from the slightest hint of scandal.

Rarely adventuresome, the girls were oblivious of everything beyond the narrow confines of their homelife. Nor did they display much yearning to expand their horizons. When they cried, which was frequently, it was to lament a lost lover; when they came up with an idea, which was rare, they inevitably cleared it with boyfriend or father, who disapproved or reshaped it into practicability. Their sole purpose, like the songs they sang, was to candify their movies and lend them emotional appeal.

But with the Big Switch of 1935, leading musical actresses were given more independence and meatier parts. Most of their characters were living on their own, usually in New York City, away from parental cosseting. More often than not, their peripheral roles as un-paid social workers was of crucial importance to the storylines. Re-taining their femininity, they progressively became liberal and assertive. No one was surprised in 1936 to hear Alice Faye dress down playboy Robert Young in *Stowaway*. When she tells him that the freewheeling, spendthrift days of Calvin Coolidge are gone forever, audiences readily agreed. When she urges him to take seriously the social ills of the day, they understood.

The young ladies' progression up the screenplay ladder was not so much a curtsy to incipient women's liberation as it was the studios' recognition that the females in their stables were as musically endowed and popular as the males, at times more so. No young woman with the extraordinary singing and dancing skills of Broadway-bred Elea-nor Powell, for example, deserved relegation to the back of the Holly-wood talent bus. Nor did Ginger Rogers, then at the top of her form, Alice Faye, Frances Langford, Ginny Simms, Shirley Ross, or the late-blooming Betty Grable.

Meanwhile, the censor's cleansing of films resulted in a number of alterations in musical production. Hollywood continued to culti-vate blonde mannequins, but now they were models of virtue. Dresses were covering more bosom and thigh. The Any-Time Annies were softened into basically good-natured, if tough-talking, ladies with Joan Blondell marshmallow hearts. Ingenues represented ideal woman-hood; they were all angels, and not fallen ones. Jean Harlow's late 1934 film, originally entitled *Born to Be Kissed,* was released under the less provocative *Girl from Missouri.* (The Howard Dietz–Arthur Schwartz theme song, however, retained the former title.) Mae West's *It Ain't No Sin* was altered into the milder *I'm No Angel.* By 1937, she was singing such songs as Irving Kahal, Sam Coslow, and Sammy Fain's "Now I'm a Lady" (in *Goin' to Town*), confessing her character reformation under duress.

Radiating childlike simplicity, the young ladies were all pretty, kittenish, perky, manicured head to foot, and marriageable. In fact, marriage was their overriding goal, a survival tactic as well as excuse for another rocky screenplay romance. They commanded respect for their naïveté, honor for their faithfulness, and bemused condescen-sion for their often exasperating feminine foibles.

The ladies' influence on the men in the cast was nothing short of bewitching. Even the ubiquitous Broadway producer, formerly portrayed as an epic womanizer, was reincarnated into a faithful, amoral friend of the aspiring actress. He remained loyal and helpful even after she had discarded him for a chorus boy, whom, more often than not, the producer had also hired for his new show. Some actresses, like Binnie Barnes and Virginia Bruce, as disarming a pair of vixens as ever stepped before the cameras, added glamour to the career-minded woman. But musicals rarely trafficked in them, except as the abrasive "other woman" who failed, with the regularity of a loser at a singles dance, to win anything, including the leading man, who invariably preferred her sweet girl-next-door rival.

"You Can't Have Everything"

When the grownups appeared opposite children, their response to the youngsters' motivating forces was predictable. Even the middle-age sourpuss who looked as if she never got a seat on a bus was amenable to turning a smiling face to the world. Kindness became an integral part of her personality, too, and she was eager to reciprocate in kind, testifying to her reformation.

Unlike earlier female singers, those of the late thirties moved front and center to perform their songs, often alone, and introduced many of the biggest film hits. *The Broadway Melody of 1936,* for example, opens with Frances Langford's singing the hit of the score, "You Are My Lucky Star," a rare assignment for an unknown newcomer. Along with the males, the ladies chimed in on the hallelujah choruses, mining ideological nuggets in lockstep with those found in the typical anti–Depression Temple tune. The 1920s concentration on over-reaching for riches, for example, is topsy-turvied by Rochelle Hudson in her Koehler-Henderson song in *Curly Top.* There will be no more grasping for the moon, she sings, but rather a return to the old-fashioned "Simple Things in Life," like strolls down lovers' lanes, delight in nature's haunts, and wedding rings.

In Alice Faye's spirited rendition of "You Can't Have Every-thing," she perfectly expresses the commandment people should adopt as their chief guide to sensible living: conspire not for riches or status. All that one really needs for the good life are a penny in the pocket and a lover in the arms. Insisting in "Wake Up and Live" that the clouds will soon vanish, she urges all to come out of their shells, show the stuff they're made of, and find their place in the sun. The message to "Pick

Yourself Up" is telegraphed by Ginger Rogers to Fred Astaire, who has slipped on the floor, in *Swing Time*. By implication, she is aiming the Dorothy Fields advice to everybody whose derrière is flat on the canvas.

In *Broadway Melody of 1938*, Eleanor Powell and George Murphy perform one of the most spirited dances of the year to Freed and Brown's "I'm Feelin' Like a Million," despite the fact that neither has the money to feed Miss Powell's racehorse, Star-Gazer, on whose fleetness of foot their livelihood depends. Earlier in the film, she gives cosmic relevance to her love for Robert Taylor, assuring him that, penniless though both are, the truly worthwhile joys of life — the stars, the moon, the seasons, and love — are "Yours and Mine."

Like many mid–1930s songs, this one merged the dreams of an attractive couple, most of their lives still before them, committed to the unshakable belief that two hearts are better than one in contending with deprivaton. This, too, shall pass, these songs lectured. Meanwhile, it is the shared anticipation of sunnier days that enables the lovers to withstand the numbing realities of the present.

The Dubin-Warren happiness song in *Gold Diggers of 1937,* which Dick Powell sings during the credits, defined the working man's opinion of money. Handy it unquestionably was, especially to dispossessed families crowded around their furniture piled up on the sidewalk by heartless landlords. But it was also the "root of all evil, / Of strife and upheaval," at least according to the lyric of "With Plenty of Money and You."

Midway through *A Day at the Races,* Allan Jones, father of singer Jack Jones, consoles a distraught Maureen O'Sullivan, the owner of a bankrupt health resort, by stripping away the layers of her anxiety to get to the rich core of optimism beneath. "Tomorrow Is Another Day," he informs her, and the new one is guaranteed to be far better than the old one. Not even Scarlett O'Hara would express hope better than Jones.

In a later scene, some 50 deliriously happy blacks sing and dance "All God's Chillun Got Rhythm," which, like Dick Powell's "pocketful of sunshine," was another coin-of-the-realm asset in the Depression years. That they perform to the piping of Harpo Marx in front of the crowded shanties they call home is of no significance whatever, except to indicate that if dirt-poor folks can laugh off the blues with a song, so should everybody else.

Confirming redneck America's theory that blacks are uniquely gifted at putting on a happy face by an inborn talent to do a fast shuffle through life, the number is nevertheless very well performed. For one thing, it is sung by Ivie Anderson, one of the finest of the 1930s female vocalists. Also mingling with the jive-jumping kiddies in the chorus is teenager Dorothy Dandridge.

Cole Porter and Irving Berlin put their individual stamps on other tunes extolling the value of dissolving troubles in a song or dance. Eleanor Powell shows how to do it in *Born to Dance,* using Porter's "Swingin' the Jinx Away" finale as her launching pad. In *On the Avenue,* Alice Faye sings Berlin's words to lament the fate of one dyspeptic fellow who is a born loser. He spends all his nights alone in his house wearing a frown, she reports. The result: he's the loneliest man in town. The reason: "He Ain't Got Rhythm."

To Bing Crosby, one of the marquee monarchs in the optimists' parade, it mattered little that money does not grow on trees. In Burke and Johnston's "Pennies from Heaven," which ranks close to the top of the entire decade's greatest film songs, Crosby reminds child actress Edith Fellows that, though showers must fall, they need not drown visions of happiness.

Just as rain reinvigorates nature, so do life's occasional problems strengthen the resolve to overcome them. Raindrops, after all, are sent from heaven, a benevolent force. Symbolically, they represent not the tears of a misbegotten world, but the down payment on the cloudless sky that will inevitably follow. The wise will collect their share of the largess by turning their umbrellas upside down to catch the falling coins of hope. They will then trade them in for the promised sunny days that lie ahead.

In *Sing You Sinners,* Crosby openly admits that "I'm no millionaire" — but he's not the type to care, either. "Happiness comes with success," he sings in "I've Got a Pocketful of Dreams," but "success is more or less / A point of view." His view is that a dream in the pocket is better than cash in the hand. Indeed, Crosby "wouldn't take the wealth on Wall Street / For a road where nature trods." Money is valuable only to purchase life's necessities; great wealth vitiates enjoyment of them. "I calculate I'm worth my weight in goldenrods," he sings, and that is plenty good enough for him.

Cast as a taxi driver in *East Side of Heaven,* the crooner cannot afford to set up housekeeping with Joan Blondell. Cruising Manhattan

Bing Crosby and child star Gloria Jean during the "I Haven't Time to Be a Millionaire" number in *If I Had My Way* (1940).

streets in search of fares to the tune of "Sing a Song of Sunbeams," Crosby underlines the vital importance of cheerfulness as a remedy for depression. People love a most happy fella with a grin on his face; what's more, a merry disposition might even get him elected president. What all people should do to feel better, Crosby insists, is take a lesson from nature. The distressing times notwithstanding, "Still the Blue Bird Sings," most likely because it never fails to "Meet the Sun Half-Way."

To persons still unable to accept his frequent reminders that making money detracts from loftier pursuits, Crosby sings, in *If I Had My Way,* that "I Haven't Time to Be a Millionaire." It is far more important to "take care of wild roses by a country road" and the "cheerful brook on a mountainside" than pan the landscape for gold. Crosby vows to remain carefree and unacquisitive, since a "friendly gang of robins / Are peeved when I forget / That I'm the second tenor in their quartet."

Familiar Refrains...

The Great Depression musicals in many ways recycled the themes of the 1929-30 period. Filmed operettas, for example, returned from limbo in stunning fashion in 1935 with the release of Victor Herbert's *Naughty Marietta,* the first of the eight Nelson Eddy–Jeanette MacDonald co-starring vehicles. Eddy was a stiff actor, and Miss MacDonald's singing voice was more suitable to light opera than grand opera, into which she occasionally ventured. But they were a handsome couple, the sets and costumes lavishly beautiful, and the music beyond reproach, having been created by the best purveyors of semi-classical tunes in the business.

Herbert's melodic magic was displayed also in *Sweethearts,* as was that of Sigmund Romberg (*Maytime* and *New Moon*), Rudolf Friml (*Rose-Marie*), and Noel Coward (*Bitter Sweet*). Romberg also furnished the pair with original songs for *The Girl of the Golden West,* previously musicalized by Puccini. As if exhumed from sarcophagi, the songs took on a new life among younger fans with only negligible knowledge of Broadway's distinguished musical past.

Eddy and MacDonald parted company several times during their heyday, he to appear opposite Eleanor Powell in Cole Porter's *Rosalie,* Ilona Massey in *Balalaika,* and, in 1941, opera star Risë Stevens in *The Chocolate Soldier;* she to team with Allan Jones for Friml's *Firefly.* To give Jones a song not part of the 26-year-old Broadway operetta, Friml and three collaborators reworked the composer's independently written "Chansonette" into the hit of the film. Its new title was "Donkey Serenade."

For the benefit of contemporary audiences, MGM wisely decided not to regard these stage properties as precious family heirlooms untouchable for sentimental reasons. The dialogue was updated here and there and a great number of subsidiary characters inserted to enliven the goings-on. Rarely had such liberties been permitted in 1929-30.

Adored as the two singing lovers were, Eddy and MacDonald were not alone in lifting the filmed operetta to its greatest heights. One of Hollywood's finest actresses and singers, Irene Dunne, was another major promoter. A favorite of Jerome Kern—she had starred as Magnolia in the first *Show Boat* stage tour in 1929—Miss Dunne was never indentured to film musicals, good as she was in them. Nominated five times for the Best Actress award, she gave stature and dignity to dramas (*Back Street, Cimarron, The Silver Cord*) and screwball comedy (*The Awful Truth*) as well as to operettas.

Her lovely presence and singing voice in Kern's *Sweet Adeline* in 1935 won her the leading feminine role in *Roberta*. Little was lost in the stage-to-film translation, and it is doubtful that anyone who heard and watched her tearful reprise of "Smoke Gets in Your Eyes," that peerless lament to lost love, forgot it. In 1936, on the eve of her 38th birthday, she again appeared as Magnolia in the second remake of *Show Boat*, with Allan Jones as Ravenal. Far the best of the three film versions, it also featured Helen Morgan and Charles Winninger, holdovers from the original 1927 cast. For the superbly talented Paul Robeson, who reprises "Ol' Man River," Hammerstein and Kern wrote "Ah Still Suits Me," which Robeson duets with Hattie Mac-Daniel, an excellent singer in her own right. For Jones they added the charming "I Have the Room Above," and for Miss Dunne, "Gallivantin' Around."

Unfortunately, the three new songs usurped "Why Do I Love You," a last-minute insertion in the 1927 stage original which is played in the background only. Adequately compensating for the loss was Miss Morgan's reprise of "My Bill," which was originally written in 1917 by Kern and P.G. Wodehouse, the author of the Jeeves novels, for *Oh Lady, Lady*, but was dropped from the score during rehearsal. Once again, Miss Morgan sings it while sitting on a piano, a personal trademark suggested to her in 1926 by composer Louis Alter, then her financé, to combat her nervousness when performing in public by gripping the sides of the instrument.

Kern also wrote the score for Miss Dunne's *High, Wide and Handsome* ("Can I Forget You?" and "Folks Who Live on the Hill") and *Joy of Living*, which contained "You Couldn't Be Cuter" and the jewel-like "Just Let Me Look at You." In *Theodora Goes Wild* (1936), she was responsible for popularizing the lovely ballad "Be Still, My Heart," written two years earlier by Allan Flynn and Jack Egan.

Opera stars were again pressed into service for a string of unremarkable films with outstanding scores. Divas Gladys Swarthout, Marion Talley, Grace Moore, and Lily Pons introduced such charmers as "The Champagne Waltz," "Follow Your Heart," "Stars in My Eyes," and "Seal It with a Kiss," the latter the loveliest of all popular soprano solos since 1934's "One Night of Love." The biggest hit among these songs, "September in the Rain," was delivered by James Melton. Composed in 1935 for the tenor's *Stars Over Broadway*, the song was ineligible for the 1937 Academy Award because Warners failed to delete it from the background of the earlier picture.

It took musical films four years to run out of steam, but by mid-1936 they were already shy of new faces for the casts. So, as in 1929-30, the studios tapped dramatic and comic stars to jump aboard the musical bandwagon, unqualified as many were to ride along. Robert Taylor sang "I've Got a Feelin' You're Foolin'" in *Broadway Melody of 1936,* and Joan Fontaine performed a mild dance with Astaire to "Things Are Looking Up" in *A Damsel in Distress,* as did Burns and Allen in the "Stiff Upper Lip" number.

Clark Gable tap danced to "Puttin' on the Ritz" in *Idiot's Delight,* and Jean Harlow and Cary Grant sang "Did I Remember" in *Suzy.* (Grant, under his real name of Archie Leach, had made his New York stage debut in *Golden Dawn,* a 1927 musical.) Olivia De Havilland and Madeleine Carroll co-starred with Dick Powell in *Hard to Get* and *On the Avenue,* respectively. In 1940, the usually villainous Basil Rathbone was cast as an incompetent composer whose reputation is made by buying other songwriters' ditties. Even a future president of the United States participated in musical films, if only from the dramatic sidelines. *Hollywood Hotel* was Ronald Reagan's first such film, to which were added *Cowboy from Brooklyn, Going Places,* and *Naughty But Nice.*

Dubbing singing voices was rare, and the two major examples were ordered for no apparent reason. For the stupendous "A Pretty Girl Is Like a Melody" production number in *The Great Ziegfeld,* Allan Jones supplied the vocalizing for Dennis Morgan, himself an excellent singer, as future musical roles would attest. In *Wake Up and Live,* Buddy Clark's voice was substituted for Jack Haley's, which was quite adequate on its own. One of the better crooners of the 1937–49 period, Clark had the misfortune of lacking the facial credentials to become a matinee idol, and so never appeared in a feature film.

Musicals perpetuated the plots of the earlier golden age. Ever intent on an innocent fling, young actors and actresses found themselves back on college campuses, in the Navy or Marines, and on the bandstand, Broadway stage, vaudeville circuit, radio, and Hollywood sound stages. Such settings revoked the previously enforced no-no clamped on all-star casts, and no studio provided more of them than

Paramount. Its *Big Broadcast of 1937* decanted a heady mix of personalities from all corners of the entertainment spectrum, ranging from Burns and Allen, Jack Benny, Martha Raye, Ray Milland, and Larry Adler, to Bob Burns, Virginia Weidler, Benny Goodman, Shirley Ross, and Benny Fields, with conductor Leopold Stowkowski thrown in for extra star power. Healthy box office revenues were obviating further husbanding of resources to keep creditors at bay. The costly extravaganza was decidedly back in vogue.

Thanks to such recent discoveries as Hermes Pan, who created many of Astaire's most animated, amusing, and elegant dances (he won the 1937 choreography Oscar for *A Damsel in Distress*), and the reliable Busby Berkeley, production numbers took on a sophistication in content and execution rarely glimpsed in 1929-30. Violent death, often the climax of melodramas choreographed by Berkeley, occurs in the "Lullaby of Broadway" finale of *Gold Diggers of 1935,* an unencumbered example of how dance can leaven a tragic plot brilliantly without detracting from it. The leading character is Winifred (Wini) Shaw, a former Ziegfeld girl with outstanding beauty and singing voice.

Playing the party girl, she is seen returning to her Brooklyn flat after another carefree night on the town. Her life of pleasure is contrasted incisively with the workaday lives of her neighbors: the milkman, who enviously watches her ascend the stairs as he makes his early morning deliveries; the ring of alarm clocks in other flats; the boiling coffee pot; the nickels pushed into subway turnstile slots; the hands clutching straps as the cars race along the tracks. At her door is a kitten, hunched between a fresh bottle of milk and the morning newspaper. The door opens and a hand pours milk into a saucer.

Darkness falls and the clock outside her bedroom window illuminates the time from beneath a neon-lighted "Credit Jewelers" sign. It is party time again, and she happily joins Dick Powell in another nightclub. The stage is flooded with dancers, their precise movements accenting the staccato rhythm of the famous Dubin and Warren tribute to the "hip hooray and ballyhoo" of Broadway. Today the production dancing still ranks as one of the finest, if not *the* finest, of all such routines on film.

Ever the madcap darling of the after-hours set, Miss Shaw is the object of a crush of admirers after the dance is completed. Backing away from them, she steps onto a balcony and inadvertently topples over the balustrade to her death. Broadway, the source of her nightly frivolities and thrills, has claimed her.

The kitten reappears outside her door, the saucer empty: this time no hand is there to refill it. Miss Shaw's head, silhouetted in blackness, reappears and turns away from the audience, as if from life itself. She lifts a half-smoked cigarette from between her lips and sings the finale of her own dirge. Her voice sturdy, her mood defiant, she cries "Let's call it a day" to her short, empty existence carousing the street she will never see again.

. . . AND A FEW DEPARTURES

The major differences between the 1929-30 and 1935-40 musicals concentrated, in most instances, on adding cohesiveness to the scripts and upgrading the acting of the leading players. *The Great Ziegfeld,* an ambitious undertaking with major dramatic results, needed only a few of the many songs associated with the producer's repertoire of stage shows, and two new Adamson-Donaldson interpolations, to lift the film to box office prominence.

Living celebrities in any field were rarely portrayed in films under their real names, but MGM selected Myrna Loy to play Billie Burke, Ziegfeld's second wife. He had died in 1932, but Miss Burke was still very much alive and kicking. Three years later, she would enchant audiences as the Good Witch of the North in *The Wizard of Oz.* Most capable as Ziegfeld was William Powell, who seven years earlier had dashed out of a recording stage after cringing at the sound of his own voice, threatening never to appear in talking pictures. *The Great Ziegfeld* was the second musical to win the Oscar for Best Picture; in her role as Anna Held, Ziegfeld's first wife, Luise Rainer became the first woman in a musical to win the Best Actress award.

The film's success spawned more whitewashed "biographies" of musical celebrities, including Johann Strauss (*The Great Waltz*), Stephen Foster (*Swanee River*), Victor Herbert, and Lillian Russell. Of all the major American composers only Irving Berlin consistently refused to permit screenwriters to tinker with his life, an ultimately wise decision verified by the later typically miscast, unchronological, and uninspired films based on the careers of Ernest R. Ball; George Gershwin; Porter; Kern; Rodgers and Hart; DeSylva, Brown, and Henderson; and Romberg.

Alexander's Ragtime Band, an excellent 1938 Fox musical, came closest to reprising Berlin's early days, and it also established a tradition. Besides the composer's new songs ("Now It Can Be Told" and "My Walking Stick"), the film reverberated with the strains of 12 of his older hits, from the title song to "When I Lost You." From that time forward, no film carrying the Berlin name would omit a selection of his best-known standards. Even *Holiday Inn* (1942), with 12 new songs, harkened back to the past by inserting Berlin's "Easter Parade" and "Lazy."

The almost total absence of Technicolor, whose cost reached beyond the budgets of producers, also distinguished the 1935–40 musicals. With the exception of *Vogues of 1938* and *The Goldwyn Follies,* no major song-and-dance film was shot in color. In *The Women,* a drama, Technicolor was used only for a fashion-show segment featuring female models displaying the latest 1939 satins and laces, their every step choreographed to the tantalizing Edward Ward background music.

"It Don't Mean a Thing..."

Coinciding with the gigantic number of songs written for 1935–40 films was the rise in the number and popularity of dance bands, which played a decisive role in bringing the tunes to even wider attention via recordings, radio shows, and cross-country one-night stands. Young Americans with only a cursory interest in jazz were intoxicated with "swing" music, which was then entering a golden age of its own.

Among the few 1930s growth industries, swing and its constant companion, the jukebox, had been around for decades. The ubiquitous jukebox was invented in 1889 by Louis Glass, proprietor of San Francisco's Palais Royale Saloon, when he fitted a nickel coin slot on an Edison phonograph machine that played songs recorded on wax cylinders. The term swing music, based on the throbbing beat of the rhythm section of jazz bands, is believed to have been coined by jazz great Jelly Roll Morton in his 1906 composition "Georgia Swing." In 1932, Duke Ellington wrote it into the title of his own "It Don't Mean a Thing (If It Ain't Got That Swing)," which his orchestra rocked and riffed into nationwide celebrity.

By 1936, clarinetist Benny Goodman, among the most significant and respected of the "Big Band" leaders and instrumentalists, had been crowned "King of Swing" after only three years of fronting his own orchestra. Along with Ellington, Cab Calloway, Tommy Dorsey, Jimmy Lunceford, Kay Kyser, and a host of lesser-known demigods of the dancehall, Goodman joined the Hollywood hoedown in the late thirties. Naturally peppy tunes, like "Pick Yourself Up," became grist for his orchestra's recording sessions. But so did numerous slow ballads, rejuvenated into fast-tempo gymnastic exercises to placate the armies of jitterbugs with a chronic craving for the new sound. The swing ensembles took even sentimental foxtrots composed by Warren, Revel, McHugh, and Whiting on figurative trips "uptown" — all the way to Harlem, which served as official headquarters for many of the upbeat maestros and synonym for their foot-stomping arrangements.

Helped immeasurably by such enormous talents as arrangers Fletcher Henderson and Sy (Melvin James) Oliver, Goodman and his contemporaries pumped vitality into popular music that earlier white bands had only dallied with. Even sedate Ben Bernie, the only violinist-turned-bandleader to study engineering at Columbia University, fell under the sway of swing. *Love and Hisses,* which promoted the make-believe running feud between Bernie and columnist Walter Winchell, suitably limbered up his orchestra for such bouncy Gordon-Revel songs as "I Wanna Be in Winchell's Column" and "Broadway's Gone Hawaii."

Also adding to the broad appeal of swing music were the "scat" singers, like Johnnie ("Scat") Davis, who in such films as *Varsity Show, Hollywood Hotel,* and *Garden of the Moon* used his voice to sidestep the regular rhythm or go at a tangent to it, substituting wah-wahs and similar meaningless doubletalk for the lyrics. Vaguely reminiscent of the 1920s jazz-singing style of Louis Armstrong, Davis's scatting of "The Girl Friend of the Whirling Dervish" foreshadowed the more complex counterpoint singing that would evolve out of be-bop in the mid–1940s.

Solo dancers likewise became more swinging, as exemplified by Bill Robinson's nimble tapping to "Got a Snap in My Fingers," one of the excellent Fields-McHugh numbers in *Hooray for Love.* Fats Waller's stride piano rendition of "Spreadin' Rhythm Around" and "Whose Baby Are You?," also by Fields and McHugh, highlighted *King of Burlesque.* Burke and Johnston's "Skeleton in the Closet" (from

Ann Miller and chorus boys in the opening "Custom House" sequence in the sprightly 1946 Latin-American musical *Thrill of Brazil.*

Pennies from Heaven) fit Louis Armstrong's voice and personality like a glove, as did Mercer and Warren's "Jeepers Creepers" two years later.

By early 1940 still another tempo was invading screen scores. Sprinting up from the Southern Hemisphere, the Latin beat captivated youngsters eager to add the rhumba, conga, and samba to their dancing expertise. Indicating the new rhythms' popularity north of the border was Gordon and Warren's "Down Argentina Way," the first "Latin-American" song to win nomination for the Academy Award. (Youmans's "Carioca" does not qualify; its beat, like Cole Porter's beguine, was the composer's own invention.) The same film (*Down Argentine Way*) reprised James McHugh's "South American Way," or "Souse American Way" in Carmen Miranda's spicy interpretation. Written in 1939 for her to sing in the stage show *Streets of Paris,* the song advanced the appeal of both Latin-based music and Miss Miranda.

Regarded by many film critics as Hollywood's greatest-ever year for drama, 1939 gave birth to a heady list of classic films, from *Gone with the Wind* to *Goodbye, Mr. Chips, Ninotchka, Mr. Smith Goes to Washington,* John Ford's *Stagecoach,* and *The Wizard of Oz.* But except for the first- and last-named films, none produced songs of note. Indeed, musicals were petering out again as they had in mid–1930, nine years earlier. The chief reasons for the decline were the temporary retirement of Warner Bros. from musical production, the death of Richard Whiting in 1938, a steep decline in the bereaved Harry Warren's output following the tragic death of his young son, and the malaise that settled over all the other overworked, tired-out tune-smiths.

Even the greatest of musical teams — Astaire and Rogers — sent a signal that the old days were dying out. In *The Story of Vernon and Irene Castle* (1939), Fred dies at the end, symbolically concluding their partnership, at least for the next ten years. (They would be reunited in 1949 for *The Barkleys of Broadway.*) For the 1938-39 season, only 3 musicals made the list of the top 16 film grossers; another 3 joined the 21 on the 1939-40 list. Among the missing was *The Story of Vernon and Irene Castle.*

An artistic spear on which the film industry had been impaled before, the film musical slump was as short-lived as radio show requests for "The Three Little Fishies," Saxie Dowell's best-selling 1939 baby-talk novelty. This time, Hollywood's musical train suffered only a comparatively minor 15-month derailment. The year 1941 witnessed a rebound in film musicals, even though the number of hit songs was fewer than the shortfall of 1939. But the new film musical revival carried over into 1942, erupting into scores of sparkling songs that announced the debut of Hollywood's third and final golden age of film music.

The direct cause of the renaissance was another catastrophe that threatened the security and well-being of the entire nation. Even more frightening than the Great Depression, the new emergency cried out for salvos of songs to help the nation relax under the grip of another consuming fear.

Once more, the songwriters proved equal to the task.

CHAPTER NINE

The Third Golden Age: 1942–1945

BESIDES ACTING as way station on the journey from peace to war in the United States, 1941 also opened theater doors to a new era in film music history. Patriotism became a major theme of most musicals, even those produced specifically as springboards into escapism, and of the numerous songs designed to heighten morale and sustain it.

The unemployment crisis receded in the mounting fear that America would soon be a participant in a fierce war that had engulfed Europe and northern Africa. The Nazi death machine seemed as unstoppable in Europe as Japan seemed bold to the point of recklessness in the Pacific. Germany invaded the Soviet Union on June 22, 1941, and six months later the Japanese bombed Pearl Harbor. President Roosevelt declared war on Japan; Germany, Italy, and Hungary retaliated by declaring war on the United States. Once again, American men were marching to the tune of "Over There."

On November 5, 1942, the writer of that famous World War I march died, six months after the release of *Yankee Doodle Dandy,* the cusp among filmed biographies and one of the greatest of all Hollywood musicals. With the versatile James Cagney delivering an unsurpassed performance as George M. Cohan, the picture played a pivotal role, along with the new war itself, in resurrecting Cohan's unashamed pride in country and the "grand old flag."

Deftly ignored was his siding with Broadway producers in the clamorous "Actors' Strike" of 1919. Entertainers, who had always regarded Cohan as one of their own despite his producing partnership with Sam H. Harris, were dismayed at his refusal to accede to their reasonable demands for higher wages. The result was that, even with appearances in Eugene O'Neill's *Ah, Wilderness!* (1933) and Rodgers and Hart's *I'd Rather Be Right* (1937), the "Prince of the American Theater" never regained his once-enviable stature as a grand vizier of the acting craft. Nor did he write a hit song during the last 23 years of his life.

With the predictability of the swallows' flight to Capistrano, the studios returned in 1942 to assembling musical pictures with the speed and uniformity of a Henry Ford gone Hollywood. Entertaining for profit was still the moguls' chief objective; everything else was ancillary to it. Thus, the 1942–45 surge in musical screenplays tended to make many of the finished products look and sound like rough drafts by the same author thrown together under tremendous deadline pressure. Once again, the songs amply supported the Hollywood cause by serving as life preservers to buoy up the 175 or so musical features released during the war years. Indeed, it was the music that lifted the most trivial from oblivion to at least obscurity.

Rarely before were so many songs written for films, or by so few practitioners, as in the 1942–45 period. Driven by the suddenness of a new imperative to lead the nation into rising above reality, the songwriters shifted into high gear, turning out an estimated 800 songs. About half of them were instant, if transitory, hits, and 150 or so of the most familiar have attained the rank of movie-music standards. Forty-six won nomination for the Academy Award, far more than the total for any other four-year span. The 14 songs nominated for the 1945 prize set the all-time record for a single year.

The familiar lines, "You went away and my heart went with you; / I speak your name in my every prayer," may have been sung by Alice Faye in an antique San Francisco setting, but World War II audiences easily adapted the sentiment of the lyric to their own recent separation from loved ones. "Say a Pray'r for the Boys Over There" served admirably as a supplication to remember the heroism and sacrifices of their servicemen and women.

Irving Kahal and Sammy Fain's "I'll Be Seeing You," heard throughout the 1945 United Artists film of the same name, took top honors in the loneliness department, even though the lyric does not refer in any way to war. Written in 1938 for the unsuccessful stage show *Right This Way,* and reprised the next year in *The Royal Palm*

Revue, the frankly sentimental song perfectly expressed the fond remembrances shared by lovers parted by circumstances beyond their control. *Right This Way,* incidentally, introduced a second Kahal-Fain perennial, "I Can Dream, Can't I?"

World War II created practically unanimous agreement on the nation's overriding goal: victory over the Axis and an end to the evils its members so clearly embodied. Its battles were waged in a markedly different America, light years away from contemporary society. Cynicism had not yet outstripped the traditional stories of brave men going out to fight for a noble cause, while their women wait staunchly at home, providing security and normalcy for the children.

Persons longing for visions of innocence uncorrupted by the latest international disaster knew exactly where to go: into the movie houses. There they could view an almost endless stream of musicals revolving around what diplomats like to call the *status quo ante*— rollbacks to Movieland's cherished happy-ending prewar years. Usually bracketed by gala production numbers, the films incorporated ballads, martial airs, Latin rhythms, swing tunes, operatic arias, vaudeville routines, minstrel numbers, and instrumentals performed by classical artists. Everything, that is, to insure the broadest audience appeal.

Songs were introduced by band vocalists, singing sisters, boys' choruses, even by dramatic stars like Bette Davis, who talked and sang her way through the Academy Award–nominated "They're Either Too Young or Too Old." Paulette Goddard struggled gamely to keep up with Fred Astaire in Johnny Mercer and Hal Borne's "I Ain't Hep to That Step, But I'll Dig It" dance in *Second Chorus.*

The musical films were mostly triumphs of mass merchandising rather than artistry. Seemingly bewitched by their own ad campaigns, producers strip-mined musical comedy almost out of relevance, burdening their pictures with plot and character duplication that overwhelmed that of any previous Hollywood era. When not flying on automatic pilot over familiar terrain, producers injected the bizarre into musical screenplays. Virginia Weidler's shepherding a prison show onto a Broadway stage in *Born to Sing* (1942) was patently ridiculous.

Perhaps rampant copycatting was inescapable. The mass of musical films released in the 1930s hung like Marley's ghost over the 1942–45 producers. Unwilling to deal with the hard-edged realities of

warfare, they rummaged through the past and welcomed its ac-
cumulated precedent into their planning sessions. Light on content
but heavy with seasoning, stories were plunked into new settings,
typically a military base or homefront canteen. Unlike wine, age did
not improve the standard film-musical formula, which increasingly
gave evidence of middle-age bulge. As Yogi Berra, the New York
Yankees' Hall of Fame catcher, would say later, and in a different context, "It was déjà vu all over again."

Something Borrowed, Something New

Just as the musicals of early 1930 had deserted the picturesque
castles and country inns of operetta mythology, so did those of 1941
depart the familiar surroundings of the more recent past. Scripts
shifted focus away from the jobless in their dreary flats to the boys in
uniform whiling away their days in barracks and evenings on leave.
Modifications were also evident in the social standing of the cast
members, who were upgraded to middle-class parents, lovers, and
friends of draftees. Their ability to buy what they needed depended
not so much on money as on the availability of scarce items and the
number of stamps in their ration books.

The charity shows of yesteryear's musicals were moved from
abandoned theaters and barns into hastily constructed stages in boot
camps. The spine of the new shows was to entertain the troops in the
cast (and civilian audiences) while shunting aside the dismal fact that
up to the American victories in the battles of the Coral Sea, Midway,
and Guadalcanal in 1942, the country's survival was very much at
risk.

The girls the Hollywood servicemen met on leave were perfection
personified: comely, sweet, understanding, sympathetic, helpful, and
musical. The back-home reminders of prewar years, they refurbished
an old, cluttered warehouse into an entertainment center for off-duty
GIs (*Two Girls and a Sailor*), marched and sang along with them on their
military bases (*Thousands Cheer* and *Star Spangled Rhythm*), and served
as apprentice mother confessors to combat loneliness (*Thank Your Lucky
Stars, Stage Door Canteen, Hollywood Canteen*). Among them was Ava
Gardner, who in her 1990 autobiography, *My Story,* candidly described
herself and other 1940s starlets as "neither intellectual nor especially
talented, just good to look at." And the latter they assuredly were.

Three sailors and their girls promenade past the Empire State Building in New York City: from left, Frank Sinatra and Betty Garrett; Jules Munshin and Ann Miller; and Gene Kelly and Vera-Ellen ("Miss Turnstiles"). The film is *On the Town*, 1949.

Also doing their bit for the war effort was the new generation of adolescent stars—Joyce Reynolds, Jeanne Crain, Gloria DeHaven, Diana Lynn, Peggy Ryan, Marcy McGuire, Susanna Foster, Ann Blyth, and Jane Powell. Their programmed enthusiasm for life created and then converted optimism into an ivy-covered wall as easily scaled by the insecure as by the stalwart. Their few screenplays that did touch on the sobering aspects of the war were quick to assure everybody that victory was imminent, since the cause was righteous.

In essence, the new celluloid youngsters preserved the same traditional values their predecessors had affirmed in the Depression musicals. Now their fathers, brothers, and boyfriends were dying on far-flung battlefields to uphold those values. The youthful musical stars were determined to prove that their deaths were not in vain, that the American way of life was irreversible.

Lana Turner, Hedy Lamarr, and Judy Garland at the head of the chorus line in *Ziegfeld Girl*, 1941.

Unlike 1934, 1941 was not a remarkable transitional film musical year, despite such enormous sound track escapist song hits as "Blues in the Night," "Chattanooga Choo Choo," "I'll Remember April," and "You Stepped Out of a Dream." More typical of the times were "Boogie Woogie Bugle Boy (of Company B)," "I Don't Want to Walk Without You," and "The Last Time I Saw Paris," which prefigured the war-based songs to come. Dedicated to Noel Coward by Hammerstein and Kern, and sung by Ann Southern in *Lady Be Good*, "The Last Time I Saw Paris" served as a bittersweet reminder of life as it once was in the French capital, then under Nazi domination, its trees dressed for spring, at peace with itself and the world. Like 1934, however, 1941 led directly into another benchmark era of film music (1942–45) that compares favorably with even the intimidating 1935–40 period.

Through the years, Hollywood has occasionally been capable of transcending criticism of its conformist tendencies. In late 1942, with theater marquees ablaze with the titles of stereotypical musicals, Paramount released *Holiday Inn,* one of the best comedies with original music on film. Tied to a show business motif, it is beautifully acted, especially by Crosby, Astaire, and Walter Abel, and propelled along its course by deft dialogue and amusing incidents supplied mostly by playwright Elmer Rice, as well as by excellent small-scale choreography.

Then there was the matchless Irving Berlin score, which included the Oscar-winning "White Christmas," as perfect a song as ever written in America. Five decades later, Crosby's Decca recording ranks as the biggest-selling Christmas single of all time. Of the other 11 Berlin songs, nine also celebrate various holidays: New Years's Day ("Let's Start the New Year Right"), Lincoln's Birthday ("Abraham"), Washington's Birthday ("I Can't Tell a Lie"), Valentine's Day ("Be Careful, It's My Heart"), Independence Day ("Let's Say It With Firecrackers" and "Song of Freedom"), Thanksgiving Day ("Plenty to Be Thankful for"), and "Happy Holiday" and "Holiday Inn," applicable to any holiday.

Throughout the war years, new claimants to the popular music throne arose in incredible numbers. But enormously talented as they were, they failed to depose the congeries of holdovers from the 1930s. Still wearing Caesar's purple mantle as commanding presences were Crosby, in movie musicals since 1930, and Astaire, since 1933, and such other luminous veterans as Alice Faye, George Murphy, John Payne, Eleanor Powell, Garland and Rooney and Durbin, Sonja Henie, and Betty Grable.

Together with the outstanding cadre of newly minted stars, like Frank Sinatra, Gene Kelly, June Allyson, Joan Leslie, Danny Kaye, Betty Hutton, Mel Tormé, Vera-Ellen, Cyd Charisse, Virginia Mayo, and Betty Garrett, the carryover performers vied for marquee power and both generations won. The elders' pictures, especially those with Crosby and doyennes Faye and Grable, attracted the heftiest box office revenues, but it became increasingly apparent that the younger set were expertly qualified to carry the musical comedy torch that one day would be passed on to them.

Kathryn Grayson revealed a loveliness of face and soprano singing voice in *Andy Hardy's Private Secretary* (1941), subsequently continuing the format set by Grace Moore of balancing popular songs and operatic arias in most of her films. Esther Williams, another coed

Fred Astaire and Rita Hayworth singing Johnny Mercer and Jerome Kern's "I'm Old Fashioned" in *You Were Never Lovelier.*

graduate of the *Andy Hardy* series, excelled at underwater ballet that surpassed those executed by the swimming damsels in *Footlight Parade* (1933). Ann Miller's extraordinary dancing skill had been largely ignored in 1938, when she appeared in *Radio City Revels,* but it resurfaced to great advantage in *Too Many Girls* (1940), leading her into a string of mostly B-picture musicals in which she was the major attraction.

Radio singer Dinah Shore, equipped with one of the best female singing voices of the war years, made her screen debut in *Thank Your Lucky Stars* in 1943; Perry Como made his in the filmed version of Cole Porter's *Something for the Boys* the next year. Also singing their way into favor were Vivian Blaine, a huge talent whose accomplishments as actress and vocalist were never duly recognized; Dick Haymes, one of the better band vocalists of the early 1940s; and the superbly gifted Lena Horne, unfortunately confined, except for *Cabin in the Sky* and *Stormy Weather,* to cameo appearances throughout her career.

Rita Hayworth, who had been appearing in films under the name Rita Cansino as early as 1935, became Astaire's third major

Ann Miller and Desi Arnaz in the 1940 film remake of Rodgers and Hart's *Too Many Girls*, **a 1939 Broadway hit.**

dancing partner, after Ginger Rogers and Eleanor Powell, in Cole Porter's *You'll Never Get Rich* in 1941. A number of young women dubbed her singing voice, but her dancing was pure Hayworth, giving off an aura of grace and glamour that complemented her face and figure. Her chorus line tap dancing with Astaire to Porter's complex "Boogie Baccarole," one of the most underappreciated of the great composer's songs, is nothing short of sensational; her ballroom dance with him to Mercer and Kern's "I'm Old Fashioned" in *You Were Never Lovelier* (1942) is as perfect as has ever been seen on film. The two dancers' jitterbug duet to Kern's "Shorty George" is similarly outstanding, causing many fans to lament the deletion of "On the Ball," one of Kern's finest uptempo songs, from the score.

ELIMINATING THE NEGATIVES

Similarly entering into a revival of activity along with a fresh crop of new songwriters were the established composers and versifiers, many of whom had been in Hollywood since the late 1920s. Back in harness were such superior lyricists as Sammy Cahn, Johnny Mercer, Leo Robin, Mack Gordon, Johnny Burke, Frank Loesser, Harold Adamson, E.Y. Harburg, and Ted Koehler. Harry Warren, at 46 the elder statesman of melody, carried on with Fox and MGM in much the same way he had with Warners, supplying at least one mammoth hit song to every musical that carried his name: "There Will Never Be Another You" (*Iceland*), "I Had the Craziest Dream" (*Springtime in the Rockies*), "No Love, No Nuthin'" and "Paducah" (*The Gang's All Here*), "You'll Never Know" (*Hello, Frisco, Hello*), "My Heart Tells Me" (*Sweet Rosie O'Grady*), "The More I See You," "I Wish I Knew," and "In Acapulco" (*Billy Rose's Diamond Horseshoe*).

Warren's two Fox pictures featuring Glenn Miller were particularly well crafted, tuneful, and fun, greatly advancing the renown of the bespectacled trombonist, whose orchestra was one of the very few that appealed to sedate middle-agers as well as to teenagers. A former arranger for the Dorsey Brothers' and Benny Goodman's orchestras, Miller had become a popular personality by 1941 from his band's appearances three times a week on Chesterfield cigarettes' 15-minute nightly radio show.

Luckily for Miller, *Sun Valley Serenade* spun off one of the finest of all the Gordon-Warren scores. Besides the Oscar-nominated "Chattanooga Choo Choo," sung and danced by the Nicholas Brothers and Dorothy Dandridge, the film also introduced "It Happened in Sun Valley," "People Like You and Me," and "I Know Why (and So Do You)," among the loveliest ballads of the decade. Killed in 1944 while on duty in the war, Miller had exited films in 1942 with *Orchestra Wives,* a musical gem that explored the domestic as well as professional

Lena Horne and Eddie ("Rochester") Anderson in *Cabin in the Sky* (1943), based on the 1940 Broadway musical. Photo courtesy of *Movie Star News*.

tribulations experienced by instrumentalists and spouses during the band's endless barnstorming of dance pavilions. The film achieved prominence by virtue of three more Gordon-Warren classics. "At Last" (also heard in the background of *Sun Valley Serenade*), is still cherished by Miller aficionados; "Serenade in Blue" remains a melodic marvel; and "I've Got a Gal in Kalamazoo" supported the most dazzling of the Nicholas Brothers' dance duets.

Composer Harry Revel in 1942 finally won his first Oscar nomination for "When There's a Breeze on Lake Louise," following it up in 1944 with his second, "Remember Me to Carolina." Lew Pollack also received a much-belated Academy nod when it nominated his very pretty "Silver Shadows and Golden Dreams." Hits by Ralph Rainger, who died in 1942, included "Here You Are" and "Oh, the Pity of It All" (from *My Gal Sal*, a purported biography of songwriter Paul Dresser), "Wishful Thinking" (*Tall, Dark and Handsome*), and "Loveliness and Love" and "You Started Something" (*Moon Over Miami*).

James McHugh compiled more hit film songs between 1942 and 1945 than he had achieved in the 1930s, three of them from the stage-based *Higher and Higher*: "The Music Stopped," "I Couldn't Sleep a Wink Last Night," and "A Lovely Way to Spend an Evening," all crooned to perfection by Sinatra. Two more came from *Nob Hill*: "I Walked in with My Eyes Wide Open" and "I Don't Care Who Knows It." *Two Girls and a Sailor* contained "My Mother Told Me" and "In a Moment of Madness"; and *Doll Face,* "Dig You Later" — the tune with the "hubba-hubba-hubba" refrain — and "Here Comes Heaven Again." James V. Monaco's "Time Alone Will Tell" was the hit of *Pin-Up Girl,* "I'm Making Believe" of *Sweet and Low-Down,* and the plaintive "We Mustn't Say Goodbye," the second of his three Academy Award contenders, of *Stage Door Canteen.*

One of the finest film scores of the era was composed by Victor Schertzinger for *The Fleet's In.* He died just before the picture was released, so he never knew to what popularity heights four of his eight songs would rise: "Not Mine," "Arthur Murray Taught Me Dancing in a Hurry," "I Remember You" (with one of Johnny Mercer's most tender lyrics), and the magnetic theme song of the toast of the Argentine, the girl with the eyes of flame and heart that belongs only to herself, "Tangerine."

Joining these composers were the biggest-name Broadway regulars, who alternated between the East and West coasts. Kern's *You Were Never Lovelier* score also included the delightful title song and "Dearly Beloved," which subsequently evolved into a popular wedding theme (Astaire sings it to celebrate a betrothal in the picture). Kern was also responsible for "Long Ago (and Far Away)" and "More and More," both of which received Oscar nomination for their respective years, 1944 and 1945.

Cole Porter won his second song nomination for "Since I Kissed My Baby Goodbye," danced by Astaire in *You'll Never Get Rich.* He later contributed "You'd Be So Nice to Come Home To," another nominee, to *Something to Shout About,* and "Don't Fence Me In" to *Hollywood Canteen.* Arthur Schwartz, one of the few distinguished American composers to write a radio theme song hit ("How High Can a Little Bird Fly?" for *The Gibson Family,* sponsored during the 1934 season by Ivory Soap), compensated for his sparse Hollywood productivity in the 1930s with three hits from a single picture. Warner Bros.'s *Thank Your Lucky Stars,* which he produced (as well as *Cover Girl* and *Night and*

Day), debuted his "I'm Ridin' for a Fall," "How Sweet You Are," and "They're Either Too Young or Too Old."

Also hired periodically was Harold Arlen, whose brilliant score requisitioned for *Blues in the Night* introduced "This Time the Dream's on Me" in addition to the classic title song. From the Astaire–Joan Leslie musical *The Sky's the Limit* emerged two more beauties, "My Shining Hour" and "One More for My Baby (and One More for the Road)."

Arlen's *Here Come the Waves* added four more hits to his impressive catalog: "There's a Fellow Waitin' in Poughkeepsie," the clever "Accent-tchu-ate the Positive," "I Promise You," and "Let's Take the Long Way Home." "Now I Know," sung by Dinah Shore, was the highlight of *Up in Arms*. "That Old Black Magic," sung by Johnny Johnston in *Star Spangled Rhythm*, remains memorable, its popularity enhanced significantly by the imaginative Mercer lyric. Ethel Waters sang Arlen's "Happiness Is Jes a Thing Called Joe" onto *Your Hit Parade* in the film version of Broadway's *Cabin in the Sky*.

Out of This World, a good-natured satire on dubbing the voice of a professional (Bing Crosby) for a non-singing pop vocalist (Eddie Bracken), was the source of Arlen's "June Comes Around Every Year" and the mesmerizing title song. As might be expected in the musical tidal wave, one of the composer's finest screen songs attracted only minimal attention. Entitled "Long Before You Came Along," it appeared in the 1942 remake of *Rio Rita*.

Hoagy Carmichael, though still contributing a few songs to motion pictures—"How Little We Know" was his best—earned most of his wartime laurels as a film actor, the only songwriter of his time to excel in front of the cameras. In one of his first films, *Topper* (1937), he was cast in his customary role as a piano player-singer, treating Cary Grant and Constance Bennett to his own tune, "Old Man Moon." In the 1940s, he regaled Humphrey Bogart and George Raft, among others, with piano and vocal solos in *To Have and Have Not* (1944) and *Johnny Angel* and *The Stork Club*, both from 1945. He reached the apex of his acting avocation in 1946 as the droll owner of a piano bar in *The Best Years of Our Lives*, the Best Picture of that year and one of the best of any year. His half-hour radio show, *Tonight at Hoagy's*, sponsored by Nu Made Mayonnaise, spanned most of 1944.

Richard Rodgers stuck closely to the Broadway theater during the war years to write *Oklahoma!* and *Carousel* with Oscar Hammerstein II,

Danny Kaye with Dinah Shore and the Goldwyn Girls in *Up in Arms* (1944).

with whom Rodgers had not collaborated since their college days at Columbia, where they wrote two of the university's varsity shows, *Fly with Me* in 1920 and *You'll Never Know* in 1921. Rodgers and Lorenz Hart, who died in 1943, wrote the uncharacteristically mundane songs for *That Night in Rio* (1941), none of which—even the lively "Cutting the Cane"—attracted strong fan approval. The picture suffered identical rejection.

In 1944, MGM called on Rodgers and Hammerstein to add the song "Boys and Girls Like You and Me" to *Meet Me in St. Louis*, and then dropped it. But the next year, the songmen were back in Lotus Land to write the extraordinary score for the first of the two remakes of Will Rogers's *State Fair*, one of Hollywood's all-time best musicals. From it came not only the Academy Award winner "It Might As Well Be Spring" but also "It's a Grand Night for Singing," "That's for Me," "Isn't It Kinda Fun?," and "All I Owe Ioway."

Expanding the Balladeer Ranks

Newly added to Hollywood's contract writers were such teams as Ralph Blane and Hugh Martin ("The Trolley Song," "Have Yourself a Merry Little Christmas," and "The Boy Next Door," all from *Meet Me in St. Louis*); Ray Evans and Jay Livingston, whose "Cat and the Canary" was a 1945 Oscar nominee; and Don Raye and Gene dePaul, nominated for "Pig Foot Pete."

Of special signficance were the film contributions of James Van Heusen, born Edward Chester Babcock, the boy from Syracuse (New York) and the only contract composer to challenge Harry Warren as the most prolific and successful in the film capital's history. (Van Heusen surpassed Warren's 11 Oscar nominations by three and his three winners by one.) Van Heusen regarded Warren as the greatest of all film composers and consciously set out to rival his idol despite their warm, career-long friendship. Actually, Van Heusen's graceful style is more akin to Harry Revel's than Harry Warren's, but he owed nothing to any of his predecessors or contemporaries. His music was especially favored by Frank Sinatra, who recorded more songs by Van Heusen— 76—than by any other composer.

The writer of numerous Broadway and independent hits—"Darn That Dream," "I Thought About You," "Deep in a Dream," "Imagination," "Blue Rain," and "Polka Dots and Moonbeams"—Van Heusen from the outset of his film career in 1940 was a master of melody, sweet to be sure, but never saccharine. His initial Hollywood score, written with Johnny Burke for Paramount's *Love Thy Neighbor,* which furthered the radio "feud" between Jack Benny and Fred Allen, produced two excellent songs, "Do You Know Why?" and "Isn't That Just Like Love." Their success earned Van Heusen a long-term contract with that studio.

In 1941 he again teamed up with Burke to write the songs for *The Road to Zanzibar.* Burke, who had specialized in writing the lyrics for most of Crosby's post–1935 screen songs, became Van Heusen's partner for the next dozen years, and together they poured out a rapid succession of classics for "Der Bingle." How compatible the two writers were, both artistically and temperamentally, and how mindful of Crosby's individual singing style, was made perfectly clear from the beginning. *Zanzibar*'s chief hit, "It's Always You," ranks among Van Heusen's most beautiful melodies, along with the lesser-known "You're Dangerous," sung by Dorothy Lamour. (Van Heusen's personal favorite, "But Beautiful," appeared in 1947's *Road to Rio.*)

Other sparkling Burke and Van Heusen wartime Crosby standards were "Moonlight Becomes You" (*The Road to Morocco*); "Sunday, Monday or Always" and "If You Please" (*Dixie*); "Going My Way," "The Day After Forever," and "Swinging' on a Star" (*Going My Way*); and "Aren't You Glad You're You" (*The Bells of St. Mary's*). In 1943, Van Heusen and Eddie DeLange's 1939 song "Heaven Can Wait" was revived to promote the Don Ameche–Gene Tierney comedy-fantasy film of the same name. In 1944, Van Heusen's "It Could Happen to You" highlighted *And the Angels Sing.* The next year, his "Sleighride in July" (*Belle of the Yukon*) won an Oscar nomination; "Like Someone in Love"was the film's second hit.

Another prominent Hollywood writer was London-born composer Jule Styne, a former child piano prodigy and man of many and diverse talents. A front-rank melodist, Styne wrote as many hit songs for the screen and independently between 1942 and 1945 as anyone else, including Warren and Van Heusen. Along the way, he was abetted by working with three exceptional lyricists, Cahn, Loesser, and Adamson.

Although Styne began writing film songs in 1938, it was not until 1942 that he hit his stride, earning his second Academy nomination for "I've Heard That Song Before" along with collaborator Cahn.

Ann Miller in a scene from Gene Autry's *Melody Ranch*, 1940.

Styne's "I Don't Want to Walk Without You," with a Loesser lyric, was another of the year's top film songs. The next year, Styne again contended, this time with Harold Adamson, for the Oscar with the pretty "Change of Heart," from *Hit Parade of 1943*.

Cahn had met the composer in 1938, when Cy Feuer, a musical director with Republic Pictures, introduced them. Styne had written most of the songs for two Gene Autry pictures, *Ridin' on a Rainbow* and *Melody Ranch,* made by that studio. The first featured the lively "Sing a Song of Laughter"; the second was used as the title of Autry's popular radio show. Feuer asked Cahn whether he would like to write words to Jule Styne's music. Cahn's classic reply, "I'd write with that fellow if his name were Frankenstein," paved the way for one of the most successful songwriting partnerships of the 1940s.

Cahn and Styne captured their second Oscar nomination in 1944 with "I'll Walk Alone," one of their, and the decade's, best-known ballads. In 1945 they made a little Hollywood history by becoming the second team to be nominated for two Academy Awards the same year, for "Anywhere" and the better-remembered "I Fall in Love Too Easily," introduced by Sinatra in *Anchors Aweigh*. Mercer and Arlen were the first to claim the double Oscar distinction in 1943; Arlen in 1945 surpassed everybody when three of his songs were placed in contention.

Other Cahn-Styne early 1940s best-sellers were "Come Out, Come Out, Wherever You Are," "As Long as There's Music," "There Goes That Song Again," "I'm Glad I Waited for You," "Five Minutes More," and "I Begged Her." The partners were equally gifted at fashioning non-production tunes that rivaled their movie songs in popularity. Among the most successful between 1943 and 1946 were "Saturday Night (Is the Loneliest Night in the Week)," "Let It Snow, Let It Snow, Let It Snow," and "It's Been a Long, Long Time." "The Things We Did Last Summer," the definitive ballad of a warm summertime love that cools off in the first frost of autumn, combines the typical lovely Styne melody with the most poignant of Cahn's lyrics.

MUSIC, MAESTRO, PLEASE

Since nothing was too good for the boys and girls in uniform, it followed that the studios would compete to put their best feet forward as America entered its second full year at war. In early 1943, musicals suddenly arrived at a bustling intersection where the brightest Hollywood stars converged with artists from a wide variety of other musical arenas. Like their 1930s predecessors, the new spectaculars expanded their casts to massive all-star proportions while reincarnating the lavishness, though rarely the grandeur, of the *Gold Diggers* and *Broadway Melody* series and *The Great Ziegfeld* of prewar years. Warners' *Thank Your Lucky Stars* fell in that category; another was *Duffy's Tavern* (1945), described by Paramount as a "musical earthquake" with 32 "starriffic luminosities," ranging from Crosby and Alan Ladd to Dorothy Lamour, Betty Hutton, and Paulette Goddard. Burke and Van Heusen's "The Hard Way" was the hit song in the film, based on the radio show of the same name, with Ed Gardner as Archie, the proprietor of the bar and grille "where the elite meet t' eat." Playing Duffy's daughter was Shirley Booth. Almost every musical film was shot in Technicolor; almost every song summoned a chorus line.

A potpourri of cameos provided limited insight into the artistry of "high-brow" musicians, such as pianist-composer José Iturbi (*Anchors Aweigh*) and Wagnerian tenor Lauritz Melchior (*Thrill of a Romance*), their brief encounters with the camera tailored like custom-made suits to display their talents to best advantage. Hired mostly to dignify the pedestrian screenplays with the sounds of classical music, and a sampling of boogie-woogie, Iturbi played his recitals before audiences far larger than any he could hope to attract in a lifetime of touring concert halls.

At the other extreme was Spike Jones, the leader of an orchestra staffed with superbly trained musicians, whose arrangements of new and older songs inserted a Three Stooges flavor, always ridiculous, sometimes inspired, into the proceedings. In between the classical and the absurd fell practically all the major bandleaders of the day, who added to their name recognition and phonograph record sales by introducing a hefty number of popular songs in the course of their frequent film appearances.

Joining Glenn Miller in the more than 30 bandstand-based World War II musicals were Benny Goodman, already a veteran of musical films, who appeared in *The Powers Girl* and *Sweet and Low-Down,* and Jimmy Dorsey (*The Fleet's In, I Dood It, Four Jills and a Jeep, Hollywood Canteen*), and brother Tommy (*Ship Ahoy, Girl Crazy, Broadway Rhythm*). The Dorseys had formed a combined orchestra in 1933, but split up the next year after protracted disagreement over musical style. Jimmy was an excellent saxophonist, Tommy among the best swing trombonists. It was from Tommy's band that Frank Sinatra struck out on his own in 1943 to appear as a soloist in *Reveille with Beverly.*

In his only two previous films, *Las Vegas Nights* (1941) and *Ship Ahoy* (1942), Sinatra had sung "Dolores," the first of his seven Oscar nominees, and "Poor You," respectively, as a member of Dorsey's Pied Pipers singing quartet, which also included Jo Stafford. Besides Sinatra, *Ship Ahoy* featured another rare talent — that of Buddy Rich, Tommy Dorsey's agile drummer — whose tom-tom rendition of Sy Oliver's "Not So Quiet, Please" fully deserved the enthusiastic reception it earned from professional musicians and jitterbugs alike.

North Carolina–born Kay Kyser, a sort of cracker-barrel Spike Jones with a Southern accent, looked like a kindly scholar, which befit his role as genial inquisitor on his long-running radio quiz show, *College of Musical Knowledge.* Together with Harry Babbitt and Sully

Mason, two most competent singers, and comedian Ish Kabibble, Kyser premiered numerous standout songs, "I'd Know You Anywhere," "There Goes That Song Again," "You Make Me Dream Too Much," "Got the Moon in My Pocket," and "How Long Did I Dream?," in eight movies between 1939 and 1944. Most had the good fortune of being sung by Ginny Simms, next to Dinah Shore and Lena Horne the finest female vocalist of the war years.

Bing Crosby's brother, Bob, fronted the excellent Dixieland band nicknamed the Bobcats, which, like the Kyser organization, appeared in several mediocre films. Operating on a higher musical plane was Xavier Cugat (Francisco de Asis Javier Cugat Mingall de Brue y Deulofeo), the Guy Lombardo of the pampas, who became a film musical fixture. Rivaling Cab Calloway as the best actor in the roster of orchestra dons, he had popularized the rumba in North America, mostly by alternating with Benny Goodman on the 1934-35 Saturday night network radio show *Let's Dance*. Cugat led his talented assemblage into a variety of Latin rhythms in five films between 1942 (*You Were Never Lovelier*) and 1945 (*Weekend at the Waldorf*). Virtually ignored in *Pin-Up Girl* (1944) and *Breakfast in Hollywood* (1945) was the King Cole Trio, which boasted pianist-crooner Nat "King" Cole as its most distinguished member.

Other movie bandleaders, a virtual *Who's Who* of the latter half of the pre-bop swing era, included Les Brown, Charlie Spivak, Jimmy Lunceford and Will Osborne (both in *Blues in the Night*), Charlie Barnet, Carmen Cavallaro (the "Poet of the Piano") Woody Herman, Sammy Kaye, Freddy Martin, and Harry James. The latter, who wielded one of popular music's most energetic trumpets, stepped out of the Benny Goodman orchestra, as did drummer Gene Krupa. James's best-known film song, "I Had the Craziest Dream," was sung by his leading female vocalist, Helen Forrest, not by star Betty Grable. But it was Betty who married Harry shortly after the film was completed.

Although most bandleaders participated in songwriting exercises, only Harry Owens and Artie Shaw, whose clarinet playing rivaled — some say surpassed — that of Goodman, were honored with an Academy Award nomination. Shaw's "Love of My Life," appeared in Fred Astaire's only film disaster, *Second Chorus*, in 1940. Shaw also collaborated with Ben Oakland and Milton Drake on the lovely ballad "If It's You," sung by Tony Martin in the Marx Brothers' *Big Store*, in 1941.

Bandleader Kay Kyser with Ann Miller and Victor Moore in *Carolina Blues*, the 1944 film that introduced Sammy Cahn and Jule Styne's "Poor Little Rhode Island."

The other song in the picture was "Tenement Symphony," also sung by Martin to words and music by Sid Kuller, Ray Golden, and Hal Borne. Unique in the evolution of popular American music, the song defines ethnic bias in 1941 terms, celebrating the "grand illusion" of harmony prevailing among Jewish, Irish, Italian, and Scottish immigrants residing in four flats of the same apartment house on the Lower East Side of New York City.

Racial discrimination had yet to find a niche in either stage or film music. Irving Caesar's "There Ain't No Color Line Around the Rainbow," written in 1931 for Al Jolson to sing in *Wonder Bar,* touched on the subject by reminding audiences that both black and white men share the same sunshine. Jolson refused to sing it, and the song languished until 1942, when Caesar inserted it into *My Dear Public.* Neither song nor show curried favor. Two years later, however, the nation's fractious race relations were addressed in Harburg and Arlen's "Eagle and Me," which forcefully advocated completion of the black emancipation begun in the post–Civil War years, in *Bloomer Girl.*

Some 1946-47 Broadway dramas (*On Whitman Avenue, Anna Lucasta, Strange Fruit, Deep Are the Roots*) and Harold Rome's musical *Call Me Mister* probed bigotry and its corrosive impact on giver and receiver alike. Rodgers and Hammerstein's "You've Got to Be Carefully Taught," written for *South Pacific* in 1949, reintroduced the subject musically, but it was almost cut from the score during tryouts. Protests by the two songwriters and author James Michener, however, saved the song from excision.

The volume of songs made popular by musical films during the war, coupled with the almost 100 percent increase in the rate of song copyrighting between 1939 and 1942, significantly increased the jockeying for airtime. Radio was a vital promoter of popular music, so it was incumbent on publishers to get their songs a hearing on radio programs, especially network shows. For the first time since the late 1920s, comparatively few of the hundreds of 1940–45 songs arose from Broadway stages or Hollywood sound tracks. Increasingly, the majority were non-production tunes, most of them by obscure writers welcomed into membership by Broadcast Music, Inc., founded in 1939 as an alternative to ASCAP, which controlled the market for stage and screen scores.

Organized within the radio industry itself, BMI sought to answer broadcasters' complaints that ASCAP charged unreasonable license fees, later distributed to songwriters as royalties, for playing show tunes on the air, and in addition limited the number and variety of available songs by severely restricting membership. Composers and lyricists of country music and, eventually, rhythm and blues and rock and roll, largely ignored by ASCAP, found a sponsor in BMI. It took chances on unknowns, beginning with Woody Guthrie and Hank Williams and, in time Chuck Berry, the Beatles, and the Rolling Stones.

The entrance of BMI into the fee-collecting business vastly enlarged the number of independent songs played on the radio, often to the detriment of production tunes, which were shunted aside in favor of non–ASCAP songs. Nevertheless, a dozen or so 1940-41 BMI songs were the equal of all but the finest of those years' film and stage counterparts. Many developed into most respectable hits, among them "Walkin' by the River," "My Sister and I," "You Walk By," "I Hear a Rhapsody," "There I Go," "High on a Windy Hill," and "It All Comes Back to Me Now." Many more equally impressive hits would follow as time went by, and BMI grew into a major competitive force in the musical marketplace. Today it represents more than 120,000 songwriters and publishers and boasts a repertoire of about 2 million songs.

More Broadway Melodies

Curiously, at a time when escapist themes were important for relieving anxiety, the film industry almost completely ignored the operetta, the only musical genre that encapsulated the comparative serenity of bygone years. Conforming over the decades with Kabuki-like reverence to identical themes played out by princes and paupers, the operetta was too placid for 1940s jitterbugs, too quaint for adults who had spent their own adolescence worried about bill collectors and were now threatened by international fascism.

The contemporary Broadway stage was not overlooked in Hollywood's search for ways to send shafts of starlight into blacked-out cities. Cole Porter was clearly the favorite target, but MGM filmed his *Panama Hattie* to disadvantage, save for Lena Horne's singing of "Just One of Those Things," which Porter had written for *Jubilee* four years earlier. *DuBarry Was a Lady* was next, followed by *Let's Face It* and *Something for the Boys* in relatively quick succession. (Porter's *Mexican Hayride,* filmed in 1948 with Abbott and Costello, was a huge disappointment.) The filming of Irving Berlin's *Louisiana Purchase* (1941) was felicitous, but it was his *This Is the Army* (1943) that won the accolades as the best stage-to-film transfer of the war years.

Joseph McCarthy and Harry Tierney's *Irene,* from 1919, was filmed in 1940; *No, No, Nanette* and Jerome Kern's *Sunny* were reprised for the second time in 1941; the Gershwins' *Lady Be Good* and *Girl Crazy* in 1941 and 1943; and Jay Gorney's *Meet the People* in 1944. Blane and

Martin's *Best Foot Forward* repeated the success of the stage original, thanks largely to the score and Nancy Walker, a mild Dead End girl, as the leading comedienne. Sinatra's *Step Lively* was a Sammy Cahn-Jule Styne musicalized revamp of the stage farce *Room Service,* remade into a Marx Brothers romp in 1938.

Many excellent songs from the stage productions were deleted by Hollywood: Rodgers and Hart's end-of-partnership "It Never Entered My Mind," for example, was missing from the filmed *Higher and Higher.* Even worse, the songs that remained intact were typically given short shrift, visiting another affront on the songwriters. So widely known were many of the leftover stage songs that the moguls stepped up their practice of switching scenes from a singer halfway through a song to other cast members in order to further the plot. Renditions of standards were frequently shot through with such dramatic holes, leaving more than just a few songs only partially heard. Absent from the Broadway stage, these interruptions annoyed not only the writers, but many performers and moviegoers as well.

Film fans increasingly grew fond of nostalgia, especially when the settings reverted to the turn of the century or the 1920s. Fewer periods evoked a fonder response than the minstrel shows and halcyon days of vaudeville, when New York's Palace Theatre served as the citadel of artistic achievement. Older viewers were delighted by Hollywood's visual chronicles of their childhood years, before the Great Depression and World War II put their optimism on hold; youngsters were fascinated by occasional trips into a past as unfamiliar as the future was uncertain. The best survey of radio's pioneering days, *The Great American Broadcast* (1941), introduced several good Gordon-Warren songs, among them the charming Alice Faye ballad "Where You Are."

The old songs held up quite well in updated performances, thanks in large measure to such flawless troupers as Charles Winniger, Al Shean (the younger brother of Minnie Marx and the second half of the famous Gallagher and Shean vaudeville team), and Eddie Cantor. The latter's black-faced reprise of "Makin' Whoopee" in *Show Business* continued to please, as did Benny Fields's recreation of a minstrel show star in Harry Revel's *Minstrel Man.*

For those seeking more backward glances at the pre–World War I entertainment industry, *For Me and My Gal,* with Judy Garland and Gene Kelly, served up several tasty morsels, not the least of them a reprise of the title tune, written in 1917 by Edgar Leslie, E. Ray Goetz, and George W. Meyer. *Irish Eyes Are Smiling* (1944) recorded the tribulations of overcoming gimlet-eyed music publishers to triumph in the songwriting business, with Dick Haymes as songman Ernest R. Ball.

Welcomed to the Hollywood scene, but playing different roles, were two men whose names define the spit and polish that distinguished so many film musicals of the 1940s and beyond. From Broadway came director Vincente Minnelli, the second of Judy Garland's five husbands and father of Liza Minnelli. He more than adequately compensated for his woefully third-class *I Dood It* with *Cabin in the Sky* and *Meet Me in St. Louis* (for the 1904 World's Fair), which pegged the presence of a major talent in choreography and set design, as well as musical direction.

Few persons in movie history have been more closely linked to musical films than Arthur Freed (Arthur Grossman), MGM's chief contract lyricist throughout the late 1920s and 1930s, and beginning in 1939 the studio's foremost producer of song-and-dance extravaganzas. A perfectionist who demanded, and got, the best from the top-notch professionals surrounding him, Freed was fortunate in that MGM from 1944 to 1958, the heart of his productive years, assembled the most formidable array of musical talent ever to work under the same roof at the same time.

Numbered among them were Busby Berkeley, who directed *Babes in Arms, Strike Up the Band, Babes on Broadway,* and *For Me and My Gal,* all produced by Freed, and Stanley Donen, director or co-director of seven MGM musicals; Minnelli, Harry Warren, composer-arrangers André Previn and Roger Edens, orchestrator Conrad Salinger, musical directors John W. Green, Saul Chaplin, and Lennie Hayton, and an unmatched stable of stars, art directors, set and costume designers, and instrumentalists. Pizazz had always marked MGM's musicals; Freed outshone every one of his predecessors in the 1950s, when he added *A Royal Wedding, Show Boat, An American in Paris, Singin' in the Rain, The Band Wagon,* and *Gigi* to his admirable body of works.

NON-MUSICAL MUSIC

Following Hollywood tradition, a number of 1942–45 dramas included both background scores and isolated theme songs of exceptional quality. Meredith (*Music Man*) Willson's superb score for *The Little Foxes* (1941) surpassed even his excellent backdrop for Chaplin's *Great Dictator* of the previous year. (Willson's "You and I" served as the theme of radio's *Maxwell House Coffee Time,* a favorite weekly variety program of the early war years that starred "Wizard of Oz" Frank Morgan and Fanny Brice as Baby Snooks.)

Similarly, Miklos Rozsa's score for *The Lost Weekend* (1945) won deserved praise, as did his theme for *Spellbound,* which achieved lasting popularity when Mack David added the lyric. Victor Young's score for *The Uninvited* (1944) gave birth to the ever-lovely "Stella by Starlight," which, after Ned Washington supplied the lyric, blossomed into one of 1946's biggest popular songs. David Raksin's outstanding contributions were "Laura," unsung in the movie of the same name, and "Slowly," from *Fallen Angel. Now, Voyager* contained Max Steiner's "It Can't Be Wrong," and *Saratoga Trunk* his "As Long As I Live."

As timing would have it, World War II had ended when the aforementioned *State Fair* was making the rounds of neighborhood houses. No other film of the time more winsomely idealized and savored the virtues of rural America as reflected in one farm family's solidarity while pursuing the simplest of pleasures despite the intrusion of problems beyond their level of sophistication.

Exuding apple pie warmth, mother Fay Bainter is properly reluctant to add brandy to her mincemeat; father Charles Winniger's greatest concern is the health of his great Hampshire sow, "Blue Boy"; shy daughter Jeanne Crain, as pretty a girl as ever appeared in musical films, temporarily loses city slicker Dana Andrews, whom she met at the fair; brother Dick Haymes is the naïve farmhand who learns one of life's harshest lessons: unrequited love is hell. But happiness carries the day. The mincemeat and the sow win first prizes, and Jeanne wins Dana. Deserted by a band singer, Dick contentedly resumes his courtship with his childhood sweetheart.

Without knowing it, Americans were on the verge of a totally new era that would significantly alter their psyche and outlook, and also the content and treatment of the film musical. Never again, once the Atomic Age began, would an original film musical with a contemporary setting reflect so graciously the innocence and gentility that most people were convinced identified the nation's character, or sincerely hoped they did. *State Fair* was the old-time film musical's last hurrah. At its conclusion, when workmen begin dismantling the concessions and amusements along the midway, their activity symbolizes not only the end of the 1945 Iowa state fair, but also the passing of an uncomplicated slice of life that cherished the annual ride on a roller coaster as much as the glass of cold lemonade on a sweltering summer's day.

Jubilation marked the celebration of V-J Day on August 15, 1945; relief and kisses were shared in cities and villages. Fears of an Armageddon vanished; the dark underside of peace was yet to surface. After a harrowing interlude of almost six years, people watched the lights come on again everywhere in the world while bluebirds made their return flight over the white cliffs of Dover.

And a nightingale sang in Berkeley Square.

CHAPTER TEN

Days of Wine and Roses: 1946–1965

HE FIRST FULL postwar year of 1946 respectably continued the outpouring of original songs that had distinguished the 1942–45 film musicals, further testifying to the seemingly endless wizardry of the contract songwriters. Pretty ballads and updated Lindy hops arose from sound tracks with almost uncanny regularity. Only the picture plots changed, and those only slightly. For the most part, the new song-and-dance screenplays clamped the lid on tales of young Americans anxiously awaiting the call to battle. So eager was the war-weary world to piece shattered lives together that not even the Korean War, which broke out five years after the end of World War II, prompted the musical moguls to dust off their old USO scenery and roll it back onto their sound stages.

Many of the new screen songs were the equal of the 1942–45 collection of standards. But in 1946, the Academy governors restricted Best Song candidates to five, in effect penalizing the songwriters and indicating to music fans that the majority of film songs, good as they might be, were unworthy of Oscar consideration. Nothing could be further from fact; 1946 and 1948 in particular were endowed with almost as many top-rung Hollywood songs as the slightly wealthier years of 1929, 1934-35, and 1942–45.

The very few musicals centering on GIs depicted them as lame ducks seeking their niche in civilian life. Cahn and Styne's ultra-professional score for *It Happened in Brooklyn* (1947), with "Time After Time" and "It's the Same Old Dream," escorted Frank Sinatra and Kathryn Grayson through a most amiable screen courtship between a recently discharged soldier and a girl from back home. Sinatra fails to win her, but no sighs are heaved, no tears shed. His true love, expressed in the only popular anthem to a city landmark, was the Brooklyn Bridge, the object of his affection and wistful serenade.

World War II intruded into the Cold War in 1949 with Betty Comden, Adolph Green, and Leonard Bernstein's *On the Town,* shoplifted from Broadway. Shy its best ballad, "Lucky to Be Me," the film sported a game, youthful cast that turned the story of three sailors (Frank Sinatra, Gene Kelly, and Jules Munshin) on leave in New York City into an MGM triumph. Two years later, Fox also imposed the old war on the new one in Korea by reissuing *Call Me Mister,* written by Harold Rome, of the Depression era's *Pins and Needles* and *Sing Out the News* fame, for 1946 Broadway. The wittiest of the doughboy-turned-civvy tales, the picture coupled Betty Grable and Dan Dailey, who revived the show's two biggest hits, "Along with Me" and that supreme satire on Latin music, "South America, Take It Away!" Martin and Lewis's *At War with the Army,* their third feature film, placed Jerry's slapstick and Dean's vocalizing ("You and Your Beautiful Eyes") squarely in a World War II context.

More to the liking of spectators were fond recollections of times and performers past, which were paraded before them in melodious little diversions set in America's antebellum years. For Arthur Freed's *Harvey Girls,* which cued viewers in on the 19th-century founding of a white-tablecloth chain of slow-food restaurants throughout the Old West, Mercer and Warren exceeded everything they had accomplished together with "On the Atchison, Topeka and Santa Fe." The number was made even more winning by Judy Garland's expert vocalizing, Ray Bolger's dancing, and one of the largest and most complex chorus routines ever filmed. A second hit was the ballad "Wait and See," sung by Kenny Baker, who was back in films again after a three-year hiatus.

Astaire and Garland's *Easter Parade* was set in an earlier, gentler New York, when congregations of upper-crust ladies and gentlemen began strolling the blocks abutting and adjacent to St. Patrick's Cathedral to model their Easter Sunday finery. A show biz ambience was sewn into the plot, and from it came four Irving Berlin sparklers: "It Only Happens When I Dance with You," "Steppin' Out with My Baby," "A Couple of Swells," a jubilant throwback to baggy-pants vaudeville, and Judy's and Berlin's greatest lament to love gone astray, "Better Luck Next Time."

The actress ended her 14-year MGM career in 1950 with *Summer Stock,* a bucolic rendering of the puttin'-on-a-show theme in a barn situated on the most attractive stretch of farmland hammered together since *State Fair.* Gene Kelly's soft-shoe routine, using newspapers instead of sand, to Harry Warren's "You, Wonderful You" was the hit of the picture, but it also featured the more substantial and melodically complex "Friendly Star," which underscored Judy's ability to strum the heartstrings with the plaintive touch of a loveless lady.

For the sports-minded, baseball in the President Theodore Roosevelt years took center stage in the Arthur Freed–produced, Busby Berkeley–directed *Take Me Out to the Ball Game,* a minor musical despite its roaring box office business, Sinatra's romancing of Esther Williams to "The Right Girl for Me," and Gene Kelly's superior dance solo to Betty Comden, Adolph Green, and Roger Edens's "The Hat My Dear Old Father Wore (Upon St. Patrick's Day)." Calling on his inherent Irishness, Kelly performs the dance with the jaunty ease of a professional leprechaun. Curiously, of all the major film musical stars, Kelly was called on to perform the least number of original songs; his forte was reinterpreting decades-old standards for a new generation.

The original "Pal Joey" in the 1941 Broadway musical, Kelly was placed in competition for male dancing honors with Astaire, also on the MGM payroll in the late 1940s and 1950s. Actually, choosing between them was a frivolous pastime, similar to the earlier fan-inspired rivalry involving Crosby and Sinatra in the crooning department. Both dancers, like the two singers, were equally gifted. Their similarities in style were more obvious than their differences, and each made unique contributions to dance on film. Astaire's 1930s popularity cleared the path for Kelly's screen stardom; Kelly, equal to the challenge, matched the master's nimbleness and precision.

A more virile dancer than Astaire, he was also a better actor and extraordinary choreographer and director. From his first film, *For Me and My Gal* (1942), Kelly's multiplicity of talents was clearly evident, as was the fact that MGM had still another major star on its roster. He expertly fulfilled his potential from 1951 to 1956 in masterpieces ranging from *An American in Paris* to *Invitation to the Dance.*

Jerome Kern's death on November 11, 1946, provided an example of how an artist's renown often depends more on creativity than publicity. His works were widely known; the man was not. A severe stroke felled the composer on New York City's Park Avenue, where medical attendants picked him up in an unconscious state and without identification. They wheeled their latest "John Doe" into a charity ward at the Welfare Island hospital. No one recognized Kern. All that was found on his person was a card bearing his ASCAP membership number, but no name. A hospital secretary called ASCAP, which identified Kern from her detailed description. He was removed to a Manhattan hospital, where he died one week later.

Among Kern's legacy of singable show music was his final score, written for *Centennial Summer,* which harkened back to America's 100th birthday in 1876. Although one of his best latter-day songs, "Two Hearts Are Better Than One," was deleted, the film showcased two other equally lovely ballads, "In Love in Vain" and the Oscar-nominated "All Through the Day." "Up with the Lark," with a lyric by Leo Robin, was so typical of the lilting melodies of Kern's Princess Theatre days that it served as a fitting conclusion to his extraordinary body of works.

Remembrances of Things Past

Also providing charming, usually frivolous insights into the bygone days of show business were the numerous "biographies" of early vaudeville and silent-picture stars and some of Broadway's favorite songwriters. Besides reprising many older tunes, these films also added numerous new songs to the reservoir of hits written expressly for the screen.

The story of the singing Dolly Sisters, for instance, introduced Gordon and Monaco's "I Can't Begin to Tell You"; Frank Loesser's "I Wish I Didn't Love You So" lent a poignant touch to Betty Hutton's madcap performance as Pearl White in *The Perils of Pauline* (she had also played Texas Guinan in 1945's *Incendiary Blonde*). Betty Grable delighted her fans by portraying a leggy chorus girl in *Mother Wore Tights,* a fictionalized account of Broadway's golden olden days that introduced two very good songs by Mack Gordon and composer newcomer Josef Myrow, "You Do" and "Kokomo, Indiana." Gordon and Myrow's score for the super nostalgic *Three Little Girls in Blue* (Vivien Blaine, Vera-Ellen, and June Haver) perfectly complemented the ambience of Atlantic City, that prewar saltwater mecca of tourism and Broadway tryouts. Both "On the Boardwalk in Atlantic City" and

"You Make Me Feel So Young" were immediate hits, as was Warren's "This Is Always."

An arcane piece of business history was recounted in *The Shocking Miss Pilgrim,* with Miss Grable playing her best role as a *fin-de-siècle* secretary-typist (nicknamed "typewriter" at the time). Adding noteworthiness to the film was the nine-song score by George Gershwin, who had died ten years earlier. His composer friend Kay Swift adapted the music from George's manuscripts with the help of brother Ira, who added the lyrics, handing Miss Grable and co-star Dick Haymes three first-rate reminders of George's heyday professionalism: "Changing My Tune," "Aren't You Glad We Did," and "For You, For Me, For Evermore," the latter the equal of any song bearing George's imprimatur.

Then there was Vincente Minnelli's *Ziegfeld Follies.* Assembled in congested variety show format by 36 scriptwriters, the film blended old and new songs ("If You Knew Susie," Freed and Warren's "This Heart of Mine," and Blane and Martin's "Love") with veteran and current entertainers (Victor Moore and Fanny Brice, Lucille Bremer and Lena Horne) in a Technicolor extravaganza that incorporated Fred Astaire's most insinuating dance solo. The song, Douglas Furber and Philip Braham's "Limehouse Blues," had been around since 1924, when it was introduced in *(André) Charlot's Revue,* but Astaire's treatment was contemporary, neatly balancing taps with ballet to superb effect.

The number also emphasized the growing importance of coordinating the visual creativity of the art director and costume designer, in this instance Cedric Gibbons and Helen Rose, with that of the choreographer and cinematographer, Robert Alton and George J. Folsey. Ingenious set design had long been a staple of film musicals in the hands of such master craftsmen as Gibbons, one of America's foremost exponents of Art Deco, and Lyle Wheeler, who designed the incredible nightclub sets for *Garden of Allah* (1936) and several musical pictures.

In *The Ziegfeld Follies,* Astaire's backdrop consists of a surreal reconstruction of London's slummy Limehouse district, replete with fog coiling up from the docks and splashes of blazing red and gold appended to the midnight black sky. Using fans to semaphore his love for a Chinese prostitute, Astaire remains a model of controlled understatement throughout the dance duet, even after Miss Bremer rejects

him. Nor is the busy background, as lavish as any in the MGM repertoire, permitted to detract from the subtle mixture of grace and ex-
oticism seen in this splendid sequence.

Summer Holiday, a musicalized version of *Ah, Wilderness!,* unfolded
lovely movable memoirs of a society that many viewers feared was
forever lost. The film was as pregnant with nostalgia as it was absent
of great tunes, even though it was Harry Warren who contributed
them. His best song, "Spring Isn't Everything," was cut out, but it
became a standard independently. "The Stanley Steamer," one of the
few hit songs with an automobile as the subject, was retained, also
blossoming into a standard.

The year 1947 witnessed one of MGM's toniest remakes, *Good
News,* moviedom's all-time best college reunion, with June Allyson
and Peter Lawford in the roles created by Bessie Love and Cliff Edwards
in the studio's swaddling-clothes 1930 version. A rollicking example of
Hollywood's skill in parlaying clichés into first-class entertainment, it
embraced everything that anyone would hope to encounter on a 1927
campus. The handsome, vain football star is there, and so are an appealing gold digger and sad-eyed assistant librarian trying cheerfully
to work her way through college, the stodgy anti-sports professor of
French, carefree flappers at fraternity parties, Victrolas, ramshackle
roadsters with rumble seats, a protective house mother, and happy-
ever-after ending, all of them wrapped in tinsel.

The picture revived four of the most popular songs to emanate
from the same Broadway musical: "The Best Things in Life Are Free,"
"Lucky in Love," "Just Imagine," and "Varsity Drag." The original
DeSylva, Brown, and Henderson score was expanded to include two
newcomers, Roger Edens's raffish "French Lesson," a minor classic in
linguistics, and the sprightly "Pass That Peace Pipe," an Oscar contender given expert treatment by the multi-talented Joan McCracken,
who had played Sylvie in the original *Oklahoma!*

Superficial tributes to songwriters flourished, beginning with
Rhapsody in Blue, the story of the Gershwins (1945), with Robert Alda,
father of Alan (M*A*S*H) Alda, handing in a superior performance
as George. Also on hand was Hazel Scott, an excellent keyboard artist
whose treatments of "The Man I Love," "Fascinating Rhythm," and
"I Got Rhythm" were worth the price of admission in themselves.
Other "biographies" committed to film were *I Wonder Who's Kissing Her
Now,* with Mark Stevens as songwriter Joseph E. Howard, and *Night*

and Day, with suave Cary Grant in the role of that master purveyor of melody and elegant lyrics, Cole Porter. *Words and Music* (1948), which perfunctorily addressed the career and works of Rodgers (Tom Drake) and Hart (Mickey Rooney), followed in 1948.

These writers' songs were usually performed out of chronological sequence, as were various incidents in their lives, but the films nonetheless earned applause for reprising about 75 of the most memorable songs composed for Broadway and Hollywood. Adding to their favorable impact were the singers and dancers. The studios tapped their top musical stars for countless cameo appearances, and the results were typically outstanding. Ginny Simms did justice to Porter's lyrics, and equally professional was Betty Garrett's rendition of Rodgers and Hart's "There's a Small Hotel," Garland and Rooney's "I Wish I Were in Love Again," and Lena Horne's "Lady Is a Tramp."

But it was *Till the Clouds Roll By,* MGM's monumental 1946 mosaic of events in the life of Jerome Kern, well played by Robert Walker, that walked off with all the honors. Authoritative to a much higher degree than any of its biographical competitors, the film spared no expense, enthusiasm, or expertise in staging the many production numbers, particularly the opening *Show Boat* sequence, packaging the huge cast in gorgeous costumes and granting unlimited permissiveness to director Richard Whorf and choreographer Robert Alton.

Kathryn Grayson and Tony Martin's duet of "Make Believe" is a respectable successor to that of Irene Dunne and Allan Jones in the 1936 *Show Boat.* Martin is also effective with "All the Things You Are," one of the finest of all popular songs. Ironically, it was largely ignored in 1939 because the stage show containing it, *Very Warm for May,* had a disappointing Broadway run of only seven weeks.

Angela Lansbury's singing of "How'd You Like to Spoon with Me?," Kern's first song smash, written in 1906 for a London show, beguilingly reflects insouciance as effectively as Dinah Shore's low-key reprises of "They Didn't Believe Me" and "The Last Time I Saw Paris" remain faithful to the gentleness of the lyrics. June Allyson's singing and dancing to the title tune and "Cleopatterer," with its mounting of love affairs on the pedestal of history in the clever P.G. Wodehouse lyric, are as enjoyable as one could wish.[8]

---

[8] *Judy Garland portrayed Marilyn Miller in this picture, dancing to "Who?" under Vincent Minnelli's direction. In* Look for the Silver Lining *(1949), June Haver played Miss Miller.*

William Warfield's "Ol' Man River" solo, slower in tempo than Paul Robeson's and more intense in delivery, is most creditable. Sinatra's repeat version, sung at the conclusion of the picture, has long been a matter of contention among music buffs. One school maintains that the song is beyond the crooner's range, and that his version therefore suffers in comparison with the bass skills of the black singers whose renditions preceded his. The second verdict holds that Sinatra's baritone is more than adequate to the grinding task of rising above the comparatively limited talent required to sing pop ballads.

As always, Sinatra's pacing is masterful, and the emotions stirred by the powerful Hammerstein lyric lead him dramatically from anger to resignation. His pauses precisely alternate between weariness of spirit and refusal to succumb to eternal depression. The sturdy finale underlines the singer's determination to live, not out of the fear of dying, but to confirm man's eventual triumph over nature's lack of interest in his fate.

Dressing Sinatra in a white tuxedo, manicured head to foot, before a stupendous, equally tailored orchestra was the flaw, and it was one of judgment rather than performance. The song properly belongs to a desperately poor man more worried about survival than appearance. But the truth is that Sinatra's voice never sounded better than in his rendition of this acknowledged classic, which continues to test the virtuosity of the singer bold enough to attempt it.

The Jolson Story was the third biggest movie of the 1947 season, and as of 1991 ranked as the ninth highest grossing film musical of all time. Cast in the leading role was Larry Parks, a veteran of undistinguished B pictures. Jolson himself was assigned to dub the songs, and the result was exceptional. Parks mastered the roguish, roving eyes of his mentor, as well as the stances, shuffles, gestures, and overall bravado that was unique to Jolson the performer. Brother Hirsch Jolson was excluded from the screenplay, but his absence was more than compensated for by the remarkable character actor William Demarest, who had appeared briefly with Jolson 19 years earlier in *The Jazz Singer* as the entertainer's tutor, manager, and lifelong friend.

Jolson was ensconsed in a ten-year career eclipse when the film was in production. His own films were few, and he had been replaced as host of radio's *Kraft Music Hall* by Bing Crosby when the variety show moved from New York City to Hollywood in 1936. But Jolson garnered so much acclaim after the picture's release that his renewed popularity rivaled that of his Winter Garden days of the teens and twenties. Practically all of his major signature songs were reprised, from "Swanee" to "About a Quarter to Nine." He also sings "Anniversary Song," which he wrote with Saul Chaplin based on Ivanovici's "Danube Waves" and interpolated as the serenade to his parents' wedding anniversary.

The picture fades out with the impending dissolution of Jolson's marriage to Ruby Keeler (renamed Julie Benson and played by Evelyn Keyes). He wants to return to performing; she insists that he remain with her in secluded retirement. As drama, *The Jolson Story* has few faults, if one is willing to forgive the omission of Jolson's numerous personality defects. As a musical, however, it is superb, occupying the same plane as *Yankee Doodle Dandy*.

The film's unresolved ending naturally invited a sequel, and along it came in 1949 under the title *Jolson Sings Again,* one of the few second-act movies as good as the first. More sedate than the earlier installment, the followup adheres more closely to biographical facts and brings the entertainer's life up to the 1946 premier of *The Jolson Story*.

The second part also permitted Parks/Jolson to sing a restrained version of "Sonny Boy." Mogul Harry Cohn had excised the song from the first part out of the justifiable fear that its towering presence would overwhelm every other song in the picture. Its appearance in *Jolson Sings Again* was commendable; it stole the show.

But it was supposed to. Temporarily out of public and professional favor, Jolson sings it at a benefit show produced by a man who has to be coerced into letting him appear in it. The bare bones stage set forces the listener to focus attention on the song without the sentimentality of the original setting of 1928's *Singing Fool,* which coupled a Christmas tree and a little boy anxiously seeking solace while hovering at death's door.

Jolson Sings Again was the highest-grossing film in all categories in 1949.

DAY BY DAY

She was born Doris von Kappelhoff, an unmemorable name virtually impossible to letter out on a marquee, but she made it big during

World War II as a vocalist with the Bob Crosby and Les Brown orchestras. In 1948, she entered a fruitful partnership with Warner Bros.' stirred that year into reflexing its attenuated musical comedy muscles, and proved to be the most versatile singing actress between Irene Dunne and Barbra Streisand, and a box office sensation. By then known as Doris Day, she lucked out by being handed a first-class assortment of hit songs by Sammy Cahn, whose lyric for "Day by Day" had inspired her change of surname, and Jule Styne for two of her first three musicals. Cahn's advocacy of Miss Day won her a screen test at Warners and her first film role.

The picture, *Romance on the High Seas,* provided the starlet with "It's Magic," one of the songwriters' best Best Song nominees, as well as "It's You or No One" and the bouncy "Put 'Em in a Box." From *It's a Great Feeling* came the popular title song, another nominee, the lovely ballad "Blame My Absent-Minded Heart," and "Fiddle Dee Dee." Between these two films, Miss Day introduced "My Dream Is Yours" and "Someone Like You," by Blane and Warren, in *My Dream Is Yours,* a respectable remake of Warners' own 1934 hit *Twenty Million Sweethearts,* with Dick Powell and Ginger Rogers. Bits and pieces of 12 earlier Warren melodies were interpolated, including the 1928 novelty "Nagasaki."

Pretty and prim and inevitably groomed to perfection, the photogenic actress in the early fifties was cast as the prototype of Miss America for any year between 1890 and 1920, tightly bodiced, wearing skirts that trailed along the floor, her blonde hair languishing over her shoulders and flashing eyes and smile entrancing her many suitors. Continuing the trend toward reviving song titles to identify their pictures, the moguls starred Miss Day in such lightweight but pleasurable sorties into the past as *Tea for Two,* based ever so slightly on *No, No, Nanette* (1950); *On Moonlight Bay* and *I'll See You in My Dreams* (1951); and *April in Paris* and *By the Light of the Silvery Moon* (1952). The well-recognized songs used for the titles were the headliners among the many standard tunes revived for the pictures. For *Lullaby of Broadway* (1950), Warners even repackaged the production-number treatment given to that Dubin-Warren song, this time with Miss Day and Gene Nelson as the dancing leads, but with far less imagination than Busby Berkeley applied to it in *Gold Diggers of 1935.*

In the mid–1950s, by which time she was being given longer stints to display her dramatic talents, Miss Day sang three more Oscar-nominated songs, bringing to five her total of such songs and tying her with Betty Grable. Her contestants were "Secret Love," "I'll Never Stop Loving You," and "Whatever Will Be, Will Be (Que Sera, Sera)."

Besides Doris Day, the closing years of the 1940s introduced another major, and eventually tragic, talent in the person of Mario Lanza, whose first film, *That Midnight Kiss* (1949), gave ample evidence of the maturation of a once-in-a-generation tenor voice that combined power and sensitivity. Born Alfredo Arnold Cacozza in Philadelphia, the ruggedly handsome, muscular star was blessed with a voice that was termed the "greatest of this century" by no less an authority than conductor Arturo Toscanini. Anyone who heard Lanza's version of "Vesti la Guibba (Put on Your Costume)" in *The Great Caruso* (1951) most likely would accede to the opinion.

Paired with Kathryn Grayson for "Be My Love" in *The Toast of New Orleans,* and with Doretta Morrow for "Because You're Mine" in the picture of the same name, Lanza was equally effective with popular ballads, his voice soaring to operatic heights without overdramatizing the simplicity of the lyrics.

Lanza appeared in a scant seven films up to his death in 1959; only his singing voice was heard in *The Student Prince,* played by Edmund Purdom, in 1954. Lacking the discipline required of an artist, and resentful of efforts to force it on him, Lanza actually lost control of his career by the end of its third year, his talent downgraded by alcohol, barbiturates, and increasing obesity. He died at age 38. In his final film, *For the First Time,* Lanza was reduced, like John Barrymore before him, to a mockery of his former self, in only a few scenes reminding audiences of the magnificent gifts that had earned their respect.

Of far greater significance than the debut of any nascent film star was the movement away from established music to the eccentric pseudo-jazz style known as rhythm and blues, boosted to prominence beginning in 1951 by disk jockey Alan Freed. Seemingly permanent in its influence, the new popular music was popularized by pianist Fats Domino. Along with singing his own songs, once described by jazz authority Hugues Panassie as "indistinguishable one from the other," Domino accompanied himself with an emphatic boogie bass and numerous trills and other freight in the right hand. It was only a matter of time — and not very much of it — before rock and roll would emerge. Elvis Presley's 1956 recording of "Don't Be Cruel" greatly advanced rock and roll and launched Presley into overnight superstardom.

Most of his 31 films, as traditional in storyline and treatment as they were avant-garde in music, were spectacularly popular, although not influential. They augured no revival of original musical comedies, nor did they breed a host of aspirants to follow in his celluloid tracks. In fact, Presley was the last star to appear in an extended series of musicals. His sole competitor was Pat Boone, a clean-cut singer in the Dick Powell image, who appeared in a handful of musicals after 1957. One of them, *State Fair* (1962), was an unremittingly banal revision of the 1945 Fox classic, despite five pleasant additions to his original score by Richard Rodgers, who also wrote the lyrics.

Presley's first film, *Love Me Tender* (1956), co-starred the singer with his most familiar, oldest, and best song, also entitled "Love Me Tender," which from the mid–19th century on had been known as "Aura Lea." His movie career began bottoming out in 1962, when he appeared as a singing boxer loosely patterned on Wayne Morris's role in the 1937 gangster thriller *Kid Galahad.*

Except for Jerry Leiber and Mike Stoller's "Treat Me Nice" (*Jailhouse Rock*) and "Loving You" (*Loving You*), both from 1957; "King Creole" (*King Creole,* 1958) and "Bossa Nova Baby" (*Fun in Acapulco,* 1961); and Sid Wayne and Jerry Livingston's "What a Wonderful Life" (*Follow That Dream,* 1962), none of Presley's pictures produced any new songs of distinction or longevity. What they did was transport the star to various glittering locales, from Hawaii to Las Vegas, New Orleans to New York City, in time periods ranging from the Civil War and the Roaring Twenties to the then-present day. Only three of his films (*It Happened at the World's Fair, Viva Las Vegas, Girl Happy*) indicated the presence of a professional scriptwriter, again underscoring how easily a popular star can surmount his material. Absent from theatrical films for his final eight years, Presley died of a heart attack at age 47 in 1977.

THE FANTASTIC FIFTIES

The 1950s ranks as the major musical decade in film musical history. Those years are still the foremost purveyors of a continuous series of spectaculars that collectively consign most earlier musicals to second-class Hollywood citizenship. Unquestionably the most professionally scripted, designed, choreographed, danced, sung, acted, orchestrated, photographed, edited, and directed, the 1950s musicals still cast the unmistakable glow of glamour on the screen, and stand as permanent tributes to the geniuses who guided them from inception to release.

The beautifully lacquered Technicolor façades of many of them, like *An American in Paris,* voted Best Picture of 1951, and *Funny Face,* have not diminished with time, nor has their ebullient good naturedness. Fighting no philosophical battles, advocating no causes, sponsoring no cultural revolution, the participants were happy to share with viewers the evident joy they took in assembling and appearing in them. Indeed, the period from 1950 to 1958 merits the title of the Golden Age of Film Musicals.

Steeped in sumptuous nostalgia verité, most of them projected the Norman Rockwell innocence of the past into the present. One of their chief purposes was to show that the time lapse between what was being shown on the screen and the real world of the 1950s was negligible. Nothing much had changed. Americans were still an idealistic people whose lives were guided by moral precepts that not even the slaughter of innocence in World War II or the Cold War with the Soviet Union, a former ally in war, could weaken.

The fifties do not, however, deserve to be acclaimed as either *the* or *a* golden age of film *music.* Very few of the pictures displayed originality. Everything they did, and the ways they did it, had been done before; the 1950s musicals simply did everything better, and with enviable consistency. These pictures' glories were mostly the result of advances in movie-making technology and acting competence, although surely no one can deny that the masterminds behind the scenes worked overtime to achieve their stunning results.

The stories were basically tuneful rehashes of earlier successes; unlike the 1930s and 1940s, original songs were almost nonexistent. Where they were present — in such examples as "That's Entertainment" and "A Woman in Love" — they were outshone by reprises of the 200 or so of the greatest standards ever written by the acknowledged masters of the songwriting craft.

The majority of the decade's film musicals fell into three categories: remakes of Broadway shows, more alleged biographies of older-generation show business personalities, and musical adaptations of Hollywood's own earlier dramas and comedies, themselves frequently having originated on the New York stage. All were designed to attract audiences by guiding them into the safe harbor of familiarity. The moguls were content to live in Broadway's substantial shadow by capitalizing on the stage's munificent post–World War II array of blockbuster musicals, which begged for the opportunity to reassert themselves in celluloid. Not that Hollywood overlooked old Broadway; borrowings from Kern, the Gershwins, Romberg, and Friml also served as armatures for dazzling film adaptations (see List #18, "Selected Broadway Song Hits by 10 American Composers").

The Broadway of 1920–40 was represented in such time capsules as *Show Boat* (third film version, 1951); *Lovely to Look At* (based on *Roberta,* 1952); *The Band Wagon* and *The Jazz Singer* (second film version, 1953); *Rose-Marie* (second film version, 1954); *The Student Prince* (second film version, 1954); *Hit the Deck* (second film version, 1955); *Anything Goes* (second film version, 1956); *The Desert Song* (third film version, 1956); *The Vagabond King* (second film version); *Funny Face* (1957); and *Porgy and Bess* (1959).

From 1941 to 1959 Broadway came *Annie Get Your Gun* (1950); *Call Me Madam, Gentlemen Prefer Blondes,* and *Kiss Me Kate* (all 1953); *Brigadoon, New Faces of 1952,* and *Top Banana* (all 1954); *Carmen Jones, Guys and Dolls, Kismet,* and *Oklahoma!* (all 1955); *Carousel* and *The King and I* (both 1956); *The Pajama Game, Pal Joey,* and *Silk Stockings* (all 1957); *South Pacific* and *Damn Yankees* (both 1958); and *Li'l Abner* (1959).

Hollywood also resurrected a few older film dramas and comedies, but with far less ingenuity. The rust that time had visited on many of these early films was irreversible, rendering them almost totally unacceptable to musical adaptation. Indeed, the 1950s spun off a plethora of remakes that rivaled the number made in the 1930s, when producers added sound and new casts to update silent pictures. Most of the 1930s reincarnations were of the highest order; those of the 1950s were poor, suffering badly when compared with the originals.

New versions of Hollywood dramas and comedies, this time bearing mostly undistinguished sprigs of songs, included *Daddy Long Legs* (the Mary Pickford original dated back to 1919, Janet Gaynor's version to 1931); *Let's Do It Again* (based on *The Awful Truth,* the 1938 classic comedy with Cary Grant and Irene Dunne); *My Sister Eileen* (the 1942 version starred Rosalind Russell and Janet Blair); *The Opposite Sex*

Ann Miller and dancing caballeros in *Small Town Girl*, 1953.

(based on *The Women*, 1939); *Small Town Girl* (the original 1936 film starred Janet Gaynor and Robert Taylor); *You're Never Too Young* (a reworking of 1942's *Major and the Minor,* with Ginger Rogers and Ray Milland); *She's Working Her Way Through College* (an inconsequential adaptation of Henry Fonda's *The Male Animal,* 1942).

Of particular interest was *A Star Is Born,* which had its roots in *What Price Hollywood,* the 1931 drama with Constance Bennett as a waitress turned motion picture star, and the 1937 Janet Gaynor–Fredric March Technicolor classic. Judy Garland's tour de force performance as Mrs. Norman Maine in the 1954 version was not only the high-water mark in her own acting career, but also the finest performance by an actress in a film musical. The story of her rise from small-band singer to Oscar-winning actress would have carried the film without any songs at all. Luckily, the inestimable Ira Gershwin and Harold Arlen provided a first-class score that included "It's a New World," "Here's What I'm Here For," and "The Man That Got Away."

For the "Born in a Trunk" interlude in *A Star Is Born* (1954), Judy Garland also sang several standard songs. One was Irving Caesar and George Gershwin's "Swanee," written in 1918, which she performed while wearing top hat, black tie, and tails.

Miss Garland's finest vocalizing is heard in Leonard Gershe's unforgettable "Born in a Trunk." The scenes accompanying the song bear more than slight resemblance to Gene Kelly's dashed-hopes visits to theatrical agents in "The Broadway Melody" number in *Singin' in the Rain*, but everything else about the sequence is original. And Judy out–Garlands herself—a pretty difficult task to begin with—in the conclusion to the song. Her struggle to enter show business has succeeded; she is on the brink of stardom. Eyes flashing, hands pumping the air to connote her victory, she completes her singing autobiography by asserting the value of perseverance as practiced by a stubborn little gamine-turned-woman who was "born in a trunk" in a theater in Idaho. This was to be Miss Garland's finest musical hour, and one of the great moments recorded on film.

A second wondrous translation was *High Society,* the 1956 reworking of *The Philadelphia Story,* first filmed in 1940. Although Crosby, Sinatra, Grace Kelly, and Celeste Holm gave Cary Grant, James Stewart, Katharine Hepburn, and Ruth Hussey a run for the money, the earlier cast was superior. What *High Society* added to the Philip Barry stage-based comedy was the best score that Cole Porter wrote for the screen. The songs ranged from the ultra-romantic ("True Love," "I Love You, Samantha," and "Mind If I Make Love to You") to the upbeat ("Now You Has Jazz" and "Well, Did You Evah?," the latter of which had been dropped from Porter's score for *Panama Hattie* in 1939) to the sophisticated ("You're Devastating"). There is not a mundane song in the picture, something that cannot be claimed for any other Porter film.

Harry Warren's final Academy Award–nominated song, "An Affair to Remember," appeared in the 1957 Cary Grant–Deborah Kerr picture with the same title, a superior recreation of Charles Boyer and Irene Dunne's *Love Affair,* released in 1939. The original version also contained an Oscar contender, "Wishing (Will Make It So)," qualifying the film as the first of only two pairs based on the same story to contain a Best Song nominee. The second were the 1954 and 1976 versions of *A Star Is Born.*

"There Goes That Song Again"

Biographies of musical stars and songwriters unfolded as never before: *Three Little Words* (Bert Kalmar and Harry Ruby, and Debbie Reynolds as Helen Kane); *I'll See You in My Dreams* (with Danny Thomas as lyricist Gus Kahn); *The I Don't Care Girl* (Eva Tanguay); *Stars and Stripes Forever* (John Philip Sousa); *So This Is Love* (Grace Moore); *I Dream of Jeanie* (Stephen Foster); *St. Louis Blues* (W.C. Handy); *With a Song in My Heart* (Jane Froman); *I'll Cry Tomorrow*

(Lillian Roth); *Love Me or Leave Me* (Ruth Etting); *Deep in My Heart* (Sigmund Romberg); *The Joker Is Wild* (nightclub singer-entertainer Joe E. Lewis); *The Eddie Cantor Story, The Gene Krupa Story, The Benny Goodman Story, The Glenn Miller Story, The Eddy Duchin Story,* and *The Helen Morgan Story; The Five Pennies* (with Danny Kaye as jazz in-strumentalist Loring "Red" Nichols); and *The Best Things in Life Are Free* (DeSylva, Brown, and Henderson), all released between 1950 and 1959.

One exceptional biography, *Hans Christian Andersen* (1952), starred Danny Kaye in his finest role as the Danish teller of fairy tales. Frank Loesser, by then writing both words and music, supplied the songs, and a sparkling collection they turned out to be. "The Inch Worm," carrying one of the most imaginative of Hollywood lyrics, never became a hit, but three of the other seven songs did: "Thumbalina," an Oscar nominee; "No Two People"; and "Wonderful Copenhagen." For *Knock on Wood* two years later, his wife, Sylvia Fine, a gifted writer of patter songs, like "Anatole of Paris" and "Soliloquy for Three Heads," gave Kaye the very pretty "All About You."

Films with standard songs as their titles included *My Blue Heaven,* among the first film musicals with a television background, *Pagan Love Song,* and *I'll Get By* (all 1950); *The Love Nest, Painting the Clouds with Sunshine,* and *The Daughter of Rosie O'Grady* (all 1951); *Singin' in the Rain* (1952); *Down Among the Sheltering Palms* and *Easy to Love* (both 1953); *There's No Business Like Show Business, The Last Time I Saw Paris,* and *White Christmas* (all 1954); *Ain't Misbehavin'* (1955); *That Certain Feeling* (1956); and *Slaughter on Tenth Avenue* (1957).

The praise showered on *Singin' in the Rain* over the past four decades is totally deserved. The Comden-Green plot would have been suitable for a non-musical comedy. The dialogue and incidents not only are amusing in themselves, but also recapture Hollywood's early talking-picture turmoil with a sardonic but friendly tone that borders on the miraculous.

Likewise, the Arthur Freed–Nacio Herb Brown songs were per-formed better than ever before or since. Gene Kelly's waterlogged um-brella dance to the title tune is wondrous, requiring neither a chorus nor elaborate sets to give zest and fascination to the solo from start to finish. If any flaw can be laid at the picture's door, it is the inclusion of "Make 'Em Laugh," which in melody and philosophy bears too heavy a resemblance to Cole Porter's "Be a Clown," from *The Pirate* (1948).

Fred Astaire (as lyricist Bert Kalmar) and Vera-Ellen performing "Mr. and Mrs. Hoofer at Home" in *Three Little Words,* 1950.

Not so for composer Brown's only other new song, "Moses Supposes (His Toeses Are Roses, But Moses Supposes Erroneously)." Comden and Green's lyric qualifies as unequalled nonsensical pitter-patter, happily complementing the eccentric dance duet by Kelly and Donald O'Connor. Only one song in the vast score was not by Brown, "Fit as a Fiddle," which Freed wrote with Al Hoffman and Al Goodhart in 1932.

Kathryn Grayson, as opera-movie star Grace Moore, in *So This Is Love*, 1953, only one of the decade's numerous filmed "biographies" of entertainers.

There's No Business Like Show Business, the title of Irving Berlin's *Annie Get Your Gun* salute to performers, remains notable for Marilyn Monroe's appearance as a showgirl. More actress than singer and dancer, she repeated her earlier role as an ingenue flirt in *Gentlemen Prefer Blondes* and *How to Marry a Millionaire* in 1953. Dietrich was sultrier, West wiser, and Harlow slinkier. Monroe had only a subconscious awareness of her vast sexual attractiveness. She was genuinely amazed when men responded vigorously to it, retreating like a little girl into shyness. Lamentably, *Business* was her last musical. Producers simply ignored her potential for developing into one of musical comedy's best practitioners since the 1930s.

Naturally, Hollywood's 1950s obsession with outclassing Broadway was influenced greatly by the increasing popularity of the movies' most potent competitor. President Roosevelt himself had appeared in the first scheduled telecast in 1939, when he spoke at the opening of the New York World's Fair on April 30. But it was in November 1950 that the rivalry between theatrical films and television heated up. That month CBS Television produced the first full-length TV movie, the 53-minute *Three Musketeers,* on *The Magnavox Theater.*

Songs and spectacle on film had helped to ween the previous generation from vaudeville and the radio. The moguls fully expected them to pose a formidable threat to the new entertainment medium, most of whose offerings were patently amateurish and unglamorous, sans color, sans original songs, sans the star power of Hollywood's household names, sans the visual excitement of intricate ensemble dancing.

Up to 1955, the Hollywood film was clearly the winner. But television had made striking professional advancements, including the use of three cameras to film *I Love Lucy* episodes, which permitted television shows to be continuously filmed in sequence before live audiences, giving them a stagelike aura. The new setup, installed by master cinematographer Karl Freund, was also responsible in large measure for TV reruns, which added still more punch to the knockout blows television was dealing to theatrical films.

"Too Late Now"

Adding to the mid-decade decline of film musicals was the fact that Hollywood had just about fished out Broadway's waters. Then, too, the contract songwriters were understandably unable to maintain the level of hit productivity that had distinguished their contributions over the previous 20 years. So the industry foraged through its substantial bag of tricks and resuscitated its oldest: experimentation.

The short-lived flirtation with "3-D," or the three-dimensional projection of mostly second-rate films (except *Kiss Me Kate*), filled the screen with objects leaping mysteriously into the audience when viewed through polaroid glasses. The novelty wore off within two years of its debut. Such wide-screen processes as Cinerama, Cinema-Scope, and VistaVision enjoyed longer popularity, even though the concept was anything but new. The conclusion of *The Big Trail* and *All Quiet on the Western Front* had provided notable 1930s examples of Magnascope, which also enlarged the images by using a special lens to project them. Because so many theater screens were too small to accept such magnification, Magnascope saw little service. But it was a worthy forerunner of CinemaScope, first used by 20th Century-Fox for *The Robe* in 1953.

For the most part, original musical screenplays were relatively few, and their impact on the box office alternated from tepid to cool. Some of the songs, like "I Can See You" and "Wonder Why," were as tuneful as ever; many of the lyrics were, in a word, brilliant. But the public was being sung to death, and a substantial percentage preferred the couch and cookie-box screen to the neighborhood movie house.

Accommodating the worldwide interest in the wedding pageant of Princess Elizabeth of England and Philip Mountbatten was *A Royal Wedding* (1951), with Astaire, Jane Powell, and Sarah Churchill, the daughter of the doughty British prime minister. The seven excellent songs by Alan Jay Lerner and Burton Lane included the popular ballad "Too Late Now" and the superlative wedding song, "The Happiest Day of My Life." "You're All the World to Me," which carries the same melody as Lane's "I Want to Be a Minstrel Man," and "Every Night at Seven," were the show-stopping dance numbers. The delightful nod to vaudeville, "How Could You Believe Me When I Said I Loved You When You Know I've Been a Liar All My Life?," holds distinction as one of the longest song titles in popular music history.

One of Harry Warren's best later scores brightened the Bing Crosby–Jane Wyman musical *Just for You.* The title tune turned into a hit ballad; "I'll Si-Si Ya in Bahia," "Zing a Little Zong," "On the 10:10 (From Ten-Ten-Tennesee)," and, above all, "The Live Oak Tree" were happy additions to the composer's catalog. His "Hey, Marty!" lent a lively backdrop to *Marty* (1954), which traced the ups and downs in the love life of an ugly ducking Bronx butcher; "That's Amore," Dean Martin's best-known film song, earned Warren his tenth Oscar nomination.

Warren, with Johnny Mercer, was also responsible for the appetizing tidbits performed by Astaire and Vera-Ellen in *The Belle of New York,* a superlatively tuneful 1952 over-the-shoulder glance at old New York, complete with a series of picture-postcard views of the lithographic art of (Nathaniel) Currier and (James Merritt) Ives, as designed and costumed prettily by Cedric Gibbons and Jack Martin Smith, and Edwin B. Willis and Richard Pefferle, respectively. "Baby Doll," actually composed in 1945, provided the catchy backdrop for the best of the two stars' dances, while "Naughty But Nice" verified the triple-threat talent of Vera-Ellen as singer, dancer, and actress. Astaire's soft-shoe to "I Wanna Be a Dancing Man" was sheer perfection.

Gene Nelson, Jane Powell, Gordon MacRae, and Jack E. Leonard in *Three Sailors and a Girl*, 1953. Photo courtesy of *Movie Star News*.

"When I'm Out with the Belle of New York" and "Oops" rounded out what was unfortunately to be Warren's final hit screen score. He continued to write songs, among them 12 for 3 Paramount films starring Jerry Lewis, whose gratuitous mugging and totally inadequate singing voice drained them of all melody and feeling, with the single exception of the lullaby "Dormi, Dormi, Dormi."

Other Hollywood-written 1950s musicals achieved scant distinction from either story or score. *Nancy Goes to Rio*, *Three Sailors and a Girl*, and *Two Weeks with Love* (all 1950); *Texas Carnival* (1951); *I Love Melvin* and *Give a Girl a Break* (both 1953); *Red Garters* (1954); the *Cinderella*-based *Glass Slipper* and *It's Always Fair Weather* (both 1955); *Happy Go Lovely*, *Let's Be Happy*, *The Girl Most Likely*, and Cole Porter's *Les Girls* (all 1957); and *Say One for Me* (1959) revolved around moss-covered plots, and most of the music evaporated along with other reminders of the pictures.

One exception was *Seven Brides for Seven Brothers* (1954), featuring a solid, if not popular, score by Johnny Mercer and Gene DePaul, and performances by Howard Keel, Jane Powell, and Russ Tamblyn.

It was the dancing, however, that isolated the film from its run-of-the-mill competitors, acrobatic, original, and executed with a rare blend of virility and gracefulness.

Another standout, based on a 1944 novella by Colette, was molded into the best 1950s musical with an original score by producer Freed and director Minnelli. The cast for *Gigi* was perfection: Leslie Caron in the title role, Louis Jourdan as the regenerative roué, and Maurice Chevalier and Hermione Gingold as the young-at-heart geriatric lovers. The Lerner–Frederick Loewe score supplied all the major participants with at least one popular song: the Oscar-winner "Gigi" to Jourdan, "The Night They Invented Champagne" (Miss Caron), "Thank Heaven for Little Girls" and "I'm Glad I'm Not Young Anymore" (Chevalier), and that most touching of ballads to aging, "I Remember It Well," shared by Chevalier and Miss Gingold. Add to the song list the decade's best original film waltz, "She Is Not Thinking of Me," and *Gigi* rises to the pinnacle of MGM musicals, past, present, and (quite possibly) future.

Why such an excellent and lucrative film failed to coax Hollywood into a new round of musical activity remains a mystery. Perhaps the moguls secretly admitted that nothing they could do would equal its many superior qualities. More likely, it was an admission that the era of the film musical was nearing its end. It had enjoyed a good run of almost three decades, a most respectable span in the entertainment industry. Appropriately, *Gigi* permitted the genre to dissolve in grand and glorious style.

THE STUNTED SIXTIES

The demise of the film musical quickened in the first half of the 1960s, even though music retained its prominent role in motion picture production. What Hollywood did was shift focus from billets-doux sung by lovers and danced by choruses to the action and atmosphere of dramatic and adventure pictures, increasingly pervading them with background scores dotted with theme songs that, when removed from the context of the films, reached astonishing heights of popularity.

The quality and variety of the theme songs, together with the highly professional orchestrations behind them, combined to enrich motion pictures both artistically and emotionally. No longer was music inserted merely to give audiences hummable melodies, although a good number of theme songs ("Emily," "Faraway Part of Town," "Second Chance," "So Little Time") qualified in that regard. Integrated into the plots with unparalleled precision, the 1960s background scores soon displaced once and for all Hollywood's practice of using similar snatches of melody to direct viewers into responding properly to the emotions expressed by the characters on the screen.

Many of the earliest sound pictures depended on hundreds of stock musical compositions neatly cataloged in cabinets and labeled to facilitate the task of writing mood music. All that a composer like Vernon Duke had to do was pull out the drawer marked Anger, Hysteria, Seduction, Passion, or Chase, and he was in business. He would often alter the melody slightly and modify the harmonic structure to prevent accusations of plagiarism, yet remain "as close to the original as possible." The practice continued for years, especially for scoring B pictures and newsreels. Even Duke conceded that the music library served a purpose. It was a "great boon in my Paramount days, when I was in a hurry and had to turn out music by the yard," he wrote in his autobiography, *Passport to Paris.*

That background music was the new pathway to songwriting success has been confirmed to such a degree that one can say without qualification that without theme songs, motion pictures over the past 35 years would have produced only a scattering of hit songs. In 1950, four of the five Oscar song nominees came from musical pictures; in 1953, three did, but in 1956 only one. From 1957 through 1965, 6 of the 45 nominees were introduced in a musical. Of the 123 Best Song contenders between 1966 and 1991, 13 appeared in the 12 pictures with at least 50 percent original songs. By contrast, 10 of the 14 nominees in 1945 made their debut in musical films.

The significant impact of background scores on films and popular music obviously did not originate overnight in 1960s Hollywood. The 1928-29 films proved that music need not be confined to musicals, but can enhance any classification of film. So commonplace did wall-to-wall sound tracks become in subsequent years that the most curious feature of the drama *Executive Suite,* released in 1954, was its almost total lack of music, even during the rolling of the credits. Except for about two minutes of music from the chimes of a furniture factory, an unseen pianist at the Stork Club, and a radio, not another note is heard throughout the picture's 105 minutes.

Dimitri Tiomkin's *High Noon* theme ("Do Not Forsake Me") high-lighted the 1952 Gary Cooper Western. Tex Ritter's nasal voice-over rendition perfectly complemented the no-frills starkness of the film, while Ned Washington's lyric abetted the suspense by foreshadowing key elements of the plot during the presentation of the credits.

Succeeding Washington-Tiomkin themes distinguished such non-musical films as *Wild Is the Wind, War Wagon, The High and the Mighty, Town Without Pity, The Alamo,* and *Return to Paradise* and attained additional stature by developing into popular songs. Victor Young's themes for *Shane* ("Eyes of Blue"), *Strategic Aid Command* ("The World Is Mine"), *Around the World in 80 Days,* and *Written on the Wind* are as beautiful as any written for the films. So were Bronislaw Kaper's "Drifting," the *Auntie Mame* background waltz; Frederick Hollander's ballet music for *The 5,000 Fingers of Dr. T,* and Elmer Bernstein's "Lovers' Gold," written for the 1958 remake of Cecil B. DeMille's 20-year-old *Buccaneer,* with Yul Brynner essaying the Fredric March part as the patriotic pirate Jean Lafitte.

Also of interest were Bernstein's theme from *The Rat Race,* "Monica" (*The Carpetbaggers*), and "Monique" (*Kings Go Forth*). His "Walk on the Wild Side" deservedly won Academy nomination in 1962, and his rousing theme for *The Magnificent Seven* has taken its place alongside Ernest Gold's "Exodus Song" as one of the movies' best-remembered themes.

Evans and Livingston's "Angela" (*Night of the Grizzly*), Morris Stoloff's "To Love Again" (*The Eddie Duchin Story*), Max Steiner's theme for *A Summer Place,* and Chaplin's "Eternally" or "The Terry Theme" (*Limelight*) are other examples of first-rate movie music, along with Alfred Newman's "Best of Everything" and love theme from *The Robe.* George W. Dunning's theme for *Picnic,* with words contributed later by comedian Steve Allen, blended so smoothly into "Moonglow," the familiar 1934 standard by Will Hudson, Eddie deLange, and Irving Mills, that recollections of that forgettable 1956 film are confined to the two songs and Kim Novak's brief, sexy solo dance.

James Van Heusen easily fell into writing pleasant themes, most carrying Sammy Cahn lyrics, such as "Wake Me When It's Over" and the love theme from *The World of Suzie Wong,* both 1960; "The Boys' Night Out" (1962); "Under the Yum-Yum Tree" and "My Six Loves" (both 1963); and "Where Love Has Gone" (1964), lending distinction to otherwise minor comedies and dramatic films.

Henry Mancini's wraparound background music, which included "Moon River," for the offbeat 1962 comedy *Breakfast at Tiffany's* was one of the most intricate and lyrical instrumentals of the decade. Charles B. Williams's "Key to Love," from *The Apartment* (1960), composed 15 years earlier, David Raksin's "Sylvia" (1964), Miklos Rozsa's "Falcon and the Dove" (1961), and Frank DeVol's "Hush, Hush, Sweet Charlotte" (1965) likewise contributed nobly to the growing statue of theme song composition.

The most active theme song writing team consisted of veteran composer Sammy Fain and lyricist Paul Francis Webster. Fain had written his first screen songs in 1929; Webster began his film career in 1935. Among the most poetic of lyricists, Webster found the ideal partner in Fain, and their songs basked in the sunshine of popularity and prestige from the 1950s into the 1970s.

Two of their songs, "Secret Love" and "Love Is a Many-Splendored Thing," won the Academy Award, while five others were nominated—"April Love," "A Certain Smile," "A Very Precious Love," "Tender Is the Night," and "Strange Are the Ways of Love." Webster was nominated seven more times for songs written with other composers, among them the superlative "Shadow of Your Smile," the 1965 Oscar winner, with music by Johnny Mandel.

Meanwhile, the teenage craze for sand, surf, and skimpy swimsuits, exemplified by the smarmy *Bikini Beach* (1964), defined the new wave of stupefying dullness better than any musical film of the 1960s. As if that Frankie Avalon picture were not sufficient to show how defective Hollywood musicals had become, along came *When the Boys Meet the Girls* (1965), an anemic Connie Francis remake of *Girl Crazy* that achieved the impossible by turning Louis Armstrong into driftwood, bleached of any vestige of his enormous talent. At the opposite end of the artistic scale were the Beatles' *Hard Day's Night* (1964) and *Help!* (1965). These films also catered to the youth market but with engaging original music and scripts rich in inventiveness that reached their climax in the singing quartet's *Yellow Submarine* in 1968.

BROADWAY BORROWINGS

Except for the ever-glorious *Sound of Music,* the 1960s Broadway-to-Hollywood transfers are of only transient interest. Stephen Sondheim and Leonard Bernstein's *West Side Story* (1962) was a most respectable, if gritty, translation with a contemporary setting that skillfully updated the *Romeo and Juliet* story to 1950s ghetto New York. Together with the music, the cinematography earned most of the film's accolades, even though the dramatic picture-opening downward view of the towers of Manhattan, rising like stalagmites from a bedrock of schist, had been used 33 years earlier at the beginning of *The Broadway Melody.* Unfortunately, *West Side Story* bore no offspring of equal caliber, and so must rank as an uninfluential but deeply satisfying curiosity.

Other rare successes were Rodgers and Hammerstein's *Flower Drum Song* (1961) and *The Music Man* (1962), thanks to the Meredith Willson songs and Robert Preston, who reprised his stage role as Professor Harold Hill. For Lerner and Loewe's *My Fair Lady* (1964), Audrey Hepburn displaced Julie Andrews as Eliza Doolittle, but Rex Harrison survived the realignment of the original stage cast of this most literate musicalized version of Shaw's *Pygmalion.* Clearly, the songs, almost all of them hits, were so well known by the time the film came out that they no longer commanded the rapturous attention that had welcomed them to Broadway in 1956.

But under the superior direction of George Cukor, *Lady* fared wealthily at the box office, helped immeasurably by Stanley Holloway's acting and spirited rendition of "Get Me to the Church on Time." The strong script also helped, giving *Lady* far more plot interest than, say, the earlier landmark *Oklahoma!*, which, when all was said and done, revolved totally around the unsuspenseful question of who's going to take Laurey to the box social.

Far more numerous were the fair-to-middling, like *The Bells Are Ringing* (1960), a stupendous bore despite Judy Holliday and such Comden-Green-Styne songs as "Just in Time" and "The Party's Over." Equally inept were E.Y. Harburg and Burton Lane's *Finian's Rainbow* (1968), notwithstanding the presence of Fred Astaire in his last film musical, and *Jumbo*, notwithstanding the lovely sounds of the 1935 Rodgers and Hart score.

It was in *The Sound of Music* in 1965 that stage star Julie Andrews made an indelible mark on films, although she, too, displaced the star who had originated the role of Maria on Broadway, Mary Martin. Complete with stunning scenery and a refreshing alfresco ambience, the film soared above the stage version, proving again that the very best of Hollywood musicals are indeed capable of improving on their sources. Although composer Rodgers considered *Carousel* to be his all-time best musical, *The Sound of Music* made a far better film and, song by song, its score is better known. Nine of the songs are standards, a record among Broadway musicals. None of them was more simple or beautiful than "Edelweiss," a song sometimes mistakenly identified as the Austrian national anthem. The finest film musical ever, *Music* still ranked first among American musical pictures in gross box office receipts and fifth among all American films, regardless of category, as recently as 1991.

As *The Sound of Music* illustrated, Hollywood had not lost its magical musical touch. What was disappearing was the audience that for decades had appreciated it. Only a few years after its release, the traditional song-and-dance spectacle was obsolete.

CHAPTER ELEVEN

Fadeout: 1966–1991

*T*HE 25 YEARS between 1966 and 1991 witnessed cataclysmic shifts in the content and visual presentation of American films. All were significant, a few were profound, and each in its own way contributed to the crumbling of the musical comedy infrastructure. The principles that had guided filmmaking for decades were displaced by a realism so inimical to musical pictures that they dwindled down to a not-so-precious few.

The motion picture camera was transformed into an x-ray machine, its meticulous dissecting of human relationships almost totally eliminating the grace and charm that one might wish to remember with fondness. As addicted to the trite as were their forebears, directors littered the film landscape with blood, sex, and profanity, sending angry reminders that all was not well with an America newly transformed into one huge stage of violence.

Reprieveless buddy-cop partnership melodramas bulged with corpses and chase scenes on wheels that ended in slow-motion crashes through plate glass windows. Flaunting the detritus of thousands of lives, big cities were pictured as virtual police states, homes as safe deposit vaults. Superhuman champions of law and order became avengers, acting as judge, jury, and executioner. Using their screenplays as Baedekers to post–1966 times and tastes, plotmakers consistently taught the lesson that an Uzi or a bomb was the most effective and fastest means of solving problems. Sequels were so common that pictures bearing the same titles had to be numbered.

Equally commonplace were stylishly ambiguous dramas that left no human degradation unplumbed and manifestos of grievances, real and assumed, that appealed to a culture separated into tribes, each deriving pleasure from what it saw through the prism of its own special interests. Romances pandered to voyeurism in the inevitable bedroom scene, while tales of scrofulous serial murderers, monsters, and mutants made such maladroit exploitative 1950s films as *Teen-Age Cave Man, Blood of Dracula,* and *The Brain Eaters* look like the kindergarten-level scare shows they were. Dispiriting depictions of alienation vitiated the spirit of social and family compatibility during stressful times, trivializing by repetition a basic human tragedy.

It was obvious that at a time when fear and cynicism had successfully routed optimism, no filmmaker with his or her wits would consider competing in the marketplace with another *Gold Diggers* or *Broadway Melody.* Songs and stories advocating sexual abstinence till the wedding night were outdated, along with innocence and subtlety, the two chief bulwarks that had held the traditional musical film in place for more than 30 years. The largely harmonious, ever-cheerful movie universe of the 1929–65 period dissolved without a whimper, a victim of the growing disdain for accepting backlot fantasy as a means of evading the depressingly large assortment of social ills demanding real-world remedies.

As rock music displaced escapist ballads on radio and records, Hollywood producers recognized the imperative of giving it a prominent role in their repackaged musicals or dispensing with the genre altogether. Status quo music had become an endangered species by the late 1950s because of decreasing originality of both lyrics and melody. As its successor, early rock and its spinoffs (including hard rock, funk, country rock, progressive rock, jazz rock, and sweet soul) smashingly reinvigorated box office revenues for the comparatively short list of filmed extravaganzas released between the early 1970s and the late 1980s.

By departing so completely from the past, however, the new music became a major force in revamping the movie musical format. The mass of the songs underscored the values — transitional rather than traditional — of adolescents continually in conflict with authority and pressured to conform to a code of conduct far different from that of their elders. Although tunes were still being written solely to entertain, far fewer than ever before sought to uplift. Hope rarely sprang from the lyrics, many of them serving instead as angry or morose ruminations by self-centered characters on the inability to cope with life's disappointments.

An estimated 98 percent of all American songs have dealt with love, be it for a person, a specific locality, or the flag and country. Rock tunes did carry on that tradition, though rarely with eloquence or restraint. Some songwriters specialized in praising youthful sexual gratification, making even more unfashionable the ritual of courtship and marriage that had animated the Golden Age lovers. Certainly, Cole Porter and Lorenz Hart were not shy about ventilating the pleasures of passionate love, but the stimulation of the pursuit and the thrill of the conquest were insinuated rather than proclaimed. Getting there was half the fun, their lyrics implied.

By diluting the romance in romantic songs, rock writers inevitably imbued the words of such older ballads as "May I Have the Next Romance with You?" and "Let's Take the Long Way Home" with a quaintness that defined irrelevancy. Gradually, these and the hundreds of other plea-bargaining petitions once issued by distraught on-screen male lovers spoke to ever-declining numbers of listeners.

For one thing, the lyrics were customarily literate. Composer Van Heusen, a lifelong exponent of grammatical correctness, for example, refused to work with any lyricist who ignored the rules "unless the tune depended on dialect or slang for humorous purposes." For another, the lyrics were to be clearly heard, not drowned out by the thundering instrumental background that typically accompanied contemporary soloists and group singers. The thumps of electrified guitars further detracted from vocal and musical harmony by provoking spasms of exhibitionism among members of the rock ensemble, exemplified by Madonna in her 1991 concert tour documentary (or "rockumentary"), *Truth or Dare,* Paul McCartney in *Get Back,* and the aging Rolling Stones in *At the Max.*

To the earliest Hollywood lyricists, a simple kiss from a decidedly unflirtatious lady was a major achievement worth celebrating in song ("A Kiss to Build a Dream On"). The idealistic suitor was compelled to admit that making the lady his own would be as gratifying as finding heaven on earth ("Cheek to Cheek"). His goddess was equipped with eyes, usually blue, that sparkled like diamonds in the sky ("Star Eyes"); her hair, usually blonde, shone like the summer sun ("I Used to Be Color Blind"); her cheeks resembled roses ("It's Always You"). Her glorious presence was enough to enthrall him ("Lovely to Look At"), even if the sight later plunged him into self-denigration ("A Sinner Kissed an Angel").

Essentially a defense mechanism, the conventional musical permitted swarms of moviegoers to fend off the intrusion of a complex, unkind outside world. It never mattered to the refugees that their favorites of both sexes, easy on the eye and ear, were unrepresentative of the population, that their fairyland misadventures were insignificant, and that the entire cast functioned in an insular Anglo-Saxon society as devoid of racial diversity as it was of defeatism. The implied philosophical lesson of the pictures was that the performers deserved admiration for embodying the values that the ordinary Jacks and Jills sitting in the dark had been taught from childhood were superior to those of any other culture.

As the swirl of post–1966 events motivated many young Americans into activism, the music they preferred began covering instead of skirting the waterfront of national and international crises. The Vietnam War loomed as a major cause célèbre, along with racial and gender discrimination, the decaying environment, and the plight of the lower economic classes. Only occasionally did the mostly confrontational songs savor humanity's triumphs, preferring to concentrate on its inconsistencies.

One significant result of focusing so sharply on youngsters' ceaseless demand for songs of social commentary was a reversal of the relative rank of the composer and lyricist. Melody, formerly the more commanding element in popular music, was frequently relegated to the back burner of creativity. It was the words, after all, that carried the message, and spreading it had been the main purpose for writing the song. If above-average composers happened to be available to supply the music, so much the better. But they were really not needed. The lyrics were sufficient to the task of stirring the emotions.

No musical offshoot has illustrated the primacy of words over music better than the rap song, which owed its increasing popularity to the rappers' formidable skill at threatening society with violence while urging the ghetto disenfranchised into self-improvement. An effective expansion of the once-playful patter song, rap uniquely explored the debilitating effects of poverty and the resentment aroused by the failure of public and private efforts to eradicate it.

The pornographic film, in the past confined to seedy theaters in the saltier parts of town, began playing at respectable urban houses in 1976. If through rear and frontal nudity the *First Nudie Musical* did not make a total mockery of the once-honored art form it proposed to satirize, it certainly attempted to do so. Filled with abysmal acting, dancing dildos, hackneyed dialogue, and throwaway jokes and songs, it gauged the depth to which the film musical had fallen by ingloriously repeating the most overworked of plots.

This time it revolves around the struggles of a neophyte director (Bruce Kimmel) to make a film musical amid a gaggle of cranky performers and hoodlum backers who demand that he complete it in two weeks — or else. In the tradition of *42nd Street,* the ingenue (Cindy Williams) lands the feminine lead, and the director to boot, and the film project succeeds.

Far too amateurish to offend, *Nudie* probed the nadir of post–1965 musical films. Even such a pleasant pastiche as 1987's groin-grinding *Dirty Dancing,* far more professional than *Nudie,* would have been relegated to the slums, despite its PG-13 rating, in the 1929–65 period.

To compare the 1930s screen children with their 1980s descendants is to discover the extent to which Hollywood has abandoned the crusading zeal for which the Depression youngsters were noted. Rarely have the newcomers plied their charm and tricks to reform anything; whatever ideals they may have stood for were drained of content, as if all problems had disappeared or were incapable of solution.

Drew Barrymore, in such a film as *Firestarter* (1984), and her generation still prevailed over crises cooked up by directors like Frank Capra, Jr., and Steven Spielberg. But the world they inhabited was that of the occult, far beyond the purview of their audiences, who merely gasped at the young performers' supernatural powers. Like their elders in *Cocoon,* the children retreated into the ultimate escapism, often finding friendship and love with extraterrestrial creatures rather than with fellow humans. By opting to get off the planet altogether, they reflected the widespread disenchantment with a cruel environment incapable of improvement, and against which neither young nor old had any defense.

If the Depression children were often too good to be true, those reared over the past five years have been too obnoxious to be tolerated. The youngsters in the two *Problem Child* films (admittedly an extreme example) were presented in the worst possible light as simple-minded delinquents with malice toward all. With no songs in their hearts, they committed mayhem on adults and shared their crude jokes; Michael Oliver, as the spiteful Junior Healy, even urinates in a pitcher of lemonade.

Meanwhile, adult characters in recent movies have often been depicted as either hostile or helpless, both roles antithetical to musical pictures. Those films' systemic cheerfulness and surmounting of misfortune no longer could be expected to please, even as occasional departures from regular film fare. To the despair of romantics, movie musicals have been unable to reconcile their past with the present; by the mid–1970s the few new ones wandered in an artistic Sinai, either pathetically unresponsive to contemporary tastes or descending into misguided lampoonery, foreshadowed in 1971 by the uninspired *Boy Friend.* (Far better as satire was *Movie Movie* 1978, the second half of it a rollicking burlesque of *42nd Street,* with George C. Scott as the harassed producer.)

"THE AGE OF NOT BELIEVING"

The first tendrils of realism became visible in the dramatic films of the early 1940s, although they only dipped rather than immersed viewers in it. But the moguls stonewalled when it came to revising the tone or theme of their musical pictures, fearing that any concession they might make would only warp the veneer of the lighthearted innocence they wanted to preserve. Music still escorted lovers wherever they went. Although such a convenience is acceptable in a Broadway theater, where the pit orchestra is in sight, even the most fervent film fans shook their heads at the sound of still another ballad looming up from a deserted street or park. Authenticity of plot, characterization, and dialogue, greatly abetted by the on-location settings for dramas, militated against further acceptance of musical comedy's artificiality. Nor did any viewer really care any longer whether the boy's show would be staged, whether his girlfriend would star in it, or whether they would cement their relationship at the end by sharing a song.

In only one area of musical films has realism been admitted, with the results typically positive. The eschewal of fiction and gloss in biographies of entertainers brought to recent pictures a credibility unmatched by their predecessors. No longer did they simply record the succession of triumphs that transformed the brash hopeful into the polished performer, with scant attention paid to the ruthlessness that most show business climbers have encountered from time immemorial.

In 1950, *Young Man with a Horn* recounted with rare dispassion the personal and professional travails of a talented neophyte — at least up to the concluding ten minutes, when Warner Bros. felt compelled to inject the traditional happy ending. Cornetist Bix Beiderbecke, on whose life the Dorothy Baker book and the film were loosely based, did not recover from the wreckage caused by his freewheeling lifestyle. In the film, "Rick Martin" not only escapes Beiderbecke's early death, but also gives the distinct impression that he was capable of reaching new career heights far greater than his alcoholic dependency warranted. (Harry James played the trumpet for star Kirk Douglas's rendition of the striking title song by musical director Ray Heindorf and all his other solos.)

Additional realistic touches were interpolated into the screenplay revolving around the rise of a fictitious rock singer in Tommy Sands' *Sing Boy Sing* in 1958, and even more into *Your Cheatin' Heart*, the 1964 biography of Hank Williams. But they were only preludes to the later fully orchestrated treatments given to *Lady Sings the Blues* (1972), with Diana Ross successfully dividing her concentration between Billy Holiday's surface glamour and the coarse and brutal events that characterized "Lady Day's" brief life; *Leadbelly* (1976), which traced the mercurial career of folk singer-guitarist Ledbetter; and *The Buddy Holly Story* (1978).

Similarly depressing yet undoubtedly truer to life than the 1940s and 1950s biographies was Bette Midler's impressive tracing of the ups and mostly downs of another rock singer in *The Rose* (1979); Willy Nelson's portrayal of a star-crossed country rock singer in *Honeysuckle Rose* (1980); and Clint Eastwood's coldly analytical portrayal of a consumptive cowboy singer in 1980's *Honky Tonk Man*.

Sparkle in 1976 presented another view of a developing singing group, this one black, but quickly descended into predictability, a major flaw that became common to even the new school of filmed biographies. *American Hot Wax* (1978), with Tim McIntire masquerading as disk jockey Alan Freed, also kept the rock flame burning under the ashes of a worn-out plot, as did *La Bamba* (1987), which centered on the brief career of rocker Ritchie Valens. Paul Simon's title song for *One-Trick Pony* helped somewhat to alleviate some of the banalities imposed on the 1980 film by adolescent dialogue and plotting and the stiff acting by Simon in the role of another rock star convulsed by incremental personal and career disintegration.

Luckily, the 1980s premiered *This Is Spinal Tap* and *Hairspray* as antidotes to the overblown drama invading musical films. The first on-the-mark spoof satirized rock music and musicians; the second targeted 1960s teenage television dance programs in its "Corny Collins Show" sequences. Except for overtones of self-pity, *All That Jazz* in 1987 succeeded in balancing the consummate artistry of choreographer Bob Fosse with the personality defects that eventually destroyed him, while 1989's *Great Balls of Fire* exposed the ritualistic downfall of Jerry Lee Lewis. As recently as 1991, *The Commitments* pursued the explosive upsurge in popularity and travails of a ten-piece soul band in Dublin, Ireland; meanwhile *Rock 'n' Roll High School Forever,* a sequel to 1979's *Rock 'n' Roll High School,* clearly showed that teenage musicals had not progressed very far over the 12 intervening years. Oliver Stone's taut direction of *The Doors,* with Val Kilmer as rocker Jim Morrison, unfortunately blew the singer's slight influence on music far out of proportion in much the same way that the recent *Bugsy* glamourized a cheap, cutthroat hood.

Contemporary producers have naturally concentrated on the types of films they felt were the most commercially acceptable, thereby justifying their errors of judgment by perpetuating them. In refusing to expand the potential of the traditional musical comedy, they narrowed the variety of films, permitting gangster and science fiction movies to maintain their staggering popularity by default. The result has been the polarization of motion picture audiences. Recent films have generally been made for and appreciated by a single age group — persons under the age of 35. This trend is a sharp reversal from the aim of earlier producers, whose films were designed to appeal to all generations.

Gimme Shelter (1971) continues to be of limited interest for its insights into the talents of the Rolling Stones rather than for plot or score. Much the same can be said of Martin Scorsese's *The Last Waltz* (1978), with Bob Dylan and Muddy Waters, among others; *The Great Rock-and-Roll Swindle* (1980), which displays the aimless "artistry" of Sid Vicious; Paul McCartney's *Give My Regards to Broad Street* (1984); *Hail! Hail! Rock 'n' Roll!* (1987), with Chuck Berry; and *Cool as Ice* (1991), an absolute classic of gross ineptness in story, music (by Stanley Clarke), and performance (by Vanilla Ice).

Xanadu (1980) ill-advisedly wrapped old-style chorus line dancing and rock music into the same package, succeeding only in embarrassing both past and present, while unforgivably reducing Gene Kelly to bemused spectator of the current music scene. *Breakin' 2: Electric Boogaloo* in 1984 tried to cash in on the old charity show routine, with the dancers staging one to save a community center. *Salsa* (1988) and *Lambada* (1990) concerned themselves with fleeting dance crazes, while *Forbidden Dance* (1990) worked in a poorly conceived save-the-environment subplot. *Sing* (1989) circumvented the adult market entirely with its childish plot about putting on a Brooklyn high school talent show without the filmmakers' hiring professionals to write, direct, or play in it.

The convenient time-divider between old and new movies is usually cited as 1966, when the U.S. Supreme Court loosened the shackles of censorship. Greater flexibility was given to the Motion Picture Producers and Distributors Association in determining what was fit to be said and shown in theaters. The once-powerful Legion of Decency became the mild National Catholic Office for Motion Pictures, which also relaxed its moral suasions. The industry took quick advantage of the new freedom of expression, devising in 1968 its first film-rating system, a much-publicized attempt to legitimize the prurient and offensive by banning the sale of tickets to anyone under the age of 13.

The court's ruling, however, was ironic. With the lifting of virtually all restrictions on subject and dialogue, older generations imposed a self-censorship that has estranged them from the box office. Their abstinence has diluted the supply of antiquarians whom old-style movie musicals logically might have been expected to attract.

Films, did however, continue as major sources of songs with originality and merit, even if they were sung only infrequently on camera by cast members. Instead of relying on a few hardy contract composers and lyricists as in the past, contemporary producers have distributed music-writing chores widely among an assortment of artists whose individual styles have provided welcome musical variety. Their lyrical themes and background scores abounded throughout 1966–91 films, much of them surpassing the finest written between 1928 and 1965. Often, the music was the most memorable reminder of the film it appeared in. Many of the best-remembered Oscar nominees, ranging from "The Way We Were" and "The Last Dance" to "Life Is What You Make It" and "The First Time It Happens," are assuredly of the highest caliber.

Older songs, however, were revived, occasionally. The Gershwins' "Someone to Watch Over Me" served nicely as the theme of the 1987 detective film of the same name; Hy Zaret and Alex North's "Unchained Melody," written for the 1955 film *Unchained,* was reprised by the Righteous Brothers in *Ghost* (1989); and Gordon and Revel's 53-year-old "Good Morning, Glory" supported the period backdrop for *Brighton Beach* in 1986. A dozen 1920s and 1930s standards were sprinkled throughout *When Harry Met Sally* (1989). For the most part, old and new songs were orchestrated and vocalized to advantage, except for such an appalling example as singer Noel Harrison's off-screen, rapid-fire, emotionless rendition of the lovely "Windmills of Your Mind" behind the credits of *The Thomas Crown Affair.*

Fame's title song and "Out Here on My Own" expertly reinforced the jaunty optimism that overlays the basic insecurity of youngsters working toward a career in the performing arts. Similar hopefulness and determination were delightfully dispensed throughout *Saturday Night Fever*, among the better of the post–1965 musicals with the ambition of would-be musical stars their pivot.

The harshness of many recent screenplays has been ameliorated by the romantic lushness of background music. James Horner's score for *Glory* (1989), which contained the most harrowing battle scenes since *All Quiet on the Western Front,* added significantly to its sweep and poignancy. Likewise, Mark Knopfler's backdrop for *Last Exit to Brooklyn* (1989) sensitized the few humane scenes in a totally brutal film, which concluded with a gang rape. Elmer Bernstein achieved a comparable level of artistry for *The Grifters* (1989), and Phillip Glass for *The Thin Blue Line* (1988).

Harkening back to the silent days was Carmine Coppola, father of director Francis Ford Coppola, who in 1981 brilliantly scored the 4½ hour restoration of Abel Gance's silent epic *Napoleon.* It had been musicalized in 1927 by Arthur Honegger, but practically the entire score was lost over the intervening 54 years.

Perhaps, after a respectable lapse of time, critics will regard the past quarter-century as another golden age of film music, for background scores and themes if not for individual pop songs. By and large, the musical accompaniments were so good that an in-depth study is warranted to gauge the melodies' staying power and whether they successfully defined the times in which they were written. The music in Arlo Guthrie's *Alice's Restaurant,* for example, is so evocative

Barbra Streisand in the first of two films in which she played singer/come-dienne Fanny Brice: *Funny Girl,* **1969.**

of the 1960s that the 1969 cult film continually fascinates persons too young to remember that decade.

Unfortunately, recent writers of music and lyrics have not been given the opportunity to add to their luster by pursuing their craft with metronomic regularity. Films no longer provide the breeding ground for another Dubin and Warren, Gordon and Revel, Robin and

Rainger, or Adamson and McHugh. On call for up to five pictures a year for much of his career, Warren typically wrote five songs for each musical to which he was assigned. (His last was the title tune for Rosalind Russell's *Rosie* in 1967.)

Equally gifted contemporaries — Henry Mancini, Burt Bacharach, and Marvin Hamlisch among them — have yet to compose a five-song score for an original Hollywood musical. Nor have Broadway's best continued the precedent established by the Gershwins, Berlin, Porter, Rodgers and Hart, and Kern and Company by contributing new scores to productions on the West as well as the East coast. Although some of their stage successes were reprised in films, Jerry Herman, Andrew Lloyd Webber, Jerry Bock, and Charles Strouse have not been bylined on the credit cards of a major original movie musical. Cy Coleman wrote the score for Broadway's remake of John Barrymore and Carole Lombard's *Twentieth Century* (renamed *On the Twentieth Century*) in 1980, but no studio has filmed it. Even Stephen Sondheim (*Gypsy*, for which he wrote lyrics only; *A Funny Thing Happened on the Way to the Forum; A Little Night Music,* in which every song is a waltz) has been restricted to writing occasional background music (*Stavisky,* 1974; *Reds,* 1981) and single songs like "Sooner or Later (I Always Get My Man)," the 1990 Oscar winner from *Dick Tracy.*

Overwhelmingly, the finest 1966–91 screen songs received nomination for the Academy Award, a praiseworthy practice formerly disregarded by that institution, which for decades considered comparatively few first-rate songs (see List #19, "Film Songs Nominated for the Academy Award, 1966–91"). Certainly, the marked decrease in the number of film songs has been the major factor in elevating such a high percentage to Academy recognition. In 1985 three, instead of the customary five, earned nomination. Only twice before, in 1935 and 1936, did the Academy, in obvious dereliction of its duty, find but three songs worthy of attention. Breaking with Academy tradition that there be only one contestant per picture, the 1980 festival admitted two songs from *Fame,* an anomaly that resurfaced in 1983, when two each came from *Flashdance* and *Yentl. Footloose* (1981), *White Knights* (1985), and *The Little Mermaid* (1989) were also the source of two candidates. At the 1992 ceremony, three songs from *Beauty and the Beast* received nomination.

Any list of, say, the most respectable 18 or so 1966–91 film songs

Warren Beatty and Madonna in *Dick Tracy* (1990); the Stephen Sondheim song "Sooner or Later (I Always Get My Man)" won an Academy Award.

that failed to receive nomination is arbitrary. Each viewer most likely would be able to furnish his or her own valid list of titles, but chances are that most of the following titles would be included in many such lists: "Barefoot in the Park" (Johnny Mercer–Neal Hefti), *Barefoot in the Park*, 1967; "Candy Man" (Leslie Bricusse–Anthony Newley), *Willy*

Wonka and the Chocolate Factory, 1971; "Crazy World" (Leslie Bricusse–Henry Mancini), *Victor/Victoria,* 1981; "Imagine" (Sammy Cahn — Francis Lai), *The Bobo,* 1967; "Mrs. Robinson" (Paul Simon), *The Graduate,* 1967; "New York, New York" (Fred Ebb–John Kander), *New York, New York,* 1977; "On Golden Pond (Main Theme)" (Dave Grusin), *On Golden Pond,* 1981; "Simply Meant to Be" (George Merrill–Henry Mancini), *Blind Date,* 1987; "The Slender Thread" (Mack David–Quincy Jones), *The Slender Thread,* 1966; "Somewhere, My Love" (Paul Francis Webster–Maurice Jarre), *Doctor Zhivago,* 1966; "Theme from Sophie's Choice" (Marvin Hamlisch), *Sophie's Choice,* 1983; "Speak Softly, Love" (Nino Rota), *The Godfather,* 1972; "Strangers in the Night" (Bert Kaempfert), *A Man Could Get Killed,* 1966; "The Summer Knows" (Marilyn and Alan Bergman–Michel Legrand), *Summer of '42,* 1971; "Too Beautiful to Last" (Paul Francis Webster–Richard Rodney Bennett), *Nicholas and Alexandra,* 1972; "Take the Money and Run (Main Theme)" (Marvin Hamlisch), *Take the Money and Run,* 1969; and "You're Going to Hear from Me" (André and Dory Previn), *Inside Daisy Clover,* 1966.

Thoroughly Modern Millie (1967) and *Star!* (1968) introduced two appealing Sammy Cahn–Van Heusen nominees, but the rest of the films' scores consisted mostly of reprises of tunes written decades earlier. Leslie Bricusse's "Talk to the Animals" and especially "When I Look in Your Eyes" revolved charmingly around the substandard plot of *Doctor Doolittle* in 1967, but even they and star Rex Harrison were unable to salvage the picture from box office disaster.

Lerner and Loewe's songs for *The Little Prince* (1974) added little to the film musical canon despite the winsome title tune. "How Lucky Can You Get," "I'm Easy," and "Do You Know Where You're Going To" were the only notable newcomers in 1975's tuneful trio of *Funny Lady, Nashville,* and *Mahogany.* Barbra Streisand wrote the music for the Oscar-winning "Evergreen," but the poorly reupholstered picture it appeared in, *A Star Is Born,* was so sophomoric that MGM's *Two Girls on Broadway* (1940), an equally slick but unoriginal updating of the studio's own *Broadway Melody,* sparkles by comparison.

Besides the realism pervading screenplays, Hollywood's musical production has been made all the more precarious by the gigantic sum of money needed to mount one. The average cost of a dramatic or adventure feature film in 1990 rose 14.2 percent from 1989 to $26.8 million, according to the Motion Picture Association of America. Add to that figure the estimated $11.6 million spent on advertising and distribution, and the cost per non-musical film soars to $38.4 million.

Because of ever-rising ticket prices, box office revenues amounted to about $5 billion in 1990, down slightly from the record set in 1989. But ticket sales dropped 7 percent in 1990 compared with the 1989 figure of 1.3 billion, virtually the same as the 1979 total. Musical pictures, traditionally the most expensive of Hollywood properties, have simply priced themselves out of a market that has grown singularly unappreciative of them to begin with.

DIMMING OF THE GREAT WHITE WAY

Broadway, too, has experienced slackened musical activity in recent years. So many New York theaters have vanished that Hollywood's ransacking the stage for material has reached its lowest point since the 1930–33 period. Since 1986, three playhouses have been demolished to make room for the Marriott Marquis Hotel; two have been converted into churches; the vacant Biltmore, in painful disuse and disrepair, continues to disintegrate; and the Longacre is in danger of becoming a community court. Then, too, the cost of producing a stage musical has become almost prohibitive, now ranging between $5 million and $7 million, further winnowing possibilities down to only the scant few that seem to have hit potential built into them. Once as reliable as spare tires and numerous as the spokes on a small fleet of trucks, Broadway shows no longer can be relied on to produce a favorable impact on the Hollywood's studios' balance sheets.

The Broadway musicals that did make it into films ranged, as always, from the thoroughly professional to the inept, even the insulting. *Fiddler on the Roof* (1971), with Topol in the leading role, was hailed as a triumph, and rightly so, since it surpassed the stage version in every detail a film can. Fred Ebb and John Kander's *Cabaret* (1972), the brittle retelling of the Christopher Isherwood–John Van Druten tale of pre–Hitler Germany (*I Am a Camera*), ranks close to the top of the finest Broadway-to-Hollywood translations. From Liza Minnelli's Oscar-winning performance to Joel Gray's serio-comic embodiment of hypocrisy and decadence in the Weimar years, every detail of the film is perfection. Similarly, *Oliver!* was a stunning 1968 recreation of the Dickens novel.

Emerging relatively unscathed from the stage was *Sweet Charity* (1969), which despite the lively Dorothy Fields–Cy Coleman songs and the radiant presence of Shrley MacLaine was a commercial failure. Also on the asset side of Hollywood's artistic ledger were *Funny Girl* (1968) and *Funny Lady* (1975), two exemplary biographies starring Barbra Streisand as Fanny Brice.

The retooling of *The Wiz,* on the other hand, suffered such a box office battering that the 1978 Diana Ross–Michael Jackson vehicle turned into one of the biggest revenue losers in film musical history, substantiating E.Y. Harburg's verdict of the original Broadway production. Harburg, the writer of the lyrics and parts of the screenplay for *The Wizard of Oz,* walked out of the theater after the first act, and later described the musical as a "disgrace to the tenderness evoked by the 1939 film it was based on." He refused to see the filmed *Wiz.*

The Best Little Whorehouse in Texas, 1776, Jesus Christ Superstar, Camelot, and even the exuberant *Hair* were instantly forgettable. *Hello, Dolly!* had several things going for it, above all Barbra Streisand and Walter Matthau, but it almost collapsed under the tonnage of visual gimmicks appended to the Broadway original. In the theater of the absurd category, *The Little Shop of Horrors* (1986) was also less than memorable, even though it had gone through two earlier practice sessions, first as a 1961 Hollywood spoof of horror movies and then as an Off Off Broadway musical.

"Hopelessly Devoted to You" was a respectable *Grease* insertion, and the film duplicated the roaring success of the stage production, grossing so much money that it still ranks as the second biggest box office musical of all time, between *The Sound of Music* and *Saturday Night Fever.* "Surprise, Surprise" added little to Marvin Hamlisch's brilliant *Chrous Line* score, which was submerged in a heavy-handed, intrusive romantic subplot that was absent from the Broadway show.

Martin Charnin and Charles Strouse's *Annie* failed to repeat its 1977–83 Broadway success on film. Replete with reminders of New Deal days, like the song "Tomorrow," when the sun will shine through again, the 1984 reenactment sported Dickensian characters, all good or all bad and rarely in between, charming children in rags singing and dancing their tears away, an ill-tempered headmistress of an orphanage, a kindly tycoon, and even President Roosevelt himself. But the audience for the Harold Gray comic strip–based picture was limited mostly to persons who shared familiarity with the Depression by having lived through it. The authors' sequel, *Annie Warbucks*, opened Off Off Broadway in mid–August 1993 to rave reviews.

Equally unfortunate were the musicalized versions of two of the screen's greatest 1930s dramas, *Lost Horizon* and *Goodbye, Mr. Chips*, again proving that although music hath charms, it requires imaginative adaptations to display them. *At Long Last Love* (1975) happily revived 20 Cole Porter songs, many of which, like the title tune, had been dormant for decades. They were performed respectfully, but the awkwardness of Burt Reynolds, who was cast in a role obviously far too sophisticated for his mild talent, turned much of the basically prosaic film into an extended amateur night.

Pennies from Heaven owed little to Bing Crosby's 1936 musical except the title song and the Depression-era setting. The 1982 picture towered over any 1930s musical in showing the stark realities of the time and the wrenching decline of hope among the victims of a crippled economy. Had it featured original songs, the Steve Martin-Bernadette Peters co-starring vehicle very well might have made film history.

Even as mesmerizing a musical personality as Prince, to a larger degree in *Graffiti Bridge* (1990) than in the earlier *Sign o' the Times, Under the Cherry Moon,* and *Purple Rain,* has been unable to recapture the feel-good ambience of the Depression musicals, although he has surely tried hard enough. Sunny song bursts have inundated his pictures, but the optimism of the juvenile lyrics has been tinctured with a dash of gloom. The performers, including the star himself, tend to sing and dance with a desperation revealing their need to cheer up not the audience, but themselves.

Such other musical personalities as Geoffrey Hines and Mikhail Baryshnikov have not been altogether fortunate in finding scripts to display their talents to advantage. Hines's appearance in *Cotton Club* and *Tap* focused on his dramatic rather than musical skills, with the result being that his extraordinary dancing was irrelevant to the plots, which ranged from the trite to the banal. In *White Knights,* Baryshnikov, too, was burdened with a poor script that placed acting prowess over dancing mastery. *Dancers* served him better, in that his dancing was not incidental to the storyline.

Without question, earlier musical pictures ran on empty in the dramatic department, but the producers were wise enough to let the songs and musical performers carry them. No bloated social significance

was given to the screenplays, nor was any mogul unwilling to shoe-
horn in another ballad to replace a few extra lines of dialogue.

Unsurprisingly, the handful of recent movie-musical stars die,
artistically, almost as quickly as they are born, a reflection in part of
the postwar implosion of the once magisterial studio system, which
kept alive many big-name performers after only traces of their
charisma were evident. Supplanting the system was the increase in independent film projects, which pick up and drop leading players
largely on the basis of popularity polls conducted among mercurial
teenagers. It is doubtful that another musical performer will chalk up
Fred Astaire's 35 years in films or Bing Crosby's 34. Lacking continuous practice making musical films, including B-rated co-features,
today's and tomorrow's "superstars" cannot be expected to develop
equal proficiency in exercising their artistry.

If only intermittently, stagegoers have been more receptive to
nostalgia than the latest generation of moviegoers, who rejected Bette
Midler's peppy late–1991 personification of a uso entertainer, half
Patti Andrews, half Martha Raye, in *For the Boys.* Despite her rendition of Diane Warwick's most respectable "Every Road Leads Back to
You," the picture's nostalgia backfired. Youngsters found it too irrelevant, oldsters too coarse, and the box office suffered.

Two other 1991 films sought success by repeating old themes.
Stepping Out, a charming anachronism starring Liza Minnelli, revived
the hopes, if not the fortunes, of a group of misfit adults who take tap
dancing lessons as therapy, eventually putting on a show to "Save the
Children." *Straight Talk,* this one with Dolly Parton, who wrote the
mediocre songs, dwells on the potential of dreaming. "Dreams do
come true . . . sometimes," read the newspaper ads for the picture,
and they do for Miss Parton, playing an unemployed, modern-day
Cinderella with big hopes. She manages to make the Big Time on talk
radio. Perhaps it was the ancient plots of the pictures, or maybe it was
the dimming star power of the actress leads, but audiences shunned
both films by the droves.

On the other hand, the wartime film musical *Meet Me in St. Louis*
was transferred to Broadway in 1989, where it enjoyed a respectable
run. All the original Ralph Blane–Hugh Martin songs were retained,
plus a half-dozen new ones by the same authors. Largely because of
Tommy Tune's award-winning choreography, *Grand Hotel: The
Musical,* served notice that the 1932 mgm dramatic film was amenable

to 1990s culture. The first half of 1992 witnessed successful revivals of Frank Loesser's *Most Happy Fella* and *Guys and Dolls,* Joe Darion and Mitch Leigh's *Man of LaMancha,* of "The Impossible Dream" fame, and *Crazy for You,* which reprised 15 standards and a half-dozen newly reconstructed songs by the Gershwins.

The Will Rogers Follies, another throwback to the thirties, courtesy of Betty Comden, Adolph Green, and Cy Coleman, was voted the best Broadway musical of 1990. The hopeful finale reverberates with unshakable faith in contemporary America's ability to muddle through its troubles once again. Included is a running commentary by humorist Rogers, played by Keith Carradine, whose wry observations on the state of the nation served a similar reassuring purpose in print and over the radio six decades earlier.

CODA

Since the film medium by its nature is overwhelmingly graphic and visceral, it is not surprising that musicals dealing in pep-pill palliatives have been unable to gain a foothold with aficionados of decapitation and frenetic slapstick. Horror and farce are hardly new to films, but their present treatments are. The power of suggestion has been sacrificed for unrelenting realism and intimacy of details. Obscenities roll off the tongue so easily that cursing no longer shocks but bores, largely because repetition has dulled the force that certain words, used sparingly, once had.

Feature films that could have provided the basis for musical comedy, such as Chevy Chase's family vacation series (e.g., *National Lampoon's Christmas Vacation* in 1988), instead played up chaos or mayhem. Comedy, a central motivator of musicals, became a primer in dullness in John Belushi, John Candy, Cheech (Marin) and (Tommy) Chong films, and the overwrought *Police Academy, Porky's,* and *Meatball* lookalikes. Character sloppiness predominated while vulgarity assailed the senses.

Rarely before has cinematography or film editing been more expert or innovative; the acting, at all levels, is usually very good, even in films that are otherwise unwatchable. Unfortunately, the traditional musical film, for so long deficient in all three categories, has not been the beneficiary of these cinematic advances.

With viewer attention riveted on the creativity of special effects departments, a revival of musical films has been further hindered, if only because of their comparative blandness. Befitting an industry that is a consortium of sciences as well as arts, dazzling effects have spectacularized adventure and science fiction films to an extraordinary degree, especially when straining credulity to the breaking point. But musical pictures do not need *Star Wars* technology; indeed its availability is of minor importance to musicals, as was exemplified by the ridiculous invasion of dysfunctional sex-starved astronauts in *Earth Girls Are Easy* in 1988. Many of the best musicals were even filmed without color.

The market for film musicals, depressed for so long, provides no evidence that a resurgence is either imminent or desired. Just as musicals are no longer needed to popularize songs, people need not buy their way into a theater to see one. Cable channels like MTV also combine audio and visual presentations of songs, often in a movie-production context. Hundreds of Hollywood musicals are available for home viewing on videocassette, and are revived periodically on commercial, public broadcasting, and cable television.

Yet, at this writing, rumors were being circulated that Andrew Lloyd Webber's *Cats,* already in its eleventh year on Broadway, would be filmed as an animated cartoon. Like the composer's other Broadway spectacular, *Phantom of the Opera, Cats* should qualify as a movie blockbuster and possibly a trendsetter as well, indicating that a musical picture revival has not been precluded after all, just deferred. In late 1991, the Disney organization's *Beauty and the Beast,* with a pleasant score by Howard Ashman and Alan Menken, was giving every indication of developing, along with *Aladdin,* into the studio's biggest hit since *Snow White and the Seven Dwarfs*.

A later Disney release, *Newsies,* was little more than a tiresome, strained live-action musical revolving around the 1899 strike by New York newsboys against publishers Joseph Pulitzer and William Randolph Hearst. The songs, like "Santa Fe," are well crafted, if unmemorable, and the film represented the first score with lyrics by Jack Feldman to Menken's music. Howard Ashman, the composer's former collaborator, died in 1991 of AIDS.

In the panoramic sweep of history, the life of the films, the songs, and the stars mentioned in the earliest chapters of this book spanned but one brief and shining moment. Overwhelmingly, they survive as flowers found pressed in the pages of old books, the dead reminders of times and places holding little significance for succeeding generations. But in the cheeriest of scenarios, future filmgoers will not dismiss Hollywood's musical past as a mere inconsequential tributary from this century's cultural mainstream, for they will never see its artistic like again.

Appendix

List 1
Most Popular 100 Songs from 1928–33 Films

All of Me (Seymour Simons–
Gerald Marks) *Careless Lady*,
1931

Am I Blue? (Grant Clarke–Harry
Akst) *On with the Show*, 1929

Angela Mia (Erno Rapée–Lew
Pollack) *Street Angel*, 1928

Beautiful Girl (Arthur
Freed–Nacio Herb Brown) *Stage
Mother*, 1933

Beyond the Blue Horizon (Leo
Robin–W. Franke Harling–
Richard A. Whiting) *Monte
Carlo*, 1930

Black Moonlight (Sam Coslow–
Arthur Johnston) *Too Much
Harmony*, 1933

Boulevard of Broken Dreams (Al
Dubin–Harry Warren) *Moulin
Rouge*, 1933

Broadway Melody (Arthur Freed–
Nacio Herb Brown) *Broadway
Melody*, 1929

By a Waterfall (Irving Kahal–
Sammy Fain) *Footlight Parade*,
1933

*Carioca (Gus Kahn–Edward
Eliscu–Vincent Youmans) *Flying
Down to Rio*, 1933

Cryin' for the Carolines (Sam
Lewis–Joe Young–Harry Warren) *Spring Is Here*, 1929

Cuban Love Song (Dorothy
Fields–Herbert Stothart–James
McHugh) *Cuban Love Song*, 1930

Day You Came Along (Sam Coslow–Arthur Johnson) *Too Much
Harmony*, 1933

Delishious (Ira and George Gershwin) *Delicious*, 1931

Did You Ever See a Dream Walking? (Mack Gordon–Harry
Revel) *Sitting Pretty*, 1933

†Don't Blame Me (Dorothy
Fields–James McHugh) *Dinner
at Eight*, 1933

Down the Ox Road (Sam Coslow–Arthur Johnston) *College
Humor*, 1933

Dream Lover (Clifford Grey–Victor Schertzinger) *Love Parade*,
1929

263

Everything I Have Is Yours
(Harold Adamson–Burton
Lane) *Dancing Lady,* 1933
Flying Down to Rio (Gus Kahn–
Edward Eliscu–Vincent You-
mans) *Flying Down to Rio,* 1933
For You (Al Dubin–Joe Burke)
Holy Terror, 1930
Forty-Second Street (Al Dubin–
Harry Warren) *42nd Street,* 1933
Give Me a Moment, Please (Leo
Robin–W. Franke Harling–
Richard A. Whiting) *Monte
Carlo,* 1930
Happy Days Are Here Again
(Jack Yellen–Milton Ager)
Chasing Rainbows, 1929
Have a Little Faith in Me (Sam
Lewis–Joe Young–Harry War-
ren) *Spring Is Here,* 1929
Here Lies Love (Leo Robin–
Ralph Rainger), *Big Broadcast,*
1932
Honeymoon Hotel (Al
Dubin–Harry Warren) *Footlight
Parade,* 1933
I Cover the Waterfront (Edward
Heyman–John W. Green) *I
Cover the Waterfront,* 1933
I Love You So Much (Bert
Kalmar–Harry Ruby) *Cuckoos,*
1930
If I Had a Talking Picture of You
(Buddy DeSylva–Lew Brown–
Ray Henderson) *Sunny Side Up,*
1929
§I'll Always Be in Love with You
(Bud Green–Herman
Ruby–Sam H. Stept) *Syncopa-
tion,* 1929
(I'm a Dreamer) Aren't We All?
(Buddy DeSylva–Lew

Brown–Ray Henderson) *Sunny
Side Up,* 1929
I'm Yours (E.Y. Harburg–John
W. Green) *Leave It to Lester,* 1930
Inka Dinka Doo (Ben Ryan–
Jimmy Durante) *Palooka,* 1933
Isn't It Romantic (Lorenz
Hart–Richard Rodgers) *Love Me
Tonight,* 1932
It Happened in Monterey (Billy
Rose–Mabel Wayne) *King of
Jazz,* 1930
It's Only a Paper Moon (Billy
Rose–E.Y. Harburg–Harold
Arlen) *Take a Chance,* 1933
I've Got a Feeling I'm Falling
(Billy Rose–Harry Link–Fats
[Thomas Wright] Waller) *Ap-
plause,* 1929
Jeannine, I Dream of Lilac Time
(L. Wolfe Gilbert–Nathaniel
Shilkret) *Lilac Time,* 1928
Jericho (Leo Robin–Richard
Myers) *Syncopation,* 1929
Just You, Just Me (Raymond
Klages–Jesse Greer) *Blondy,*
1929
Keepin' Myself for You (Sidney
Clare–Vincent Youmans) *Hit
the Deck,* 1930
Laugh, Clown, Laugh (Joe
Young–Sam M. Lewis–Ted
Fiorito) *Great Gabbo,* 1929
Let Me Sing and I'm Happy (Ir-
ving Berlin) *Mammy,* 1930
Little by Little (Bobby Dolan–
Walter O'Keefe) *Sophomore,* 1929
Little Kiss Each Morning (Harry
Woods) *Vagabond Lover,* 1929
Livin' in the Sunlight — Lovin' in
the Moonlight (Al Lewis–Al
Sherman) *Big Pond* 1930

Lonesome Road (Gene Austin–Nathaniel Shilkret) *Show Boat,* 1929

Louise (Leo Robin–Richard A. Whiting) *Innocents of Paris,* 1928

Love, Your Magic Spell Is Everywhere (Elsie Janis–Edmund Goulding) *Trespasser,* 1931

Lover (Lorenz Hart–Richard Rodgers) *Love Me Tonight,* 1932

Marie (Irving Berlin) *Awakening,* 1928

Mimi (Lorenz Hart–Richard Rodgers) *Love Me Tonight,* 1932

Moon Song (That Wasn't Meant for Me) (Sam Coslow–Arthur Johnston) *Hello Everybody,* 1932

Moonstruck (Sam Coslow–Arthur Johnston) *College Humor,* 1933

My Baby Just Cares for Me (Gus Kahn–Walter Donaldson) *Whoopee!,* 1930

My Future Just Passed (George Marion, Jr.–Richard A. Whiting) *Safety in Numbers,* 1933

My Ideal (Leo Robin–Newell Chase–Richard A. Whiting) *Playboy of Paris,* 1930

My Love Parade (Clifford Grey–Victor Schertzinger) *Love Parade,* 1929

My Mother's Eyes (L. Wolfe Gilbert–Abel Baer) *Lucky Boy,* 1929

One Hour with You (Leo Robin–Richard A. Whiting) *One Hour with You,* 1932

Orchids in the Moonlight (Gus Kahn–Edward Eliscu–Vincent Youmans) *Flying Down to Rio,* 1933

Out of Nowhere (Edward Heyman–John W. Green) *Dude Ranch,* 1931

Pagan Love Song (Arthur Freed–Nacio Herb Brown) *Pagan,* 1929

Painting the Clouds with Sunshine (Al Dubin–Joe Burke) *Gold Diggers of Broadway,* 1929

Paradise (Gordon Clifford–Nacio Herb Brown) *A Woman Commands,* 1932

Please (Leo Robin–Ralph Rainger) *Big Broadcast,* 1932

Precious Little Thing Called Love (Lou Davis–J. Fred Coots) *Shopworn Angel,* 1929

Puttin' on the Ritz (Irving Berlin) *Puttin' on the Ritz,* 1929

Reaching for the Moon (Irving Berlin) *Reaching for the Moon,* 1931

Remember My Forgotten Man (Al Dubin–Harry Warren) *Gold Diggers of 1933,* 1933

River, Stay 'Way from My Door (Harry Woods) *Swanee River,* 1931

Romance (Edgar Leslie–Walter Donaldson) *Cameo Kirby,* 1929

Shadow Waltz (Al Dubin–Harry Warren) *Gold Diggers of 1933,* 1933

Shanghai Lil (Al Dubin–Harry Warren) *Footlight Parade,* 1933

Should I? (Arthur Freed–Nacio Herb Brown) *Lord Byron of Broadway,* 1929

Shuffle Off to Buffalo (Al Dubin–Harry Warren) *42nd Street,* 1933

Sing You Sinners (Sam Coslow–W. Franke Harling) *Honey, 1930*

Singin' in the Rain (Arthur
Freed– Nacio Herb Brown)
Hollywood Revue of 1929,
1929
Sonny Boy (Al Jolson–Buddy
DeSylva–Lew Brown–Ray
Henderson) *Singing Fool,*
1928
Sunny Side Up (Buddy DeSylva–
Lew Brown–Ray Henderson)
Sunny Side Up, 1929
Temptation (Arthur Freed–Nacio
Herb Brown) *Going Hollywood,*
1933
Thanks (Sam Coslow–Arthur
Johnston) *Too Much Harmony,*
1933
There's a Rainbow 'Round My
Shoulder (Al Jolson–Billy Rose–
Dave Dreyer) *Singing Fool,*
1928
Three Little Words (Bert Kalmar–
Harry Rub) *Check and Double
Check,* 1930
Tip Toe Through the Tulips
(with Me) (Al Dubin–W.
Franke Harling–Joe Burke)
Gold Diggers of Broadway, 1929
We Will Always Be Sweethearts
(Leo Robin–Oscar Straus) *One
Hour with You,* 1932
Weary River (Grant Clarke–Louis
Silvers) *Weary River,* 1929
Wedding of the Painted Doll (Ar-
thur Freed–Nacio Herb Brown)
Broadway Melody, 1929
We'll Make Hay While the Sun

Shines (Arthur Freed–Nacio
Herb Brown) *Going Hollywood,*
1933
We're in the Money (a.k.a. Gold
Diggers Song) (Al Dubin–
Harry Warren) *Gold Diggers of
1933,* 1933
When I Take My Sugar to Tea
(Irving Kahal–Pierre Norman–
Sammy Fain) *Monkey Business,*
1931
When Your Lover Has Gone
(E.A. Swan) *Blonde Crazy,*
1931
While Hearts Are Singing (Clif-
ford Grey–Oscar Straus) *Smiling
Lieutenant,* 1931
Who's Afraid of the Big Bad
Wolf? (Anne Ronell–Frank
Churchill) *Three Little Pigs,*
1933
Why Am I So Romantic? (Bert
Kalmar–Harry Ruby) *Animal
Crackers,* 1930
You Are Too Beautiful (Lorenz
Hart–Richard Rogers) *Hallelu-
jah, I'm a Bum!,* 1933
You Brought a New Kind of Love
to Me (Irving Kahal–Pierre
Norman–Sammy Fain) *Big
Pond,* 1930
You Were Meant for Me (Arthur
Freed–Nacio Herb Brown)
Broadway Melody, 1929
You're Getting to Be a Habit with
Me (Al Dubin–Harry Warren)
42nd Street, 1933

* *Nominated for the 1934 Academy Award.*
† *Dropped from the film before release.*
§ *The song had been played previously in the background of* Stepping High *in 1928.*

List 2
Selected "Western" Songs from American Films

Along the Santa Fe Trail (Al Dubin–Edwina Coolidge–Will Grosz) *Santa Fe Trail*, 1940

*Ballad of Cat Ballou (Mack David–Jerry Livingston) *Cat Ballou*, 1965

*Be Honest with Me (Gene Autry–Fred Rose) *Ridin' on a Rainbow*, 1941

*Blazing Saddles (Mel Brooks–John Morris) *Blazing Saddles*, 1974

Blue Shadows on the Trail (Eliot Daniel) *Melody Time*, 1948

**Buttons and Bows (Ray Evans–Jay Livingston) *Paleface*, 1948

*Cowboy and the Lady (Arthur Quenzer–Lionel Newman) *Cowboy and the Lady*, 1938

Don't Fence Me In (Cole Porter) *Hollywood Canteen*, 1944

*Dust (Johnny Marvin) *Under Western Stars*, 1938

Empty Saddles (Billy Hill) *Rhythm on the Range*, 1936

End of the Lonesome Trail (Herman Ruby–Ray Perkins) *Great Divide*, 1929

Funny Old Hills (Leo Robin–Ralph Rainger) *Paris Honeymoon*, 1938

*Gal in Calico (Leo Robin–Arthur Schwarts) *Time, the Place and the Girl*, 1947

**High Noon (Ned Washington–Dimitri Tiomkin) *High Noon*, 1952

I Gotta Ride (Frank Loesser–Burton Lane) *Las Vegas Nights*, 1941

I'm an Old Cow Hand (Johnny Mercer) *Rhythm on the Range*, 1936

I'm Ridin' for a Fall (Frank Loesser–Arthur Schwartz) *Thank Your Lucky Stars*, 1943

In Our Little Shanty of Dreams (Gene Autry–Johnny Marvin) *Shooting High*, 1940

Jingle Jangle Jingle (Frank Loesser–Joseph T. Lilley) *Forest Rangers*, 1942

*Marmalade, Molasses, and Honey (Marilyn and Alan Bergman–Maurice Jarre) *Life and Times of Judge Roy Bean*, 1972

*Melody from the Sky (Sidney D. Mitchell–Louis Alter) *Trail of the Lonesome Pine*, 1936

*Mule Train (Fred Glickman–Hy Heath–Johnny Lange) *Singing Guns*, 1950

My Little Buckaroo (Jack Scholl–M.K. Jerome) *Cherokee Strip*, 1937

Nevada (Mort Greene–Walter Donaldson) *What's Buzzin', Cousin?*, 1943

*Ole Buttermilk Sky (Jack Brooks–Hoagy Carmichael) *Canyon Passage*, 1946

On the Sunny Side of the Rockies (Roy Ingraham–Harry Tobias) *Roll Along, Cowboy*, 1937

**Raindrops Keep Fallin' on My Head (Hal David–Burt

Bacharach) *Butch Cassidy and the
Sundance Kid,* 1969

Ridin' Home (Harold Adam-
son–James McHugh) *Road to
Reno*

Roll On, Prairie Moon (Ted Fior-
ito–Harry MacPherson–Albert
Von Tilzer) *Here Comes the
Band,* 1935

Silver on the Sage (Leo Robin–
Ralph Rainger) *Texans,* 1938

Streets of Laredo (Jay Livingston–
Ray Evans) *Streets of Laredo,*
1949

*True Grit (Don Black–Elmer
Bernstein) *True Grit,* 1969

Tumblin' Tumbleweeds (Bob
Nolan) *Tumblin' Tumbleweeds,*
1934

Twilight on the Trail (Sidney D.
Mitchell–Louis Alter) *Trail of
the Lonesome Pine,* 1936

Nominated for the Academy Award.
**Winner of the Academy Award.*

List 3
Academy Award–Nominated Songs from
Walt Disney Productions

Age of Not Believing (Richard M.
and Robert B. Sherman)
Bedknobs and Broomsticks, 1971

Baby Mine (Ned Washington–
Frank Churchill) *Dumbo,* 1941

Bare Necessities (Terry Gilkyson)
Jungle Book, 1967

Be Our Guest (Howard Ashman–
Alan Menken) *Beauty and the
Beast,* 1991

**Beauty and the Beast (Howard
Ashman–Alan Menken) *Beauty
and the Beast,* 1991

Belle (Howard Ashman–Alan
Menken) *Beauty and the Beast,*
1991

Bibbidy-Bobbidi-Boo (Mack
David–Al Hoffman–Jerry Livingston) *Cinderella,* 1950

Candle on the Water (Al
Kasha–Joel Hirschhorn) *Pete's
Dragon,* 1977

**Chim Chim Cher-ee (Richard
M. and Robert B. Sherman)
Mary Poppins, 1964

Kiss the Girl (Howard
Ashman–Alan Menken) *Little
Mermaid,* 1989

Lavender Blue (Larry Morey–
Eliot Daniel) *So Dear to My
Heart,* 1949

Love (Floyd Huddleston–George
Bruns) *Robin Hood,* 1973

Love Is a Song (Larry Morey–
Frank Churchill) *Bambi,* 1942

Saludos Amigos (Ned Washington–Charles Wolcott) *Saludos
Amigos,* 1943

Someone's Waiting for You (Carol
Connors–Ayn Robbins–Sammy
Fain) *Rescuers,* 1977

**Sooner or Later (I Always Get
My Man) (Stephen Sondheim)
Dick Tracy, 1990

**Under the Sea (Howard Ashman–Alan Menken) *Little Mermaid,* 1989
**When You Wish Upon a Star (Ned Washington–Leigh

Harline) *Pinocchio,* 1940
**Zip-a-Dee-Doo-Dah (Ray Gilbert–Allie Wrubel) *Song of the South,* 1947

**Winner of the Academy Award.*

List 4
Most Popular 60 Songs from 1934 Films

All I Do Is Dream of You (Arthur Freed–Nacio Herb Brown) *Sadie McKee*

Baby, Take a Bow (Lew Brown–Jay Gorney) *Stand Up and Cheer!*

†Blue Moon (Lorenz Hart–Richard Rodgers) *Manhattan Melodrama*

Carolina (Lew Brown–Jay Gorney) *Carolina*

Cocktails for Two (Sam Coslow–Arthur Johnston) *Murder at the Vanities*

**The Continental (Herb Magidson–Con Conrad) *Gay Divorcee*

Dames (Al Dubin–Harry Warren) *Dames*

Don't Let It Bother You (Mack Gordon–Harry Revel) *Gay Divorcee*

Don't Say Goodnight (Al Dubin–Harry Warren) *Wonder Bar*

Earful of Music (Gus Kahn–Walter Donaldson) *Kid Millions*

Ev'ry Day (Irving Kahal–Sammy Fain) *Sweet Music*

Fair and Warmer (Al Dubin–Harry Warren) *Twenty Million Sweethearts*

Fare Thee Well, Annabelle (Mort Dixon–Sammy Fain) *Sweet Music*

Flirtation Walk (Mort Dixon–Allie Wrubel) *Flirtation Walk*

Goin' to Heaven on a Mule (Al Dubin–Harry Warren) *Wonder Bar*

Happiness Ahead (Irving Kahal–Allie Wrubel) *Happiness Ahead*

Here Is My Heart (Leo Robin–Ralph Rainger) *Here Is My Heart*

Hold My Hand (Jack Yellen–Irving Caesar–Ray Henderson) *George White's Scandals*

How Do I Know It's Sunday (Irving Kahal–Sammy Fain) *Harold Teen*

I Only Have Eyes for You (Al Dubin–Harry Warren) *Dames*

I'll String Along with You (Al Dubin–Harry Warren) *Twenty Million Sweethearts*

I'm a Black Sheep Who's Blue (Leo Robin–Ralph Rainger) *Little Miss Marker*

Popular screen lovers Dick Powell and Ruby Keeler performing the "Flirtation Walk" sequence in the Warner Bros. picture of the same name (1934). The lyrics were by Mort Dixon, the melody by Allie Wrubel.

I'm Hummin', I'm Whistlin', I'm
  Singin' (Mack Gordon–Harry
  Revel) *She Loves Me Not*
It Was Sweet of You (Sidney
  Clare–Richard A. Whiting)

Transatlantic Merry-Go-Round
I've Had My Moments (Gus
  Kahn–Walter Donaldson)
  Hollywood Party
June in January (Leo Robin–

Ralph Rainger) *Here Is My Heart*

Keep Romance Alive (Bert Kalmar–Harry Ruby) *Hips, Hips, Hooray!*

Let's Fall in Love (Ted Koehler–Harold Arlen) *Let's Fall in Love*

Let's Give Three Cheers for Love (Mack Gordon–Harry Revel) *College Rhythm*

*Love in Bloom (Leo Robin–Ralph Rainger) *She Loves Me Not*

Love Is Just Around the Corner (Leo Robin–Louis Gensler) *Here Is My Heart*

Love Is Love Anywhere (Ted Koehler–Harold Arlen) *Let's Fall in Love*

Love Songs of the Nile (Arthur Freed-Nacio Herb Brown) *Barbarian*

Love Thy Neighbor (Mack Gordon–Harry Revel) *We're Not Dressing*

May I? (Mack Gordon–Harry Revel) *We're Not Dressing*

Mr. and Mrs. Is the Name (Mort Dixon–Allie Wrubel) *Flirtation Walk*

My Hat's on the Side of My Head (Claude Hulbert–Harry Woods) *Jack Ahoy*

My Old Flame (Sam Coslow–Arthur Johnston) *Belle of the Nineties*

Needle in a Haystack (Herb Magidson–Con Conrad) *Gay Divorcee*

New Moon Is Over My Shoulder (Arthur Freed-Nacio Herb Brown) *Student Tour*

On Account-a I Love You (Bud Green–Sam H. Stept) *Baby, Take a Bow*

On the Good Ship Lollipop (Sidney Clare–Richard A. Whiting) *Bright Eyes*

Once in a Lifetime (Gus Kahn–Walter Donaldson) *Operator 13*

One Night of Love (Gus Kahn–Victor Schertzinger) *One Night of Love*

She Reminds Me of You (Mack Gordon–Harry Revel) *We're Not Dressing*

Simple and Sweet (Irving Kahal–Sammy Fain) *Harold Teen*

Stay as Sweet as You Are (Mack Gordon–Harry Revel) *College Rhythm*

Straight from the Shoulder, Right from the Heart (Mack Gordon–Harry Revel) *She Loves Me Not*

Sweet Music (Al Dubin–Harry Warren) *Sweet Music*

Take a Lesson from the Lark (Leo Robin–Ralph Rainger) *Thank Your Stars*

Take a Number from One to Ten (Mack Gordon–Harry Revel) *College Rhythm*

That's Love (Lorenz Hart–Richard Rodgers) *Nana*

This Is Our Last Night Together (Lew Brown–Jay Gorney) *Stand Up and Cheer!*

Tonight Is Mine (Gus Kahn–W. Franke Harling) *Stingaree*

Waitin' at the Gate for Katy (Leo Robin–Richard A. Whiting) *Bottoms Up*

When My Ship Comes In (Gus
Kahn–Walter Donaldson) *Kid
Millions*
Why Do I Dream Those Dreams
(Al Dubin–Harry Warren)
Wonder Bar
With Every Breath I Take (Leo
Robin–Ralph Rainger) *Here Is
My Heart*

With My Eyes Wide Open I'm
Dreaming (Mack Gordon–
Harry Revel) *Shoot the
Works*
Your Head on My Shoulder
(Harold Adamson–Burton
Lane) *Kid Millions*

*Nominated for the Academy Award.
**Winner of the Academy Award.
†Under the title of "The Good in Every Man," the song was dropped from the film before release.*

List 5
25 Biggest Shirley Temple Film Songs

Animal Crackers in My Soup
(Ted Koehler–Irving
Caesar–Ray Henderson) *Curly
Top,* 1935
At the Codfish Ball (Sidney D.
Mitchell–Lew Pollack) *Captain
January,* 1936
*Baby, Take a Bow (Lew Brown–
Jay Gorney) *Stand Up and
Cheer!,* 1934
Be Optimistic (Walter Bullock–
Harold Spina) *Little Miss Broad-
way,* 1938
*But Definitely (Mack Gordon–
Harry Revel) *Poor Little Rich
Girl,* 1936
†Curly Top (Ted Koehler–Ray
Henderson) *Curly Top,* 1935
Dixie-Anna (Ted Koehler–James
McHugh) *Dimples,* 1936
Fifth Avenue (Mack Gordon–
Harry Warren) *Young People,*
1940
*Goodnight, My Love (Mack

Gordon–Harry Revel)
Stowaway, 1936
I Wouldn't Take a Million (Mack
Gordon–Harry Warren) *Young
People,* 1940
Laugh, You Son of a Gun (Leo
Robin–Ralph Rainger) *Little
Miss Marker,* 1934
Little Miss Broadway/I'll Build a
Broadway for You (Walter
Bullock–Harold Spina) *Little
Miss Broadway,* 1938
Oh, My Goodness (Mack Gor-
don–Harry Revel) *Poor Little
Rich Girl,* 1936
Old Straw Hat (Mack Gordon–
Harry Revel) *Rebecca of Sun-
nybrook Farm,* 1938
On Account-a I Love You (Bud
Green–Sam H. Stept) *Baby,
Take a Bow,* 1934
On the Good Ship Lollipop
(Sidney Clare–Richard A.
Whiting) *Bright Eyes,* 1934

Picture Me Without You (Ted Koehler–James McHugh) *Dimples*, 1936

Polly-Wolly-Doodle (Sidney Clare–Buddy DeSylva) *Littlest Rebel*, 1935 (revised version)

Right Somebody to Love (Jack Yellen–Lew Pollack) *Captain January*, 1936

That's What I Want for Christmas (Irving Caesar–Gerald Marks) *Stowaway*, 1936

This Is a Happy Little Ditty (Walter Bullock–Harold Spina) *Just Around the Corner*, 1938

§Toy Trumpet (Sidney D. Mitchell–Lew Pollack–Raymond Scott) *Rebecca of Sunnybrook Farm*, 1938

Tra-La-La-La (Mack Gordon–Harry Warren) *Young People*, 1940

When I Grow Up (Edward Heyman–Ray Henderson) *Curly Top*, 1935

*When I'm with You (Mack Gordon–Harry Revel) *Poor Little Rich Girl*, 1936

*Special lyric added.
†Dance only.
§*Scott was the brother of Mark Warnow, leader of radio's* Your Hit Parade *orchestra.*

List 6
Most Popular 75 Songs from 1935 Films

About a Quarter to Nine (Al Dubin–Harry Warren) *Go Into Your Dance*

According to the Moonlight (Jack Yellen–Herb Magidson–Joseph Meyer) *George White's 1935 Scandals*

Alone (Arthur Freed–Nacio Herb Brown) *Night at the Opera*

Animal Crackers in My Soup (Ted Koehler–Irving Caesar–Ray Henderson) *Curly Top*

Bon Jour, Mam'selle (Mack Gordon–Harry Revel) *Paris in the Spring*

Champagne Waltz (Con Conrad–Ben Oakland–Milton Drake) *Champagne Waltz*

*Cheek to Cheek (Irving Berlin) *Top Hat*

Curly Top (Ted Koehler–Ray Henderson) *Curly Top*

Don't Give Up the Ship (Al Dubin–Harry Warren) *Shipmates Forever*

Down by the River (Lorenz Hart–Richard Roders) *Mississippi*

Hear What My Heart Is Saying (Harold Adamson–Burton Lane) *Reckless*

Here's to Romance (Herb Magidson–Con Conrad) *Here's to Romance*

I Dream Too Much (Dorothy

Al Jolson and Ruby Keeler, then man and wife in real life, practice Al Dubin and Harry Warren's "About a Quarter to Nine" routine in *Go Into Your Dance* (1935).

Fields–Jerome Kern) *I Dream Too Much*

I Feel a Song Comin' On (Dorothy Fields–George Oppenheimer–James McHugh) *Every Night at Eight*

I Feel Like a Feather in the Breeze (Mack Gordon–Harry Revel) *Collegiate*

I Found a Dream (Don Hartman–Jay Gorney) *Redheads on Parade*

I Won't Dance (Oscar Hammerstein II–Otto Harbach–Dorothy Fields–James McHugh–Jerome Kern) *Roberta*

I'd Rather Listen to Your Eyes (Al Dubin–Harry Warren) *Shipmates Forever*

If I Should Lose You (Leo Robin–Ralph Rainger) *Rose of the Rancho*

I'm Goin' Shoppin' with You (Al Dubin–Harry Warren) *Gold Diggers of 1935*

I'm in Love All Over Again (Dorothy Fields–James McHugh) *Hooray for Love*

I'm in the Mood for Love (Dorothy Fields–James McHugh) *Every Night at Eight*

I'm Livin' in a Great Big Way

(Dorothy Fields–James McHugh) *Hooray for Love*

I'm Shooting High (Ted Koehler–James McHugh) *King of Burlesque*

I'm Sittin' High on a Hill Top (Gus Kahn–Arthur Johnston) *Thanks a Million*

In the Middle of a Kiss (Sam Coslow) *College Scandal*

Isn't This a Lovely Day (to Be Caught in the Rain)? (Irving Berlin) *Top Hat*

It's All So New to Me) Edward Heyman–Ray Henderson) *Curly Top*

It's Easy to Remember (Lorenz Hart–Richard Rodgers) *Mississippi*

I've Got a Pocket Full of Sunshine (Gus Kahn–Arthur Johnston) *Thanks a Million*

Jockey on the Carrousel (Dorothy Fields–Jerome Kern) *I Dream Too Much*

Keep Your Fingers Crossed (Sam Coslow–Richard A. Whiting) *Coronado*

Lady in Red (Mort Dixon–Allie Wrubel) *In Caliente*

Let's Make a Wish (Bert Kalmar–Harry Ruby) *Walking on Air*

Little Things You Used to Do (Al Dubin–Harry Warren) *Go Into Your Dance*

Little White Gardenia (Sam Coslow) *All the King's Horses*

Lonely Gondolier (Al Dubin–Harry Warren) *Broadway Gondolier*

(Lookie, Lookie, Lookie) Here Comes Cookie (Mack Gordon)

Love in Bloom

Love Me Forever (Gus Kahn–Victor Schertzinger) *Love Me Forever*

Lovely Lady (Ted Koehler–James McHugh) *King of Burlesque*

*Lovely to Look At (Dorothy Fields–James McHugh–Jerome Kern) *Roberta*

**Lullaby of Broadway (Al Dubin–Harry Warren) *Gold Diggers of 1935*

Lulu's Back in Town (Al Dubin–Harry Warren) *Gold Diggers of 1935*

Mammy, I'll Sing about You (Al Dubin–Harry Warren) *Go Into Your Dance*

Midnight in Paris (Herb Magidson–Con Conrad) *Here's to Romance*

One Rainy Afternoon (Jack Stern–Harry Tobias–Ralph Erwin) *One Rainy Afternoon*

Paris in the Spring (Mack Gordon–Harry Revel) *Paris in the Spring*

Penny in My Pocket (Leo Robin–Ralph Rainger) *Millions in the Air*

Piccolino (Irving Berlin) *Top Hat*

Rhythm of the Rain (Jack Meskill–Jack Stern) *Folies Bergère de Paris*

Roll Along, Prairie Moon (Ted Fiorito–Harry MacPherson–Albert Von Tilzer) *Here Comes the Band*

Rose in Her Hair (Al Dubin–Harry Warren) *Broadway Gondolier*

She's a Latin from Manhattan (Al

Dubin–Harry Warren) *Go Into Your Dance*

Simple Things in Life (Ted Koehler–Ray Henderson) *Curly Top*

So Nice Seeing You Again (Mort Dixon–Allie Wrubel) *We're in the Money*

Soon (Lorenz Hart–Richard Rodgers) *Mississippi*

Tender Is the Night (Walter Donaldson) *Here Comes the Band*

Thanks a Million (Gus Kahn–Arthur Johnston) *Thanks a Million*

Then It Isn't Love (Leo Robin–Ralph Rainger) *Devil Is a Woman*

Top Hat, White Tie and Tails (Irving Berlin) *Top Hat*

Twenty-four Hours a Day (Arthur Swanstrom–James F. Hanley) *Sweet Surrender*

Two for Tonight (Mack Gordon–Harry Revel) *Two for Tonight*

Two Together (Gus Kahn–Arthur Johnston) *Girl Friend*

What's the Reason (I'm Not Pleasin' You)? (Coy Poe–Jimmy Grier–Pinky Tomlin–Earl Hatch) *Times Square Lady*

When I Grow Too Old to Dream (Oscar Hammerstein II–Sigmund Romberg) *The Night Is Young*

Where Am I (Am I in Heaven)? (Al Dubin–Harry Warren) *Stars Over Broadway*

Why Do They Call It Gay Paree? (Mack Gordon–Harry Revel) *Paris in the Spring*

Will I Ever Know? (Mack Gordon–Harry Revel) *Collegiate*

With All My Heart (Gus Kahn–James McHugh) *Her Master's Voice*

Without a Word of Warning (Mack Gordon–Harry Revel) *Two for Tonight*

Words Are in My Heart (Al Dubin–Harry Warren) *Gold Diggers of 1935*

Would There Be Love (Mack Gordon–Harry Revel) *Stolen Harmony*

You Took the Words Right Out of My Mouth (Harold Adamson–Burton Lane) *Folies Bergère de Paris*

You're an Angel (Dorothy Fields–James McHugh) *Hooray for Love*

You're an Eyeful of Heaven (Mort Dixon–Allie Wrubel) *Bright Lights*

*Nominated for the Academy Award.
**Winner of the Academy Award.

List 7
Most Popular 100 Songs from 1936 Films

All My Life (Sidney D. Mitchell–Sam H. Stept) *Laughing Irish Eyes*

At the Codfish Ball (Sidney D. Mitchell–Lew Pollack) *Captain January*

Awake in a Dream (Leo Robin–
Frederick Hollander) *Desire*
Bojangles of Harlem (Dorothy
Fields–Jerome Kern) *Swing
Time*
Broadway Rhythm (Arthur
Freed–Nacio Herb Brown)
Broadway Melody of 1936
But Definitely (Mack Gordon–
Harry Revel) *Poor Little Rich Girl*
But Where Are You (Irving
Berlin) *Follow the Fleet*
*Did I Remember (Harold Adam-
son–Walter Donaldson) *Suzy*
Double Trouble (Leo Robin–
Richard A. Whiting–Ralph
Rainger) *Big Broadcast of 1936*
Easy to Love (Cole Porter) *Born to
Dance*
Empty Saddles (Billy Hill) *Rhythm
on the Range*
An Evening with You (Al Dubin–
Harry Warren) *Colleen*
Fancy Meeting You (E.Y. Har-
burg–Harold Arlen) *Stage Struck*
A Fine Romance (Dorothy Fields–
Jerome Kern) *Swing Time*
Follow Your Heart (Sidney D.
Mitchell–Victor Schertzinger)
Follow Your Heart
Goodnight, My Love (Mack Gor-
don–Harry Revel) *Stowaway*
House Jack Built for Jill (Leo
Robin–Frederick Hollander)
Rhythm on the Range
I Adore You (Leo Robin–Ralph
Rainger) *College Holiday*
I Can't Escape from You (Leo
Robin–Ralph Rainger–Richard
A. Whiting) *Rhythm on the Range*
I Don't Have to Dream Again (Al
Dubin–Harry Warren) *Colleen*

I Don't Want to Make History
(Leo Robin–Ralph Rainger)
Palm Springs
I Have the Room Above (Oscar
Hammerstein II–Jerome Kern)
Show Boat
I Wished on the Moon (Dorothy
Parker–Ralph Rainger) *Big
Broadcast of 1936*
I'd Rather Lead a Band (Irving
Berlin) *Follow the Fleet*
I'll Sing You a Thousand Love
Songs (Al Dubin–Harry War-
ren) *Cain and Mabel*
I'm an Old Cow Hand (Johnny
Mercer) *Rhythm on the Range*
I'm Putting All My Eggs in One
Basket (Irving Berlin) *Follow the
Fleet*
In Your Own Quiet Way (E.Y.
Harburg–Harold Arlen) *Stage
Struck*
†It's Been So Long (Harold
Adamson–Walter Donaldson)
Great Ziegfeld
It's Love I'm After (Sidney D.
Mitchell–Lew Pollack) *Pigskin
Parade*
It's the Animal in Me (Mack Gor-
don–Harry Revel) *Big Broadcast
of 1936*
It's You I'm Talking About (Mack
Gordon–Harry Revel) *Florida
Special*
I've Got a Feelin' You're Foolin'
(Arthur Freed–Nacio Herb
Brown) *Broadway Melody of
1936*
*I've Got You Under My Skin
(Cole Porter) *Born to Dance*
Je Vous Adore (Sam Coslow–Vic-
tor Young) *Fatal Lady*

Let Yourself Go (Irving Berlin) *Follow the Fleet*

Let's Call a Heart a Heart (Johnny Burke–Arthur Johnston) *Pennies from Heaven*

Let's Face the Music and Dance (Irving Berlin) *Follow the Fleet*

Let's Sing Again (Gus Kahn–James McHugh) *Let's Sing Again*

Little House That Love Built (Al Dubin–Harry Warren) *Sing Me a Love Song*

Lookin' Around Corners for You (Mack Gordon–Harry Revel) *Head Over Heels in Love*

May I Have the Next Romance with You? (Mack Gordon–Harry Revel) *Head Over Heels in Love*

*Melody from the Sky (Sidney D. Mitchell–Louis Alter) *Trail of the Lonesome Pine*

Miss Brown to You (Leo Robin–Ralph Rainger) *Big Broadcast of 1936*

Moonburn (Edward Heyman–Hoagy Carmichael) *Anything Goes*

Moonlight and Shadows (Leo Robin–Frederick Hollander) *Jungle Princess*

Moonlit Waltz (Sidney D. Mitchell–Lew Pollack) *One in a Million*

My Kingdom for a Kiss (Al Dubin–Harry Warren) *Hearts Divided*

Never Gonna Dance (Dorothy Fields–Jerome Kern) *Swing Time*

Oh, My Goodness (Mack Gordon–Harry Revel) *Poor Little Rich Girl*

On a Sunday Afternoon (Arthur Freed–Nacio Herb Brown) *Broadway Melody of 1936*

One, Two, Button Your Shoe (Johnny Burke–Arthur Johnston) *Pennies from Heaven*

One in a Million (Sidney D. Mitchell–Lew Pollack) *One in a Million*

One Never Knows, Does One? (Mack Gordon–Harry Revel) *Stowaway*

*Pennies from Heaven (Johnny Burke–Arthur Johnston) *Pennies from Heaven*

Pick Yourself Up (Dorothy Fields–Jerome Kern) *Swing Time*

Picture Me Without You (Ted Koehler–James McHugh) *Dimples*

Rainbow on the River (Paul Francis Webster–Louis Alter) *Rainbow on the River*

Rap, Tap on Wood (Cole Porter) *Born to Dance*

Rendezvous with a Dream (Leo Robin–Ralph Rainger) *Poppy*

Right Somebody to Love (Jack Yellen–Lew Pollack) *Captain January*

San Francisco (Gus Kahn–Bronislaw Kaper–Walter Jurmann) *San Francisco*

Shake It Off with Rhythm (E.Y. Harburg–Harold Arlen) *Strike Me Pink*

Sing, Baby, Sing (Jack Yellen–Lew Pollack) *Sing, Baby, Sing*

Skeleton in the Closet (Johnny Burke–Arthur Johnston) *Pennies from Heaven*

Smoke Dreams (Arthur Freed–

Nacio Herb Brown) *After the Thin Man*

So Do I (Johnny Burke–Arthur Johnston) *Pennies from Heaven*

§Stars in My Eyes (Dorothy Fields–Fritz Kreisler), *King Steps Out*

Summer Night (Al Dubin–Harry Warren) *Sing Me a Love Song*

Sweetheart Waltz (Ralph Freed–Burton Lane) *College Holiday*

That's What I Want for Christmas (Irving Caesar–Gerald Marks) *Stowawauy*

There's Something in the Air (Harold Adamson–James McHugh) *Banjo on My Knee*

A Thousand Dreams of You (Paul Francis Webster–Louis Alter) *You Only Live Once*

Thru the Courtesy of Love (Jack Scholl–M.K. Jerome) *Tattler*

Trust in Me (Ned Wever–Jean Schwartz–Milton Ager) *Let's Sing Again*

Twilight on the Trail (Sidney D. Mitchell–Louis Alter) *Trail of the Lonesome Pine*

Twinkle, Twinkle, Little Star (Herb Magidson–Ben Oakland) *Hats Off*

Waltz in Swing Time (Dorothy Fields–Jerome Kern) *Swing Time*

**The Way You Look Tonight (Dorothy Fields–Jerome Kern) *Swing Time*

When April Comes Again (Al J. Neiburg–Marty Symes–Jerry Levison) *Hollywood Revels of 1936*

*When Did You Leave Heaven? (Walter Bullock–Richard A.

Whiting) *Sing, Baby, Sing*

When I'm with You (Mack Gordon–Harry Revel) *Poor Little Rich Girl*

When You Are Dancing the Waltz (Lorenz Hart–Richard Rodgers) *Dancing Pirate*

Where Are You? (Harold Adamson–James McHugh) *Top of the Town*

Where Have You Been All My Life? (Herb Magidson–Ben Oakland) *Hats Off*

Where Is My Heart? (Leo Robin–Ralph Rainger) *Three Cheers for Love*

Where the Lazy River Goes By (Harold Adamson–James McHugh) *Banjo on My Knee*

Who's Afraid of Love? (Sidney D. Mitchell–Lew Pollack) *One in a Million*

Who's that Knocking at My Heart? (Frank Loesser–Burton Lane) *College Holiday*

Why Dream? (Leo Robin–Ralph Rainger–Richard A. Whiting) *Big Broadcast of 1936*

Why Stars Come Out at Night (Ray Noble) *Big Broadcast of 1936*

Would You (Arthur Freed–Nacio Herb Brown) *San Francisco*

You (Harold Adamson–Walter Donaldson) *Great Ziegfeld*

You Are My Lucky Star (Arthur Freed–Nacio Herb Brown) *Broadway Melody of 1936*

You Do the Darn'dest Things, Baby (Sidney D. Mitchell–Lew Pollack) *Pigskin Parade*

You Gotta Know How to Dance (Al Dubin–Harry Warren) *Colleen*

You Never Looked So Beautiful
(Harold Adamson–Walter
Donaldson) *Great Ziegfeld*
You Turned the Tables on Me
(Sidney D. Mitchell–Louis
Alter) *Sing, Baby, Sing*

You're Slightly Terrific (Sidney
D. Mitchell–Lew Pollack)
Pigskin Parade
You're the Cure for What Ails
Me (E.Y. Harburg–Harold
Arlen) *Singing Kid*

Nominated for the Academy Award.
**Winner of the Academy Award.*
†*Dropped from the picture before release.*
§*Kreisler revised the melody from his own "Who Can Tell?," which appeared in the 1919 operetta*
Apple Blossom.

List 8
Most Popular 125 Songs from 1937 Films

Afraid to Dream (Mack Gor-
don–Harry Revel) *You Can't
Have Everything*
All God's Chillun Got Rhythm
(Gus Kahn–Bronislaw Kaper–
Walter Jurman) *Day at the Races*
All You Want to Do Is Dance
(Johnny Burke–Arthur
Johnston) *Double or Nothing*
All's Fair in Love and War (Al
Dubin–Harry Warren) *Gold
Diggers of 1937*
Am I in Love? (Al Dubin–Harry
Warren) *Mr. Dodd Takes the Air*
Beginner's Luck (Ira and George
Gershwin) *Shall We Dance*
Bei Mir Bist Du Schoen (Sammy
Cahn–Saul Chaplin–Jacob
Jacobs–Shalom Segunda) *Love,
Honor and Behave*
Blossoms on Broadway (Leo
Robin–Ralph Rainger) *Blossoms
on Broadway*
Blue Hawaii (Leo Robin–Ralph
Rainger) *Waikiki Wedding*
The Call to Arms (Edward

Heyman–Arthur Schwartz) *That
Girl from Paris*
Can I Forget You? (Oscar Ham-
merstein II–Jerome Kern) *High,
Wide and Handsome*
'Cause My Baby Says It's So (Al
Dubin–Harry Warren) *Singing
Marine*
Danger, Love at Work (Mack
Gordon–Harry Revel) *You Can't
Have Everything*
Did Anyone Ever Tell You?
(Harold Adamson–James
McHugh), *When Love Is
Young*
Donkey Serenade (Bob Wright–
Chet Forrest–Rudolf Friml–
Herbert Stothart) *Firefly*
Don't Ever Change (Walter
Hirsch–Lou Handman) *Rhythm
in the Clouds*
Don't Save Your Love (for a
Rainy Day) (Walter Bullock–
Harold Spina) *52nd Street*
Easy Living (Leo Robin–Ralph
Rainger) *Easy Living*

Ebb Tide (Leo Robin-Ralph Rainger) *Ebb Tide*

Every Day's a Holiday (Sam Coslow-Barry Trivers) *Every Day's a Holiday*

First Time I Saw You (Allie Wrubel-Nathaniel Shilkret) *Toast of New York*

Foggy Day (Ira and George Gershwin) *Damsel in Distress*

Folks Who Live on the Hill (Oscar Hammerstein II-Jerome Kern) *High, Wide and Handsome*

Girl on the Police Gazette (Irving Berlin) *On the Avenue*

Good Night, Angel (Herb Magidson-Allie Wrubel) *Radio City Revels*

Got a Pair of New Shoes (Arthur Freed-Nacio Herb Brown) *Thoroughbreds Don't Cry*

Have You Got Any Castles, Baby? (Johnny Mercer-Richard A. Whiting) *Varsity Show*

Here's Love in Your Eye (Leo Robin-Ralph Rainger) *Big Broadcast of 1937*

High, Wide and Handsome (Oscar Hammerstein II-Jerome Kern) *High, Wide and Handsome*

Hooray for Hollywood (Johnny Mercer-Richard A. Whiting) *Hollywood Hotel*

How Could You? (Al Dubin-Harry Warren) *San Quentin*

I Could Use a Dream (Walter Bullock-Harold Spina) *Sally, Irene and Mary*

I Hit a New High (Harold Adamson-James McHugh) *Hitting a New High*

I Know Now (Al Dubin-Harry Warren) *Singing Marine*

I Still Love to Kiss You Goodnight (Walter Bullock-Harold Spina) *52nd Street*

I Wanna Be in Winchell's Column (Mack Gordon-Harry Revel) *Love and Hisses*

I Want a New Romance (Sam Coslow-Burton Lane) *Love on Toast*

If I Put My Heart in My Song (Sam Coslow-Al Siegel) *Mountain Music*

I'll Take Romance (Oscar Hammerstein II-Ben Oakland) *I'll Take Romance*

I'm Bubbling Over (Mack Gordon-Harry Revel) *Wake Up and Live*

I'm Like a Fish Out of Water (Johnny Mercer-Richard A. Whiting) *Hollywood Hotel*

In a Little Hula Heaven (Leo Robin-Ralph Rainger) *Waikiki Wedding*

In Old Chicago (Mack Gordon-Harry Revel) *In Old Chicago*

In the Still of the Night (Cole Porter) *Rosalie*

Is It Love or Infatuation (Sam Coslow-Frederick Hollander) *This Way, Please*

It's Raining Sunbeams (Sam Coslow-Frederick Hollander) *100 Men and a Girl*

It's the Natural Thing to Do (Johnny Burke-Arthur Johnston) *Double or Nothing*

I've a Strange New Rhythm in My Heart (Cole Porter) *Rosalie*

I've Got My Heart Set on You

(Mack Gordon–Harry Revel)
Ali Baba Goes to Town

I've Got My Love to Keep Me
Warm (Irving Berlin) *On the
Avenue*

I've Hitched My Wagon to a Star
(Johnny Mercer–Richard A.
Whiting) *Hollywood Hotel*

I've Taken a Fancy to You
(Sidney D. Mitchell–Lew
Pollack) *In Old Chicago*

Just a Quiet Evening (Johnny
Mercer–Richard A. Whiting)
Ready, Willing and Able

La Bomba (Leo Robin–Ralph
Rainger) *Big Broadcast of 1937*

Lady Who Couldn't Be Kissed (Al
Dubin–Harry Warren) *Singing
Marine*

Let That Be a Lesson to You
(Johnny Mercer–Richard A.
Whiting) *Varsity Show*

Let's Call the Whole Thing Off
(Ira and George Gershwin)
Shall We Dance

Let's Give Love Another Chance
(Harold Adamson–James
McHugh) *Hitting a New High*

Let's Put Our Heads Together
(E.Y. Harburg–Harold Arlen)
Gold Diggers of 1937

Love Is Never Out of Season
(Lew Brown–Sammy Fain) *New
Faces of 1937*

Love Is on the Air Tonight
(Johnny Mercer–Richard A.
Whiting) *Varsity Show*

Loveliness of You (Mack Gordon–Harry Revel) *You Can't
Have Everything*

Lovely One (Frank Loesser–Man-
ning Sherwin) *Vogues of 1938*

Mama, I Wanna Make Rhythm
(Jerome Jerome–Richard
Byron–Walter Kent) *Manhattan
Merry-Go-Round*

Melody for Two (Al
Dubin–Harry Warren) *Melody
for Two*

Moon Got in My Eyes (Johnny
Burke–Arthur Johnston) *Double
or Nothing*

Moon of Manakoora (Frank
Loesser–Alfred Newman) *Hur-
ricane*

Music in My Heart (Paul Francis
Webster–Louise Alter–Oscar
Straus) *Make a Wish*

My Little Buckaroo (Jack
Scholl–M.K. Jerome) *Cherokee
Strip*

My Silver Dollar Man (Al
Dubin–Harry Warren) *Marked
Woman*

Nearness of You (Ned Washington–Hoagy Carmichael)
Romance in the Rough

Never in a Million Years (Mack
Gordon–Harry Revel) *Wake Up
and Live*

Nice Work If You Can Get It (Ira
and George Gershwin) *Damsel
in Distress*

Night in Manhattan (Leo
Robin–Ralph Rainger) *Big
Broadcast of 1937*

Night Over Shanghai (Johnny
Mercer–Harry Warren) *Singing
Marine*

Our Penthouse on Third Avenue
(Lew Brown–Sammy Fain) *New
Faces of 1937*

Our Song (Dorothy Fields–Jerome
Kern) *When You're in Love*

Over Night (Sidney D. Mitchell–
Lew Pollack) *Thin Ice*
*Remember Me? (Al Dubin–
Harry Warren) *Mr. Dodd Takes
the Air*
Rosalie (Cole Porter) *Rosalie*
Roses in December (Herb Magid-
son–Allie Wrubel) *Life of the
Party*
Seal It with a Kiss (Edward
Heyman–Arthur Schwartz) *That
Girl from Paris*
September in the Rain (Al
Dubin–Harry Warren) *Melody
for Two*
Seventh Heaven (Sidney D.
Mitchell–Lew Pollack) *Seventh
Heaven*
Shall We Dance (Ira and George
Gershwin) *Shall We Dance*
Silhouetted in the Moonlight
(Johnny Mercer–Richard A.
Whiting) *Hollywood Hotel*
Slap that Bass (Ira and George
Gershwin) *Shall We Dance*
Slumming on Park Avenue (Ir-
ving Berlin) *On the Avenue*
Smarty (Ralph Freed–Burton
Lane) *Double or Nothing*
Song of the Marines (Al
Dubin–Harry Warren) *Singing
Marine*
Stiff Upper Lip (Ira and George
Gershwin) *Damsel in Distress*
Stop! You're Breakin' My Heart
(Ted Koehler–Burton Lane)
Artists and Models
Sweet as a Song (Mack Gor-
don–Harry Revel) *Sally, Irene
and Mary*
Sweet Heartache (Ned Washing-
ton–Sam H. Stept) *Hit Parade*

Sweet Is the Word for You (Leo
Robin–Ralph Rainger) *Waikiki
Wedding*
**Sweet Leilani (Harry Owens)
Waikiki Wedding
Sweet Someone (Mack Gor-
don–Harry Revel) *Love and
Hisses*
Sweet Varsity Sue (Charles
Tobias–Al Lewis–Murray
Mencher) *Life Begins in College*
Swing High, Swing Low (Ralph
Freed–Burton Lane) *Swing
High, Swing Low*
Swing Is Here to Sway (Mack
Gordon–Harry Revel) *Ali Baba
Goes to Town*
Talking Through My Heart (Leo
Robin–Ralph Rainger) *Big
Broadcast of 1937*
*That Old Feeling (Lew
Brown–Sammy Fain) *Vogues of
1938*
There's a Lull in My Life (Mack
Gordon–Harry Revel) *Wake Up
and Live*
There's a New Moon (Over the
Old Mill) (Herb Magid-
son–Allie Wrubel) *Radio City
Revels*
They All Laughed (Ira and
George Gershwin) *Shall We
Dance*
*They Can't Take That Away
from Me (Ira and George
Gerswhin) *Shall We Dance*
Things Are Looking Up (Ira and
George Gershwin) *Damsel in
Distress*
This Never Happened Before
(Harold Adamson–James
McHugh) *Hitting a New High*

Ruby Keeler and Lee Dixon dance on the keys of a mammoth typewriter while duetting Johnny Mercer and Richard A. Whiting's "Too Marvelous for Words" in Ready, Willing and Able, **1937. Photo courtesy** Movie Star News.

This Year's Kisses (Irving Berlin) On the Avenue

Tomorrow Is Another Day (Gus Kahn–Bronislaw Kaper–Walter Jurmann) Day at the Races

Too Marvelous for Words (Johnny Mercer–Richard A. Whiting) Ready, Willing and Able

True Confession (Sam Coslow–Frederick Hollander) True Confession

Turn Off the Moon (Sam Coslow) Turn Off the Moon

Wake Up and Live (Mack Gordon–Harry Revel) Wake Up and Live

Was It Rain? (Walter Hirsch–Lew Handman) Hit Parade

We're Working Our Way Through College (Johnny Mercer–Richard A. Whiting) Varsity Show

What a Beautiful Beginning (Sidney Clare–Harry Akst) Sing and Be Happy

When Love Is Young (Harold Adamson–James McHugh) When Love Is Young

*Whispers in the Dark (Leo Robin–Frederick Hollander) Artist and Models

Who Knows? (Cole Porter) Rosalie

With Plenty of Money and You
(Al Dubin–Harry Warren) *Gold
Diggers of 1937*
Yankee Doodle Band (Herb
Magidson–Allie Wrubel) *Life of
the Party*
You Can't Have Everything

(Mack Gordon–Harry Revel)
You Can't Have Everything
You Can't Run Away from Love
Tonight (Al Dubin–Harry War-
ren) *Singing Marine*
You're Laughing at Me (Irving
Berlin) *On the Avenue*

*Nominated for the Academy Award.
**Winner of the Academy Award.*

List 9
Most Popular 100 Songs from 1938 Films

Alone with You (Sidney D.
Mitchell–Lew Pollack) *Rebecca of
Sunnybrook Farm*
*Always and Always (Bob
Wright–Chet Forrest–Edward
Ward) *Mannequin*
April in My Heart (Helen
Meinardi–Hoagy Carmichael)
Say It in French
Beside a Moonlit Stream (Sam
Coslow–Frederick Hollander)
Booloo
By a Wishing Well (Mack Gor-
don–Harry Revel) *My Lucky
Star*
*Change Partners (Irving Berlin)
Carefree
Chapel Bells (Harold Adam-
son–James McHugh) *Mad About
Music*
Could You Pass in Love? (Mack
Gordon–Harry Revel) *My Lucky
Star*
*Cowboy and the Lady (Arthur
Quenzer–Lionel Newman)
Cowboy and the Lady
Cowboy from Brooklyn (Johnny

Mercer–Harry Warren) *Cowboy
from Brooklyn*
Daydreaming (All Night Long)
(Johnny Mercer–Harry War-
ren) *Gold Diggers in Paris*
Don't Let That Moon Get Away
(Johnny Burke–James V.
Monaco) *Sing You Sinners*
Dreamy Hawaiian Moon (Harry
Owens) *Cocoanut Grove*
*Dust (Johnny Marvin) *Under
Western Stars*
Everybody Sing (Arthur
Freed–Nacio Herb Brown)
Broadway Melody of 1938
For the First Time (Harold
Adamson–James McHugh)
Youth Takes a Fling
Funny Old Hills (Leo Robin–
Ralph Rainger) *Paris Honeymoon*
Garden of the Moon (Al Dubin–
Johnny Mercer–Harry Warren)
Garden of the Moon
Girl Friend of the Whirling Der-
vish (Al Dubin–Johnny Mercer–
Harry Warren) *Garden of the
Moon*

A Gypsy Told Me (Jack Yellen–
Sam Pokrass) *Happy Landing*
Havin' Myself a Time (Leo Robin–
Ralph Rainger) *Tropic Holiday*
Heart and Soul (Frank Loesser–
Hoagy Carmichael) *A Song Is
Born*
Heigh-Ho (Larry Morey–Frank
Churchill) *Snow White and the
Seven Dwarfs*
How'dja Like to Love Me (Frank
Loesser–Burton Lane) *College
Swing*
I Have Eyes (Leo Robin–Ralph
Rainger) *Paris Honeymoon*
I Hum a Waltz (Mack Gordon–
Harry Revel) *This Is My Affair*
I Love to Whistle (Harold Adam-
son–James McHugh) *Mad About
Music*
I Used to Be Color Blind (Irving
Berlin) *Carefree*
I Wanna Go Back to Bali
(Johnny Mercer–Harry War-
ren) *Gold Diggers in Paris*
I Was Doing All Right (Ira and
George Gershwin) *Goldwyn
Follies*
I'll Dream Tonight (Johnny
Mercer–Harry Warren) *Cowboy
from Brooklyn*
I'm Feelin' Like a Million (Arthur
Freed–Nacio Herb Brown)
Broadway Melody of 1938
I'm in My Glory (Harold Adam-
son–James McHugh) *Merry-Go-
Round of 1938*
I'm Wishing (Larry Morey–Frank
Churchill) *Snow White and the
Seven Dwarfs*
In Any Language (Mack Gordon–
Harry Revel) *Josette*

In Between (Roger Edens) *Love
Finds Andy Hardy*
Invitation to Love (Mack Gor-
don–Harry Revel) *Straight, Place
and Show*
I've Got a Date with a Dream
(Mack Gordon–Harry Revel)
My Lucky Star
I've Got a Pocketful of Dreams
(Johnny Burke–James V.
Monaco) *Sing You Sinners*
*Jeepers Creepers (Johnny
Mercer–Harry Warren) *Going
Places*
Joobalai (Leo Robin–Ralph Rain-
ger) *Paris Honeymoon*
Just Let Me Look at You
(Dorothy Fields–Jerome Kern)
Joy of Living
Latin Quarter (Al Dubin–Harry
Warren) *Gold Diggers in Paris*
Little Kiss at Twilight (Leo
Robin–Ralph Rainger) *Give Me
a Sailor*
Little Miss Broadway/I'll Build a
Broadway for You (Walter
Bullock–Harold Spina) *Little
Miss Broadway*
Love Is Here to Stay (Ira and
George Gershwin) *Goldwyn
Follies*
Love Is Where You Find It
(Johnny Mercer–Harry Warren)
Garden of the Moon
Love Walked In (Ira and George
Gershwin) *Goldwyn Follies*
Lovelight in the Starlight (Ralph
Freed–Frederick Hollander) *Her
Jungle Love*
Mama, That Moon Is Here Again
(Leo Robin–Ralph Rainger) *Big
Broadcast of 1938*

Eleanor Powell and George Murphy sing and dance their financial woes away with Arthur Freed and Nacio Herb Brown's "I'm Feelin' Like a Million" in *Broadway Melody of 1938.*

May I Drop a Petal in Your Glass of Wine? (Mack Gordon–Harry Revel) *Josette*

Meet the Beat of My Heart (Mack Gordon–Harry Revel)

Love Finds Andy Hardy

*Merrily We Live (Arthur Quenzer–Phil Craig) *Merrily We Live*

*Mist Over the Moon (Oscar

Hammerstein II–Ben Oakland)
Lady Objects

Moments Like This (Frank
Loesser–Burton Lane) *College
Swing*

My Fine Feathered Friend
(Harold Adamson–James
McHugh) *You're a Sweetheart*

My Heart Is Taking Lessons
(Johnny Burke–James V.
Monaco) *Dr. Rhythm*

*My Own (Harold Adamson–
James McHugh) *That Certain
Age*

My Walking Stick (Irving Berlin)
Alexander's Ragtime Band

*Now It Can Be Told (Irving
Berlin) *Alexander's Ragtime
Band*

Old Apple Tree (Jack
Scholl–M.K. Jerome) *Swing
Your Lady*

Old Straw Hat (Mack Gordon–
Harry Revel) *Rebecca of Sunnybrook Farm*

On the Sentimental Side (Johnny
Burke–James V. Monaco) *Dr.
Rhythm*

The One I Love (Gus Kahn–
Bronislaw Kaper–Walter Jurmann) *Everybody Sing*

Ride, Tenderfoot, Ride (Johnny
Mercer–Richard A. Whiting)
Cowboy from Brooklyn

Say It with a Kiss (Johnny
Mercer–Harry Warren) *Going
Places*

Says My Heart (Frank Loesser–
Burton Lane) *Cocoanut Grove*

Serenade to the Stars (Harold
Adamson–James McHugh) *Mad
About Music*

Silver on the Sage (Leo Robin–
Ralph Rainger) *Texans*

Small Fry (Frank Loesser–Hoagy
Carmichael) *Sing You Sinners*

Some Day My Prince Will Come
(Larry Morey–Frank Churchill)
Snow White and the Seven Dwarfs

Someone to Care for Me (Gus
Kahn–Bronislaw Kaper–Walter
Jurmann) *Three Smart Girls*

Stolen Heaven (Ralph Freed–
Frederick Hollander) *Stolen
Heaven*

Sun Up to Sun Down (Gus
Kahn–Sigmund Romberg) *Girl
of the Golden West*

Thanks for Ev'rything (Mack
Gordon–Harry Revel) *Thanks
for Everything*

**Thanks for the Memory (Leo
Robin–Ralph Rainger) *Big
Broadcast of 1938*

There's a Sunny Side to Every
Situation (Johnny Mercer–
Harry Warren) *Hard to Get*

This Is My Night to Dream
(Johnny Burke–James V.
Monaco) *Dr. Rhythm*

This May Be the Night (Mack
Gordon–Harry Revel) *My Lucky
Star*

Thrill of a Lifetime (Sam
Coslow–Frederick Hollander)
Thrill of a Lifetime

Toy Trumpet (Sidney D.
Mitchell–Lew Pollack–Ray-
mond Scott) *Rebecca of Sunnybrook Farm*

Two Sleepy People (Frank
Loesser–Hoagy Carmichael)
Thanks for the Memory

What Goes on Here in My

Heart? (Leo Robin-Ralph Rainger) *Give Me a Sailor*

What Have You Got That Gets Me (Leo Robin-Ralph Rainger) *Artists and Models Abroad*

When You're in Love (Bob Wright-Chet Forrest) *Girl Downstairs*

Where in the World (Mack Gordon-Harry Revel) *Josette*

Whistle While You Work (Larry Morey-Frank Churchill) *Snow White and the Seven Dwarfs*

Who Are We to Say? (Gus Kahn-Sigmund Romberg) *Girl of the Golden West*

The Yam (Irving Berlin) *Carefree*

You Appeal to Me (Walter Bullock-Harold Spina) *Happy Landing*

You Couldn't Be Cuter (Dorothy Fields-Jerome Kern) *Joy of Living*

You Leave Me Breathless (Ralph Freed-Frederick Hollander) *Cocoanut Grove*

You Must Have Been a Beautiful Baby (Johnny Mercer-Harry Warren) *Hard to Get*

You Took the Words Right Out of My Heart (Leo Robin-Ralph Rainger) *Big Broadast of 1938*

Your Broadway and My Broadway (Arthur Freed-Nacio Herb Brown) *Broadway Melody of 1938*

You're a Sweet Little Headache (Leo Robin-Ralph Rainger) *Paris Honeymoon*

You're a Sweetheart (Harold Adamson-James McHugh) *You're a Sweetheart*

You're Lovely, Madame (Leo Robin-Ralph Rainger) *Artists and Models Abroad*

You're Pretty as a Picture (Harold Adamson-James McHugh) *That Certain Age*

Yours and Mine (Arthur Freed-Nacio Herb Brown) *Broadway Melody of 1938*

*Nominated for the Academy Award.
**Winner of the Academy Award.

List 10
Most Popular 50 Songs from 1939 Films

Angel in Disguise (Kim Gannon-Paul Mann-Stephan Weiss) *It All Came True*

The Answer Is Love (Charles Newman-Sam H. Stept) *That's Right, You're Wrong*

Apple for the Teacher (Johnny Burke-James V. Monaco) *Star Maker*

At the Balalaika (Bob Wright-Chet Forrest-George Posford) *Balalaika*

Blue Nightfall (Frank Loesser-Burton Lane) *St. Louis Blues*

Bluebirds in the Moonlight (Silly Idea) (Sammy Timberg-Winston Sharples) *Gulliver's Travels*

Ding-Dong! The Witch Is Dead
(E.Y. Harburg–Harold Arlen)
Wizard of Oz
East Side of Heaven (Johnny
Burke–James V. Monaco) *East
Side of Heaven*
*Faithful Forever (Leo Robin–
Ralph Rainger) *Gulliver's Travels*
For Ev'ry Lonely Heart (Gus
Kahn–Herbert Stothart–Edward
Ward) *Broadway Serenade*
†Gone with the Wind (Herb
Magidson–Allie Wrubel)
Good Morning (Arthur Freed–
Nacio Herb Brown) *Babes in
Arms*
Hang Your Heart on a Hickory
Limb (Johnny Burke–James V.
Monaco) *East Side of Heaven*
I Live Again (Ned Washington–
Victor Young) *All Women Have
Secrets*
I Never Knew Heaven Could
Speak (Mack Gordon–Harry
Revel) *Rose of Washington
Square*
*I Poured My Heart into a Song
(Irving Berlin) *Second Fiddle*
If I Only Had a Brain (E.Y. Har-
burg–Harold Arlen) *Wizard of
Oz*
I'll Remember (Frank Loesser–
Burton Lane) *She Married a Cop*
I'm Sorry for Myself (Irving
Berlin) *Second Fiddle*
In a Moment of Weakness
(Johnny Mercer–Harry War-
ren) *Naughty But Nice*
It's a Hap-Hap-Happy Day
(Sammy Timberg–Winston
Sharples) *Gulliver's Travels*
Kinda Lonesome (Leo Robin–

Sam Coslow–Hoagy Car-
michael) *St. Louis Blues*
Lady's in Love with You (Frank
Loesser–Burton Lane) *Some Like
It Hot*
Little Joe (Frank Loesser–Frederick
Hollander) *Destry Rides Again*
Love with a Capital "You" (Leo
Robin–Ralph Rainger) *$1,000 a
Touchdown*
Lydia, the Tattooed Lady (E.Y.
Harburg–Harold Arlen) *At the
Circus*
A Man and His Dreams (Johnny
Burke–James V. Monaco) *Star
Maker*
Merry Old Land of Oz (E.Y.
Harburg–Harold Arlen) *Wizard
of Oz*
My First Impression of You
(Charles Tobias–Sam H. Stept)
Having Wonderful Time
Only When You're in My Arms
(Herman Ruby–Bert Kalmar–
Con Conrad) *Story of Vernon and
Irene Castle*
**Over the Rainbow (E.Y. Har-
burg–Harold Arlen) *Wizard of
Oz*
Prom Waltz (Leo Robin–Ralph
Rainger) *Tempo of Tomorrow*
See What the Boys in the Back
Room Will Have (Frank Loes-
ser–Frederick Hollander) *Destry
Rides Again*
Sing, My Heart (Ted Koehler–
Harold Arlen) *Love Affair*
Sing a Song of Sunbeams
(Johnny Burke–James V.
Monaco) *East Side of Heaven*
Song of the Metronome (Irving
Berlin) *Second Fiddle*

Still the Bluebird Sings (Johnny Burke–James V. Monaco) *Star Maker*

Strange Enchantment (Frank Loesser–Frederick Hollander) *Man About Town*

That Sentimental Sandwich (Frank Loesser–Frederick Hollander) *Man About Town*

That Sly Old Gentleman (from Featherbed Lane) (Johnny Burke–James V. Monaco) *East Side of Heaven*

This Night (Will Be My Souvenir) (Gus Kahn–Harry Warren) *Honolulu*

Two Blind Loves (E.Y. Harburg–Harold Arlen) *At the Circus*

We're All Together Now (Leo Robin–Ralph Rainger) *Gulliver's Travels*

We're Off to See the Wizard (E.Y. Harburg–Harold Arlen) *Wizard of Oz*

When Winter Comes (Irving Berlin) *Second Fiddle*

Where Else But Here? (Gus Kahn–Sigmund Romberg) *Let Freedom Ring*

Who Told You I Cared? (George Whiting, Jr.–Bert Reisfeld) *Kid Nightingale*

*Wishing (Will Make It So) (Buddy DeSylva) *Love Affair*

Wonderful Wizard of Oz (E.Y. Harburg–Harold Arlen) *Wizard of Oz*

You've Got That Look (Frank Loesser–Frederick Hollander) *Destry Rides Again*

Nominated for the Academy Award.
**Winner of the Academy Award.*
†*Written in 1937 as a promotional song only.*

List 11
Most Popular 40 Songs from 1940 Films

Ain't It a Shame About Mame (Johnny Burke–James V. Monaco) *Rhythm on the River*

Along the Santa Fe Trail (Al Dubin–Edwina Coolidge–Will Grosz) *Santa Fe Trail*

April Played the Fiddle (Johnny Burke–James V. Monaco) *If I Had My Way*

Because of You (Arthur Hammerstein–Dudley Wilkinson) *I Was an American Spy*

Between You and Me (Cole Porter) *Broadway Melody of 1940*

Blue Lovebird (Gus Kahn–Bronislaw Kaper) *Lillian Russell*

*Down Argentina Way (Mack Gordon–Harry Warren) *Down Argentine Way*

Dreaming Out Loud (Sam Coslow) *Dreaming Out Loud*

Hi-Diddle-Dee-Dee (An Actor's Life for Me) (Ned Washington–Leigh Harline) *Pinocchio*

Eleanor Powell and George Murphy performing Cole Porter's "Between You and Me" in *Broadway Melody of 1940.*

I Concentrate on You (Cole Porter) *Broadway Melody of 1940*

I Haven't Time to Be a Millionaire (Johnny Burke–James V. Monaco) *If I Had My Way*

I Wouldn't Take a Million (Mack Gordon–Harry Warren) *Young People*

*I'd Know You Anywhere (Johnny Mercer–James McHugh) *You'll Find Out*

Intermezzo (a.k.a. A Love Story) (Robert Henning–Heinz Provost) *Intermezzo*

Isn't That Just Like Love (Johnny Burke–James Van Heusen) *Love Thy Neighbor*

*It's a Blue World (Bob Wright–Chet Forrest) *Music in My Heart*

It's a Great Day for the Irish (Roger Edens) *Little Nellie Kelly*

I've Got My Eyes on You (Cole Porter) *Broadway Melody of 1940*

*Love of My Life (Johnny Mercer–Artie Shaw) *Second Chorus*

Meet the Sun Half-Way (Johnny Burke–James V. Monaco) *If I Had My Way*

Moon and the Willow Tree (Johnny Burke–Victor Schertzinger) *Road to Singapore*

Moon Over Burma (Frank Loesser–Frederick Hollander) *Moon Over Burma*

Oh! What a Lovely Dream (Bob Wright–Chet Forrest) *Music in My Heart*

One Look at You (Ned Washington–Earl Carroll–Victor Young) *Night at Earl Carroll's*

*Only Forever (Johnny Burke–James V. Monaco) *Rhythm on the River*

*Our Love Affair (Arthur Freed–Roger Edens) *Strike Up the Band*

Rhythm on the River (Johnny Burke–James V. Monaco) *Rhythm on the River*

Say It (Over and Over Again) (Frank Loesser–James McHugh) *Buck Benny Rides Again*

Sweet Potato Piper (Johnny Burke–James V. Monaco) *Road to Singapore*

That's for Me (Johnny Burke–James V. Monaco) *Rhythm on the River*

Too Romantic (Johnny Burke–James V. Monaco) *Road to Singapore*

Two Dreams Met (Mack Gordon–Harry Warren) *Down Argentine Way*

*Waltzing in the Clouds (Gus Kahn–Robert Stolz) *Spring Parade*

**When You Wish Upon a Star (Ned Washington–Leigh Harline) *Pinocchio*

Where Was I? (Al Dubin–W. Franke Harling) *'Til We Meet Again*

*Who Am I? (Walter Bullock–Jule Styne) *Hit Parade of 1941*

Wishful Thinking (Leo Robin–Ralph Rainger) *Tall, Dark and Handsome*

You Say the Sweetest Things (Baby) (Mack Gordon–Harry Warren) *Tin Pan Alley*

Your Dream Is the Same as My
   Dream (Dorothy Fields–Jerome
   Kern) *One Night in the Tropics*

You've Got Me This Way
   (Johnny Mercer–James
   McHugh) *You'll Find Out*

Nominated for the Academy Award.
** *Winner of the Academy Award.*

List 12
Most Popular 50 Songs from 1941 Films

*Baby Mine (Ned Washington–
   Frank Churchill) *Dumbo*
*Be Honest with Me (Gene Autry–
   Fred Rose) *Ridin' on a Rainbow*
*Blues in the Night (Johnny Mer-
   cer–Harold Arlen) *Blues in the
   Night*
Boa Noite (Good-Night) (Mack
   Gordon–Harry Warren) *That
   Night in Rio*
*Boogie Woogie Bugle Boy (of
   Company B) (Don Raye–Hugh
   Prince) *Buck Privates*
*Chattanooga Choo Choo (Mack
   Gordon–Harry Warren) *Sun
   Valley Serenade*
Chica Chica Boom Chic (Mack
   Gordon–Harry Warren) *That
   Night in Rio*
Dancing on a Dime (Frank Loes-
   ser–Burton Lane) *Dancing on a
   Dime*
*Dolores (Frank Loesser–Louis
   Alter) *Las Vegas Nights*
Hi, Neighbor (Jack Owens) *San
   Antonio Rose*
Honorable Moon (Ira Gersh-
   win–E. Y. Harburg–Arthur
   Schwartz) *Princess O'Rourke*
How Long Did I Dream (Johnny
   Burke–James Van Heusen)

Playmates
Humpty Dumpty Heart (Johnny
   Burke–James Van Heusen)
   Playmates
I Don't Want to Walk Without
   You (Frank Loesser–Jule Styne)
   Sweater Girl
I Hear Music (Frank Loesser–
   Burton Lane) *Dancing on a Dime*
I Know Why (and So Do You)
   (Mack Gordon–Harry Warren)
   Sun Valley Serenade
I Said No (Frank Loesser–Jule
   Styne) *Sweater Girl*
I Take to You (Mack Gordon–
   Harry Warren) *Great American
   Broadcast*
I, Yi, Yi, Yi, Yi (I Like You Very
   Much) (Mack Gordon–Harry
   Warren) *That Night in Rio*
If It's You (Ben Oakland–Artie
   Shaw–Milton Drake) *Big Store*
I'll Never Let a Day Pass By
   (Frank Loesser–Victor Schertz-
   inger) *Kiss the Boys Goodbye*
I'll Remember April (Don
   Raye–Gene DePaul–Pat
   Johnston) *Ride 'Em Cowboy*
I'm Still Crazy for You (Leo
   Robin–Ralph Rainger) *Footlight
   Serenade*

It Happened in Sun Valley (Mack
Gordon–Harry Warren) *Sun
Valley Serenade*

It's Always You (Johnny
Burke–James Van Heusen)
Road to Zanzibar

Katy-Did, Katy-Didn't (Frank
Loesser–Hoagy Carmichael)
Mr. Bug Goes to Town

Kindergarten Conga (Leo Robin–
Ralph Rainger) *Moon Over
Miami*

Kiss the Boys Goodbye (Frank
Loesser–Victor Schertzinger)
Kiss the Boys Goodbye

**Last Time I Saw Paris (Oscar
Hammerstein II–Jerome Kern)
Lady Be Good

Long Ago Last Night (Mack Gordon–Harry Warren) *Great
American Broadcast*

Love Is Such an Old Fashioned
Thing (Frank Loesser–Victor
Schertzinger) *Glamour Boy*

Loveliness and Love (Leo
Robin–Ralph Rainger) *Moon
Over Miami*

Man with the Lollipop Song
(Mack Gordon–Harry Warren)
Weekend in Havana

Miami (Leo Robin–Ralph Rainger) *Moon Over Miami*

Minnie from Trinidad (Roger
Edens) *Ziegfeld Girl*

*Out of the Silence (Lloyd B.
Norlind) *All American Co-Ed*

Sand in My Shoes (Frank
Loesser–Victor Schertzinger)

Kiss the Boys Goodbye

*Since I Kissed My Baby Good-
bye (Cole Porter) *You'll Never
Get Rich*

†Sinner Kissed an Angel (Mack
David–Ray Joseph)

Starlight, Starbright (Don Raye–
Gene DePaul) *In the Navy*

This Time the Dream's on Me
(Johnny Mercer–Harold Arlen)
Blues in the Night

§Too Beautiful to Last (Marty
Symes–Ruth Lowe) *Ziegfeld
Girl*

Waiter, the Porter, and the
Upstairs Maid (Johnny
Mercer) *Birth of the Blues*

We're the Couple in the Castle
(Frank Loesser–Hoagy Car-
michael) *Mr. Bug Goes to Town*

When I See an Elephant Fly (Ned
Washington–Frank Churchill)
Dumbo

Where You Are (Mack Gor-
don–Harry Warren) *Great
American Broadcast*

You Started Something (Leo
Robin–Ralph Rainger) *Moon
Over Miami*

You Stepped Out of a Dream
(Gus Kahn–Nacio Herb Brown)
Ziegfeld Girl

Your Words and My Music
(Arthur Freed–Roger Edens)
Lady Be Good

You're the One for Me (Johnny
Mercer–James McHugh) *You're
the One*

Nominated for the Academy Award.
**Winner of the Academy Award.*
†*Written to promote the film* Hold Back the Dawn.
§*Heard in the background only.*

List 13
Most Popular 100 Songs from 1942–43 Films

Abraham (Irving Berlin) *Holiday Inn,* 1942

All Through the Night (Johnny Mercer–Arthur Schwartz) *All Through the Night,* 1942

*Always in My Heart (Kim Gannon–Ernesto Lecuona) *Always in My Heart,* 1942

And Russia Is Her Name (E.Y. Harburg–Jerome Kern) *Song of Russia,* 1943

Arthur Murray Taught Me Dancing in a Hurry (Johnny Mercer–Victor Schertzinger) *Fleet's In,* 1942

At Last (Mack Gordon–Harry Warren) *Orchestra Wives,* 1942

Be Careful, It's My Heart (Irving Berlin) *Holiday Inn,* 1942

Candlelight and Wine (Harold Adamson–James McHugh) *Around the World,* 1943

Can't Get Out of This Mood (Frank Loesser–James McHugh) *Seven Days Leave,* 1942

*Change of Heart (Harold Adamson–Jule Styne) *Hit Parade of 1943,* 1943

Conchita Marquita Lolita Pepita Rosita Juanita Lopez (Frank Loesser–Jule Styne) *Priorities on Parade,* 1942

Constantly (Johnny Burke–James Van Heusen) *Road to Morocco,* 1942

Cow-Cow Boogie (Don Raye–Gene DePaul) *Swing Symphony,* 1942

*Dearly Beloved (Johnny Mercer–Jerome Kern) *You Were Never Lovelier,* 1942

Don't Believe Everything You Dream (Harold Adamson–James McHugh) *Around the World,* 1943

Don't Sit Under the Apple Tree (Lew Brown–Charles Tobias–Sam H. Stept) *Private Buckaroo,* 1942

Don't Worry (Kim Gannon–Jule Styne) *Salute for Three,* 1943

The Dreamer (Frank Loesser–Arthur Schwartz) *Thank Your Lucky Stars,* 1943

Fuddy Duddy Watchmaker (Frank Loesser–James McHugh) *Happy-Go-Lucky,* 1943

Got the Moon in My Pocket (Johnny Burke–James Van Heusen) *My Favorite Spy,* 1942

*Happiness Is Jes a Thing Called Joe (E.Y. Harburg–Harold Arlen) *Cabin in the Sky,* 1943

Happy Holiday (Irving Berlin) *Holiday Inn,* 1942

Heavenly, Isn't It? (Mort Greene–Harry Revel) *Mayor of 44th Street,* 1942

Here You Are (Leo Robin–Ralph Rainger) *My Gal Sal,* 1942

Hit the Road to Dreamland (Johnny Mercer–Harold Arlen) *Star Spangled Rhythm,* 1943

*How About You? (Ralph Freed–Burton Lane) *Babes on Broadway,* 1942

How Sweet You Are (Frank Loesser–Arthur Schwartz) *Thank Your Lucky Stars,* 1943

I Always Knew (Cole Porter) *Something to Shout About,* 1943

I Dug a Ditch (in Wichita) (Lew Brown–Ralph Freed–Burton Lane) *Thousands Cheer,* 1943

I Get the Neck of the Chicken (Frank Loesser–James McHugh) *Seven Days Leave,* 1942

I Had the Craziest Dream (Mack Gordon–Harry Warren) *Springtime in the Rockies,* 1942

I Remember You (Johnny Mercer–Victor Schertzinger) *Fleet's In,* 1942

If You Please (Johnny Burke–James Van Heusen) *Dixie,* 1943

I'll Take Tallulah (E.Y. Harburg–Burton Lane) *Ship Ahoy,* 1942

I'm Old Fashioned (Johnny Mercer–Jerome Kern) *You Were Never Lovelier,* 1942

I'm Ridin' for a Fall (Frank Loesser–Arthur Schwartz) *Thank Your Lucky Stars,* 1943

In My Arms (Frank Loesser–Ted Grouya) *See Here, Private Hargrove,* 1943

It Can't Be Wrong (Charlotte's Theme) (Kim Gannon–Max Steiner) *Now, Voyager,* 1942

*I've Got a Gal in Kalamazoo (Mack Gordon–Harry Warren) *Orchestra Wives,* 1942

*I've Heard That Song Before (Sammy Cahn–Jule Styne) *Youth on Parade,* 1942

Jingle Jangle Jingle (Frank Loesser–Joseph J. Lilley) *Forest Rangers,* 1942

Johnny Doughboy Found a Rose in Ireland (Kay Twomey–Al Goodhart) *Johnny Doughboy,* 1942

The Joint Is Really Jumping (Ralph Blane–Hugh Martin) *Thousands Cheer,* 1943

Journey to a Star (Leo Robin–Harry Warren) *Gang's All Here,* 1943

Lady in the Tutti-Frutti Hat (Leo Robin–Harry Warren) *Gang's All Here,* 1943

Last Call for Love (E.Y. Harburg–Margery Cummings–Burton Lane) *Ship Ahoy,* 1942

Later Tonight (Leo Robin–Nacio Herb Brown) *Wintertime,* 1943

Let's Get Lost (Frank Loesser–James McHugh) *Happy-Go-Lucky,* 1943

Let's Start the New Year Right (Irving Berlin) *Holiday Inn,* 1942

*Love Is a Song (Larry Morey–Frank Churchill) *Bambi,* 1942

Mister Five By Five (Don Raye–Gene DePaul) *Behind the 8 Ball,* 1942

Moonlight Becomes You (Johnny Burke–James Van Heusen) *Road to Morocco,* 1942

Murder, He Says (Frank Loesser–James McHugh) *Happy-Go-Lucky,* 1943

My Heart Tells Me (Mack Gordon–Harry Warren) *Sweet Rosie O'Grady,* 1943

*My Shining Hour (Johnny Mercer–Harold Arlen) *Sky's the Limit,* 1943

Nevada (Mort Greene–Walter Donaldson) *What's Buzzin', Cousin?,* 1943

No Love, No Nothin' (Leo Robin–Harry Warren) *Gang's All Here,* 1943

Not Mine (Johnny Mercer–Victor
Schertzinger) *Fleet's In,* 1942
Oh, the Pity of It All (Leo
Robin–Ralph Rainger) *My Gal
Sal,* 1942
Old Music Master (Johnny
Mercer–Hoagy Carmichael)
True to Life, 1943
One for My Baby (Johnny
Mercer–Harold Arlen) *Sky's the
Limit,* 1943
Out of This World (Kim Gannon–
Jule Styne) *Powers Girl,* 1942
Paducah (Leo Robin–Harry War-
ren) *Gang's All Here,* 1943
*Pennies for Peppino (Chet For-
rest–Bob Wright–Edward
Ward) *Flying with Music,* 1942
People Like You and Me (Mack
Gordon–Harry Warren) *Or-
chestra Wives,* 1942
*†Pig Foot Pete (Don Raye–Gene
DePaul) *Hellzapoppin',* 1942
Plenty to Be Thankful For (Irving
Berlin) *Holiday Inn,* 1942
Polka Dot Polka (Leo Robin–
Harry Warren) *Gang's All Here,*
1943
Poor You (E.Y. Harburg–Burton
Lane) *Ship Ahoy,* 1942
Road to Morocco (Johnny
Burke–James Van Heusen)
Road to Morocco, 1942
Run, Little Raindrop, Run
(Mack Gordon–Harry Warren)
Springtime in the Rockies, 1942
*Saludos Amigos (Ned Washing-
ton–Charles Wolcott) *Saludos
Amigos,* 1943
*Say a Pray'r for the Boys Over
There (Herb Magidson–James
McHugh) *Hers to Hold,* 1943

Serenade in Blue (Mack Gor-
don–Harry Warren) *Orchestra
Wives,* 1942
Shoo-Shoo Baby (Phil Moore)
Three Cheers for the Boys, 1943
Sing a Tropical Song (Frank Loes-
ser–James McHugh) *Happy-Go-
Lucky,* 1943
Sing Me a Song of the Islands
(Mack Gordon–Harry Owens)
Sing Me a Song of the Islands, 1942
The Son of a Gun Who Picks on
Uncle Sam (E.Y. Harburg–
Burton Lane) *Panama Hattie,* 1942
Star Eyes (Don Raye–Gene
DePaul) *I Dood It,* 1943
Sunday, Monday or Always
(Johnny Burke–James Van
Heusen) *Dixie,* 1943
Take It from There (Leo Robin–
Ralph Rainger) *Coney Island,*
1942
Tangerine (Johnny Mercer–Vic-
tor Schertzinger) *Fleet's In,* 1942
Thank Your Lucky Stars (Frank
Loesser–Arthur Schwartz)
Thank Your Lucky Stars, 1943
*That Old Black Magic (Johnny
Mercer–Harold Arlen) *Star
Spangled Rhythm,* 1943
There Will Never Be Another
You (Mack Gordon–Harry
Warren) *Iceland,* 1942
*They're Either Too Young or
Too Old (Frank Loesser–Arthur
Schwartz) *Thank Your Lucky
Stars,* 1943
Three Dreams (Kim Gannon–Jule
Styne) *Powers Girl,* 1942
Touch of Texas (Frank Loesser–
James McHugh) *Seven Days
Leave,* 1942

*We Mustn't Say Goodbye (Al Dubin–James V. Monaco) *Stage Door Canteen*, 1943
*When There's a Breeze on Lake Lousie (Mort Greene–Harry Revel) *Mayor of 44th Street*, 1942
**White Christmas (Irving Berlin) *Holiday Inn*, 1942
Wishing Waltz (Mack Gordon–Harry Warren) *Sweet Rosie O'Grady*, 1943
You and the Waltz and I (Paul Francis Webster–Walter Jurmann) *Seven Sweethearts*, 1942
You Can't Hold a Memory in Your Arms (Hy Zaret–Arthur Altman) *What's Cookin'*, 1942
You Can't Say "No" to a Soldier

(Mack Gordon–Harry Warren) *Iceland*, 1942
You Were Never Lovelier (Johnny Mercer–Jerome Kern) *You Were Never Lovelier*, 1942
*You'd Be So Nice to Come Home To (Cole Porter) *Something to Shout About*, 1943
**You'll Never Know (Mack Gordon–Harry Warren) *Hello, Frisco, Hello*, 1943
You're in Love with Someone Else (But I'm in Love with You) (Frank Loesser–Jule Styne) *Priorities on Parade*, 1942
You're the Rainbow (Leo Robin–Ralph Rainger) *Riding High*, 1943

Nominated for the Academy Award.
**Winner of the Academy Award.*
†*Also sung in 1941 by Martha Raye in* Keep 'Em Flying.

List 14
Most Popular 125 Songs from 1944–45 Films

*Ac-cent-tchu-ate the Positive (Johnny Mercer–Harold Arlen) *Here Come the Waves*, 1945
All I Owe Ioway (Oscar Hammerstein II–Richard Rodgers) *State Fair*, 1945
(All of a Sudden) My Heart Sings (Harold Rome–Jamblan and Herpin) *Anchors Aweigh*, 1945
And Then You Kissed Me (Sammy Cahn–Jule Styne) *Step Lively*, 1944
And There You Are (Ted Koehler–Sammy Fain) *Weekend at the Waldorf*, 1945

Angel (Arthur Freed–Harry Warren) *Yolanda and the Thief*, 1945
Any Moment Now (E.Y. Harburg–Jerome Kern) *Can't Help Singing*, 1945
*Anywhere (Sammy Cahn–Jule Styne) *Tonight and Every Night*, 1945
Apple Blossoms in the Rain (Mort Greene–Lew Pollack) *Seven Days Ashore*, 1944
*Aren't You Glad You're You (Johnny Burke–James Van Heusen) *Bells of St. Mary's*, 1945
As Long as I Live (Charles

Tobias–Max Steiner) *Saratoga Trunk*, 1945

As Long as There's Music (Sammy Cahn–Jule Styne) *Step Lively*, 1944

Beloved (Ted Koehler–Burton Lane) *Rainbow Island*, 1944

The Boy Next Door (Ralph Blane–Hugh Martin) *Meet Me in St. Louis*, 1944

Californ-i-ay (E.Y. Harburg–Jerome Kern) *Can't Help Singing*, 1945

Can't Help Singing (E.Y. Harburg–Jerome Kern) *Can't Help Singing*, 1945

*Cat and the Canary (Ray Evans–Jay Livingston) *Why Girls Leave Home*, 1945

The Charm of You (Sammy Cahn–Jule Styne) *Anchors Aweigh*, 1945

Coffee Time (Arthur Freed–Harry Warren) *Yoland and the Thief*, 1945

Come Out, Come Out, Wherever You Are (Sammy Cahn–Jule Styne) *Step Lively*, 1944

Day After Forever (Johnny Burke–James Van Heusen) *Going My Way*, 1944

Did You Happen to Find a Heart (This Morning)? (Herb Magidson–Lew Pollack) *Music in Manhattan*, 1944

Dig You Later (A Hubba-Hubba-Hubba) (Harold Adamson–James McHugh) *Doll Face*, 1945

Doctor, Lawyer, Indian Chief (Paul Francis Webster–Hoagy Carmichael) *Stork Club*, 1945

Don't Fence Me In (Cole Porter) *Hollywood Canteen*, 1944

*Endlessly (Kim Gannon–Walter Kent) *Earl Carroll Vanities*, 1945

A Friend of Yours (Johnny Burke–James Van Heusen) *Great John L.*, 1944

Going My Way (Johnny Burke–James Van Heusen) *Going My Way*, 1944

Have Yourself a Merry Little Christmas (Ralph Blane–Hugh Martin) *Meet Me in St. Louis*, 1944

Here Comes Heaven Again (Harold Adamson–James McHugh) *Doll Face*, 1945

Here It Is Monday (Kim Gannon–Walter Kent) *Song of the Open Road*, 1944

His Rocking Horse Ran Away (Johnny Burke–James Van Heusen) *And the Angels Sing*, 1944

How Blue the Night (Harold Adamson–James McHugh) *Four Jills and a Jeep*, 1944

How Little We Know (Johnny Mercer–Hoagy Carmichael) *To Have and Have Not*, 1944

How Many Times Do I Have to Tell You? (Harold Adamson–James McHugh) *Four Jills and a Jeep*, 1944

How Would You Like to Kiss Me in the Moonlight? (Harold Adamson–James McHugh) *Princess and the Pirate*, 1944

I Begged Her (Sammy Cahn–Jule Styne) *Anchors Aweigh*, 1945

*I Couldn't Sleep a Wink Last Night (Harold Adamson–James McHugh) *Higher and Higher*, 1944

I Don't Care Who Knows It (Harold Adamson–James McHugh) *Nob Hill*, 1945

*I Fall in Love Too Easily

(Sammy Cahn–Jule Styne) *Anchors Aweigh*, 1945

I Promise You (Johnny Mercer–Harold Arlen) *Here Come the Waves*, 1945

I Should Care (Sammy Cahn–Axel Stordahl) *Thrill of a Romance*, 1944

I Walked In (with My Eyes Wide Open) (Harold Adamson–James McHugh) *Nob Hill*, 1945

I Wish I Knew (Mack Gordon–Harry Warren) *Billy Rose's Diamond Horseshoe*, 1945

I Wish We Didn't Have to Say Good-night (Harold Adamson–James McHugh) *Something for the Boys*, 1944

I'd Rather Be Me (Sam Coslow–Eddie Cherkose–Felix Bernard) *Out of This World*, 1945

If I Had a Dozen Hearts (Paul Francis Webster–Harry Revel) *Stork Club*, 1945

If I Had a Wishing Ring (Marla Shelton–Louis Alter) *Breakfast in Hollywood*, 1945

*I'll Buy That Dream (Herb Magidson–Allie Wrubel) *Sing Your Way Home*, 1945

*I'll Walk Alone (Sammy Cahn–Jule Styne) *Follow the Boys*, 1944

I'm Glad I Waited for You (Sammy Cahn–Jule Styne) *Tars and Spars*, 1945

*I'm Making Believe (Mack Gordon–James V. Monaco) *Sweet and Low-Down*, 1944

In a Moment of Madness (Ralph Blane–James McHugh) *Two Girls and a Sailor*, 1944

In Acapulco (Mack Gordon–Harry Warren) *Billy Rose's Diamond Horseshoe*, 1945

In the Middle of Nowhere (Harold Adamson–James McHugh) *Something for the Boys*, 1944

In the Spirit of the Moment (Bernie Grossman–Walter Jurmann) *His Butler's Sister*, 1944

Irresistible You (Don Raye–Gene DePaul) *Broadway Rhythm*, 1944

Isn't It Kinda Fun (Oscar Hammerstein II–Richard Rodgers) *State Fair*, 1945

It Could Happen to You (Johnny Burke–James Van Heusen) *And the Angels Sing*, 1944

**It Might as Well Be Spring (Oscar Hammerstein II–Richard Rodgers) *State Fair*, 1945

It's a Grand Night for Singing (Oscar Hamemrstein II–Richard Rodgers) *State Fair*, 1945

June Comes Around Every Year (Johnny Mercer–Harold Arlen) *Out of This World*, 1945

Laura (Johnny Mercer–David Raksin) *Laura*, 1944

Let's Take the Long Way Home (Johnny Mercer–Harold Arlen) *Here Come the Waves*, 1945

Like Someone in Love (Johnny Burke–James Van Heusen) *Belle of the Yukon*, 1945

*Linda (Ann Ronell) *Story of G.I. Joe*, 1945

*Long Ago (and Far Away) (Ira Gershwin–Jerome Kern) *Cover Girl*, 1944

Love Is a Merry-Go-Round

(Sammy Cahn–Jule Styne) *Tars and Spars,* 1945

*Love Letters (Edward Heyman–Victor Young) *Love Letters,* 1945

Love Me (Sammy Cahn–Jule Styne) *Stork Club,* 1945

Love on a Greyhound Bus (Ralph Blane–Kay Thompson–George Stoll) *No Leave, No Love,* 1945

A Lovely Way to Spend an Evening (Harold Adamson–James McHugh) *Higher and Higher,* 1944

Make Way for Tomorrow (Ira Gershwin–Jerome Kern) *Cover Girl,* 1944

Memphis in June (Paul Francis Webster–Hoagy Carmichael) *Johnny Angel,* 1945

Milkman, Keep Those Bottles Quiet (Don Raye–Gene DePaul) *Broadway Rhythm,* 1944

*More and More (E.Y. Harburg–Jerome Kern) *Can't Help Singing,* 1945

The More I See You (Mack Gordon–Harry Warren) *Billy Rose's Diamond Horseshoe,* 1945

The Music Stopped (Harold Adamson–James McHugh) *Higher and Higher,* 1944

My Dreams Are Getting Better All the Time (Mann Curtis–Vic Mizzy) *In Society,* 1944

My Mother Told Me (Ralph Freed–James McHugh) *Two Girls and a Sailor,* 1944

*Now I Know (Ted Koehler–Harold Arlen) *Up in Arms,* 1944

Out of This World (Johnny Mercer–Harold Arlen) *Out of This World,* 1945

Personality (Johnny Burke–James Van Heusen) *Road to Utopia,* 1945

Please Don't Say "No" (Ralph Freed–Sammy Fain) *Thrill of a Romance,* 1945

Poor Little Rhode Island (Sammy Cahn–Jule Styne) *Carolina Blues,* 1944

*Remember Me to Carolina (Paul Francis Webster–Harry Revel) *Minstrel Man,* 1944

*Rio De Janeiro (Ned Washington–Ary Barroso) *Brazil,* 1944

*Silver Shadows and Golden Dreams (Charles Newman–Lew Pollack) *Lady Let's Dance,* 1944

Skip to My Lou (Ralph Blane–Hugh Martin) *Meet Me in St. Louis,* 1944 (revised version)

*Sleighride in July (Johnny Burke–James Van Heusen) *Belle of the Yukon,* 1945

Slowly (Kermit Goell–David Raksin) *Fallen Angel,* 1945

*Some Sunday Morning (Ted Koehler–Ray Heindorf–M.K. Jerome) *San Antonio,* 1945

Somebody's Walking in My Dreams (Harold Adamson–James McHugh) *Doll Face,* 1945

Someday, I'll Meet You Again (Ned Washington–Max Steiner) *Passage to Marseille,* 1944

*So-o-o-o-o in Love (Leo Robin–David Rose) *Wonder Man,* 1945

Spellbound (Mack David–Miklos Rozsa) *Spellbound,* 1945

Spring Will Be a Little Late This Year (Frank Loesser) *Christmas Holiday,* 1944

Suddenly, It's Spring (Johnny Burke–James Van Heusen) *Lady in the Dark,* 1944

Sure Thing (Ira Gershwin–Jerome
Kern) *Cover Girl,* 1944
*Sweet Dreams, Sweetheart (Ted
Koehler–M.K. Jerome)
Hollywood Canteen, 1944
**Swingin' on a Star (Johnny
Burke–James Van Heusen) *Going My Way,* 1944
Ten Days with Baby (Mack Gordon–James V. Monaco) *Sweet
and Low-Down,* 1944
Tess's Torch Song (Ted Koehler–
Harold Arlen) *Up in Arms,* 1944
That's for Me (Oscar Hammerstein
II–Richard Rodgers) *State Fair,*
1945
There Goes That Song Again
(Sammy Cahn–Jule Styne)
Carolina Blues, 1944
There's a Fella Waitin' in
Poughkeepsie (Johnny
Mercer–Harold Arlen) *Here
Come the Waves,* 1945
Three Caballeros (Charles Wolcott) *Three Caballeros,* 1945
Tico–Tico (Ervin Drake–Zequinha
Abreu) *Bathing Beauty,* 1944
Time Alone Will Tell (Mack Gordon–James V. Monaco) *Pin Up
Girl,* 1944
Time Waits for No One (Cliff
Friend–Charles Tobias) *Shine on
Harvest Moon,* 1944
Tonight and Every Night (Sammy
Cahn–Jule Styne) *Tonight and
Every Night,* 1945
*Too Much in Love (Kim Gannon–Walter Kent) *Song of the
Open Road,* 1944

*Trolley Song (Ralph Blane–Hugh
Martin) *Meet Me in St. Louis,* 1944
Two Silhouettes (Ray Gilbert–
Charles Wolcott) *Make Mine
Music,* 1945
Welcome to My Dream (Johnny
Burke–James Van Heusen)
Road to Utopia, 1945
What Are You Doin' the Rest of
Your Life? (Ted Koehler–Burton Lane) *Hollywood Canteen,* 1944
When I'm Walkin' Arm in Arm
with Jim (Harry Harris–Lew
Pollack) *Girl Rush,* 1944
Who Said Dreams Don't Come
True? (Harry Akst–Benny Davis–
Al Jolson) *Impatient Years,* 1944
The Wish I Wish Tonight (Jack
Scholl–M.K. Jerome) *Christmas
in Connecticut,* 1945
Wouldn't It Be Nice? (Harold
Adamson–James McHugh)
Something for the Boys, 1944
You Belong to My Heart (Ray
Gilbert–Agustin Lara) *Three
Caballeros,* 1945
You Make Me Dream Too Much
(Sammy Cahn–Jule Styne)
Carolina Blues, 1944
You May Not Remember (George
Jessel–Ben Oakland) *Show
Business,* 1944
You Moved Right In (Harold
Adamson–James McHugh)
Bring on the Girls, 1945
You're My Little Pin-Up Girl
(Mack Gordon–James V.
Monaco) *Pin-Up Girl,* 1944

Nominated for the Academy Award.
**Winner of the Academy Award.*

List #15
Most Popular 45 Songs from 1946 Films

All the Time (Ralph Freed–Sammy Fain) *No Leave, No Love*

*All Through the Day (Oscar Hammerstein II–Jerome Kern) *Centennial Summer*

Anniversary Song (Saul Chaplin–Al Jolson) *Jolson Story*

Beside You (Ray Evans–Jay Livingston) *My Favorite Brunette*

Beware, My Heart (Sam Coslow) *Carnegie Hall*

Do You Know What It Means to Miss New Orleans (Eddie deLange–Louis Alter) *New Orleans*

Do You Love Me (Harry Ruby) *Do You Love Me*

Either It's Love or It Isn't (Doris Fisher–Allan Roberts) *Dead Reckoning*

Five Minutes More (Sammy Cahn–Jule Styne) *Sweetheart of Sigma Chi*

From This Day Forward (Mort Greene–Leigh Harline) *From This Day Forward*

Give Me the Simple Life (Harry Ruby–Rube Bloom) *Wake Up and Dream*

Golden Earrings (Ray Evans–Jay Livingston) *Golden Earrings*

Have I Told You Lately? (Harold Adamson–James McHugh) *Calendar Girl*

*I Can't Begin to Tell You (Mack Gordon–James V. Monaco) *Dolly Sisters*

I Didn't Mean a Word I Said (Harold Adamson–James McHugh) *Do You Love Me*

I Love an Old Fashioned Song (Sammy Cahn–Jule Styne) *Kid from Brooklyn*

If I'm Lucky (Eddie DeLange–Josef Myrow) *If I'm Lucky*

In Love in Vain (Leo Robin–Jerome Kern) *Centennial Summer*

I've Never Forgotten (Sammy Cahn–Jule Styne) *Earl Carroll's Sketchbook*

Love (Ralph Blane–Hugh Martin) *Ziegfeld Follies*

Love Is the Darndest Thing (Johnny Burke–James Van Heusen) *Cross My Heart*

My Heart Goes Crazy (Johnny Burke–James Van Heusen) *My Heart Goes Crazy*

*Ole Buttermilk Sky (Jack Brooks–Hoagy Carmichael) *Canyon Passage*

**On the Atchison, Topeka and Santa Fe (Johnny Mercer–Harry Warren) *Harvey Girls*

On the Boardwalk (in Atlantic City) (Mack Gordon–Josef Myrow) *Three Little Girls in Blue*

Put the Blame on Mame (Doris Fisher–Allan Roberts) *Gilda*

(Running Around in Circles) Getting Nowhere (Irving Berlin) *Blue Skies*

Somewhere in the Night (Mack Gordon–Josef Myrow) *Three Little Girls in Blue*

†Spring Isn't Everything (Ralph Blane–Harry Warren) *Summer Holiday*

Stanley Steamer (Ralph Blane–
Harry Warren) *Summer Holiday*

Stella By Starlight (Ned Washington–Victor Young) *Uninvited*

Swing Your Partner Round and
Round (Johnny Mercer–Harry
Warren) *Harvey Girls*

That Little Dream Got Nowhere
(Johnny Burke–James Van
Heusen) *Cross My Heart*

That's What Christmas Means to
Me (Harry Revel) *It Happened
on Fifth Avenue*

There's Beauty Everywhere (Arthur Freed–Harry Warren)
Ziegfeld Follies

This Heart of Mine (Arthur Freed–
Harry Warren) *Ziegfeld Follies*

This Is Always (Mack Gordon–
Harry Warren) *Three Little Girls
in Blue*

§To Each His Own (Ray
Evans–Jay Livingston)

To Me (Don George–Allie
Wrubel) *Fabulous Dorseys*

†Two Hearts Are Better Than
One (Johnny Mercer–Jerome
Kern) *Centennial Summer*

Wait and See (Johnny Mercer–
Harry Warren) *Harvey Girls*

What Am I Gonna Do About
You? (Sammy Cahn–Jule
Styne) *Ladies Man*

*You Keep Coming Back Like a
Song (Irving Berlin) *Blue Skies*

You Make Me Feel So Young
(Mack Gordon–Josef Myrow)
Three Little Girls in Blue

You're the Cause of It All (Sammy
Cahn–Jule Styne) *Kid from
Brooklyn)*

Nominated for the Academy Award.
**Winner of the Academy Award.*
†*Dropped from the film before release.*
§*Used to promote the film of the same name.*

List 16
Most Popular 100 Songs from 1947–49 Films

Again (Dorcas Cochran–Lionel
Newman) *Road House,* 1948

Another Night Like This (Harry
Ruby–Ernesto Lecuona) *Carnival in Costa Rica,* 1947

Aren't You Kind of Glad We
Did? (Ira and George Gershwin) *Shocking Miss Pilgrim,* 1947

As Long As I'm Dreaming
(Johnny Burke–James Van

Heusen) *Welcome Stranger,* 1947

As Years Go By (Charles Tobias–
Peter De Rose, *Song of Love,*
1947

**Baby, It's Cold Outside (Frank
Loesser) *Neptune's Daughter,* 1949

Be a Clown (Cole Porter) *Pirate,*
1948

Better Luck Next Time (Irving
Berlin) *Easter Parade,* 1948

Blame My Absent-Minded Heart
(Sammy Cahn–Jule Styne) *It's a
Great Feeling,* 1949
Busy Doing Nothing (Johnny
Burke–James Van Heusen) *A
Connecticut Yankee in King Arthur's
Court,* 1948
But Beautiful (Johnny Burke–
James Van Heusen) *Road to
Rio,* 1947
**Buttons and Bows (Ray Evans–
Jay Livingston) *Paleface,* 1948
By the Way (Mack Gordon–
Joseph Myrow) *When My Baby
Smiles at Me,* 1948
Changing My Tune (Ira and
George Gershwin) *Shocking Miss
Pilgrim,* 1947
Couple of Swells (Irving Berlin)
Easter Parade, 1948
Dickey-Bird Song (Howard Dietz–
Sammy Fain) *Three Daring
Daughters,* 1948
Don't Call It Love (Ned Washing-
ton–Allie Wrubel) *I Walk Alone,*
1947
Dream Girl (Ray Evans–Jay Liv-
ingston) *Dream Girl,* 1948
§Egg and I (Harry Akst–Herman
Ruby–Bert Kalmar–Al Jolson)
1949
†Ever Homeward (Sammy
Cahn–Jule Styne) *Miracle of the
Bells,* 1948
Every Time I Meet You (Mack
Gordon–Josef Myrow) *Beautiful
Blonde from Bashful Bend,* 1949
Ev'ry Day I Love You (Just a Lit-
tle Bit More) (Sammy Cahn–
Jule Styne) *Two Guys from
Texas,* 1948
Experience (Johnny Burke–James

Van Heusen) *Road to Rio,* 1947
Farewell, Amanda (Cole Porter)
Adam's Rib, 1949
Fella with an Umbrella (Irving
Berlin) *Easter Parade,* 1948
Fiddle Dee Dee (Sammy Cahn–
Jule Styne) *It's a Great Feeling,*
1949
*For Every Man There's a
Woman (Leo Robin–Harold
Arlen) *Casbah,* 1948
For You, for Me, for Evermore
(Ira and George Gershwin)
Shocking Miss Pilgrim, 1947
*Gal in Calico (Leo Robin–Ar-
thur Schwartz) *Time, Place and
the Girl,* 1947
Gotta Get Me Somebody to Love
(Allie Wrubel) *Duel in the Sun,*
1947
Hankerin' (Sammy Cahn–Jule
Styne) *Two Guys from Texas,*
1948
Harmony (Johnny Burke–James
Van Heusen) *Variety Girl,* 1947
Havin' a Wonderful Wish (Time
You Were Here) (Ray Evans–
Jay Livingston (*Sorrowful Jones,*
1949
He Can Waltz (Frank Loesser)
Variety Girl, 1947
Hooray for Love (Leo Robin–
Harold Arlen) *Casbah,* 1948
I Believe (Sammy Cahn–Jule
Styne) *It Happened in Brooklyn,*
1947
*I Wish I Didn't Love You So
(Frank Loesser) *Perils of Pauline,*
1947
It Happens Every Spring (Mack
Gordon–Josef Myrow) *It Hap-
pens Every Spring,* 1949

It Only Happens When I Dance with You (Irving Berlin) *Easter Parade,* 1948

It Was Written in the Stars (Leo Robin–Harold Arlen) *Casbah,* 1948

*It's a Great Feeling (Sammy Cahn–Jule Styne) *It's a Great Feeling,* 1949

It's a Most Unusual Day (Harold Adamson–James McHugh) *Date with Judy,* 1948

*It's Magic (Sammy Cahn–Jule Styne) *Romance on the High Seas,* 1948

It's the Same Old Dream (Sammy Cahn–Jule Styne) *It Happened in Brooklyn,* 1947

It's You or No One (Sammy Cahn–Jule Styne) *Romance on the High Seas,* 1948

Ivy (Hoagy Carmichael) *Ivy,* 1947

Judaline (Don Raye–Gene DePaul) *Date with Judy,* 1948

Kokomo, Indiana (Mack Gordon–Josef Myrow) *Mother Wore Tights,* 1947

*Lavender Blue (Larry Morey–Eliot Daniel) *So Dear to My Heart,* 1949

Life Can Be Beautiful (Harold Adamson–James McHugh) *Smash Up,* 1947

Look at Me (Jack Brooks–Walter Scharf) *Yes Sir, That's My Baby,* 1949

Love Is Where You Find It (Edward Heyman-Earl Brent-Nacio Herb Brown) *Kissing Bandit,* 1949

Love of My Life (Cole Porter) *Pirate,* 1948

Love That Boy (Don Raye–Gene DePaul) *Race Street,* 1947

Lucky Us! (Ray Evans–Jay Livingston) *Great Lover,* 1949

Mam'selle (Mack Gordon–Edmund Goulding) *Razor's Edge,* 1947

Miss Julie July (Ray Evans–Jay Livingston) *Isn't It Romantic,* 1948

My Dream Is Yours (Ralph Blane–Harry Warren) *My Dream Is Yours,* 1948

*My Foolish Heart (Ned Washington–Victor Young) *My Foolish Heart,* 1949

My Heart Is a Hobo (Johnny Burke–James Van Heusen) *Welcome Stranger,* 1947

My, How the Time Goes By (Harold Adamson–James McHugh) *If You Knew Susie,* 1948

My One and Only Highland Fling (Ira Gershwin–Harry Warren) *Barkleys of Broadway,* 1949

The Night Has a Thousand Eyes (Buddy Bernier–Jerry Brainin) *The Night Has a Thousand Eyes,* 1948

Nina (Cole Porter) *Pirate,* 1948

Oh, But I Do (Leo Robin–Arthur Schwartz) *Time, the Place and the Girl,* 1947

On an Island with You (Edward Heyman–Nacio Herb Brown) *On an Island with You,* 1948

Once and for Always (Johnny Burke–James Van Heusen) *Connecticut Yankee in King Arthur's Court,* 1948

One Sunday Afternoon (Ralph Blane) *One Sunday Afternoon,* 1948

*Pass That Peace Pipe (Ralph Blane-Hugh Martin-Roger Edens) *Good News,* 1947

Poppa, Don't Preach to Me (Frank Loesser) *Perils of Pauline,* 1947

††Portrait of Jenny (Gordon Burdge-J. Russel Robinson) 1949

Put 'Em in a Box (Sammy Cahn-Jule Styne) *Romance on the High Seas,* 1948

Rainy Night in Rio (Leo Robin-Arthur Schwartz) *Time, the Place and the Girl,* 1947

Right Girl for Me (Betty Comden-Adolph Green-Roger Edens) *Take Me Out to the Ball Game,* 1949

Shoes with Wings On (Ira Gershwin-Harry Warren) *Barkleys of Broadway,* 1949

Someone Like You (Ralph Blane-Harry Warren) *My Dream Is Yours,* 1948

Something in the Wind (Leo Robin-John W. Green) *Something in the Wind,* 1947

Sometime Remind Me to Tell You (Mort Greene-Leigh Harline) *Station West,* 1948

Sooner or Later (Ray Gilbert-Charles Wolcott) *Song of the South,* 1947

Steppin' Out with My Baby (Irving Berlin) *Easter Parade,* 1948

Streets of Laredo (Ray Evans-Jay Livingston) *Streets of Laredo,* 1949

Takin' Miss Mary to the Ball

(Edward Heyman-Nacio Herb Brown) *On an Island with You,* 1948

Tallahassee (Frank Loesser) *Variety Girl,* 1947

3rd Man Theme (Harry Lime Theme) (Walter Lord-Anton Karas) *3rd Man,* 1949

*This Is the Moment (Leo Robin-Frederick Hollander) *That Lady in Ermine,* 1948

A Thousand Violins (Ray Evans-Jay Livingston) *Great Lover,* 1949

*Through a Long and Sleepless Night (Mack Gordon-Alfred Newman) *Come to the Stable,* 1949

Through a Thousand Dreams (Leo Robin-Arthur Schwartz) *Time, the Place and the Girl,* 1947

Time After Time (Sammy Cahn-Jule Styne) *It Happened in Brooklyn,* 1947

Turntable Song (Leo Robin-John W. Green) *Something in the Wind,* 1947

What Did I Do? (Mack Gordon-Josef Myrow) *When My Baby Smiles at Me,* 1948

What's Wrong with Me (Edward Heyman-Nacio Herb Brown) *Kissing Bandit,* 1949

When Is Sometime? (Johnny Burke-James Van Heusen) *Connecticut Yankee in King Arthur's Court,* 1948

(Where Are You) Now that I Need You (Frank Loesser) *Red, Hot and Blue,* 1949

*Woody Woodpecker Song (Ramey Idriss-George Tibbles) *Wet Blanket Policy,* 1948

*You Do (Mack Gordon–Josef Myrow) *Mother Wore Tights,* 1947

You Don't Have to Know the Language (Johnny Burke–James Van Heusen) *Road to Rio,* 1947

You'd Be Hard to Replace (Ira Gershwin–Harry Warren) *Barkleys of Broadway,* 1949

Your Heart Calling Mine (Frank Loesser) *Variety Girl,* 1947

**Zip-a-Dee-Doo-Dah (Ray Gilbert–Allie Wrubel) *Song of the South,* 1947

*Nominated for the Academy Award.
** Winner of the Academy Award.
†Based on a melody by K. Lubomirski.
§Used to promote the film of the same name.
†† "Inspired" by the film of the same name.

List 17
Most Popular 200 Songs from 1950–65 Films

Accidents Will Happen (Johnny Burke–James Van Heusen) *Mr. Music,* 1950

*Affair to Remember (Harold Adamson–Harry Warren) *Affair to Remember,* 1957

Ain't That a Kick in the Head? (Sammy Cahn–James Van Heusen) *Ocean's 11,* 1960

All My Tomorrows (Sammy Cahn–James Van Heusen) *Hole in the Head,* 1959

**All the Way (Sammy Cahn–James Van Heusen) *Joker Is Wild,* 1957

All the Way Home (Stanley Styne–Jule Styne) *All the Way Home,* 1963

*Almost in Your Arms (Ray Evans–Jay Livingston) *Houseboat,* 1958

*Am I in Love (Jack Brooks) *Son of Paleface,* 1951

And Then You'll Be Home (Johnny Burke–James Van Heusen) *Mr. Music,* 1950

And There You Are (Mack Gordon–Josef Myrow) *I Love Melvin,* 1953

Anywhere I Wander (Frank Loesser) *Hans Christian Andersen,* 1952

*April Love (Paul Francis Webster–Sammy Fain) *April Love,* 1957

Around the World (Harold Adamson–Victor Young) *Around the World in 80 Days,* 1956

†Baby Doll (Johnny Mercer–Harry Warren) *Belle of New York,* 1951

†Baby Doll (Bernie Hanighen–Kenyon Hopkins) *Baby Doll,* 1956

*Bachelor in Paradise (Mack David–Henry Mancini) *Bachelor in Paradise,* 1961

*Ballad of Cat Ballou (Mack David–Jerry Livingston) *Cat Ballou,* 1965

Ballad of the War Wagon (Ned Washington–Dimitri Tiomkin) *War Wagon,* 1957

*Be My Love (Sammy Cahn–Nicholas Brodszky) *Toast of New Orleans,* 1950

*Because You're Mine (Sammy Cahn–Nicholas Brodszky) *Because You're Mine,* 1952

*Best of Everything (Sammy Cahn–Alfred Newman) *Best of Everything,* 1959

Best Things Happen While You're Dancing (Irving Berlin) *White Christmas,* 1954

*Bibbidy-Bobbidi-Boo (Mack David–Al Hoffman–Jerry Livingston) *Cinderella,* 1950

Birds and the Bees (Mack David–Harry Warren) *Birds and the Bees,* 1956

*Blue Pacific Blues (Sadie Thompson's Song) (Ned Washington–Lester Lee) *Miss Sadie Thompson,* 1953

Bonne Nuit (Goodnight) (Ray Evans–Jay Livingston) *Here Comes the Groom,* 1951

Boys' Night Out (Sammy Cahn–James Van Heusen) *Boys' Night Out,* 1962

Ça, C'est l'Amour (Cole Porter) *Les Girls,* 1957

**Call Me Irresponsible (Sammy Cahn–James Van Heusen) *Papa's Delicate Condition,* 1963

Call Me Tonight (Leo Robin–Harry Warren) *Just for You,* 1952

*A Certain Smile (Paul Francis Webster–Sammy Fain) *A Certain Smile,* 1958

*Charade (Johnny Mercer–Henry Mancini) *Charade,* 1963

Cherry Pink and Apple Blossom White (Mack David–Louiguy) *Underwater,* 1955

**Chim Chim Cher-ee (Richard M. and Robert B. Sherman) *Mary Poppins,* 1964

Closer You Are (Leo Robin–Jule Styne) *Two Tickets to Broadway,* 1950

*Count Your Blessings (Instead of Sheep) (Irving Berlin) *White Christmas,* 1954

**Days of Wine and Roses (Johnny Mercer–Henry Mancini) *Days of Wine and Roses,* 1962

*Dear Heart (Ray Evans–Jay Livingston–Henry Mancini) *Dear Heart,* 1964

Don't Let This Night Get Away (Harold Adamson–Burton Lane) *Jupiter's Darling,* 1955

Dormi-Dormi-Dormi (Sammy Cahn–Harry Warren) *Rock-a-Bye Baby,* 1958

A Dream Is a Wish Your Heart Makes (Mack David–Al Hoffman–Jerry Livingston) *Cinderella,* 1950

Emily (Johnny Mercer–Johnny Mandel) *Americanization of Emily,* 1964

Eternally (The Terry Theme) (Geoffrey Parsons–Charles Chaplin) *Limelight,* 1953

Ev'ry Street's a Boulevard (in Old New York) (Bob Hilliard–Jule Styne) *Living It Up,* 1954

Exodus Song (Pat Boone–Ernest
Gold) *Exodus,* 1960
Eyes of Blue (Wilson Stone–Victor Young) *Shane,* 1953
*Facts of Life (Johnny Mercer)
Facts of Life, 1960
*Falcon and the Dove (Paul Francis Webster–Miklos Rozsa) *El
Cid,* 1961
*Faraway Part of Town (Dory
Langdon–André Previn) *Pepe,*
1960
*The Five Pennies (Sylvia Fine)
The Five Pennies, 1959
*Follow Me (Paul Francis
Webster–Bronislaw Kaper)
Mutiny on the Bounty, 1962
Friendly Star (Mack Gordon–
Harry Warren) *Summer Stock,*
1950
From Here to Eternity (Bob
Wells–Fred Karger) *From Here
to Eternity,* 1953
**Gigi (Alan Jay Lerner–Frederick
Loewe) *Gigi,* 1958
*Green Leaves of Summer (Paul
Francis Webster–Dimitri
Tiomkin) *Alamo,* 1960
*Hanging Tree (Mack David–Jerry
Livingston) *Hanging Tree,* 1959
He Doesn't Know (Jack
Brooks–Harry Warren) *Ladies
Man,* 1961
*High and the Mighty (Ned
Washington–Dimitri Tiomkin)
High and the Mighty, 1954
**High Hopes (Sammy Cahn–
James Van Heusen) *Hole in the
Head,* 1959
**High Noon (Ned
Washington–Dimitri Tiomkin)
High Noon, 1952

High on the List (Johnny
Burke–James Van Heusen) *Mr.
Music,* 1950
Hi-Lili, Hi-Lo (Helen Deutsch–
Bronislaw Kaper) *Lili,* 1952
Hold Me Close to You (Ralph
Blane–Harry Warren) *Skirts
Ahoy!,* 1952
*Hold My Hand (Jack
Lawrence– Richard Myers)
Susan Slept Here, 1954
How to Be Very, Very Popular
(Sammy Cahn–Jule Styne)
How to Be Very, Very Popular,
1955
*Hush, Hush, Sweet Charlotte
(Mack David–Frank DeVol)
Hush, Hush, Sweet Charlotte,
1964
I Can See You (Sammy Cahn–
Nicholas Brodszky) *Rich, Young
and Pretty,* 1951
I Do! I Do! I Do! (Ray Evans–
Jay Livingston) *Stars Are Singing,* 1953
I Know a Dream When I See
One (Mack David–Jerry
Livingston) *Jumping Jacks,*
1952
I Like Myself (Betty Comden–
Adolph Green–André Previn)
It's Always Fair Weather,
1955
I Remember It Well (Alan Jay
Lerner–Frederick Loewe) *Gigi,*
1958
I Speak to the Stars (Paul Francis
Webster–Sammy Fain) *Lucky
Me,* 1954
I Wanna Be a Dancing Man
(Johnny Mercer–Harry Warren
Belle of New York, 1951

Leslie Caron singing Helen Deutsch and Bronislaw Kaper's "Hi-Lili, Hi-Lo" to puppet friends in *Lili,* **1953.**

*I Will Wait for You (Jacques Demy–Norman Gimbel–Michel Legrand) *Umbrellas of Cherbourg,* 1965

If Someone Had Told Me (Charles Tobias–Peter DeRose) *About Face,* 1952

If You Feel Like Singin', Sing (Mack Gordon–Harry Warren) *Summer Stock,* 1950

I'll Always Love You (Querida Mia) (Ray Evans–Jay Livingston) *My Friend Irma Goes West*, 1950

*I'll Never Stop Loving You (Sammy Cahn–Nicholas Brodszky) *Love Me or Leave Me*, 1955

I'll Remember Tonight (Paul Francis Webster–Sammy Fain) *Mardi Gras*, 1958

**In the Cool, Cool, Cool of the Evening (Johnny Mercer–Hoagy Carmichael) *Here Comes the Groom*, 1951

Innamorata (Jack Brooks–Harry Warren) *Artists and Models*, 1956

It Doesn't Cost a Dime to Dream (Ray Evans–Jay Livingston) *Lemon Drop Kid*, 1951

It Looks Like Love (Paul Francis Webster–Sammy Fain) *Hollywood or Bust*, 1956

*It's a Mad, Mad, Mad, Mad World (Mack David–Ernest Gold) *It's a Mad, Mad, Mad, Mad World*, 1963

It's a Woman's World (Sammy Cahn–Cyril Mockridge) *Woman's World*, 1954

*Julie (Tom Adair–Leith Stevens) *Julie*, 1956

Just for You (Leo Robin–Harry Warren) *Just for You*, 1952

Key to Love (John Moran–Charles Williams) *Apartment*, 1960

*§Kiss to Build a Dream On (Bert Kalmar–Oscar Hammerstein II–Harry Ruby) *The Strip*, 1951

Life Is So Peculiar (Johnny Burke–James Van Heusen) *Mr. Music*, 1950

Long Before I Knew You (Sammy Cahn–Jule Styne) *West Point Story*, 1950

(Love Is a) Career (Sammy Cahn–James Van Heusen) *Career*, 1959

Love Is a Lovely Thing (Sammy Cahn–Harry Warren) *Rock-a-Bye Baby*, 1958

**Love Is a Many-Splendored Thing (Paul Francis Webster–Sammy Fain) *Love Is a Many-Splendored Thing*, 1955

*(Love Is) The Tender Trap (Sammy Cahn–James Van Heusen) *The Tender Trap*, 1955

Love with the Proper Stranger (Johnny Mercer–Elmer Bernstein) *Love with the Proper Stranger*, 1963

Lovers' Gold (Mack David–Elmer Bernstein) *Buccaneer*, 1958

Magic Window (Johnny Burke–James Van Heusen) *Little Boy Lost*, 1953

*Man That Got Away (Ira Gershwin–Harold Arlen) *Star Is Born*, 1954

Mating Season (Ray Evans–Jay Livingston) *Mating Season*, 1951

Me 'n' You 'n' the Moon (Sammy Cahn–James Van Heusen) *Pardners*, 1956

**Mona Lisa (Ray Evans–Jay Livingston) *Captain Carey, USA*, 1950

Monique (Sammy Cahn–Elmer Bernstein) *Kings Go Forth*, 1958

*Moon Is Blue (Sylvia Fine–Herschel Burke Gilbert) *Moon Is Blue*, 1953

**Moon River (Johnny Mercer–
Henry Mancini) *Breakfast at
Tiffany's*, 1961

*More (Norman Newell–Riz Or-
tolani–Nino Oliviero) *Mondo
Cane*, 1963

*Mule Train (Fred Glickman–Hy
Heath–Johnny Lange) *Singing
Guns*, 1950

My Beloved (Ray Evans–Jay Livingston) *Aaron Slick from Punkin
Creek*, 1951

*My Flaming Heart (Leo
Robin–Nicholas Brodszky)
Small Town Girl, 1953

*My Kind of Town (Chicago Is)
(Sammy Cahn–James Van
Heusen) *Robin and the Seven
Hoods*, 1964

*Never (Eliot Daniel–Lionel
Newman) *Golden Girl*, 1951

Never Before (Mack David–Jerry
Livingston) *Sailor Beware*,
1952

**Never on Sunday (Manos Had-
jidakis) *Never on Sunday*, 1960

The Night They Invented Champagne (Alan Jay Lerner–
Frederick Loewe) *Gigi*, 1958

No Two People (Frank Loesser)
Hans Christian Andersen, 1951

Not as a Stranger (Buddy
Kaye–James Van Heusen) *Not
as a Stranger*), 1955

An Occasional Man (Ralph
Blane–Hugh Martin) *Girl Rush*,
1955

Our Very Own (Jack Elliott–Victor Young) *Our Very Own*, 1950

Paris Holiday (Sammy Cahn–
James Van Heusen) *Paris Holiday*, 1958

Paris Is a Lonely Town (E.Y.
Harburg–Harold Arlen) *Gay
Purr-ee*, 1964

Pass Me By (Carolyn Leight–Cy
Coleman) *Father Goose*, 1964

Pete Kelly's Blues (Sammy
Cahn–Ray Heindorf) *Pete Kelly's
Blues*, 1955

Picnic (Theme) (Steve Allen–
George W. Duning) *Picnic*,
1956

Pink Panther Theme (Johnny
Mercer–Henry Mancini) *The
Pink Panther*, 1964

Pleasure of His Company (Sammy
Cahn–Alfred Newman) *Pleasure
of His Company*, 1961

*Pocketful of Miracles (Sammy
Cahn–James Van Heusen)
Pocketful of Miracles, 1961

Return to Paradise (Ned Washington–Dimitri Tiomkin) *Return
to Paradise*, 1953

Right or Wrong (Ray Evans–Jay
Livingston) *Off Limits*, 1953

The Robe (Love Theme) (Alfred
Newman) *The Robe*, 1953

Rose Tattoo (Jack Brooks–Harry
Warren) *Rose Tattoo*, 1955

Ruby (Mitchell Parish–Heinz
Roemheld) *Ruby*, 1953

Say One for Me (Sammy Cahn–
James Van Heusen) *Say One for
Me*, 1959

Sayonara (Irving Berlin) *Sayonara*,
1957

The Search Is Through (Ira
Gershwin–Harold Arlen) *Country Girl*, 1954

*Second Chance (Dory Langdon–
André Previn) *Two for the
Seesaw*, 1962

Second Star to the Right (Sammy
Cahn–Sammy Fain) *Peter Pan,*
1951
*Second Time Around (Sammy
Cahn–James Van Heusen) *High
Time,* 1960
**Secret Love (Paul Francis
Webster–Sammy Fain) *Calamity
Jane,* 1953
Seeing's Believing (Johnny
Mercer–Harry Warren) *Belle of
New York,* 1951
**Shadow of Your Smile (Paul
Francis Webster–Johnny
Mandel) *Sandpiper,* 1965
Silver Bells (Ray Evans–Jay Liv-
ingston) *Lemon Drop Kid,* 1951
Sisters (Irving Berlin) *White
Christmas,* 1954
Sleep Safe and Warm (Larry
Kusik–Eddie Snyder–
Christopher Komeda) *Rosemary's
Baby,* 1958
§§Smile (John Turner–Geoffrey
Parsons–Charles Chaplin)
*So Little Time (Paul Francis
Webster–Dimitri Tiomkin) *55
Days at Peking,* 1963
So This Is Love (Mack David–Al
Hoffman–Jerry Livingston)
Cinderella, 1950
So Warm, My Love (Paul Francis
Webster–Pete King) *Family
Jewels,* 1965
Somebody (Jack Brooks–Harry
Warren) *Cinderfella,* 1961
*Something's Gotta Give (Johnny
Mercer) *Daddy Long Legs,* 1955
*Strange Are the Ways of Love
(Ned Washington–Dimitri
Tiomkin) *Young Land,* 1959
Style (Sammy Cahn–James Van

Heusen) *Robin and the Seven
Hoods,* 1964
A Summer Place (Theme) (Max
Steiner) *A Summer Place,* 1959
Sunshine Cake (Johnny
Burke–James Van Heusen)
Riding High, 1950
Supercalifragilisticexpialidocious
(Richard M. and Robert B.
Sherman) *Mary Poppins,* 1964
*Sweetheart Tree (Johnny Mer-
cer–Henry Mancini) *Great Race,*
1965
Sylvia (Paul Francis Webster–
David Raksin) *Sylvia,* 1964
*Tammy (Ray Evans–Jay Liv-
ingston) *Tammy and the Bachelor,*
1957
Teamwork (Sammy Cahn–James
Van Heusen) *Road to Hong
Kong,* 1962
*Tender Is the Night (Paul Fran-
cis Webster–Sammy Fain)
Tender Is the Night, 1962
Thank Heaven for Little Girls
(Alan Jay Lerner–Frederick
Loewe) *Gigi,* 1958
*That's Amore (Jack Brooks–
Harry Warren) *Caddy,* 1953
That's Entertainment (Howard
Dietz–Arthur Schwartz) *Band
Wagon,* 1953
That's What Makes Paris Paree
(Sammy Cahn–Vernon Duke)
April in Paris, 1952
*Thee I Love (Paul Francis
Webster–Dimitri Tiomkin)
Friendly Persuasion, 1956
There's Music in You (Oscar
Hammerstein II–Richard
Rodgers) *Main Street to Broad-
way,* 1952

**Three Coins in the Fountain (Sammy Cahn–Jule Styne) *Three Coins in the Fountain*, 1954
*Thumbelina (Frank Loesser) *Hans Christian Andersen*, 1952
To Love Again (Main Theme) (Ned Washington–Morris Stoloff-George Sidney) *Eddie Duchin Story*, 1956
*To Love and Be Loved (Sammy Cahn–James Van Heusen) *Some Came Running*, 1958
To See You Is to Love You (Johnny Burke–James Van Heusen) *Road to Bali*, 1952
*Too Late Now (Alan Jay Lerner–Burton Lane) *Royal Wedding*, 1951
*Town Without Pity (Ned Washington–Dimitri Tiomkin) *Town Without Pity*, 1961
*True Love (Cole Porter) *High Society*, 1956
*Unchained Melody (Hy Zaret–Alex North) *Unchained*, 1955
*A Very Precious Love (Paul Francis Webster–Sammy Fain) *Marjorie Morningstar*, 1958
Wake Me When It's Over (Sammy Cahn–James Van Heusen) *Wake Me When It's Over*, 1960
*Walk on the Wild Side (Mack David-Elmer Bernstein) *Walk on the Wild Side*, 1962
What Good Is a Gal (Without a Guy)? (Ralph Blane–Harry Warren) *Skirts Ahoy!*, 1952
**Whatever Will Be, Will Be (Que Sera, Sera) (Ray Evans–Jay Livingston) *Man

Who Knew Too Much*, 1956
*What's New Pussycat? (Hal David–Burt Bacharach) *What's New Pussycat?*, 1965
When I Fall in Love (Edward Heyman–Victory Young) *One Minute to Zero*, 1952
When You Love Someone (Ray Evans–Jay Livingston) *Here Come the Girls*, 1953
When You're in Love (Johnny Mercer–Gene DePaul) *Seven Brides for Seven Brothers*, 1954
Where Is Your Heart (William Engvick–Georges Auric) *Moulin Rouge*, 1953
*Where Love Has Gone (Sammy Cahn–James Van Heusen) *Where Love Has Gone*, 1964
Why Fight the Feeling? (Frank Loesser) *Let's Dance*, 1950
*Wild Is the Wind (Ned Washington–Dimitri Tiomkin) *Wild Is the Wind*, 1957
*Wilhelmina (Mack Gordon–Josef Myrow) *Wabash Avenue*, 1950
Wives and Lovers (Hal David–Burt Bacharach) *Wives and Lovers*, 1963
A Woman in Love (Frank Loesser) *Guys and Dolls*, 1955
*Wonder Why (Sammy Cahn–Nicholas Brodszky) *Rich, Young and Pretty*, 1951
Wonderful Copenhagen (Frank Loesser) *Hans Christian Andersen*, 1952
*Written on the Wind (Sammy Cahn–Victor Young) *Written on the Wind*, 1956
You and Your Beautiful Eyes (Mack David–Jerry Livingston)

At War with the Army, 1950

You, Wonderful You (Jack Brooks–Saul Chaplin–Harry Warren) *Summer Stock,* 1950

Young at Heart (Carolyn Leigh– Johnny Richards) *Young at Heart,* 1954

You're All the World to Me (Alan Jay Lerner–Burton Lane) *Royal Wedding,* 1951

You're Sensational (Cole Porter) *High Society,* 1956

You're the Right One (Jack Brooks– Harry Warren) *Caddy,* 1953

*Zing a Little Zong (Leo Robin– Harry Warren) *Just for You,* 1952

* *Nominated for the Academy Award.*
** *Winner of the Academy Award.*
† *Since song titles cannot be copyrighted, duplicate titles have occasionally been used for different songs.*
§ *Written in 1935.*
§§ *The lyric was written in 1954. The melody, which Chaplin revised slightly, was written in 1936 as the theme song for his* Modern Times.

List 18
Selected Broadway and Non-Production Song Hits by 10 American Composers

Throughout the history of sound pictures, Hollywood studios have inserted numerous Broadway songs into their films. Usually, entire scores were transferred, as in the film versions of stage shows or in the "biographies" of various composers. Other times, stage songs were picked up for use in an original Hollywood musical ("A Pretty Girl Is Like a Melody," in *The Great Ziegfeld*) or as the title of one ("Stormy Weather," "Easter Parade," "At Long Last Love"). Some songs were used as titles for dramas ("The Man I Love," "Embraceable You"). Hollywood also drew upon the songwriters' independent or non-production tunes for specialty numbers, background themes, and film titles ("Lazy," "Yes Sir, That's My Baby," "My Blue Heaven").

Following is a selection of Broadway and independent songs by major composers. The shows for which they were originally written and the year of production are included.

Harold Arlen

As Long as I Live, *Cotton Club Parade,* 1935

Between the Devil and the Deep Blue Sea, *Rhyth-Mania,* 1931

Come Rain or Come Shine, *St.*

Louis Woman, 1946

Eagle and Me, *Bloomer Girl,* 1944

Evelina, *Bloomer Girl,* 1944

Get Happy, *Nine-Fifteen Revue,* 1931

Happy as the Day Is Long, *Cotton Club Parade*, 1933

I Gotta Right to Sing the Blues, *Earl Carroll's Vanities*, 1932

I Love a Parade, *Cotton Club Revue*, 1931

I've Got the World on a String, *Cotton Club Parade*, 1933

Kickin' the Gong Around, *Rhyth-Mania*, 1931

Legalize My Name, *St. Louis Woman*, 1946

Let's Take a Walk Around the Block, *Life Begins at 8:40*, 1934

Right as the Rain, *Bloomer Girl*, 1944

Stormy Weather, *Cotton Club Parade*, 1933

You're a Builder Upper, *Life Begins at 8:40*, 1934

Irving Berlin

Broadway Songs

Alexander's Ragtime Band, *Merry Whirl*, 1911

Anything You Can Do, *Annie Get Your Gun*, 1946

Best Thing For You (Would Be Me), *Call Me Madam*, 1950

Blue Skies, *Betsy*, 1927

Doin' What Comes Naturally, *Annie Get Your Gun*, 1946

Easter Parade, *As Thousands Cheer*, 1933

Girl on the Magazine Cover, *Stop, Look and Listen*, 1915

Girl That I Marry, *Annie Get Your Gun*, 1946

Heat Wave, *As Thousands Cheer*, 1933

How's Chances?, *As Thousands Cheer*, 1933

I Got Lost in His Arms, *Annie Get Your Gun*, 1946

I Left My Heart at the Stage Door Canteen, *This Is the Army*, 1942

I Love a Piano, *Stop, Look and Listen*, 1915

I'm Getting Tired So I Can Sleep, *This Is the Army*, 1942

It's a Lovely Day Today, *Call Me Madam*, 1950

It's a Lovely Day Tomorrow, *Louisiana Purchase*, 1939

I've Got the Sun in the Morning, *Annie Get Your Gun*, 1946

Lady of the Evening, *Music Box Revue of 1922*, 1922

Let's Have Another Cup of Coffee, *Face the Music*, 1932

Let's Take an Old-Fashioned Walk, *Miss Liberty*, 1949

Mandy, *Ziegfeld Follies of 1919*, 1919

Marrying for Love, *Call Me Madam*, 1950

Oh, How I Hate to Get Up in the Morning, *Yip-Yip-Yaphank*, 1918

A Pretty Girl Is Like a Melody, *Ziegfeld Follies of 1919*, 1919

Russian Lullaby, *Oh, la Vicieuse*, 1927

Say It with Music, *Music Box Revue of 1921*, 1921

Shakin' the Blues Away, *Ziegfeld Follies of 1927*, 1927

Simple Melody, *Watch Your Step*, 1914

Soft Lights and Sweet Music, *Face the Music*, 1932

There's No Business Like Show Business, *Annie Get Your Gun,* 1946

They Say It's Wonderful, *Annie Get Your Gun,* 1946

This Is the Army, Mr. Jones, *This Is the Army,* 1942

What'll I Do?, *Vive la Femme,* 1924

With My Head in the Clouds, *This Is the Army,* 1942

You'd Be Surprised, *Ziegfeld Follies of 1919,* 1919

You're Just in Love, *Call Me Madam,* 1950

Non-Production Songs

All Alone (1924); All By Myself (1921); All of My Life (1945); Always (1925); Any Bonds Today (1941); Everybody's Doin' It (1911); *God Bless America (1938); How Deep Is the Ocean (1932); I Want to Go Back to Michigan Down on the Farm (1914); (I'll See You in) Cuba (1920); International Rag (1913); I've Got My Captain Working for Me Now (1919); Lazy (1924); Remember (1925); Say It Isn't So (1932); Snooky Ookums (1913); The Song Is Ended (1927); When I Lost You (1912); When That Midnight Choo-Choo Leaves for Alabam' (1912)

* *Written in 1918 and dropped from the stage show* Yip-Yip-Yaphank *by Berlin himself, who thought the song was too sentimental.*

Walter Donaldson

Broadway Songs

Carolina in the Morning, *Passing Show of 1922,* 1922

Love Me or Leave Me, *Whoopee!,* 1928

Makin' Whoopee, *Whoopee!,* 1928

My Mammy, *Sinbad,* 1921

Non-Production Songs

At Sundown (1927); Back Home in Tennessee (1925); Beside a Babbling Brook (1923); Daughter of Rosie O'Grady (1917); How Ya Gonna Keep 'Em Down on the Farm (After They've Seen Paree)? (1919); *(I've Grown So Lonesome) Thinking of You (1926); Just Like a Melody Out of the Sky (1928); Little White Lies (1930); Mr. Meadowlark (1940); My Blue Heaven (1926); My Buddy (1922); Never a Day Goes By (1931); Sam the Accordion Man (1924); That Certain Party (1925); Until the Stars Fall Down (1927); (What Can I Say) After I Say I'm Sorry? (1926); Yes Sir, That's My Baby (1925); You're Driving Me Crazy (What Did I Do)? (1930).

* *The theme song of the Kay Kyser Orchestra.*

George Gershwin

Broadway Songs

Babbitt and the Bromide, *Funny Face,* 1927

Bess, You Is My Woman, *Porgy and Bess,* 1935

Bidin' My Time, *Girl Crazy,* 1930

But Not for Me, *Girl Crazy,* 1930

By Strauss, *Show Is On,* 1936

Clap Yo' Hands, *Oh, Kay!,* 1926

Do, Do, Do, *Oh, Kay!,* 1926

Do It Again, *French Doll,* 1926

*Embraceable You, *Girl Crazy,* 1930

Fascinating Rhythm, *Lady Be Good!,* 1924

Funny Face, *Funny Face,* 1927

He Loves and She Loves, *Funny Face,* 1927

†How Long Has This Been Going On?, *Rosalie,* 1927

I Got Plenty o' Nuttin', *Porgy and Bess,* 1935

I Got Rhythm, *Girl Crazy,* 1930

I Was So Young; You Were So Beautiful, *Good Morning, Judge,* 1920

I'll Build a Stairway to Paradise, *George White's Scandals of 1922,* 1922

Isn't It a Pity? *Pardon My English,* 1932

It Ain't Necessarily So, *Porgy and Bess,* 1935

I've Got a Crush on You, *Treasure Girl,* 1928

Let's Kiss and Make Up, *Funny Face,* 1927

Liza, *Show Girl,* 1929

Love Is Sweeping the Country, *Of Thee I Sing,* 1931

§The Man I Love, *Strike Up the Band,* 1930

Maybe, *Oh, Kay!,* 1926

Mine, *Let 'Em Eat Cake,* 1933

Of Thee I Sing, *Of Thee I Sing,* 1931

Oh, Lady Be Good, *Lady Be Good!,* 1924

Somebody Loves Me, *George White's Scandals of 1924,* 1924

Someone to Watch Over Me, *Oh, Kay!,* 1926

Soon, *Strike Up the Band,* 1930

Strike Up the Band, *Strike Up the Band,* 1930

Summertime, *Porgy and Bess,* 1935

Swanee, *Sinbad,* 1919

Sweet and Low Down, *Tip-Toes,* 1925

'S Wonderful, *Funny Face,* 1927

That Certain Feeling, *Tip-Toes,* 1925

Tra-La-La, *For Goodness Sake,* 1922

Who Cares?, *Of Thee I Sing,* 1931

Wintergreen for President, *Of Thee I Sing,* 1931

A Woman Is a Sometime Thing, *Porgy and Bess,* 1935

Non-Production Works

Rhapsody in Blue (1924); Concerto in F (Major) (1925); Five Piano Preludes (1926); Second Rhapsody (1932); Cuban Overture (1932)

Dropped from Funny Face, *also 1927.*
†*Written originally for the unproduced Florenz Ziegfeld musical* Ming Toy *in 1929.*
§*Dropped from* Lady Be Good!, *1924.*

Jerome Kern

All the Things You Are, *Very Warm for May,* 1939

Can't Help Lovin' Dat Man, *Show Boat,* 1927

Cleopatterer, *Leave It to Jane,* 1917

Don't Ever Leave Me, *Sweet Adeline,* 1929

Here Am I, *Sweet Adeline,* 1929

How'd You Like to Spoon with Me?, *Earl and the Girl,* 1906

I've Told Ev'ry Little Star, *Music in the Air,* 1932

Ka-Lu-a, *Good Morning, Dearie,* 1921

Land Where the Good Songs Go, *Miss 1917,* 1917

Leave It to Jane, *Leave It to Jane,* 1917

Life Upon the Wicked Stage, *Show Boat,* 1927

Look for the Silver Lining, *Sally,* 1920

Make Believe, *Show Boat,* 1927

*My Bill, *Show Boat,* 1927

Night Was Made for Love, *Cat and the Fiddle,* 1931

Ol' Man River, *Show Boat,* 1927

Once in a Blue Moon, *Stepping Stones,* 1922

One More Dance, *Music in the Air,* 1932

She Didn't Say "Yes," *Cat and the Fiddle,* 1931

Smoke Gets in Your Eyes, *Roberta,* 1933

The Song Is You, *Music in the Air,* 1932

Sunny, *Sunny,* 1925

They Didn't Believe Me, *Girl from Utah,* 1914

Till the Clouds Roll By, *Oh, Boy!,* 1917

Touch of Your Hand, *Roberta,* 1933

Try to Forget, *Cat and the Fiddle,* 1931

Whippoorwill, *Sally,* 1920

Who (Stole My Heart Away)? *Sunny,* 1925

Why Do I Love You? *Show Boat,* 1927

Why Was I Born? *Sweet Adeline,* 1929

Wild Rose, *Sally,* 1920

Yesterdays, *Roberta,* 1933

You Are Love, *Show Boat,* 1927

Written originally for Oh Lady, Lady!, *1917.*

James McHugh

Broadway Songs

Blue Again, *Vanderbilt Revue,* 1930

Diga Diga Do, *Blackbirds of 1928,* 1928

Exactly Like You, *International Revue,* 1930

I Can't Give You Anything But Love (Baby), *Blackbirds of 1928,* 1928

I Got Lucky in the Rain, *As the Girls Go,* 1948

I Must Have that Man!, *Blackbirds of 1928,* 1928

A Latin Tune, a Manhattan Moon, and You, *Keep Off the Grass,* 1940

Lost in a Fog, *Ben Marden's Riviera Revue,* 1934

On the Sunny Side of the Street, *International Revue,* 1930

Out Where the Blues Begin, *Hello, Daddy,* 1928

Rendezvous Time in Paree, *Streets of Paris,* 1939

South American Way, *Streets of Paris,* 1939

*Thank You for a Lovely Evening, *Palais Royal Revue,* 1934

Non-Production Songs

Comin' in on a Wing and Prayer (1943); I Can't Believe That You're in Love with Me (1927); My Dream of the Big Parade (1926); There's a New Star in Heaven To-Night (Rudolph Valentino) (1926); When My Sugar Walks Down the Street (All the Little Birdies Go Tweet-Tweet-Tweet) (1924)

*Used as the theme song for the 1936 MGM film Wife vs. Secretary, without screen credit to McHugh.

Cole Porter

Ace in the Hole, *Let's Face It,* 1941

All of You, *Silk Stockings,* 1954

All Through the Night, *Anything Goes,* 1934

Allez-vous-en, Go Away, *Can-Can,* 1953

Always True to You in My Fashion, *Kiss Me Kate,* 1949

Another Op'nin', Another Show, *Kiss Me Kate,* 1949

Anything Goes, *Anything Goes,* 1934

At Long Last Love, *You Never Know,* 1938

Begin the Beguine, *Jubilee,* 1935

Blow, Gabriel, Blow, *Anything Goes,* 1934

C'est Magnifique, *Can-Can,* 1953

Do I Love You?, *DuBarry Was a Lady,* 1939

Down in the Depths (on the Ninetieth Floor), *Red, Hot and Blue,* 1936

Every Time We Say Goodbye, *Seven Lively Arts,* 1944

Everything I Love, *Let's Face It,* 1941

Friendship, *DuBarry Was a Lady,* 1939

From This Moment On, *Out of This World,* 1950

Get Out of Town, *Leave It to Me,* 1938

Hey, Good-Lookin', *Something for the Boys,* 1942

How Could We Be Wrong?, *Nymph Errant,* 1933

I Get a Kick Out of You, *Anything Goes,* 1934

I Love Paris, *Can-Can,* 1953

I Love You, *Mexican Hayride,* 1944

I'm in Love Again, *Greenwich Village Follies of 1924,* 1924

It Was Written in the Stars, *DuBarry Was a Lady,* 1939

It's All Right with Me, *Can-Can,* 1953

It's D'-Lovely, *Red, Hot and Blue,* 1936

Just One of Those Things, *Jubilee,* 1935

Katie Went to Haiti, *DuBarry Was a Lady,* 1939
Let's Be Buddies, *Panama Hattie,* 1940
Let's Do It, *Paris,* 1928
Let's Misbehave, *Paris,* 1928
Love for Sale, *New Yorkers,* 1929
My Heart Belongs to Daddy, *Leave It to Me,* 1938
Night and Day, *Gay Divorcee,* 1932
Old Fashioned Garden, *Hitchy Coo of 1922,* 1922
Ridin' High, *Red, Hot and Blue,* 1936
Should I Tell You I Love You?,
Around the World, 1946
So in Love, *Kiss Me Kate,* 1949
Too Darn Hot, *Kiss Me Kate,* 1949
What Is This Thing Called Love?, *Wake Up and Dream,* 1929
Why Can't You Behave?, *Kiss Me Kate,* 1949
Why Shouldn't I?, *Jubilee,* 1935
Wunderbar, *Kiss Me Kate,* 1949
You Do Something to Me, *Fifty Million Frenchmen,* 1928
You're the Top, *Anything Goes,* 1934
You've Got That Thing, *Fifty Million Frenchmen,* 1928

As a Yale student, Porter wrote two football songs, "Bingo Eli Yale" (1910) and "Bulldog Yale" (1911). He also wrote a rare non-production hit, "Miss Otis Regrets She's Unable to Lunch Today," in 1934.

Richard Rodgers
(With Lorenz Hart as Lyricist)

Bewitched (Bothered and Bewildered), *Pal Joey,* 1941
Blue Room, *Girl Friend,* 1926
Dancing on the Ceiling, *Evergreen,* 1931
Everything I've Got, *By Jupiter,* 1942
Falling in Love with Love, *Boys from Syracuse,* 1938
Girl Friend, *Girl Friend,* 1926
Give It Back to the Indians, *Too Many Girls,* 1939
Have You Met Miss Jones?, *I'd Rather Be Right,* 1937
Here in My Arms, *Dearest Enemy,* 1925
I Could Write a Book, *Pal Joey,* 1941
I Didn't Know What Time It Was, *Too Many Girls,* 1939
I Married an Angel, *I Married an Angel,* 1938
I Wish I Were in Love Again, *Babes in Arms,* 1937
It Never Entered My Mind, *Higher and Higher,* 1940
I've Got Five Dollars, *America's Sweetheart,* 1931
Johnny One-Note, *Babes in Arms,* 1937
Lady Is a Tramp, *Babes in Arms,* 1937
Little Girl Blue, *Jumbo,* 1935
Love Never Went to College, *Too Many Girls,* 1939
Manhattan, *Garrick Gaieties of 1925,* 1925
Most Beautiful Girl in the World, *Jumbo,* 1935
Mountain Greenery, *Garrick Gaieties of 1926,* 1926
My Funny Valentine, *Babes in Arms,* 1937

My Heart Stood Still, *Connecticut Yankee,* 1927
My Romance, *Jumbo,* 1935
Over and Over Again, *Jumbo,* 1935
Sentimental Me and Romantic You, *Garrick Gaieties of 1925,* 1925
Ship Without a Sail, *Heads Up,* 1929
Sing for Your Supper, *Boys from Syracuse,* 1938
Slaughter on Tenth Avenue, *On Your Toes,* 1936 (instrumental)
Spring Is Here, *I Married an Angel,* 1938
Ten Cents a Dance, *Simple Simon,* 1930
There's a Small Hotel, *On Your Toes,* 1936
This Can't Be Love, *Boys from Syracuse,* 1938
Thou Swell, *Connecticut Yankee,* 1927
To Keep My Love Alive, *Connecticut Yankee* (1943 revival)
Tree in the Park, *Peggy Ann,* 1926
You Took Advantage of Me, *Present Arms,* 1928
Wait Till You See Her, *By Jupiter,* 1942
Where or When, *Babes in Arms,* 1937
Where's the Rainbow?, *Peggy Ann,* 1926
With a Song in My Heart, *Spring Is Here,* 1929

(With Oscar Hammerstein II as Lyricist)

All at Once You Love Her, *Pipe Dream,* 1957
Bali Ha'i, *South Pacific,* 1949
Climb Ev'ry Mountain, *Sound of Music,* 1959
Cock-Eyed Optimist, *South Pacific,* 1949
*Do I Love You (Because You're Beautiful), *Cinderella,* 1957
Do-Re-Mi, *Sound of Music,* 1959
Edelweiss, *Sound of Music,* 1959
Fellow Needs a Girl, *Allegro,* 1947
Gentleman Is a Dope, *Allegro,* 1947
Getting to Know You, *King and I,* 1951
Happy Talk, *South Pacific,* 1949
Hello, Young Lovers, *King and I,* 1951
Hundred Million Miracles, *Flower Drum Song,* 1958
†I Cain't Say No, *Oklahoma!,* 1943
I Enjoy Being a Girl, *Flower Drum Song,* 1958
I Haven't Got a Worry in the World, *Happy Birthday,* 1946
I Whistle a Happy Tune, *King and I,* 1951
If I Loved You, *Carousel,* 1944
I'm Gonna Wash That Man Right Out of My Hair, *South Pacific,* 1949
June Is Bustin' Out All Over, *Carousel,* 1944
Kansas City, *Oklahoma!,* 1943
Keep It Gay, *Me and Juliet,* 1953
Many a New Day, *Oklahoma!,* 1943
Maria, *Sound of Music,* 1959
Marriage Type Love, *Me and Juliet,* 1953
Mister Snow, *Carousel,* 1944
My Favorite Things, *Sound of Music,* 1959

§No Other Love, *Me and Juliet,*
1953
Oh, What a Beautiful Morning,
Oklahoma!, 1943
Oklahoma!, *Oklahoma!,* 1943
Out of My Dreams, *Oklahoma!,*
1943
People Will Say We're in Love,
Oklahoma!, 1943
Shall We Dance?, *King and I,*
1951
Sixteen Going on Seventeen,
Sound of Music, 1959
So Far, *Allegro,* 1947
Soliloquy ("My Boy Bill"),
Carousel, 1944
Some Enchanted Evening, *South
Pacific,* 1949
Something Wonderful, *King and I,*
1951

Sound of Music, *Sound of Music,*
1959
Sunday, *Flower Drum Song,* 1958
Surrey with the Fringe on Top,
Oklahoma!, 1943
Ten Minutes Ago, *Cinderella,* 1957
There Is Nothing Like a Dame,
South Pacific, 1949
We Kiss in a Shadow, *King and I,*
1951
What's the Use of Wond'rin',
Carousel, 1944
A Wonderful Guy, *South Pacific,*
1949
You Are Beautiful, *Flower Drum
Song,* 1958
You'll Never Walk Alone,
Carousel, 1944
Younger Than Springtime, *South
Pacific,* 1949

*Cinderella *was a CBS network television presentation.*
†*Originally entitled* Away We Go *for its New Haven tryout,* Oklahoma! *was based on Lynn
Riggs's 1931 play* Green Grow the Lilacs, *which starred Franchot Tone as Curly.*
§*The original title of this song was "Tango," and it appeared as a background theme in Rodgers's
score for* Victory at Sea, *a 1952-53 television series.*

Sigmund Romberg

Auf Wiedersehen, *Blue Paradise,*
1915
Close as Pages in a Book, *Up in
Central Park,* 1945
Deep in My Heart, Dear, *Student
Prince,* 1924
Desert Song, *Desert Song,* 1926
Drinking Song, *Student Prince,* 1924
Golden Days, *Student Prince,* 1924
Lover, Come Back to Me, *New
Moon,* 1928
Marianne, *New Moon,* 1928
One Alone, *Desert Song,* 1926
One Kiss, *New Moon,* 1928

Riff Song, *Desert Song,* 1926
Romance, *Desert Song,* 1926
Serenade, *Student Prince,* 1924
Silver Moon, *My Maryland,* 1927
Softly as in a Morning Surnise,
New Moon, 1928
Stout Hearted Men, *New Moon,*
1928
Wanting You, *New Moon,* 1928
When Hearts Are Young, *Lady in
Ermine,* 1925
When You Walk in the Room,
Up in Central Park, 1945
Will You Remember? ("Sweetheart,

Sweetheart, Sweetheart"), *Maytime,* 1917
Your Land and My Land, *My*

Maryland, 1927
Your Smile, Your Tears, *Nina
Rosa,* 1930

Arthur Schwartz

Alone Together, *Flying Colors,*
1932
By Myself, *Between the Devil,* 1937
Dancing in the Dark, *Band Wagon,*
1931
Haunted Heart, *Inside USA,* 1948
High and Low, *Band Wagon,* 1931
I Guess I'll Have to Change My
Plan, *Little Show,* 1929
I Love Louisa, *Band Wagon,* 1931
I See Your Face Before Me, *Be-
tween the Devil,* 1937
If There Is Someone Lovelier
than You, *Revenge with Music,*
1934
Louisiana Hayride, *Flying Colors,*
1932

Love Is a Dancing Thing, *At
Home Abroad,* 1935
Love Is the Reason, *A Tree Grows
in Brooklyn,* 1951
Make the Man Love Me, *A Tree
Grows in Brooklyn,* 1951
New Sun in the Sky, *Band Wagon,*
1931
Shine on Your Shoes, *Flying
Colors,* 1932
Something to Remember You By,
Three's a Crowd, 1930
This Is It, *Stars in Your Eyes,* 1939
Triplets, *Between the Devil,* 1937
You and I Know, *Virginia,* 1937
You and the Night and the
Music, *Revenge with Music,* 1934

List 19
Film Songs Nominated for the
Academy Award, 1966–1990

After All (Dean Pitchford–Tom
Snow) *Chances Are,* 1989
Against All Odds ("Take a Look
at Me Now") (Phil Collins)
Against All Odds, 1984
Age of Not Believing (Richard M.
and Robert B. Sherman)
Bedknobs and Broomsticks, 1971
Alfie (Hal David–Burt Bacharach)
Alfie, 1966
All His Children (Alan and Mari-
lyn Bergman–Henry Mancini)
Sometimes a Great Notion, 1971

All That Love Went to Waste
(Sammy Cahn–George Barrie)
Touch of Class, 1973
Ave Satani (Jerry Goldsmith) *The
Omen,* 1976
Bare Necessities (Terry Gilkyson)
Jungle Book, 1967
Be Our Guest (Howard
Ashman–Alan Menken) *Beauty
and the Beast,* 1991
*Beauty and the Beast (Howard
Ashman–Alan Menken) *Beauty
and the Beast,* 1991

Belle (Howard Ashman–Alan
Menken) *Beauty and the Beast,*
1991
Ben (Don Black–Walter Scharf)
Ben, 1972
*Best That You Can Do (Carole
Bayer Sager–Christopher
Cross–Peter Allen–Burt
Bacharach) *Arthur,* 1981
Blaze of Glory (Jon Bon Jovi)
Young Guns II, 1990
Blazing Saddles (Mel Brooks–
John Morris) *Blazing Saddles,*
1974
Bless the Beasts and Children
(Barry DeVorzon–Perry Botkin,
Jr.) *Bless the Beasts and Children,*
1971
*Born Free (Don Black–John
Barry) *Born Free,* 1966
Calling You (Bob Telson) *Bagdad
Cafe,* 1988
Candle on the Water (Al
Kasha–Joel Hirschhorn) *Pete's
Dragon,* 1977
Chitty Chitty Bang Bang
(Richard M. and Robert B.
Sherman) *Chitty Chitty Bang
Bang,* 1968
Come Follow, Follow Me (Mar-
sha and Fred Karlin) *Little Ark,*
1972
Come Saturday Morning (Dory
Previn–Fred Karlin) *Sterile
Cuckoo,* 1969
Come to Me (Don Black–Henry
Mancini) *Pink Panther Strikes
Again,* 1976
Cry Freedom (George Fenton–
Jonas Gwangwa) *Cry Freedom,*
1987
Do You Know Where You're Go-

ing To (Gerry Goffin–Michael
Masser) *Mahogany,* 1975
Endless Love (Lionel Richie)
Endless Love, 1981
*Evergreen (Paul Williams–
Barbra Streisand) *Star Is Born,*
1976
(Everything I Do) I Do It for
You (Bryan Adams–Robert
John Lange–Michael Kamen)
Robin Hood: Prince of Thieves,
1991
Eye of the Tiger (Jim Peterik–
Frankie Sullivan III) *Rocky III,*
1982
The Eyes of Love (Bob Russell–
Quincy Jones) *Banning,* 1967
*Fame (Dean Pitchford–Michael
Gore) *Fame,* 1980
First Time It Happens (Joe
Raposo) *Great Muppet Caper,*
1981
*Flashdance ... What a Feeling
(Keith Forsey–Irene Cara–
Giorgio Moroder) *Flashdance,*
1983
Footloose (Kenny Loggins–Dean
Pitchford) *Footloose,* 1984
*For All We Know (Robb Royer–
James Griffin–Arthur James–
Fred Karlin) *Lovers and Other
Strangers,* 1970
For Love of Ivy (Bob Russell–
Quincy Jones) *For Love of Ivy,*
1968
For Your Eyes Only (Mick
Leeson–Bill Conti) *For Your Eyes
Only,* 1981
Funny Girl (Bob Merrill–Jule
Styne) *Funny Girl,* 1968
Georgy Girl (Jim Dale–Tom
Springfield) *Georgy Girl,* 1966

Ghostbusters (Ray Parker, Jr.) *Ghostbusters,* 1984

Girl Who Used to Be Me (Alan and Marilyn Bergman–Marvin Hamlisch) *Shirley Valentine,* 1989

Glory of Love (Peter Cetera–Diana Nini–David Foster) *Karate Kid Part II,* 1986

Gonna Fly Now (Carol Connors–Ayn Robbins–Bill Conti) *Rocky,* 1976

Hopelessly Devoted to You (John Farrar) *Grease,* 1978

How Do You Keep the Music Playing? (Alan and Marilyn Bergman–Michel Legrand) *Best Friends,* 1982

How Lucky Can You Get (Fred Ebb–John Kander) *Funny Lady,* 1975

I Feel Love (Betty and Euel Box) *Benji,* 1974

*I Just Called to Say I Love You (Stevie Wonder) *Woman in Red,* 1984

I Love to See You Smile (Randy Newman) *Parenthood,* 1989

If We Were in Love (Alan and Marilyn Bergman–John Williams) *Yes, Giorgio,* 1982

I'll Never Say "Goodbye" (Alan and Marilyn Bergman–David Shire) *The Promise,* 1979

I'm Checkin' Out (Shel Silverstein) *Postcards from the Edge,* 1990

*I'm Easy (Keith Carradine) *Nashville,* 1975

*It Goes Like It Goes (Norman Gimbel–David Shire) *Norma Rae,* 1979

It Might Be You (Alan and Marilyn Bergman–Dave Grusin) *Tootsie,* 1982

It's Easy to Say (Robert Wells–Henry Mancini) *10,* 1979

*(I've Had) the Time of My Life (Franke Previte–John De-Nicola–Donald Markowitz) *Dirty Dancing,* 1987

Jean (Rod McKuen) *Prime of Miss Jean Brodie,* 1969

Kiss the Girl (Howard Ashman–Alan Menken) *Little Mermaid,* 1989

*Last Dance (Paul Jabara) *Thank God It's Friday,* 1978

Last Time I Felt Like This (Alan and Marilyn Bergman–Marvin Hamlisch) *Same Time, Next Year,* 1978

*Let the River Run (Carly Simon) *Working Girl,* 1988

Let's Hear It for the Boy (Tom Snow–Dean Pitchford, *Footloose,* 1984

Life in a Looking Glass (Leslie Bricusse–Henry Mancini) *That's Life,* 1986

Life Is What You Make It (Johnny Mercer–Marvin Hamlisch) *Kotch,* 1971

Little Prince (Alan Jay Lerner–Frederick Loewe) *Little Prince,* 1974

Live and Let Die (Paul and Linda McCartney) *Live and Let Die,* 1973

Look of Love (Hal David–Burt Bacharach) *Casino Royale,* 1967

Love (Floyd Huddleston–George Bruns) *Robin Hood,* 1973

Maniac (Michael Sembello–Dennis Matkosky) *Flashdance,* 1983

Marmalade, Molasses and Honey

(Marilyn and Alan Bergman–
Maurice Jarre) *Life and Times of
Judge Roy Bean,* 1972

Mean Green Mother from Outer
Space (Howard Ashman–Alan
Menken) *Little Shop of Horrors,*
1986

Miss Celie's Blues (Sister) (Quincy
Jones–Rod Temperton– Lionel
Richie) *Color Purple,* 1985

*The Morning After (Al
Kasha–Joel Hirschhorn)
Poseidon Adventure, 1972

My Wishing Doll (Mack David–
Elmer Bernstein) *Hawaii,* 1966

Nice to Be Around (Paul and John
Williams) *Cinderella Liberty,* 1973

Nine to Five (Dolly Parton) *Nine
to Five,* 1980

Nobody Does It Better (Carole
Bayer Sager–Marvin Hamlisch)
Spy Who Loved Me, 1977

Nothing's Gonna Stop Us Now
(Albert Hammond–Diane Warren) *Mannequin,* 1987

Now That We're in Love (Sammy
Cahn–George Barrie) *Whiffs,*
1975

On the Road Again, (Willie
Nelson) *Honeysuckle Rose,* 1980

One More Hour (Randy
Newman) *Ragtime,* 1981

Out Here on My Own (Lesley
and Michael Gore) *Fame,* 1980

Over You (Austin Roberts–Bobby
Hart) *Tender Mercies,* 1983

Papa, Can You Hear Me? (Alan
and Marilyn Bergman–Michel
Legrand) *Yentl,* 1983

People Alone (Wilbur Jennings–
Lalo Schifrin) *The Competition,*
1980

Pieces of Dreams (Alan and
Marilyn Bergman–Michel
Legrand) *Pieces of Dreams,* 1970

Power of Love (Huey Lewis–
Chris Hayes–Johnny Colla)
Back to the Future, 1985

Promise Me You'll Remember
(John Bettis–Carmine Coppola)
Godfather Part III, 1990

Rainbow Connection (Paul
Williams–Kenny Ascher) *Muppet Movie,* 1979

*Raindrops Keep Fallin' on My
Head (Hal David–Burt Bacharach) *Butch Cassidy and the Sundance Kid,* 1969

Ready to Take a Chance Again
(Norman Gimbel–Charles Fox)
Foul Play, 1978

Richard's Window (Norman
Gimbel–Charles Fox) *Other Side
of the Mountain,* 1975

*Say You, Say Me (Lionel
Richie) *White Nights,* 1985

Separate Lives (Stephen Bishop)
White Nights, 1985

*Shaft (Theme) (Isaac Hayes)
Shaft, 1971

Shakedown (Harold Faltermeyer–
Keith Forsey–Bob Seger) *Beverly
Hills Cop II,* 1987

Slipper and the Rose Waltz (He
Danced with Me/She Danced
with Me) (Richard M. and
Robert B. Sherman) *Slipper and
the Rose,* 1977

Someone's Waiting for You (Carol
Connors–Ayn Robbins–Sammy
Fain) *Rescuers,* 1977

Somewhere in My Memory (Leslie Bricusse–John Williams)
Home Alone, 1990

Somewhere Out There (Cynthia Weil–James Horner–Barry Mann) *An American Tail,* 1986

*Sooner or Later (I Always Get My Man) (Stephen Sondheim) *Dick Tracy,* 1990

Star! (Sammy Cahn–James Van Heusen) *Star!,* 1968

Storybook Love (Willy DeVille) *Princess Bride,* 1987

Strange Are the Ways of Love (Paul Francis Webster–Sammy Fain) *Stepmother,* 1972

Surprise, Surprise (Edward Kleban–Marvin Hamlisch) *A Chorus Line,* 1985

*Take My Breath Away (Tom Whitlock–Giorgio Moroder) *Top Gun,* 1986

*Talk to the Animals (Leslie Bricusse) *Doctor Dolittle,* 1967

Thank You Very Much (Leslie Bricusse) *Scrooge,* 1970

Thoroughly Modern Millie (Sammy Cahn–James Van Heusen) *Thoroughly Modern Millie,* 1967

Through the Eyes of Love (Carole Bayer Sager–Marvin Hamlisch) *Ice Castles,* 1979

Till Love Touches Your Life (Arthur Hamilton–Riz Ortolani) *Madron,* 1970

A Time for Love (Paul Francis Webster–Johnny Mandel) *American Dream,* 1966

True Grit (Don Black–Elmer Bernstein) *True Grit,* 1969

Two Hearts (Phil Collins–Lamont Dozier) *Buster,* 1988

*Under the Sea (Howard Ashman–Alan Menken) *Little Mermaid,* 1989

*Up Where We Belong (Will Jennings–Jack Nitzsche–Buffy Sainte-Marie) *Officer and a Gentleman,* 1982

The Way He Makes Me Feel (Alan and Marilyn Bergman–Michel Legrand) *Yentl,* 1983

*The Way We Were (Alan and Marilyn Bergman–Marvin Hamlisch) *The Way We Were,* 1973

*We May Never Love Like This Again (Al Kasha–Joel Hirschhorn) *Towering Inferno,* 1974

What Are You Doing the Rest of Your Life? (Alan and Marilyn Bergman–Michel Legrand) *Happy Ending,* 1969

When You're Alone (Leslie Bricusse–John Williams) *Hook,* 1991

When You're Loved (Richard M. and Robert B. Sherman) *Magic of Lassie,* 1978

Wherever Love Takes Me (Don Black–Elmer Bernstein) *Gold,* 1974

Whistling Away the Dark (Johnny Mercer–Henry Mancini) *Darling Lili,* 1970

*Windmills of Your Mind (Alan and Marilyn Bergman–Michel Legrand) *Thomas Crown Affair,* 1968

World that Never Was (Paul Francis Webster–Sammy Fain) *Half a House,* 1976

*You Light Up My Life (Joseph Brooks) *You Light Up My Life,* 1977

Winner of the Academy Award.

Bibliography

Books

Abels, Jules. *In the Time of Silent Cal.* New York: G.P. Putnam's Sons, 1969.

Baxter, John. *Hollywood in the Thirties.* New York: A.S. Barnes & Co., 1968.

Black, Shirley Temple. *Child Star.* New York: McGraw-Hill Publishing Co., 1988.

Buxton, Frank and Bill Owen. *Radio's Golden Age.* New York: Easton Valley Press, 1966.

Croce, Arlene. *The Fred Astaire and Ginger Rogers Book.* New York: Outerbridge & Lazard, Inc., 1972.

Curtiss, Thomas Quinn. *Von Stroheim.* New York: Vintage Books (Random House), 1973.

David, Lester and Irene David. *The Shirley Temple Story.* New York: G.P. Putnam's Sons, 1983.

Duke, Vernon. *Passport to Paris.* Boston: Little, Brown & Co., 1955.

Eames, John Douglas. *The M-G-M Story.* New York, Crown, 1975.

Edwards, Ann. *Shirley Temple: American Princess.* William Morrow, 1988.

Farnsworth, Marjorie. *The Ziegfeld Follies.* London: Peter Davies, 1956.

Galbraith, John Kenneth. *The Great Crash: 1929.* Boston: Houghton Mifflin, 1954.

Harvey, Stephen. *Directed by Vincente Minnelli.* New York: The Museum of Modern Art/Harper & Row, 1990.

Katz, Ephraim. *The Film Encyclopedia.* New York: G.P. Putnam's Sons, 1979.

Kimball, Robert and Alfred Simon. *The Gershwins.* New York: Bonanza Books, 1973.

Leuchtenburg, William E. *In the Shadow of FDR.* Ithaca, N.Y.: Cornell University Press, 1983.

McElvaine, Robert S. *The Great Depression: America, 1929–41.* New York: Times Books, 1984.

Mancini, Henry (with) Gene Lees. *Did They Mention the Music?* Chicago: Contemporary Books, 1990.

Panassie, Hugues and Madeleine Gautier. *Jazz.* Boston: Houghton Mifflin, 1956.

Pratt, George C. *Spellbound in Darkness.* Greenwich, Conn.: New York Graphic Society Ltd., 1966.

Robinson, David. *The History of World Cinema.* New York: Stein and Day, 1973.

Rooney, Mickey. *Life Is Too Short.* New York: Villard Books, 1991.

Schwartz, Charles. *Gershwin: His Life and Music.* New York: Bobbs-Merrill Co., 1973.

Taylor, Deems. *Some Enchanted Evenings.* New York: Harper & Brothers, 1953.

Thomas, Tony. *Harry Warren and the Hollywood Musical.* Secaucus, NJ: Citadel Press, 1975.

United States Bureau of the Census. *The Statistical History of the United States from Colonial Times to the Present.* New York: Basic Books, 1976.

Vidor, King. *A Tree Is a Tree.* Harcourt Brace & Co., New York, 1953.

Waters, Edward N. *Victor Herbert.* New York: Macmillan, 1955.

Wilk, Max. *They're Playing Our Song.* New York: Atheneum, 1973.

Wodehouse, P.G., and Guy Bolton. *Bring on the Girls.* New York: Simon and Shuster, 1953.

Zukor, Adolph. *The Public Is Never Wrong.* New York: G.P. Putnam's Sons, 1953.

Interviews

Personal interviews with the following songwriters were conducted between 1976 and 1988.

Harold Adamson	Sam Coslow	Mitchell Parish
Louis Alter	Edward Eliscu	Richard Rodgers
Leonard Bernstein	Jay Gorney	Jule Styne
Irving Caesar	E.Y. Harburg	Dana Suesse
Sammy Cahn	Edward Heyman	Kay Swift
Hoagy Carmichael	Burton Lane	James Van Heusen
J. Fred Coots	Gerald Marks	Harry Warren

Index

333